The Ancient Urban Maya

ANCIENT CITIES OF THE NEW WORLD

UNIVERSITY PRESS OF FLORIDA

Florida A&M University, Tallahassee
Florida Atlantic University, Boca Raton
Florida Gulf Coast University, Ft. Myers
Florida International University, Miami
Florida State University, Tallahassee
New College of Florida, Sarasota
University of Central Florida, Orlando
University of Florida, Gainesville
University of North Florida, Jacksonville
University of South Florida, Tampa
University of West Florida, Pensacola

THE ANCIENT
URBAN
MAYA

Neighborhoods, Inequality, and Built Form

Scott R. Hutson

Foreword by John W. Janusek,
Michael E. Smith, Marilyn A. Masson

UNIVERSITY PRESS OF FLORIDA
Gainesville / Tallahassee / Tampa / Boca Raton
Pensacola / Orlando / Miami / Jacksonville / Ft. Myers / Sarasota

23 22 21 20 19 18   6 5 4 3 2 1

First cloth printing, 2016
First paperback printing, 2018

Library of Congress Cataloging-in-Publication Data
Names: Hutson, Scott, author. | Janusek, John Wayne, 1963– author of
  introduction, etc. | Smith, Michael Ernest, 1953– author of introduction,
  etc. | Masson, Marilyn A., author of introduction, etc.
Title: The ancient urban Maya : neighborhoods, inequality, and built form / Scott R. Hutson ;
  foreword by John W. Janusek, Michael E. Smith, Marilyn A. Masson.
Other titles: Ancient cities of the New World.
Description: Gainesville : University Press of Florida, [2016] | Series:
  Ancient cities of the new world | Includes bibliographical references and index.
Identifiers: LCCN 2015040941 | ISBN 9780813062761 (cloth: alk. paper)
ISBN 9780813064796 (pbk.)
Subjects: LCSH: Mayas—Urban residence. | Mayas—Antiquities. | City
  planning—Mexico. | Urbanization.
Classification: LCC F1435.3.U72 H87 2016 | DDC 972/.6—dc23
LC record available at http://lccn.loc.gov/2015040941

The University Press of Florida is the scholarly publishing agency for the State University
System of Florida, comprising Florida A&M University, Florida Atlantic University, Florida
Gulf Coast University, Florida International University, Florida State University, New
College of Florida, University of Central Florida, University of Florida, University of North
Florida, University of South Florida, and University of West Florida.

University Press of Florida
15 Northwest 15th Street
Gainesville, FL 32611-2079
http://upress.ufl.edu

Contents

List of Figures   vii

List of Tables   ix

Foreword   xi

Acknowledgments   xv

1. Cities and Urban Centers: Definitions, Challenges, and Attractions   1

2. Ancient Maya Cities and Urban Centers   29

3. Identifying Neighborhoods and Other Intermediate Social Units   70

4. Neighborhoods at Chunchucmil   97
   Scott Hutson and Jacob Welch

5. The Spatial Experience of Inequality   139

6. The Allure of Maya Cities   170

7. Conclusions and Contributions   202

References   209

Index   253

Figures

1.1. Maps showing most locations mentioned in the text 5

2.1. Map of Mayapan, Yucatan, Mexico 34

2.2. Map showing 7.5 square kilometers of the center of Tikal, Peten, Guatemala 36

2.3. Map of Palenque, Chiapas, Mexico 43

2.4. Map showing 9.3 square kilometers of the center of Chunchucmil, Yucatan, Mexico 45

2.5. Map of a residential portion of Coba, Quintana Roo, Mexico 47

2.6. Map of Sayil, Yucatan, Mexico 49

2.7 Map of Copan, Honduras 50

3.1. Map of a settlement cluster to the southwest of the site core, Dzibilchaltun, Yucatan, Mexico 75

3.2. Map of twentieth-century Paste, Chiapas, Mexico 77

3.3. Schematic map of zones I and VI at Coba, Quintana Roo, Mexico 79

3.4. Map of the core of Río Bec, Campeche, Mexico 83

3.5. The San Lorenzo settlement cluster 85

3.6. Map of the Tlajinga barrio 93

4.1. Two models of circulation patterns within cities 101

4.2. Map of paths 103

4.3. Map of all buildings taller than 4 meters 110

4.4. Distribution of all buildings 5.5 meters high or taller 111

4.5. Portion of the Chunchucmil map showing how spokes 10 and 11 articulate with the Picholte and Copo quadrangles 113

4.6. Portion of the Chunchucmil map showing an example of a pair of open spaces in cluster 13 crossed by the cluster 13 spoke 117

4.7. Portion of the Chunchucmil map showing an example of a pair of open spaces next to the cluster 12 spoke but not entered by any paths 118

4.8. Map of Chunchucmil showing *chichbes*, causeways, and monumental compounds 121

4.9. Map showing the locations of the 159 architecturally focused excavation operations 125

4.10. Schematic representation of the central 9.3 square kilometers of Chunchucmil 133

4.11. Schematic representation of the central 9.3 square kilometers of Chunchucmil, divided into 250-meter-by-250-meter blocks 134

4.12. Map of a portion of Chunchucmil showing Area D from figure 4.11 135

5.1. Histogram of volume of residences (n = 884), Chunchucmil 145

5.2. Histogram of surface area of buildings (n = 128), Chunchucmil 146

5.3. Histogram of volume of architecture of house lots (n = 392), Chunchucmil 146

6.1. Major features of the Tikal site core 175

6.2. Causeway systems extending out from the site cores of Caracol, Coba, and Chichen Itza 187

6.3. Plazas at the sites of Coba, Caracol, and Dzibilchaltun 189

Tables

4.1. Population estimates for each spoke cluster and estimates of the amount of patio space in the large monumental compounds that pertain to spoke clusters 107

4.2. Open spaces and wells per spoke cluster at Chunchcumil 116

4.3. Total architectural groups at Chunchucmil and number of excavated architectural groups sorted by group type and by the one-square-kilometer block within which they are located 126

5.1. Measures of wealth inequality for a sample of Maya cities 156

Foreword

The status of Maya centers as cities has been debated for decades. In this book, Scott Hutson settles this debate using abundant data, innovative methodologies, and a grounded theoretical perspective. His extensive research at the Maya site of Chunchucmil provides primary data that form the core of the book's myriad contributions. The archaeological study of cities considers the material characteristics of cities—their size, density, social differentiation, specialized functions, image, and built form,—but Hutson emphasizes, along with George Cowgill, that "cities are notoriously hard to define." Rather than focusing on specific measures, which have driven archaeologists down countless rabbit holes, Huston refreshingly considers the *urban* character of Maya cities. Rejuvenating ideas generated in the Chicago school of sociology in the early twentieth century, he suggests that what is most important about Maya urbanism is the way of life it created, one in which socially distant people—strangers—find themselves in close proximity to one another. Tackling the traditional notion that Maya centers were "non-cities" or, at best, "low-density cities," this book makes a strong case that many Maya centers were urban places from a fundamentally social perspective.

Whether New York or Tikal, urban centers offer challenges and opportunities to their residents. The author argues that decisions to move to and reside in Maya cities resulted from negotiated, conscious choices made initially by rural populations. Coercion would have been an ineffective strategy for retention of urban residents, and it is questionable whether Maya rulers had the social or political power essential to accomplish forced settlement. In Scott Hutson's view, people of diverse occupations, kin groups, and status would have chosen city life, at least some of the time. The social life of residents helped shape urban environments and, equally, social identity and lived experiences were shaped by the context of urban spaces. Yet urban challenges are well known: crowding, anonymity, interpersonal anomie, trenchant inequality, diseases, and rats. Maya cities had most of these problems as well as those arising from their lowland, karstic, and, in many cases, fragile forest environments. Why did Maya farmers, craft specialists, merchants, and elites choose to live in cities? How did people of such diverse stripes make cities work for them?

Cities, including those of the Maya area, also have their enticements. Many Maya urban centers thrived for generations; some occupations spanned hundreds of years, even millennia. Hutson compares Maya and other Mesoamerica cities in order to understand just what attracted people to urban places in ancient Mexico and Central America. Urban life played out in the context of close-knit neighborhoods of mutually familiar people who shared kin ties or other bonds of social identity that were created by residential proximity.

The neighborhood was a central focus of investigation and urban development for the scholars of the Chicago school of sociology, and Hutson presents compelling evidence for neighborhood development at Chunchucmil and some other Maya cities. The socioeconomic importance of neighborhoods in Mesoamerican cities in general is an ambiguous and debated topic of research that is unresolved even at Teotihuacan, a massive city that contains walled apartment compounds and ethnic clusters. Hutson's contributions reveal the variation and key differences in the organizational features of Mesoamerican cities. Despite hints of real or symbolic social boundaries within some Maya cities, the constituent parts were linked by key features of the built environment, such as stone-lined thoroughfares, raised roads, gates, and walls. Recognizing the full array of diverse urban forms is an essential first step toward resolving debates regarding the institutions that bound together New World cities. This volume's major strength lies in its examination of the city from a holistic perspective that considers the strategies of exalted governors along with those of the humble urban farmers and crafting households.

Hutson draws attention to a comprehensive suite of factors that would have drawn migrants to Maya urban places. First is the prospect of *multiplicity*: the exciting possibility of new and unstructured interactions with strangers of diverse backgrounds, occupations, and economic statuses in a single place. Much of this interaction undoubtedly occurred in marketplaces. Second, the monumentality of Maya centers was designed to impress and awe.

Such striking features of Maya cityscapes have not lost their renown, even today, given their regular appearance in multimillion-dollar Hollywood film sets. The largest Maya cities were eminently *imageable* and alluring. Yet towering Maya monuments also embodied a host of specific meanings related to politico-religious power. They enclosed the tombs of deceased royalty within human-wrought caves and they were rendered as potent houses of the gods. Monumental plazas provided staging grounds for massive gatherings where people of diverse occupation, kinship, and status congregated for major state events. Monumental components of cities were an essential part of defining an urban place.

This book is the fifth in the Ancient Cities of the New World series. Books in this series provide accessible portrayals of urbanism in places where publication has not kept up with fieldwork and archival research. While the study of any past urban center can claim to be about ancient cities or urbanism, this book series features studies that employ specific theories, models, and approaches drawn from the scholarly literature on cities and urbanism. Volumes in this series will complement introductory textbooks as in-depth, theoretically driven case studies of urbanism in pre-Columbian Mesoamerica and South America.

John W. Janusek, Michael E. Smith, Marilyn A. Masson
Series editors

Acknowledgments

A number of people have helped me with this manuscript. Before I mention them individually, I want to say that I am extremely fortunate to have such kind and thoughtful colleagues. It's a huge privilege to work in their good company and add, if just a little, to the remarkable foundations they have built. First and foremost, Marilyn Masson supplied overwhelmingly positive encouragement from the beginning of this project to the end and stepped in more than once to help the book clear hurdles. She also made several comments that improved the manuscript. Cynthia Robin gave valuable feedback on the entire book, catching many lapses in my reasoning and writing while also pointing me to new ideas. An anonymous reviewer provided several useful suggestions for revision. I thank both Cynthia and the anonymous reviewer for their support and investment. Cliff Brown, Charles Golden, Mike Smith, and Glenn Storey explained a number of things to me and in some cases gave me access to unpublished manuscripts. Their help definitely clarified a number of points in the book. Marshall Becker, Steve Houston, Zach Hruby, Art Joyce, and Shannon Plank each read portions of the book and gave me comments that truly helped me improve it. Conversations with Bruce Dahlin, Traci Ardren, and Aline Magnoni, all of whom I got to know while working at Chunchucmil, have deeply impacted my thinking about Maya cities. I owe a large debt to them and other key members of the Chunchucmil crew (Maestro Gualberto Tzuc Mena, David Hixson, Daniel Mazeau, Soco Jimenez, Geni Mansell, Tara Bond, Tim Beach, Sheryl-Luzzadder Beach, and Jamie Forde).

Some of the ideas in this book received helpful questions and comments from audiences in Providence, Austin, and Philadelphia. I thank Katherine Harrington and Linda Gosner for the invitation to speak to the Mellon

Graduate Workshop on Daily Deeds and Practiced Patterns at the Joukowski Institute, Brown University. I thank Tim Beach and Sheryl Luzzadder-Beach for the invitation to speak at the Department of Geography and the Environment Colloquium at the University of Texas. I thank Whitt Schroeder for the invitation to speak at the Department of Anthropology Colloquium at the University of Pennsylvania. All hosts at these three venues provided exceptional hospitality and warm support for the half-baked propositions I laid on their doorsteps.

Dean Mark Kornbluh of the College of Arts and Sciences at the University of Kentucky granted me a sabbatical leave during which I wrote most of this book. I thank Mary Anglin, former chair of the Department of Anthropology, for advocating for this sabbatical and facilitating many other kinds of research support. Charlotte Arnauld, Wendy Ashmore, Ed Barnhart, Arlen and Diane Chase, Willie Folan, Timothy Hare, Marilyn Masson, Dominique Michelet, Jeremy Sabloff, Rebecca Storey, and Jason Yaeger granted me permission to use their maps. At the University Press of Florida, Meredith Babb and Marthe Walters have shepherded this manuscript with judiciousness and alacrity. Shannon Plank, my wife, boosted my confidence on a nearly daily basis while at the same time serving as a model of intellect and scholarship who inspires me to do better. Finally, River and Gabriel make it all worthwhile.

1

Cities and Urban Centers

Definitions, Challenges, and Attractions

> The city is something more than a congeries of individuals and of social conveniences: streets, buildings, electric lights. . . . The city is, rather, a state of mind.
>
> Park (1925, 1)

> The city often represents a locality and dense settlement of dwellings forming a colony so extensive that personal reciprocal acquaintance of the inhabitants is lacking.
>
> Weber ([1921] 1958, 65)

What could entice a person to live in a "colony so extensive" that one is often surrounded by strangers? City life, modern and ancient, presents myriad complications. Urban dwellers are beleaguered by crowding and the problems it entails—the possibility of emotional and social alienation; the potential for squalor, vermin, and noxious odors; the health threats caused by inadequate sewage disposal, water contamination, and the sheer proximity of others. Nevertheless, people made cities work for them, and over hundreds of years they remade them, remodeled them, and renewed them. The fact that ancient Maya cities persisted for many centuries clearly demonstrates that these places exerted a magnetism that smaller settlements could not bring to bear. How did people make cities not merely livable but attractive? How did cities lure people to them? How did they render themselves irresistible?

This book takes the position that people from a variety of social positions—farmers, women of commerce, royalty—exercise a degree of agency in shaping the enticements upon which a city's viability rests. I begin this introduction by exploring the complications of cities and probing the notion that both very powerful and less powerful people actively shaped cities. I then discuss the definition of city and other key terms. Later in the book I explore new demographic data that shows that some Maya cities were in fact quite densely settled, a finding that should effectively defuse lingering controversy over whether Maya centers should be classified as cities.

In the final part of this introduction I present four attractions that entice people to live in cities: neighborhoods, multiplicity, built form, and economy. Neighborhoods meet a range of social challenges, in part by providing a sense of familiarity and distinction amid a sea of anonymous faces. This book presents a uniquely fine-grained case study of neighborhoods in a Maya city. Multiplicity refers to the intermingling of large numbers of widely different people. Chance encounters between people of different occupations and different levels of wealth do not just give zest to social life, they afford chances to expand social networks and social capital. I argue that spatial layouts and social milieus in Maya cities were fertile ground for such encounters. Regarding built form, Maya cities contained a range of civic spaces that hosted compelling ceremonies and made favorable symbolic and aesthetic impressions, perhaps drawing people to cities and giving them reasons to stay, to tolerate and even enjoy close proximity to many neighbors. Finally, many urban economies featured marketplaces that streamlined exchange while also providing entertaining spectacles.

Central Issues

Urbanism refers to a condition in which people are both socially distant and physically close (Wirth 1940, 752). At the beginning of the twentieth century, Georg Simmel argued that the condition of urbanism has a profound psychological effect (see also Milgram 1970). In particular, Simmel (2002, 14) maintained that unceasing contact with multitudes of strangers encouraged a "negative type of social conduct." To conserve emotional energy (and to avoid getting scammed!) people had to cultivate a blasé attitude and a bearing of aloofness and reserve. For Simmel, urban life produces a state of mind very different from that of village life, a state of mind that many well-known literary and scholarly figures—Nietzsche, Ruskin, Spengler—found repulsive. Though people in cities might gain freedom from the cumbersome kinship commitments that come with village life, some have argued that such emancipation comes with a price tag of anomie: a lack of identification with others and a sense of rootlessness in the absence of traditions. Robert Park, whom I quoted in the epigram, established an entire research tradition— the Chicago School of Sociology—dedicated to understanding how people adapt to and even overturn the psychological, social, and economic problems of urbanism. Research on cities has burgeoned since then, and scholars have systematically documented other problems. Social inequality looms large here, and I will have quite a lot to say about it (see chapter 5). Comparative research on contemporary cities shows that as settlements grow, crime rates increase 15 percent more than the growth rate of the settlement's population (Bettencourt and West 2010, 913). Such scalar factors probably operated in the past as well (Ortman et al. 2015).

Urbanism also creates health problems. Cholera plagues cities that lack plumbing or other sanitary measures. Furthermore, crowding, a basic condition of urban life, spreads disease (measles, rubella, smallpox, influenza; Trigger 2003, 123). Archival data indicate that before the industrial revolution, which brought improvements in public health, urban populations such as those of sixteenth- and seventeenth-century London and imperial Rome had high mortality rates and low life expectancy compared to the rural areas surrounding them (Finlay 1981; Russell 1958). Bioarchaeological data from medieval Denmark show that epidemic disease had a greater impact in cities than in rural areas (Peterson et al. 2006). In tropical lowland cities such as those of the ancient Maya, warm temperatures exacerbate problems associated with poor water quality (Miksic 1999). Studying the effects of poor health, demographers of early modern European cities coined the Law of Urban Natural Decrease (De Vries 1984; Wrigley 1969), which states that pre-industrial cities could not maintain stable population levels without constant migration from rural hinterlands.

Since the New World lacked most of the kinds of diseases, infections, and epidemics that afflicted densely crowded cities in the Old World, some have assumed that pre-Conquest New World cities had better mortality rates (McNeill 1976). In 1519, when the Spaniards first laid eyes on Tenochtitlan, the very densely populated Aztec capital in the Basin of Mexico, they remarked on its exceptional cleanliness (Diaz del Castillo 1956; see figure 1.1 for a map of Maya and Mesoamerican cities mentioned in this book). Rebecca Storey's (1992a, 266) bioarchaeological analyses from the non-Maya first millennium CE city of Teotihuacan show, however, that "the effects of dense population upon mortality and health where public sanitation systems are inadequate are likely to be fairly uniform across environments and cultures." Though epidemics of the specific diseases in Old World cities may not have tormented people at Teotihuacan, infection and malnutrition were common and often chronic in this densely populated center. The population of Teotihuacan, just like that of London and Rome, would have declined without in-migration (Storey 1992a, 266).

Skeletal analysis from Maya cities such as Tikal (Haviland 1967) and Copan (Whittington 1989) reveals generally poor health (see also Saul 1972), although the small size of skeletal samples from rural areas prevent a comparison. At Copan, a very densely populated city that has provided the largest sample of burials in the Maya region (600 individuals), child mortality was high and enamel defects in deciduous teeth indicate that infants suffered from disease and malnutrition (Storey 1992b). Recent isotopic analysis of large samples of skeletons from ancient Copan shows that between 20 percent and 40 percent of the city's residents came from outside the city (Miller 2015), thus supporting the notion that urban centers required migrants. Haviland (1967) proposed that health declined as population density increased at Tikal (see also Storey 1992b, 166). Although Wright and White (1996) argue that burials in Maya cities show no consistent evidence for a deterioration of health over time, they agree that the Maya experienced a health burden similar to that of other complex preindustrial cities.

Given these problems with urban life, George Cowgill (2003a) and others (Fletcher 1995) have asked how cities persist. What motivates people to move to them? Why do they put up with urban problems? How do they create lives of meaning and value amid a variety of potential discomforts and inconveniences? Each of these questions gets at the experience of the actual people who lived in them (A. Smith 2003). In archaeology, one finds a broad literature on cities, and cities rightly deserve attention for many different reasons. The most cited work about ancient complex societies is Gordon Childe's 1950 paper about cities: "The Urban Revolution" (Smith 2009, 3). Childe's paper is popular because several of the processes critical to his understanding of cities—the relationship between cities and states, the development of occupational specialization, the production and extraction of

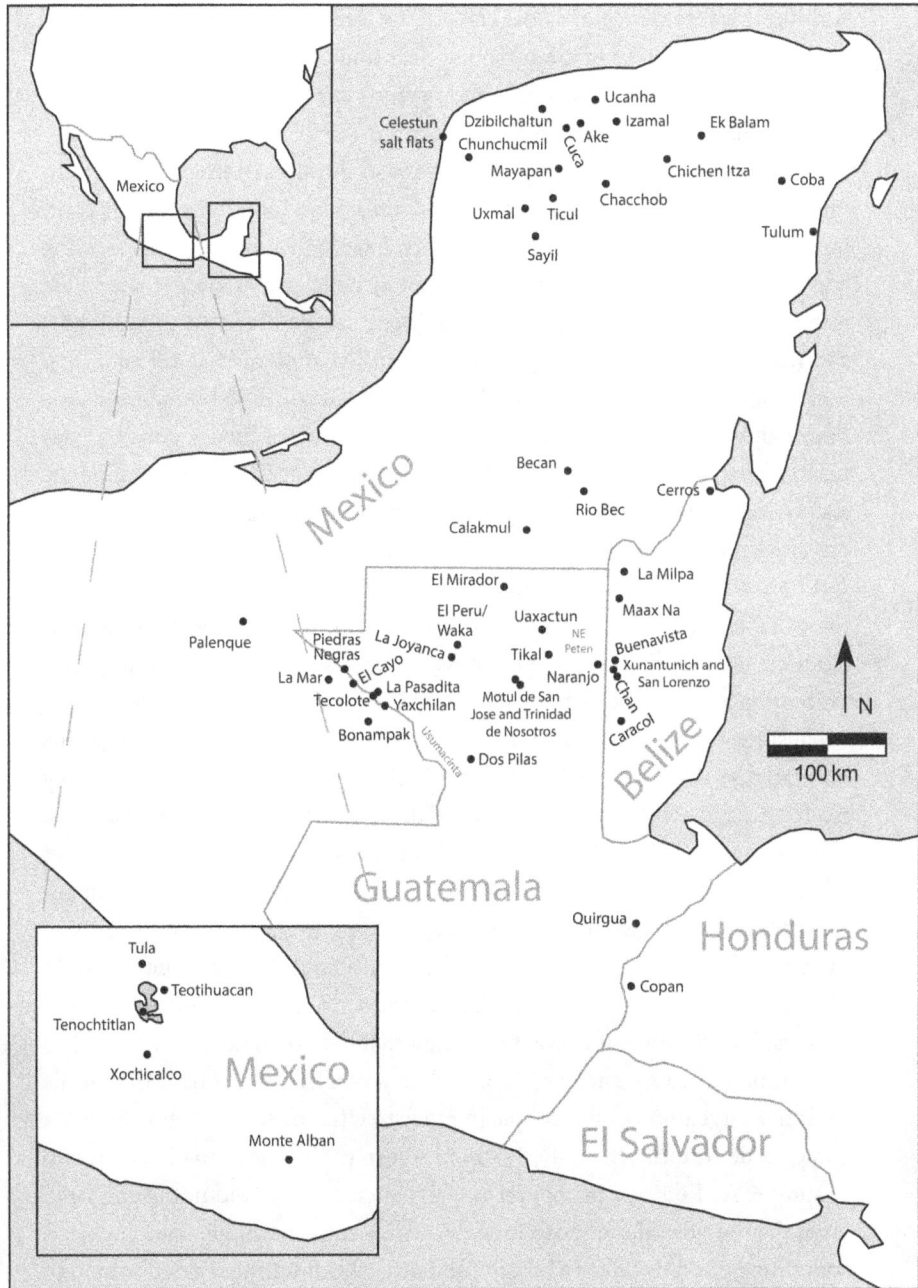

Figure 1.1. Maps showing most locations mentioned in the text.

surplus, the emergence of social classes, the intensification of long-distance trade, and the creation of monuments—continue to motivate research today (see also Smith 2009, 11–13). Childe (1950, 9) explicitly excluded the Maya from his discussion of cities, a decision I return to in the following chapter.

After Childe, an equally important realm of questions centering on catchment analysis and links between city and hinterland (see, for example, Dahlin et al. 2005) emerged from processual archaeologists' interests in sampling and regional approaches (e.g., Binford 1964; Hole et al. 1969). Researchers interested in comparative perspectives focus on the broad variety of cities and why some cities thrive and others do not (Marcus and Sabloff 2008, 25). Some aspects of ancient cities, such as density, sprawl, fluid boundaries, economic opportunity, wealth inequality, consumption of luxury goods as status markers, development of neighborhoods, and placement of monuments, also characterize modern cities, thus making comparative studies of premodern cities relevant to contemporary questions and vice versa (Fletcher 2009; Ortman et al. 2015; M. L. Smith 2003, 6). Undoubtedly, as more and more of the world's population moves from rural areas to cities, understanding how cities create wealth, poverty, happiness, waste, knowledge, and crime (Glaeser 2011; Jacobs 1969) has direct effects on our well-being.

Despite the abundance of fruitful questions about ancient cities, this book sticks to the question of why people chose to live in them and how they made them livable. By focusing on the decisions and lives of city dwellers, it links itself to other attempts to envision ancient societies as the product of willing participation from a wide array of actors. Discussing cities in ancient Middle Niger, McIntosh (2005, 149–150) notes that the vast majority of urban dwellers are "members of ordinary households" and that cities would not exist without their labor, economic production, and attendance at ceremonies. For the ancient Maya, the notion that people *chose* to produce cities is legitimate because ancient Maya leaders probably did not have the means to coerce large numbers of people to move to cities or stay in them (Inomata 2004; cf. de Montmollin 1989, 87–93). I return to the question of coercion in chapter 6. As I discuss in chapter 2, many ancient Maya did not live in large cities. Those who did choose to live in cities must have felt that cities had something good to offer (M. L. Smith 2003, 2), something valuable enough to mitigate the downsides of urban life.

By beginning from the premise that people could have chosen not to live in cities—that people could have done otherwise—this book aligns itself with a pillar of practice theory as elaborated by Anthony Giddens. Giddens (1984, 9, 14) defined agency as an actor's ability to choose; to "intervene in the world, or to refrain from such intervention, with the effect of influencing a specific process or state of affairs." Though such a choice may not produce the outcome that the actor intended, Giddens and other writers (Scott 1985, 1990) have developed persuasive arguments that even some of the most oppressed actors, such as prisoners, can act otherwise. All actors have at least some knowledge and control over their physical bodies and gain a degree of empowerment from such human resources (Sewell 1992, 10).

A wide array of ancient actors, not just leaders, willingly participated in the creation of cities. Monica Smith (2006, 109) has phrased this well:

> There has been a tendency to view cities as being primarily inhabited and directed by elites. . . . But the willing presence of [non-elites] is a necessary component of political action. . . . In considering the appeal to ordinary inhabitants, I propose that the workings of urban centers were the product of negotiation, compromise, and consensus among many different individuals and groups.

In this book I follow Smith's perspective, which is also visible in other work (e.g., Joyce 2009). Although the socially heterogeneous nature of cities (see below) suggests that there might be no such thing as what Trigger (2003, 121) called an "ordinary person" or what McIntosh called an "ordinary household," it is difficult to find a decent shorthand term for such people. The term commoner also falls short since it implies a specious homogeneity among the people compressed into this category (Lohse and Valdez 2004, 3). Nevertheless, I use the term when I can't find a substitute.

Asking what people found attractive about cities and how they created lives of meaning and dignity under adverse conditions does not mean that that this book takes an exclusively bottom-up perspective. Such a perspective privileges the decisions of people at or near the bottom of the social pyramid, but a holistic view requires attending just as much to choices and strategies of people at the top of the hierarchy. If, as Monica Smith and Art Joyce have emphasized, urban life resulted from negotiations between and among elites and non-elites regarding resources and cultural meanings, then elites are just as important as anyone else in cities. In Maya cities, there are always at least two parties to a negotiation; recent work on ancient Maya cities makes this quite clear.

For example, research in and around the large Late Classic city of Xunantunich in Belize (LeCount 1999; Yaeger 2000, 2003) has shown that rulers used gifts and feasts to court the loyalty of neighborhood leaders in the hope that such middlemen could deliver to the rulers the support of neighborhood constituencies (see also Ashmore et al. 2004; Peuramaki-Brown 2013). In concert with the idea that several Maya cities grew around the courts of Maya kings (Grube 2000; see also Inomata and Houston 2000), Houston and colleagues (2003) have argued that Piedras Negras, located along the Usumacinta River in the Department of Peten, Guatemala, came into being as a center not because of attractive economic resources but because of a moral order sustained by the holy ruler. People offered surplus goods and labor to the rulers, who made good on their followers' commitments to them by upholding covenants with supernatural beings that helped ensure good harvests. Rulers also performed rituals that made followers believe that their kings were successfully embodying the moral values continuously renewed as legitimate. Houston and colleagues clearly state that when kings transgress the moral order or fail to uphold their obligations, followers could rebel or leave (see also Demarest 1992; Inomata 2004). Finally, Golden and Scherer (2013, 402) have placed the notion of moral order in a perspective that prioritizes events in which everyone participated. They argue that the "trust needed to maintain a coherent political unit above the level of the household or the hamlet was only accessible and realizable through communal activities. . . . For actors not in daily contact with one another, highly charged events, such as marketing, feasting, participation in royal spectacles, warfare, and collaboration in construction efforts, among others, served to reinforce the sense of morality and trustworthiness." When trust breaks down, cities fall.

In sum, if farmers, fishers, cooks, and crafters made Maya cities, so did kings (cf. Tourtellot 1993, 227), although this need not be true of all cities in the world (McIntosh 2005, 10–11). The examples from Belize and the Usumacinta show that city-making was a two-way process: both top down and bottom up. Therefore, when examining how urbanites sustain their cities, this book adopts a relational perspective in which identity derives not from a bounded, individualized set of self-representations but from relations with other people and things and the activities that link these entities (Hutson 2010). In the context of this book, a relational perspective emphasizes interactions between people, attempting to see how people and strategies at one level of the social hierarchy intermingle with, complement, or challenge the goals of other actors.

Components of Cities

Some concepts in archaeology are new enough that an enumeration of the different definitions provided for them takes up less than a page, as was the case not long ago with the concept of agency (Dobres and Robb 2000, table 1). The concept "city" is so old that enumerating the various ways people have defined it requires an entire book. Outside the field of archaeology, people began to note the proliferation of different definitions at least by the 1930s (Wirth 1938, 3). Archaeologists came to note this at least by 1950 when Childe began his famous essay with the words: "The concept of city is notoriously hard to define" (see also Cowgill 2004, 526). Fortunately, most definitions contain one or more components, and several of these components show up regularly. The most common components include 1) size; 2) density; 3) social differentiation; 4) way of life; 5) specialized functions; 6) form; and 7) identification. Each of these components plays a role in this book. The number of definitions expands from these seven components, depending on which components authors emphasize and which they neglect. I will discuss these components one by one before settling on a definition that guides this book.

- Size refers to the number of people in a city. Burgess (1926, 118) wrote that a city should have at least 5,000 people. In the first half of the twentieth century, the U.S. census designated as urban any community with more than 2,500 people. However, many writers criticize the use of a minimum number of occupants as a criterion for defining a city (Hannerz 1980, 66; McIntosh 2005, 169; Trigger 2003, 120; Wheatley 1972, 620; Wirth 1938, 69). The problem is that settlements that people call cities in one part of the world might be substantially smaller than settlements that people call villages in another part of the world. Nevertheless, many prominent authors agree that cities should have a "relatively" large number of people in them (Wirth 1938), or, from a historical perspective, the first cities should at least have more people in them than villages from preceding time periods (e.g. Childe 1950, 9). In considering what counts as large, I find utility in Weber's criterion quoted in the epigraph: a settlement counts as large when "personal reciprocal acquaintance of the inhabitants is lacking." In other words, a settlement is large when there are so many people that one person can no longer know at least one member of a majority of the settlement's households on a face-to-face basis (see also Kurjack 1974, 5; Redfield 1941). Settlements with 5,000 people might meet this criterion, those with 25,000 definitely meet it.

- Density refers to the spacing of people. Density is an important factor of human settlement because when large numbers of people live physically closer to each other, the number of social interactions per unit of time increases, which both makes it possible for political and economic organization to expand (Sanders and Price 1968, 201) and at the same time threatens public health. For example, higher population density makes craft specialization cost effective because travel costs (either the producers traveling to the buyers or the buyers traveling to the producers) are no longer prohibitive. When people specialize in crafts, social diversity (the next component discussed below) increases. Comparative studies of modern cities show increasing returns to scale: when double the amount of people can come into contact, productivity more than doubles (Bettencourt 2013). A test of such increasing returns to scale in the pre-Hispanic Basin of Mexico suggests that this scalar principle may also characterize ancient cities (Ortman et al. 2014, 2015). Such scalar logic animates Louis Glaeser's (2011, 6) recent statement, in his boosterish book *Triumph of the City*, that "cities are proximity, density, closeness."

Yet density alone does not a city make. Catal Hoyuk provides a very informative case study. James Mellart's excavations in the 1960s revealed that the tell contained wall-to-wall houses, enough to suggest thousands of inhabitants packed so closely that one would have to exit a house from the roof. Such findings have led to misinterpretations that have fueled landmark books which have themselves influenced later and equally misguided statements about cities. For example, Jane Jacobs (1969) based her erroneous thesis that technological advances such as domestication always originate in cities on the notion that settlements such as Catal Hoyuk, much like London or San Francisco, would have been filled with entrepreneurs getting bright ideas from regular interaction with dynamic and diverse fellow urbanites. But Catal Hoyuk lacked both diversity and venues for interaction, even though it housed anywhere from 3,000 and 8,000 people densely packed together (Hodder 2006, 95). There were no public places, few craft specialists, and no places of specialized function, and this also applies to other Near Eastern settlements at the dawn of farming and pastoralism (Emberling 2003). More recently, using the same misunderstanding of Catal Hoyuk, Soja (2000) anchored his book *Postmetropolis* on the false premise that cities predated and produced the agricultural revolution.

- Social differentiation refers to heterogeneity among the people who live in a settlement. Heterogeneity comes from a variety of sources: different occupations, different levels of wealth, different levels of authority, different ethnic identities, and so forth. Social differentiation has been a central concern of archaeologists wrestling with cities, starting perhaps with the ten criteria that Gordon Childe used to define a city. These criteria are in fact not random traits, as some authors characterize them (Wheatley 1972, 612), but are logically interrelated consequences (Renfrew 1994; Smith 2009, 11) of two similar processes: internal differentiation (Smith 2006) and the institutionalization of authority (A. Smith 2003, 187). For example, although Childe's first criterion is a combination of size and density as described above, criteria two through ten (2 = full time craft specialists, 3 = taxation of surplus, 4 = public buildings as product and symbol of surplus, 5 = surplus supports elites, 6 = recording system developed for administrating surplus, 7 = development of math for calculating surplus and calendars for improving agriculture, 8 = specialists in art, 9 = trade for materials to support specialists and ideologies, 10 = specialists' livelihood is secure enough to reside in cities and abandon itinerancy) all have to do with occupational specializations and/or the way leaders legitimate and maintain the authority they have acquired. Stated differently, Childe's city is about social differentiation along vertical and horizontal axes.

In the case of different occupations, social differentiation has ties with Durkheim's notion of organic solidarity in the sense that a specialist devoted to craft production depends on other people for food and other products. While ancient cities certainly had craft specialists, many people living in ancient cities produced food. For example, writers from Weber ([1921] 1958) to Finley (1963) to Hansen (2000a, 159) all emphasize that most people in most ancient Greek city-states were in fact farmers. Childe (1950, 4) calmly wrote that most ancient city dwellers were farmers who worked the lands near cities (cf. Sanders 1962). We should also remember that some craft producers can also farm or embed themselves within households whose other members farm.

- Urbanization consists of changes that enable people to cope with life in large, dense, socially differentiated settlements. Urbanization is a way of life. Wirth notes that the aspects of city life presumed by writers such as Simmel—anonymity and secularism—derive from the three components listed above: size, density, and differentiation. However, I list urbanization as a component in itself—the fourth of the seven components—because it plays a large role in definitions provided by a wide array of writers (Betz 2002; Park 1925; Rotenberg 2002; Wheatley 1972; Wirth 1938). The kinds of changes that enable people to cope with cities might involve everyday habits for dealing with overload, such as aloofness toward strangers in public places (Milgram 1970, 1462) or dressing in a way that simplifies recognition of identity (Wirth 1938, 74; Park 1952, 47; Sjoberg 1960, 126) or replacing an unstated moral order with clearly stipulated contracts. Urbanization can refer to new orientations to the world, such as secularization and rationality (Simmel 2002; Smith 1972, 569). Park's epigraph bears out urbanization as a new way of thinking: "The city is something more than a congeries of individuals and of social conveniences: streets, buildings, electric lights. . . . The city is, rather, a state of mind." At the same time, we should not minimize the importance of what Park calls social conveniences because these are also the result of changes geared toward making urban centers bearable. In addition to building and maintaining streets, people in urban settings create institutions, such as arrangements to handle trash or judicial bodies to deal with disputes.
- Specialized functions: Max Weber's ([1921] 1958) book on the city is an early use of this component; he stated that cities must have a marketplace and government (see also Alston 1998, 197). Though Weber's specific requirements are too restrictive (Sanders and Webster 1988, 522), many agree with his broader point that cities provide services not found in villages. Lewis Mumford (1961, 85) also caught the gist of this fifth component in his statement that "the city is not so much a mass of structures as a complex of interrelated and constantly interacting functions." Archaeologists commonly cite Bruce Trigger's definition of a city as "a unit of settlement which performs specialized functions in relation to a broader hinterland" (Trigger 1972, 577; see also Grove 1972; Blanton 1976, 253). Notice, however, that in Trigger's hands, this particular component of cities becomes the only component that matters. Such a unidimensional definition of cities invites a predictable critique. A hamlet at the edge of

a quarry certainly qualifies as a unit of settlement that performs a specialized function—provisioning of lithic material—in relation to its hinterland, but nobody would mistake such a hamlet for a city. Michael Smith (2008, 6) has asked how many special functions a settlement must have before it can be called a city. In an update to his definition, Trigger (2003, 120) takes these criticisms into account by noting that small settlements that provide specialized functions should not always be considered cities. This caveat introduces the important distinction between a center, which is merely a place that provides a service not found in neighboring settlements, and a city, which should be something more; something that Monica Smith (2006, 105) glosses as "the synergy and liveliness that are the product of population density and interconnectedness."

Some use the word functional to refer to definitions of city that emphasize only specialized functions (Smith 2010, 138). Cowgill (2003b) notes a shift in popularity toward functional definitions: for example, cities as places that host certain institutions or practices. Having specialized functions can be an important component of cities, but approaches that focus too much on function carry three risks. First, when archaeologists discuss centralizing functions, their discussion usually zooms in on government and administration. As several writers have noted (Cowgill 2004, 526; Smith 2006, 104–105), discussions of this sort (e.g. Childe 1950) often elide "city" and "state." This elision promotes the point of view that cities only exist as part of states (Trigger 1972, 2003). Archaeologists commonly define a state as a polity with centralized leadership, professional administrators, multiple levels of settlement hierarchy, and pronounced vertical and horizontal social differentiation (e.g. Flannery 1972). Hansen (2000b, 14–15), McIntosh (2005), and M. L. Smith (2003, 2006) provide strong support that in places such as Africa and South Asia, settlements that most people would consider cities exist in the absence of states. Second, emphasizing function risks resuscitating an outmoded functionalist perspective in which societies are seen as smoothly operating organisms devoid of internal conflicts. This perspective takes attention away from humans as actors with varied agendas and places too much focus on higher-level institutions. Mention of such institutions introduces the third risk: getting stuck in a top-down perspective. The most important functions presented in functional approaches are hierarchical, drawing the researcher's attention to leaders and the ideology of monuments. Trigger (2003, 121) writes that "major cities impressed visitors by their scale, richness, and architectural magnificence and the grandeur of what went on in them. These attributes stressed the insignificance of the ordinary person, the power and legitimacy of the ruler, and the concentration of supernatural power. It is therefore not surprising that the development of cities was strongly promoted by the upper classes, who used them to pursue their personal and collective goals." I agree that upper classes pursued their goals in cities (and elsewhere), but Trigger provides no evidence that the hierarchical features of cities render ordinary people insignificant. Trigger himself may or may not have seen ordinary people as insignificant, but his phrasing suggests that only upper-class people took initiative, that only upper-class people pursued their goals in cities. I intend to show in this book that the existence of cities depends just as much on the goals and actions of those of other classes (see also Joyce 2009, 191; Robin 2013).

- Built form: Betz (2002, 12) argues that although writers usually refer only vaguely to a city's form, some notion of form underlies all definitions of city (see also J. Marcus 1983, 196–198). Betz's argument begins with the points that cities are settings and that all settings have structural form. She then stresses that the form of a settlement plays a large role in attracting people to it, thus making the settlement a city (see also Boone and Redman 1982, 29). Thus, form is critical. This point of view builds from Lynch's (1960, 30) argument that people always have a visual image of the city in which they live.

- Identification: The notion of people's images of the city brings up the final and most controversial component of definitions of city. Using ethnographic evidence, Rotenberg (2002, 97) argues that city people's sense of who they are is bound up with the powerful images, generated through everyday life, of the city in which they live (see also Ardren 2015, 21–50; Magnoni et al. 2014). In archaeology, Emberling (2003, 254) uses inhabitants' identification with the city as one of three elements of his definition of city. People create cities not just physically but also socially. In other words, urban dwellers create meaningful relations with each other and generate a positive impression of their city, both of which make city life desirable and compelling (see also Rotenberg 2002, 105). I agree that a person in an ancient or modern city can recognize their city as a salient entity distinguished from other nearby settlements and can come to identify themselves as a person from that city. Yet city dwellers do not always have an emic concept of city. The classical Greeks distinguished city from country: the term *asty* refers to a nucleated settlement, as does one sense of the word *polis*. The term *demos* can refer to suburbs or country villages, while one sense of the word *chora* refers to the hinterland. Yet whereas *demos* can refer to a person from the countryside, the Greeks had no term to refer to a person specifically from a city; terms such as *astos* and *polites* simply mean "citizen," not necessarily a city dweller (Hansen 2000a, 152–154). Things were trickier among the Nahua, the majority population in central Mexico at the time of the Spanish conquest. In the Nahuatl language, the closest word for city, *altepetl*, referred not just to a nucleated settlement but to the ruler, the ruler's territory, and the inhabitants of the territory as whole, within and beyond the nucleated settlement. The "meaningful unit," according to J. Marcus (1983, 207), is not the nucleated settlement but the realm: land and people. Hirth (2003a, 63) goes a step further and argues that "throughout Mesoamerica, urban centers were not viewed as places qualitatively distinct and separate entities from the countryside as they were in western society." Since the *altepetl*, as opposed to the nucleated settlement, was the jurisdictional unit among the Nahua, Hirth argues that urban clusters were epiphenomenal; they were merely the households that clustered around the *altepetl*'s civic ceremonial apparatus. As we will see in chapter 2, the ancient Maya likely lacked a precise term equivalent to city. My own point of view is that people can have a strong identification with place, be it a quarry, a village, or a city, regardless of whether their culture contains a linguistically marked category to which their place pertains (Tuan 1977). This raises a question: If people identify with all kinds of settlements, should identification with a city serve as a key component in defining a city?

Definitions: City and Urbanism/Urban

What should we do with each of these seven components? Is it worth using some combination of them to form a definition of city? On the one hand, several authors note that every city might be unique (J. Marcus 1983, 198; Wirth 1925, 175). Even in a particular region, such as the Maya area, there is no typical city and there can be huge variety between neighboring cities (Chase et al. 1990; Hutson et al. 2008; Isendahl and Smith 2013, 142; Morley 1997, 44–45; Pyburn 1997, 161; Smith 1989; see also Smith 2006, 106–107). On the other hand, some of these same authors (Wirth 1938; Isendahl and Smith 2013, 135) note that most cities have some things in common, even if such commonalities are at the level of processes and trends as opposed to forms or types (Bettencourt 2007; Morley 1997, 44–45; Wheatley 1972). Since I agree with Cowgill (2004, 256) that a clear analysis requires definitions of key terms, I prefer settling on a definition, even if it is fuzzy. Given the difficulty of finding criteria that apply to all cities, an approach using a polythetic as opposed to a nomothetic set of components works best. Monica Smith (2006) provides such a polythetic set of components in her triaxial approach. Smith begins with four of the components described above (size, density, social differentiation, and specialized functions), reduces them to three by combining size and density into a single component (the "demographic" component), and states that as long as a settlement exhibits two of the three components, it qualifies as a city. I agree with Smith's approach but believe that size and density should not be combined into one component.

Thus, settlements qualify as cities if they possess three of the following four characteristics: specialized functions, social differentiation, large size, and high density. This definition works well with how most Mayanists use the term (see chapter 2). What about the three components that are excluded from this definition: identification, built form, and urbanization? As noted above, identification is problematic. Though I believe it is an important process, it is by no means unique to cities. Built form is also not unique to cities. All settlements exhibit form, and some cities may lack the kind of form that would be considered striking. In this book, I take the position that built form does not define cities; rather, certain forms make cities attractive and help draw people to them whether or not the builders intended this. Thus, built form plays an important role in this book (see below and chapter 6), but it does not need to be part of the definition of a city.

Finally, what about urbanization? The title of this book hints that I see urbanization as quite important. To reiterate what I wrote in the previous section, urbanization is a set of changes, both physical and attitudinal, that respond to life in a place that features the first three components: large size, high density, and significant social differentiation. Urbanization need not develop in all settlements that qualify as cities. According to my definition, a settlement can qualify as a city if it has social differentiation, specialized functions, and large size yet lacks high settlement density. This is important because we have much to gain from considering low-density cities in the same context as modern cities, making lessons from ancient low-density cities applicable to challenges in today's city-dominated world (see also chapter 2; Chase and Scarborough 2014; Costanza et al. 2007). The terms urban and urbanism are closely related to urbanization, and I see a distinction not just between city and urbanization, but between city and urban/urbanism as well. Precisely what, then, do urban and urbanism mean?

According to Wirth (1938) and Sjoberg (1960, 11), size, density, and social differentiation—components one through three above—make a place urban. In this book, urban and urbanism mean the same thing, though one is an adjective and the other a noun. Urbanism refers to a condition in which socially distant people find themselves physically close. Social distance results both from large size (too many people for one person to know many others) and from social differentiation (some of the people whom a person encounters in an urban environment will be quite different from that person). Being physically close results from density. Milgram (1970, 1462) equated the condition of urbanism with an "overloaded social environment." Urbanization, which I have described above as one of the seven common components of definitions of cities, refers to how people respond to urbanism. It refers to the changes that enable people to cope with life in large, dense, socially differentiated settlements. As such urbanism begets urbanization. Urbanization results from living in an urban center. All urban centers are cities, but not all cities have overloaded social environments. Thus, some cities, particularly low-density ones, may not be urban.

Readers may note that my definitions of urban/urbanism and urbanization differ from other highly visible definitions, such as those put forth by Cowgill (2004, 527), who defines urban as "city-ness," urbanism as "the prevalence of urban places in a society," and urbanization as "the creation of cities by a society that formerly lacked urban settlements." My choice to embrace the definition of urban Wirth, Sjoberg, and others used puts me in conflict with trending nomenclature such as "low-density urbanism" (e.g. Fletcher 2009). Since high density is part of how I define urbanism, "low-density urbanism" is an oxymoron that I would replace with the phrase "low-density cities" (see also Stark and Ossa 2007). I stick to my own definitions because they are well established in anthropology (see, for example, Beals 1951) and they have foundations beyond anthropology, even if they are a bit old school.

In the context of the claim that not all cities may seem urban, the title of this book—*Ancient Urban Maya*—implies that I will only be discussing

Maya cities that "count" as urban. While this book does indeed focus on the larger and sometimes more densely populated Maya cities, I put quotation marks around the word "count" because, operationally, I can't pinpoint size and density thresholds at which a city unequivocally qualifies as urban. For example, to get to the condition where people are both socially distant and physically close, the population must be dense enough for there to be opportunities for strangers on foot (the ancient Maya had no vehicles, mountable quadrupeds, or beasts of burden) to encounter each other somewhat regularly. But how regularly? Precisely how dense? And how does a larger population size offset a lower population density in terms of creating more opportunities for social encounters? I don't know the answers to these questions. While settlements with fewer than 5,000 people probably do not count as urban and settlements with 25,000 people inside 16 square kilometers probably do count as urban, the space between these poles is blurry; better to see urbanism as a continuum. Instead of entering that blurry continuum and adjudicating the matter of which cities do or do not count as urban, we should see cities as more versus less urban. Although I present data in chapter 2 that show that several Maya cities had a higher settlement density than what usually comes to mind for the Maya area, calling attention to the overlooked urbanism of Maya cities is only a starting point for analysis. Presuming that social and health problems beset large Maya cities, this book seeks to understand how cities attracted people and how people made cities livable.

Urban Attractions

Despite the disadvantages—crowding, unhealthy conditions—of urbanism, large cities formed in many parts of the world and often persisted for hundreds of years. People had to work to overcome those disadvantages and make cities not just livable but attractive. What made Maya urban centers not just bearable but vibrant? Knowing that cities had to attract newcomers to grow and/or maintain population (if city dwellers had high birth rates, high mortality rates more than canceled these out) sensitizes us to new interpretations of ancient places and practices. An important point of this book is that approaching urban centers from the perspective of the experience of the people who had to live in them advances our understanding of ancient Maya cities. In this section, I revisit the social challenges of ur-

banism and outline four things that counterbalance such challenges: neighborhoods, multiplicity, built form, and economy. I treat each of these as
attractions, although some city dwellers may see multiplicity as dystopian.
Later chapters expand on each of these four: economic attractions surface
in Chapters 2 and 6, neighborhoods take center stage in chapters 3 and 4,
multiplicity appears to different degrees in chapters 5 and 6, and built form
is prominent in chapter 6 but also manifests itself in the spatial relations discussed in all other chapters.

Neighborhoods

Raymond Williams (1973) exposed negative stereotypes about cities as a
common trope in English literature going back to the times of Chaucer. For
millennia people have called attention to the contrast between village and
city (Wheatley 1972, 602). Foundational figures in anthropology formalized
this contrast of ideal types in the nineteenth century. For Henry Maine and
Lewis Henry Morgan, personal relations in villages were based on kin, status, and tradition, while relations in cities were formal and contractual (see
also Redfield 1941; Beals 1951, 9). The distinction between cities and villages
is in fact not as stark as was once supposed (Lewis 1965), but the social consequences are worth pursuing in greater detail. According to earlier social
scientists, when people move from village to city they emancipate themselves from the overbearing kinship obligations and rigorous norms that
make villages the close-knit, intimate units they are imagined to be. Though
people gain a new freedom of expression, they risk losing the morale and
sense of participation that comes from living in a homogeneous, integrated
society (Simmel 2002, 18; Wirth 1938, 73). Another social challenge of the
shift from rural to urban is compartmentalization. In a large society where
one does not know many people well, one's co-worker is likely to be very
different from one's neighbor, who is very different from one's butcher, one's
cousin, and so forth. Thus, family relationships are distinct from work relationships, which are distinct from leisure relationships and relationships of
other kinds. Acquaintances tend toward the superficial as deeper, more ful-
filling human contact decreases (Simmel 2002; Wirth 1938). Finally, though
not exhaustively, cities may contain spaces where people find themselves in
the midst of a bewildering variety of strangers, some of whom might wish
them ill. The following quote from Allan Pred's analysis of nineteenth-

century Stockholm highlights this discomfort: "Nowhere did many of the Bourgeoisie sense more heightened apprehension or greater threat than amidst the welter of activities and bustling movement of the city's streets. There one might be cast adrift in a . . . sea of pedestrian promiscuity, where the banker and the bum, the wholesaler and whore, the retailer and the ragpicker, the respectable and the disrespectful, the high and the low, the clean and the dirty, flowed and jostled, side by side, over the same spaces" (Pred 1990, 129).

Urban planners have come up with several strategies to combat these challenges. The most drastic one, Ebenezer Howard's (1902) Garden City, does away with large cities by resettling people into smaller towns. Howard's idea (see also chapter 4) has inspired authors, planners, and architects from Mumford (1961) to Le Corbusier (1987). Recognizing, however, that many people in cities choose not to return to smaller towns, I focus on the ways people within cities confront these challenges and discomforts. Erving Goffman (1963), for example, explored a variety of body idioms and gestures through which people manage their co-presence with strangers. The formation of neighborhoods, which are more archaeologically accessible than bodily comportment, also responds to the challenges of anomie and compartmentalization. While neighborhoods are perhaps an attraction of city life, they could also be considered a solution to one of the problems of city life. Neighborhoods create nodes of community and integration that offset anonymity and compartmentalization. Oscar Lewis's (1965) ethnographic work in Mexico City has shown that migrants to the city did not live lives bereft of enduring, multilayered social relations. Rather, Lewis found that extended family ties had increased. Within the city, Lewis's subjects to some extent created villages in which compartmentalization was largely absent: family relations spilled over into work relations and leisure relations (Hannerz 1980, 111–112). Neighborhoods do not always need to be kin-based, but household archaeology in the urban center of Tiwanaku, Bolivia, shows that kin ties remained important for integrating different divisions in that city (Janusek and Blom 2006). This work calls into question the notion that kinship diminishes in cities (see also McIntosh 2005, 150; M. L. Smith 2003, 21).

Neighborhoods are attractive because the mutual familiarity of people within them helps foster "networks of small-scale, everyday public life and thus of trust and social control" (Jacobs 1961, 119). Such networks accomplish many things—they protect both neighbors and strangers, they nudge children toward responsible social roles—and give an urban context to the phrase "it takes a village." Chapter 3 discusses precisely what a neighborhood is and how it differs from other social divisions larger than the household. Chapter 3 also discusses methods for detecting neighborhoods archaeologically and how archaeologists have deployed these methods in the Maya area. Chapter 4 gives an extended example of the hunt for neighborhoods at the urban center of Chunchucmil. Although neighborhoods within cities might have the effect of reproducing the relations of trust found in village life, I will argue in chapter 4 that successful neighborhoods are not replicas of villages.

Jostled by the dirty and the disrespectful, the nineteenth-century bourgeoisie of Stockholm craved exclusive, class-based neighborhoods. So did the wealthiest residents of Mexico City in the late eighteenth century, but, living in the very center of the city, they had to interact with pollution and the poor (Bailey Glasco 2010). As David Harvey (1985) has documented, the commoditization of real estate and Haussmann's transformation of the city plan of mid-nineteenth-century Paris resulted in the creation of wealth-based neighborhoods, an early example of gentrification that minimized uneasy encounters between high and low, banker and bum. In chapter 5, I address the notion of wealth-based neighborhoods in Maya cities. That chapter pays specific attention to whether or not wealth inequality was high and whether people of various levels of wealth were spatially segregated or interspersed.

Multiplicity

I use multiplicity as shorthand for what Pred (1990) called a "sea of pedestrian promiscuity." I also gloss multiplicity as unstructured contact with strangers. Words such as crowding, traffic, and meshing also capture some aspects of the concept, but I stick with the clumsily Latinate "multiplicity" because dictionaries note the sense of diversity implied by this word. A sea of pedestrian promiscuity implies not just many people in a single place but many *diverse* people in a single place. Though Pred's quote about the wholesalers, whores, retailers, and ragpickers frames multiplicity as dystopian, multiplicity can also be an attraction. Authors who see frequent encounters with strangers as a negative form of overload from which people seek refuge have also noted that unstructured contact with strangers can provide psychological excitement and spontaneous integration (Milgram 1970, 1462; see also Betz 2002, 3). Ulf Hannerz (1980, 112–113) discusses a number of attractive aspects of unstructured contact with strangers. From such contacts a person may overhear conversations, see bold clothing, get new ideas. One feature of chance encounters with strangers is the possibility of striking up a personal relation that can expand one's social network. Social networks are valuable because they can result in access to resources, be they economic, social, spiritual, or political (Kadushin 2012; Putnam 2000). In other words, multiplicity promotes the expansion of social capital. "If economic capital is in people's bank accounts and human capital is inside their heads, social capital inheres in the structure of their relationships" (Portes 1998, 7). Despite its recent association with the Internet, the notion of social networks is a classic concept in sociology (e.g., Simmel 1950) with broad relevance. Social networking certainly exists outside urban centers, but the throngs of people and the broad array of human resources one finds in cities expand the possibilities for gaining social capital. Sjoberg (1960) rejected the possibility that contact with strangers created opportunities, arguing that social roles and statuses in cities were so clearly marked by dress that people could see who was different from them and would only contact people similar to themselves (homophily). Contemporary research on social capital and social networks is less dismissive of the effects of homophily (Mouw 2006). Furthermore, following Toynbee's earlier idea that unexpected encounters and juxtapositions are a motor of historical change, Lewis Mumford (1961, 96) argued that cities are eminently important because it is only in cities that chance interactions and transactions multiply the opportunities for shock and stimuli.

Multiplicity as an attraction is important not just because it is common in cities but also because archaeologists have a good chance of detecting the places where people crowd. Chapter 5 explores the distribution of wealth across Maya cities in order to determine whether or not people of different levels of wealth had frequent contact in residential zones. In chapter 6, I discuss ceremonial plazas, marketplaces, and other locales with an eye toward the possibility that these places provided opportunities for people of diverse walks of life to intermingle. It is important to note that not all public spaces are likely to host multiplicities. Paths that weave through neighborhoods can be considered public but might have a predictable or even homogeneous set of people treading them in comparison to a central plaza or marketplace (cf. Isbell 2009, 213). Space falls on a spectrum from homogeneous to heterogeneous.

Built Form

The discussion of multiplicity entertains the possibility that people designed aspects of cities with the goal of enhancing sociability in the past (Betz 2002, 59). In 1937, Lewis Mumford put forth an influential idea of the city as theater, that cities are unique because they host the social drama of the coexistence of a wide variety of people. Built form is critical: "The physical organization of the city may deflate this drama or . . . make the drama more richly significant, as a stage-set, well-designed, intensifies and underlines the gestures of the actors and the action of the play" (Mumford [1937] 2002, 93). As Mumford and many others knew very well, built form is not just a setting for drama; it can both attract and repel people. Did built forms make Maya urban centers attractive or even vibrant? Built form includes specific buildings but also the way multiple buildings are arranged with respect to each other, the intentionally planned open spaces between them, and the routes that connect them. Built form also intersects with neighborhood layouts and the spatial distribution of wealth, but I treat these two topics as subjects of their own (chapters 3–5). Built form can be attractive because of the symbolic meanings it conveys and the ways that people moving through them might experience those forms perceptually. In some cases, meaning and perception blend together.

In terms of symbolic meaning, Wheatley (1971) famously described Chinese cities as axis mundi. They were built with very precise arrangements in order to approximate spiritual and symbolic conceptions of a properly ordered world and, more importantly, to guarantee the accessibility of the sacred. Michael Smith (2007, 30–35) has argued that it is very difficult for archaeologists to assess the extent to which ancient people planned aspects of their cities to look like cosmograms or replicas of sacred symbols. However, most cities did have built forms that were intended to manifest and reinforce some aspect of a supernaturally sanctioned world view. Settlers in and around such cities likely recognized that such elements served as variably concealed strategies for legitimating authority. Even so, most people probably also believed that they could benefit from living as close as possible to a center whose exemplary built features placed its inhabitants in the gods' favor. People might have felt small in the presence of these features but privileged compared with those who lived elsewhere (Cowgill 2003a, 44). As Janusek (2002, 53) argues, the long-term stability of Tiwanaku in the first millennium CE "was a function of its ability to promote an attractive vision of the cosmos and society, a vision that groups adopted, internalized and reformulated as their own." The notion of the cosmic referents of Maya buildings has been worked to the point of exhaustion but merits revisiting in chapter 6 from the perspective of urban attraction and stability.

Furthermore, using prominent landmarks such as massive temples as part of heavily attended ceremonies can cause people to identify with such landmarks, creating a popular consciousness of belonging, a sense of community that strengthens attachment to place. The image of the city can be "an aesthetic symbol of collective unity" (Mumford [1937] 2011, 93). Cowgill (2003a, 44) has made this point for the colossal pyramids at Teotihuacan. Though these landmarks may have satisfied the egos of the leaders, they "very likely made anyone who could identify with the grandeur feel proud and important to be a part of it all." People who may have been critical of the centralized leaders would have experienced such forms quite differently.

Attachment to place brings up a notion of the city as image elaborated by Kevin Lynch, a student of Frank Lloyd Wright. On the basis of years of talking to people in cities, Lynch (1960) argued that people create mental images of the city that provide a sense of order. Some images feature routes, others feature edges, others feature landmarks, and so forth. Cities can be designed to facilitate these attempts at organization or to frustrate them. The cities that are the easiest to image are the most alluring.

Economy

Finally, the economy of urban centers can be attractive. Production, consumption, and distribution all improve when settlements exhibit the first two components of urbanism: large population and high density. Lampard (1955) and Wolf (1966) each note that locating multitudes of producers and consumers close to each other and placing a wide variety of operations in the same settlement lead to increased efficiency. Recent work suggests this is also true of ancient cities (Ortman et al. 2014, 2015). Such efficiency, which is not limited to cost effectiveness, enhances production, consumption, and distribution.

Regarding production, "the concentration of specialized labor, including specialized administration and control . . . provides the context for invention and development in a variety of technological, artistic and intellectual endeavors" (Emberling 2003, 256). In dense urban spaces, ideas spread quickly, stoking creativity and innovation (Glaeser 2011, 19). Innovation leads to new kinds of products and more variety. While the variety of products attracts consumers, the dynamic conditions of production attract producers. Cities have more elites, and elites seek goods to show their status and increase their comfort (Trigger 1972, 582). Thus, elites seek to bring more people and producers to cities. Of course, elites are not the only ones who seek opportunities to consume for comfort and style (Pyburn 2008). To the extent that urban centers inspire the elaboration of peculiar personalities (Simmel 2002, 18) or that people in cities seek specific attire to signify social affiliation (a kind of signification that was not necessary in settlements that are small enough that most people know each other), processes of social differentiation in cities also spur consumption.

Trigger (1972, 582–584) highlights how the clustering of producers and consumers spurs innovation but also makes the production of labor-intensive goods cost effective. For example, producing fancy pottery for serving food took a lot of work. Since a potter could produce only a rather low output (compared to an obsidian blade maker, for example) in the course of a year, that potter must have been handsomely remunerated in order to make production worthwhile (Sanders and Webster 1988). Fancy pots may or may not have been sold at market, but when the price is high, the number of buyers is low. In an area with low population, such as a rural area, the number of people with the resources to buy fancy pottery might not have been large enough to support the potter. But in more densely populated areas, such as an urban center, the potter would have had access to many more consumers with the resources to buy fine pottery. Simply because of access to more buyers, cites therefore make specialization, even if the craftsperson specialized only part-time, a viable economic strategy.

Cities therefore provide the incentive for the development of diverse economies with multiple kinds of specialists. Of course, Trigger's logic presumes that producers must be supported entirely by sales of their craft. The idea here is that production of some goods is so complex or engrossing that it requires full-time dedication. The specialist does not have time to grow food on the side. This may be true for some crafts, but such producers might also be part of kin groups who farm. In this case, the kin group can subsidize the full-time specialist with food so that the crafter does not need to break even with his/her craft.

Finally, urban economies are attractive because they select for an efficient and desirable form of distribution: marketplace exchange. Marketplaces are attractive to both producers and consumers because much of one's buying and selling can occur at a single place, thus saving someone from having to travel to a different location for each good or buyer they seek. Marketplace exchange is not the only kind of exchange in complex societies: it undoubtedly occurred alongside reciprocity between neighbors, gifts across various social strata, and centralized forms of redistribution in which leaders controlled the circulation of exotic goods (Hirth 1998; Hirth and Pillsbury 2013, 5–6; McAnany 1992). Given that leaders concerned with intrapolity factionalism, interpolity diplomacy, revenue generation, ritual performance, and other enterprises would not have had the time or resources to organize the redistribution of common goods such as stone tools, pots, baskets, food, lime, clothing, medicine, and so forth, much was left to the market (Masson and Freidel 2013, 207; Stark and Garraty 2010, 44). Though rural areas can support marketplaces, urban centers are obvious places for them because a high number of producers and consumers are closely packed within them. Thus, urban marketplaces tend not only to be larger but also to feature a broader variety of goods. To the extent that people find variety attractive, marketplaces can help a city grow (Ardren 2015; Masson and Freidel 2012, 461). In the Maya area, leaders controlled the production of only a limited range of goods but marketplaces gave them a chance to benefit from the distribution of the overwhelming amount of goods they were not involved in producing. By sponsoring marketplaces, they could perhaps levy a charge on vendors who wanted to use a booth at the market (Shaw 2012). Even if leaders could not benefit economically from marketplaces, they could gain a degree of prestige or symbolic capital from hosting them (Hirth 2010), they could gain an outlet for converting into wealth goods the staple goods they collected as tribute (Garraty 2010, 20–21), or they could stimulate the kinds of consumption that reaffirmed their ability to control taste and set standards of excellence (Pyburn 2008).

For a number of reasons, Maya economies have only recently come to be understood as complex. With the exception of a small number of studies (e.g. Wurtzburg 1991; Jones 1996), serious consideration of Maya marketplaces did not begin until about fifteen years ago. Chapter 2 reports on a torrent of new work that has prompted a reconsideration of Maya economies. In particular, it highlights the marketplaces that made Maya cities attractive. Chapter 6 revisits marketplaces from a social perspective, arguing that the large marketplaces at the center of some Maya cities could have been alluring spaces of multiplicity and spectacle. Chapter 5 focuses on wealth inequality, a common feature of complex economies. Among other discussions, that chapter treats the question of how to measure wealth in cities and how it relates to status and class.

Conclusion

Settlements qualify as cities if they have three of the following four characteristics: specialized functions, social differentiation, large size, and high settlement density. Urban centers are cities that may have a broad array of characteristics but must have social differentiation, large size, and high density. In the next chapter, I propose that some ancient Maya cities shared characteristics with urban centers in other parts of the world, past and present. High density, large populations, and appreciable social differentiation brought socially distant people physically close. Ancient Maya urbanites had to cope with some of the downsides of urbanism: crowding, many strangers, health risks. Yet many people chose to live in urban centers. Did they take measures to adapt to these downsides? Given an absence of predictable or systemic shortcomings with rural life (see chapter 6), at least some of the people who moved to Maya cities could have stayed in the country. Something must have attracted them to cities. In the chapters that follow, I argue that these attractions consisted of commercialized economies (chapters 2, 6), neighborhoods (chapters 3, 4), multiplicities (chapters 5, 6), and built form (chapter 6). All four can be studied archaeologically. From a relational perspective, I argue that people at all positions of the social hierarchy worked to create these attractions. They worked together because satisfying their own self-interests first required that they satisfy the broader, foundational issue of making cities livable.

Hannerz (1980, 99) writes that when analyzing cities, one could easily "glance over one's shoulder" and get distracted by political economy or some other body of theory and not attend to the notion of cities as interesting places. Life in a dense, heterotopic place has characteristics that are different from those that prevail elsewhere. Hannerz thus emphasized that urban anthropology, as opposed to anthropology done in urban settings, should take stock of the sense of place, the senses of experience that people get, and how they modify that experience to meet their needs. I titled the book "Urban Maya," as opposed to, say, "Maya Cities," because I wanted to draw attention to the notion that some Maya cities were characterized by high settlement density and had to manage or offset the complications that accompany such density. At the same time, the book considers many large cities where settlement densities may not be unequivocally urban. This is because cities and urban centers are part of a continuum that does not offer a clear point of division between the two. Furthermore, as I discuss in the next chapter, nonurban locations are also important for understanding urban ones.

Finally, some disclaimers. This book is not a comprehensive treatment of Maya cities. Because of a shortage of extensive maps or other information, I do not even mention cities that would make anyone's "top ten" list in terms of size, such as El Mirador (Hansen 2001) and Izamal (Millet Cámara and Burgos Villanueva 2006). I also do not focus on the collapse of cities. The depopulation of Maya cities has generated a lot of scholarship in the last decade (e.g., Demarest et al. 2004; Webster 2002). How cities managed to reach their peak populations in the first place requires more study. In focusing on cities I do not mean to imply that smaller settlements were somehow less important. Smaller settlements beyond cities were complex, viable, and innovative (Iannone and Connell 2003; Yaeger and Robin 2004; see also chapter 6), not to mention healthier. Cities therefore had to offer a lot in order to get people to move to them. Some readers may say that no Maya were urban. Others may say that I don't consider enough ancient Maya people to have been urban. In the following chapters, critics from both sides should nevertheless find contributions to themes of broad interest, such as wealth distributions across large sites and units of social organization intermediate in size between households and sites.

2

Ancient Maya Cities and Urban Centers

The place of which I am speaking was beyond all
doubt once a large populous and highly civilized city.

Stephens (1841, 413)

When John Lloyd Stephens traveled across Yucatan and Central America in
the 1830s, he frequently used the word city to refer to ruins such as Copan,
Palenque, Quirigua, and Uxmal, the referent in the epigraph. Other nineteenth-century explorers, such as Del Río (1822), Walker and Caddy (Pendergast 1967, 123), Waldeck (1838), and Maudslay (1889–1902, 5, part 3, 10),
also referred to Maya ruins as cities. They did so because they thought that
large populations clustered near the largest buildings and that these populations featured a complex class structure (Becker 1979, 4). These thoughts
imply that Maya sites fulfilled three of the components of cities—size, density, social differentiation—presented in chapter 1. Other nineteenth-century
writers, such as Lewis Henry Morgan (1880, 73–74), argued that Maya society was egalitarian and communal. Morgan explicitly criticized Stephens
for his liberal use of the word city, stating that Stephens applied the word
to any and all clusters of ruined buildings. Instead, Morgan claimed that the
Maya lived in a series of small villages spread evenly across the landscape
(see also Kurjack 1974, 20–21). Of course, all of these claims, whether for or
against cities, were impressionistic and indefensible because they lacked the
systematic demographic data necessary to back them up. The debate could
not advance until the middle of the twentieth century, when archaeologists
looked beyond site cores and carried out research designs that systematically
documented the extent of outlying residential areas (Willey 1956a, 113–114).

Despite a pioneering effort at Uaxactun in the 1930s (Ricketson and Ricketson 1937), demographic data from large sites did not emerge until the early 1960s, when maps of Tikal and Dzibilchaltun revealed the full extent of these two behemoths (Andrews 1965; W. Coe 1965).

Yet the maps of Tikal (Carr and Hazard 1961) and Dzibilchaltun (first circulated in 1960 but published in 1979 by Stuart and colleagues) did not settle the question of whether or not large Maya ruins were cities. Instead, the debate shifted to disagreements over types of cities, with the naysayers relegating large Maya sites to a lesser category of city known as the regal-ritual city (Sanders and Webster 1988), which I define later in this chapter. As many archaeologists have noted, lumping all Maya cities into a single category oversimplifies the actual diversity of Maya cities and therefore distorts our understanding of the ancient Maya (Chase et al. 1990; Hutson et al. 2008; Smith 1989). As I explain below, calling all Maya cities regal-ritual also implies that Maya cities are second-tier cities, not fully comparable to impressive ruins elsewhere in the world. The fault lines in the debate center on several issues, including settlement density, degree of occupational specialization, economic complexity, and commercialization. Although very few archaeologists today doubt that the Maya had cities comparable to those elsewhere in the world, in this chapter I review the debate for many reasons. To begin with, such a review provides the opportunity to present some actual Maya cities. Whereas chapter 1 introduced general ways of thinking about cities, working through competing perspectives about large Maya sites localizes the concept of city for the Maya area, providing an orientation for later chapters. Looking closely at questions of settlement density, economic complexity, and the importance of markets also permits synthesis of new data. Such synthesis permits us to talk not just about Maya cities but also about Maya urbanism. To set the stage, I begin by presenting the intellectual landscape that existed prior to the production of the Tikal and Dzibilchaltun maps.

Debating Maya Cities

Nobody denies that Maya sites with massive temples meet an important requirement of some definitions of cities: they serve a specialized ceremonial/ritual function in relation to a broader hinterland (Trigger 1972, 577). The debate centers instead on population size, population density, social differentiation, and commercial development. This chapter discusses all four themes.

Shortly before research was undertaken at Tikal and Dzibilchaltun, the balance of data and many well-respected Mayanists—Kidder, Shook, Proskouriakoff, Morley, de Borhegyi—supported the notion that large Maya ruins were cities in the sense of large population centers with significant social differentiation (see Becker 1979 for a useful review). The first serious contribution to suggest that large Maya ruins were not cities came from Oliver Ricketson's survey of Uaxactun. Ricketson surveyed four 400-yard-wide transects, each one starting from a seasonal wetland a few hundred meters south of Group A and extending 1.8 kilometers in each of the cardinal directions. He believed that his survey results showed that the density of housemounds around the Uaxactun site core was low (82 structures per square kilometer of habitable land) and that the housemounds extended out from the temples at the site core with no end, thus challenging the idea that residents clustered near the site core (Ricketson and Ricketson 1937, 15). Using an ethnographic analogy with the highland Guatemalan towns of Sololá and Chichicastenango, Ricketson proposed that Uaxactun hosted large festivals and ceremonies but housed few permanent residents. In other words, Uaxactun was like a vacant ceremonial center: mostly empty except during celebrations. Becker (1979) notes that most other towns in highland Guatemala are in fact not like those Ricketson chose for his analogy with Uaxactun. In his popular, nonscholarly publications, Eric Thompson (1931, 334) presented an argument similar to Ricketson's, explicitly using the term "ceremonial center" to refer to sites with large temples but low population. Yet Thompson did not provide data in support of the idea of the vacant ceremonial center and did not discuss it in his scholarly work (Becker 1979).

Ricketson's Uaxactun research design—systematic survey of cruciform transects that extend out from a site core—was a huge advance in field methods. Mayanists still use cruciform transects today (Healy et al. 2007; Hutson et al. 2008; Ringle and Andrews 1990). However, Ricketson did not survey the transects carefully enough and did not extend them far enough away from the Uaxactun site core. In the 1960s, Dennis Puleston (1974, 1983) resurveyed Ricketson's south transect while completing a survey transect between Tikal and Uaxactun, a distance of about 19 kilometers. On Ricketson's south transect, Puleston found 2.5 times the number of mounds that Ricketson had found: approximately 200 mounds per square kilometer of habitable (e.g., nonswamp) land. Puleston's longer survey transect also showed that settlement density dropped as the distance from the Uaxactun site core increased (Ricketson's transects did not go far enough out from the Uaxactun site core to see this). Puleston estimated a settlement density of eighty-eight mounds per square kilometer of habitable land in between Tikal and Uaxactun, less than half of the settlement density within Uaxactun.

Research by Gordon Willey and William Bullard renewed Ricketson's ideas and established a model of the Maya as rural and relatively egalitarian. In the period 1953 to 1956, Willey (1956b, 778) surveyed along the Belize River Valley and found housemound clusters "in a more or less continuous distribution" over a stretch of about 50 kilometers. At Barton Ramie, Willey documented a density of 106 mound clusters per square kilometer. Since these house clusters usually contained two or three mounds, the settlement density would exceed 200 mounds per square kilometer. After walking a distance of 250 kilometers along a network of trails in northeast Peten, Guatemala, and mapping arbitrarily selected chunks of land at two locations, Bullard (1960) reported evenly dispersed mounds in rural areas and noted that these mounds exhibited a higher density (178 mounds per square kilometer) than what Ricketson found at Uaxactun. Along with Bullard and Willey's new settlement data came a new ethnographic analogy. Whereas Ricketson had compared Uaxactun to highland Guatemalan towns, ethnographer Evon Vogt (1969) showed that Zinacantan, a twentieth-century regional center in highland Chiapas, was populated heavily only during annual ceremonies. For the rest of the year, most people lived in hamlets dispersed beyond Zinacantan. Vogt noted that while more compact settlement patterns could be found in places such as Yucatan during the twentieth century, he maintained that such compaction resulted from Spanish colonial disturbance. Vogt (1969, 590) argued that classic period Maya settlement patterns, consisting of the small, dispersed hamlets Bullard and Willey found, were "astonishingly close" to what he documented in and around Zinacantan.

Bullard and Willey argued that the social structure of the ancient Maya was relatively egalitarian because the well-built and spacious houses they encountered on their surveys suggested that the farmers spread across the landscape were all "reasonably prosperous" (Willey 1956a, 779). In response to the idea that the massive buildings in ceremonial centers imply that the ancient Maya must have had an elite class of rulers and priests, Vogt (1969) countered with another analogy based on his ethnographic fieldwork in Chiapas. In what is called the cargo system, offices of religious and political leadership required large outlays of personal resources but rotated every few years. The system thus provided a leveling mechanism that maintained social equality: people who had become wealthy would lose their wealth through the burden of office holding. Similar mechanisms would have maintained egalitarianism in ancient Maya societies. Willey dismissed abundant ethno-historical documentation that identified nobles, commoners, and slaves in sixteenth-century Maya societies by arguing that such social differentiation was imported into the Maya area as a result of contact with class-based societies in central Mexico during the Postclassic period and contact with the Spanish after the conquest. Likewise, when systematic settlement data from Late Postclassic Mayapan emerged in the 1950s (Shook 1952; Proskouriakoff 1955) and proved that this city contained 4.2 square kilometers of dense settlement clustered inside a wall (figure 2.1), critics (Sanders 1963, 224–230; Willey and Bullard 1965, 370) responded that Mayapan's leaders, who claimed central Mexican ancestry, brought this compact urban style of settlement to Mayapan from Central Mexico, which had a deep precedent of compact cities going back to Teotihuacan at the beginning of the first millennium CE. In other words, researchers claimed that the Maya themselves did not create cities: other people forced cities onto them (see Kurjack 1974, 27 for a similar summary).

Bullard and Willey's field projects were methodological advances in the sense that they were the first to focus attention on broad areas beyond large site cores. However, they did not systematically map terrain extending from site centers to hinterlands. Bullard (1960, 355) acknowledged that his goal was to "get around and see as much as possible . . . rather than provide the accurate quantitative data that result from careful mapping and test excavating." Willey's evidence of over 200 mounds per square kilometer in rural areas along the Belize River was misleading because it came from Barton Ramie, which is a small but complex and relatively dense site (Yaeger 2003). Systematic surveys conducted more recently in rural areas of the Belize River Valley show high settlement densities in fertile upland soils, but these are a fraction of habitable zones. On average, settlement densities remain below 100 mounds per square kilometer (Ford and Fedick 1992; Yaeger 2010). Decisively resolving the question of whether the Maya had cities required systematic maps that began at site cores and extended well into the periphery.

Against this backdrop, research at Tikal blazed new trails, literally and figuratively. Carr and Hazard's (1961) map of Tikal revealed a density of 275 structures per square kilometer in the central 9 square kilometers. In his re-

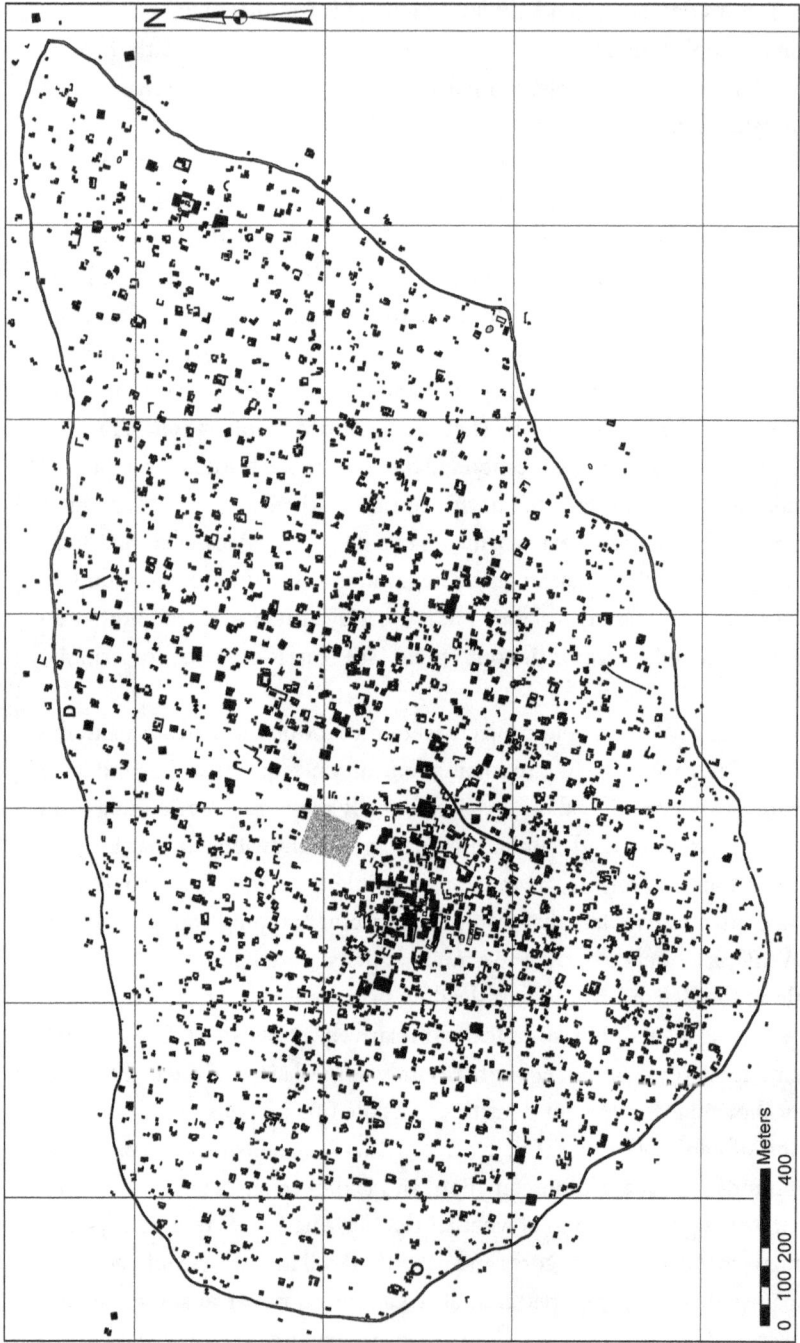

Figure 2.1. Map of Mayapan, Yucatan, Mexico, highlighting settlement within the wall; structures shown in black. Adapted from Timothy Hare's digitization of the Carnegie Project base map (Pollock et al. 1962).

view of the map, Willey (1962) raised two points, both of which suggested that residential settlement did not cluster around Tikal's major temples and palaces. He first noted that Carr and Hazard's map showed no site limits. He then stated that Tikal's settlement density approximates rural settlement densities he and Bullard had documented in areas far away from major ceremonial centers. Puleston's surveys beyond the nine-square-kilometer map, also part of the University of Pennsylvania project, rebutted both of Willey's points. Puleston expanded the Tikal map from 9 square kilometers to 16 square kilometers by mapping an additional 500 meters in all directions beyond the Carr and Hazard map. More importantly, beyond the sixteen-square-kilometer square, Puleston mapped 500-meter-wide "strips" that extended 12 kilometers out from Tikal in the east, west, north, and south and additional strips measuring 3.45 kilometers and 6 kilometers that reached Uaxactun (Puleston 1973, 1983). Puleston's survey, which covered over 30 square kilometers, definitively demonstrated clustering at the Tikal site core (figure 2.2).

On the basis of Tikal Project data, Haviland (1969, 1970) estimated that 39,000 people lived in the central 63 square kilometers (620 people per square kilometer) and 6,000 in the peripheral 60 square kilometers (100 people per square kilometer). Culbert and colleagues (1990, 116–117) have proposed more nuanced figures: 922 people per square kilometer for the central 9 square kilometers, 711 people per square kilometer for the next 7 square kilometers, 440 people per square kilometer for the next 104 square kilometers, and 153 people per square kilometer for the outlying rural area. In other words, Tikal was not only large, it was much more densely occupied than the rural hinterlands. I should clarify, though, that the lines dividing cities from hinterlands were blurry. Although Maya cities exhibit clustering, they generally lack a sharp threshold between the denser city center and the less dense rural dispersion. Only one Maya city—Mayapan—has a wall that appears to mark an important drop-off in density (Russell 2008). Although other cities—such as Aké, Ek Balam, Dos Pilas, Cuca, Tulum, Chunchucmil, Becan, Uxmal, and Chacchob—had encircling walls, these delimited a ceremonial precinct or a core to be defended, not the edge of the city where domestic settlement density drops (Dahlin 2000; Webster 1976, 1979).

Unlike the Tikal survey work, mapping at Dzibilchaltun did not extend deeply into the rural area. Stuart and colleagues (1979) mapped a nineteen-square-kilometer block, roughly 6 kilometers east-west by 3 kilometers

Figure 2.2. Map showing 7.5 square kilometers of the center of Tikal, Peten, Guatemala. Contour lines represent five-meter intervals; structures are shown in black. Courtesy of Penn Museum.

north-south. The site core was about 500 meters east of the exact center of the block. A certain patchiness in the site's settlement (large empty tracts here and there; see Kurjack 1974, figure 24) and the existence of several small settlement clusters make it harder to infer from the nineteen-square-kilometer map a single pattern of clustering around the site core. Yet if one looks only at the distribution of vaulted structures, clustering near the site core is clear. The Dzibilchaltun map stands out for its high overall settlement density: 8,390 structures (and Kurjack [1974, 80] admitted to missing small structures) within 19 square kilometers, which converts to 442 structures per square kilometer.

In response to suggestions that population density was in fact quite low because very few houses at sites such as Tikal and Dzibilchaltun were occupied at the same time (Sanders 1963; Sanders and Price 1968, 165; Thompson 1971), Haviland (1972, 2014) replied that excavations in 117 structures at Tikal showed that most buildings had multiple renovations during the Late Classic period, demonstrating that they were occupied through much of that period. Excavations or surface collections in over 700 architectural contexts at Dzibilchaltun produced similar results (Andrews 1965; Andrews and Andrews 1980; Kurjack 1974).

If Puleston's systematic survey of intersite areas provided the first empirical proof that rural settlement density estimates like that of Bullard's 178 mounds per square kilometer could not be applied broadly across the lowlands, rural surveys since the 1960s have further circumscribed the applicability of Bullard's figure (Ford 1986; Hutson et al. 2008; Hutson and Covarrubias Reyna 2011; Rice and Rice 1990; Yaeger 2010). At the same time, settlement beyond centers such as Tikal and Dzibilchaltun consists not just of dispersed hamlets but also numerous villages and minor centers, such as Barton Ramie, where population densities exceeded those of rural areas (Ashmore 1981b). In comparison to Mesopotamia, a higher proportion of the total Maya lowland population lived outside cities, thus giving support to the notion of a dispersed settlement pattern and raising inquiries about the political and economic consequences of that pattern (see also Freidel 1981a).

Finally, research at both Tikal and Dzibilchaltun produced evidence of social differentiation. At Dzibilchaltun, the extreme diversity in the costliness of houses suggested social differentiation in terms of wealth (Kurjack 1974, 93). The Tikal research produced similar evidence and demonstrated the existence of hereditary social inequality by showing that individuals buried in tombs with rich offerings (probably kings) had higher stature than everyone else, implying that they enjoyed special diets beginning in early childhood (Haviland 1966). The Tikal excavations also produced evidence for horizontal differentiation in terms of craft specialization. Becker (1973) marshaled excavation data for knappers, dentists, sculptors, masons, potters, and woodworkers (see also Haviland 1974). Finally, the extraordinary material culture (musical instruments, feather headdresses, jade and shell adornments, etc.) seen in tombs and painted pots and on murals from the site of Bonampak implied the presence of several other specialists (Adams 1970; Coe 1973). Although most craft specialization in the Maya area took place part-time in household contexts as opposed to workshops (McAnany 1993b, but see Shafer and Hester 1983, 537), this is not terribly different from what archaeologists have determined for cities in central Mexico (Hirth 2009a).

In sum, archaeologists working at Tikal (W. Coe 1965; Haviland 1969, 430; Haviland 2008, 271) and Dzibilchaltun (Andrews 1965; Kurjack 1974, 93–94) argue that these sites are cities because of their size, density, and social differentiation (vertical and horizontal) (see also Andrews 1975, 15–18). The massive temples and administrative buildings stand as evidence for the specialized functions these centers served, a point that was never doubted even by archaeologists who were once skeptical of the idea of Maya cities. These two sites thus satisfy all four of the criteria for defining cities presented in chapter 1. Unsurprisingly, as a result of the research at Tikal and Dzibilchaltun, Ashmore and Willey stated in a 1981 summary of Maya settlement patterns research that "there has been a growing consensus that the great lowland Maya centers were considerably more like true cities than some of the opponents of this idea had originally supposed" (Ashmore and Willey 1981, 16). In W. Coe's words (1965, 52), "Tikal unquestionably was more than a ceremonial center. A relatively dense population lived there." Andrews wrote (1965, 58), "Dzibilchaltun was heavily urbanized. It must have been supported by tribute or trade with a large surrounding area." As noted in chapter 1, Childe purposefully omitted Maya sites from his consideration of ancient cities. I believe that if he had had access to the data from Tikal and Dzibilichaltun and data from later projects at Coba (Folan et al. 1983), Calakmul (Folan, Fletcher, et al. 2001), and Caracol (Chase et al. 2011), he would have changed his mind and classified these sites as cities, given the fact that they meet many of the criteria of his definition: craft working, political leadership, surplus extraction, long distance-trade.

Yet in 1988, Sanders, who had been skeptical of the existence of Maya cities at least since the 1960s, and Webster took a different position, arguing that the word city should refer only to the largest and most complex settlements. They wrote: "Our definition is a quantitative one, but our position is that certain qualitative changes in human relationships occur when communities reach a certain critical size" (Sanders and Webster 1988, 427). This position aligns with the definition of urban I presented in chapter 1. To get to a situation of physical closeness among socially distant people, a situation that prompts changes in how people live, a large quantity of diverse people must be living in a small quantity of space. In line with their definition, Sanders and Webster sought an approach to cities that has change/process at its core but accommodates quantitative measures. Richard Fox's (1977) typology of Old World cities gave them just such an approach, since it categorizes cities primarily on the basis of function, although quantification of population size and density is important in terms of what functions a city can perform.

Fox presented three types of city: regal-ritual, administrative, and mercantile. He argued that the prime function of regal-ritual cities is leadership and its ritual expression. Leaders in regal-ritual centers presided over small, weakly centralized polities. The centers themselves were small, a bit larger than villages, ranging from a few hundred to a few thousand permanent residents (Sanders and Webster 1988, 524). Since population was small, there was not a large market for luxury goods, so producers of these goods could survive only if they were attached to and subsidized by the leaders. Surely royal courts anchored many Maya cities (Inomata and Houston 2000; Houston and Inomata 2009). Sanders and Webster suggest, however, that these cities held little more than the expanded household of the king. In contrast, administrative centers are larger, denser, and more heterogeneous (Sanders and Webster 1988, 525). Sanders and Webster argued that only capitals of large polities qualify as administrative centers. I return later to Fox's third type of city, the commercial center. Sanders and Webster placed all Maya cities in Fox's regal-ritual category (see also Arnauld 2008, 21). Such a construal of Fox's typology enabled Sanders and Webster to grant Maya centers the status of city (appeasing most Mayanists?) while minimizing their scale and importance.

Sanders and Webster's use of Fox's typology has drawbacks. One could look more closely and critically at the general practice of categorizing cities into types, a practice seen clearly in Max Weber's work ([1921] 1958), although such scrutiny is beyond the scope of this chapter. For now I draw attention to the strong correlation Sanders and Webster made between polity size and city development. In their article, the only cities that qualify as administrative centers are capitals of large, expansionist polities, such as Tenochtitlan and Monte Alban. Trigger (2003, 110–112) notes that in other parts of the world, cities are not as populous in territorial states as they are in city-states. Regardless, because Sanders and Webster did not recognize any Maya cities as capitals of large polities (a valid position, but see Martin and Grube [1995] for the possibility that Tikal and Calakmul were capitals of "superstates"), they presumed that no large Maya cities developed. Yet, as we will see below, several Maya cities grew to be larger than the presumed administrative center Monte Alban, which had fewer than 30,000 inhabitants (Blanton 1978). Whether or not Maya cities were more heterogeneous than Monte Alban is difficult to determine. Recognizing that cities and states do not always go hand in hand (see chapter 1; Smith 2006; McIntosh 2005), I argue that when evaluating cities, we need to focus on the cities themselves and less on the size of ancient polities. Put differently, classifying a polity as a large state or a small state (Webster 1997, 142) does not settle the issue of whether the polity had a large capital city or a small capital city.

If we focus on the cities themselves, we find variation across Mesoamerica (Smith 1989) and within the Maya area specifically (Hutson et al. 2008). Yet Sanders and Webster placed all but four cities—Tenochtitlan, Teotihuacan, Monte Alban, and Tula—into the regal-ritual type. A type that is meant to contain cities of at most a few thousand must accommodate everything from Tikal to Ticul (an ancient minor center in Yucatan, Mexico, better known as the name of a contemporary town with several potters; Arnold 1985). Since Sanders and Webster discussed only one Maya city (Copan), their article hides variation among Maya cities. Expanding the discussion to cities such as Tikal, Calakmul, and Caracol shows that some Maya cities definitively do not fit the regal-ritual category. Although there are important differences among these three cities, each has populations ten times larger than what Fox had in mind, too much administrative architecture to be merely the extended household of a king, producers of luxury goods who were not attached to rulers, and commercial systems for exchanging goods (Chase and Chase 2014; Chase et al. 1990; Jones 2015; Martin 2012). In other words, large Maya cities may indeed have been "court centers" (Webster and Houston 2003, 427) containing the extended household of the ruler but they also had much more than this. As Rice (2006, 275) notes, Maya cities fall on a continuum between regal-ritual and administrative centers, with some closer to the latter. Recent economic data suggest that large Maya cities had some of the characteristics of Fox's commercial center (Dahlin 2009, 347; Masson and Freidel 2012, 476). We might be better off attempting to proceed without Fox's types in the first place.

In highlighting the lack of fit between certain Maya cities and the regal-ritual category, I do not mean to suggest that these cities lacked regal rituals. Maya kings certainly did host spectacular and well-attended rites and celebrations, and many have argued that the king's ritual performance was critical to maintaining both cosmological balance and the support of the masses (Demarest 1992; Houston et al. 2003; Sharer and Golden 2004). As I discuss in chapter 6, such events are definitely an aspect of cities that attracted people. The point of the current chapter is that Maya cities had more going for them than just regal rituals.

Population Density and Ancient Maya Cities

In 1997, Webster put forth a slightly modified case against the idea that Maya centers were cities "as we think of them" (Webster 1997, 135). Webster thought Maya centers were different from cities in other parts of the world because they lacked large nucleated populations (Webster 1997, 139). Nucleation can refer to two distinct concepts: high population density and clustering of population. A settlement with relatively low population density can still exhibit clustering of population as long as the settlement's population density is higher than that of its hinterland. Because these two concepts are distinct, I treat them separately. I begin with high population density, about which two misconceptions have hindered better understanding of Maya cities. The first has to do with the notion that Maya cities have low population densities compared to cities from other parts of the world. As I discuss below, this is only partially true. The second misconception has to do with the argument that low-density settlements should not be considered cities.

High Density Cities

There is no denying that a city such as Tikal, which had a density of 922 people per square kilometer in its central 9 square kilometers in the Late Classic period (Culbert et al. 1990), was less dense than the non-Maya, roughly contemporaneous Central Mexican city of Teotihuacan (6,000 people per square kilometer; Millon 1981). One should keep in mind, however, that Teotihuacan was unique in Mesoamerica for its time (Manzanilla 2012). In fact, the density of most other Central Mexican cities was not appreciably higher than in Maya cities (Marken 2011, 111; Smith 1989). In addition, at least two-thirds of the population at Teotihuacan (and possibly at Tenochtitlan) were farmers (Millon 1976, 228; Smith 1996). These facts have led to the conclusion that Central Mexican cities are not categorically different from Maya cities (Haviland 1969; Isendahl and Smith 2013).

Putting Maya cities in a worldwide context of settlement density estimates makes it possible to compare them with the kinds of cities that Webster (1997) likely had in mind. Glenn Storey (1997, 120), who compiled data from 600 Old World cities, showed that the mean density approached 13,000 people per square kilometer. Storey estimated a density of 17,670 per square kilometer for Pompei and 27,438 for Ostia. These figures are stunning, especially when compared to the density of modern cities. According to the 2000 U.S. census, New York City, the most densely populated U.S. city, has a lower population density (10,406 people per square kilometer) than the mean density of Old World cities. The next most densely populated major U.S. cities are San Francisco (6,659), Boston (5,143) and Chicago (4,582). Of course, many Old World cities are not nearly as dense as the mean of 13,000 people per square kilometer, and the median is less than the mean (see also Pyburn 2008). Although they are at the bottom of the Old World scale, several Maya cities discussed below had a population density close to or exceeding 2,000 people per square kilometer.

Palenque

Palenque sits on a natural terrace with a view north toward the coastal plain of the Gulf of Mexico (figure 2.3). Although Palenque's hieroglyphic texts reach back to the fifth century CE (Martin and Grube 2000, 154), its largest buildings and most illustrious rulers date to the seventh and eighth centuries and a series of excavations beyond the site core produced exclusively Late Classic ceramics (Barnhart 2001, 75; Gonzalez Cruz 1993; Miller 1999, 35–43). Edwin Barnhart mapped 2.2 square kilometers of the city and located 1,481 structures. The natural terrace, and most likely the city itself, contin-

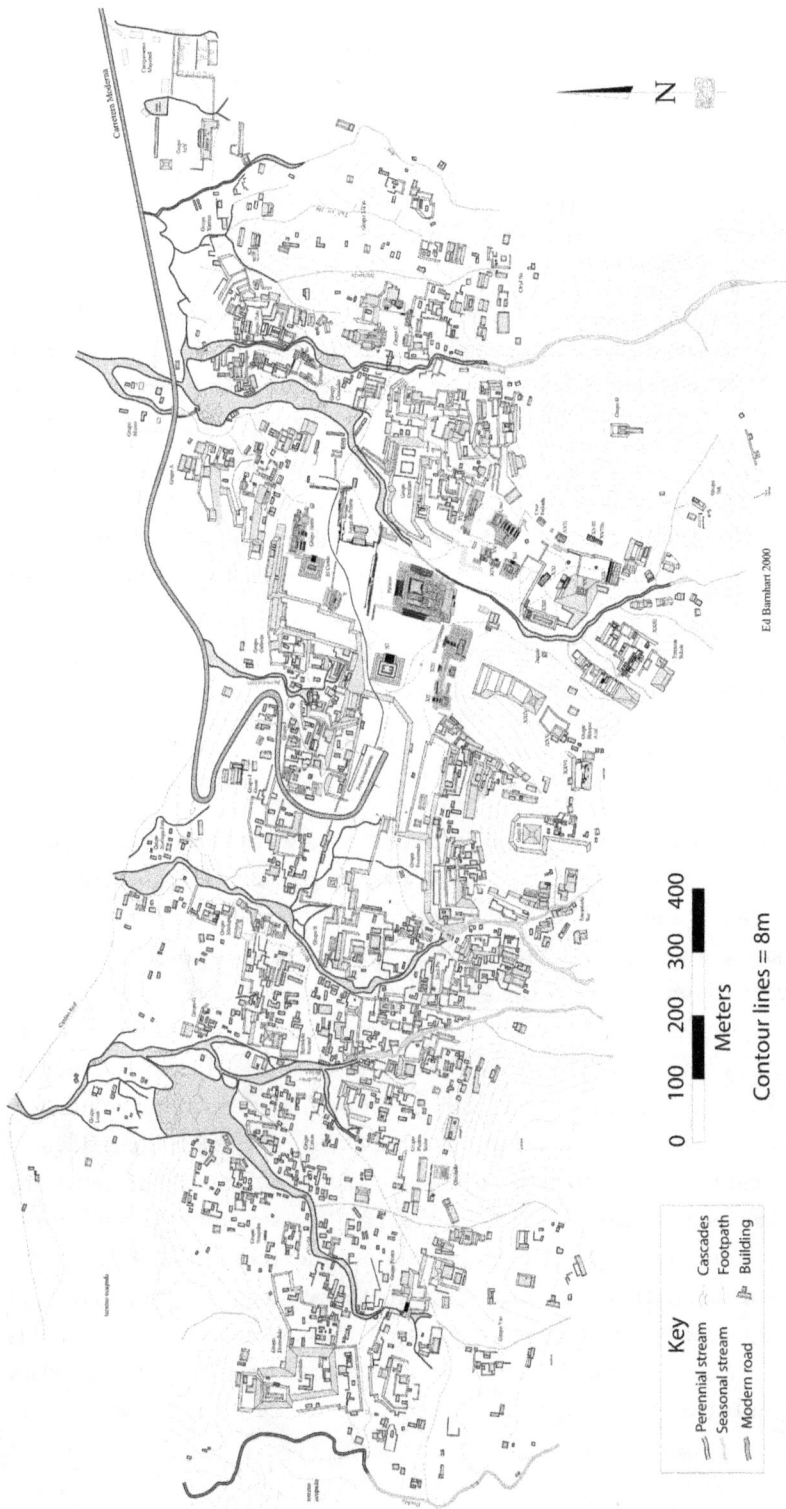

Key

— Perennial stream   Cascades
— Seasonal stream   Footpath
— Modern road   Building

0   100   200   300   400

Meters

Contour lines = 8m

Ed Barnhart 2000

Figure 2.3. Map of Palenque, Chiapas, Mexico. Reproduced courtesy of Edward Barnhart.

ues for another kilometer to the west of Barnhart's map. Since some of these structures were not houses and since it is not likely that every house was occupied at the same time, Barnhart chose to reduce the number of structures by 30 percent in order to arrive at the number of residences. Assuming between four and six people per residence, Barnhart estimated a population of between 4,147 and 6,220 (this figure could grow perhaps by thousands depending on the size of the habitable terrain to the west of Barnhart's map) and a density of between 1,885 and 2,827 people per square kilometer. Since Palenque was very densely inhabited, Barnhart believed that there was little room for hidden or perishable structures and therefore did not adjust his estimates upward for such structures. However, because it is located in hilly terrain, Palenque's ground surface is quite uneven, creating the potential that eroded sediments from slopes may have buried smaller structures. Barnhart also did not factor in the possibility of perishable structures. Due to the potential for buried and/or perishable structures I favor a population estimate near the high end of Barnhart's range for the 2.2-square-kilometer mapped area: perhaps 6,000. This estimate yields a density estimate of 2,727 people per square kilometer for the Late Classic period.

Chunchucmil

Chunchucmil is located on the plains of the Northern Maya lowlands in the northwest corner of the state of Yucatan. As part of the Pakbeh Regional Economy Program (Dahlin and Ardren 2002), archaeologists mapped 11.7 square kilometers of the site (figure 2.4). The site consists of a center of 0.55 square kilometers surrounded by a dense residential core of an estimated 5.85 square kilometers and a residential periphery of an estimated 8.7 square kilometers (Hutson et al. 2008; Hutson et al. 2016a). The site reached its peak in the sixth and early seventh centuries. All but a handful of architectural groups were occupied at this time (Magnoni 2008). The residential core contains 1,064 structures per square kilometer. To be conservative, my colleagues and I assume that 37.5 percent of these structures were either not houses or were not all occupied at the same time. Thus, with 664 houses per square kilometer and five people per house, we get a population density of 3,325 people per square kilometer, covering nearly 6 square kilometers. This estimate is likely to be too low because these calculations exclude all *chi'ich* mounds (low, amorphous piles of cobble). *Chi'ich* mounds exceeding 20 square meters have been considered houses elsewhere (Ringle and Andrews 1990; Tourtellot et al. 1990). If we assume that half the number of *chi'ich* mounds per square kilometer (about fifty *chi'iches*) housed families of four individuals, this brings the population density estimate to 3,525 per square kilometer. Over 30,000 people lived at Chunchucmil during its peak (Magnoni et al. 2012).

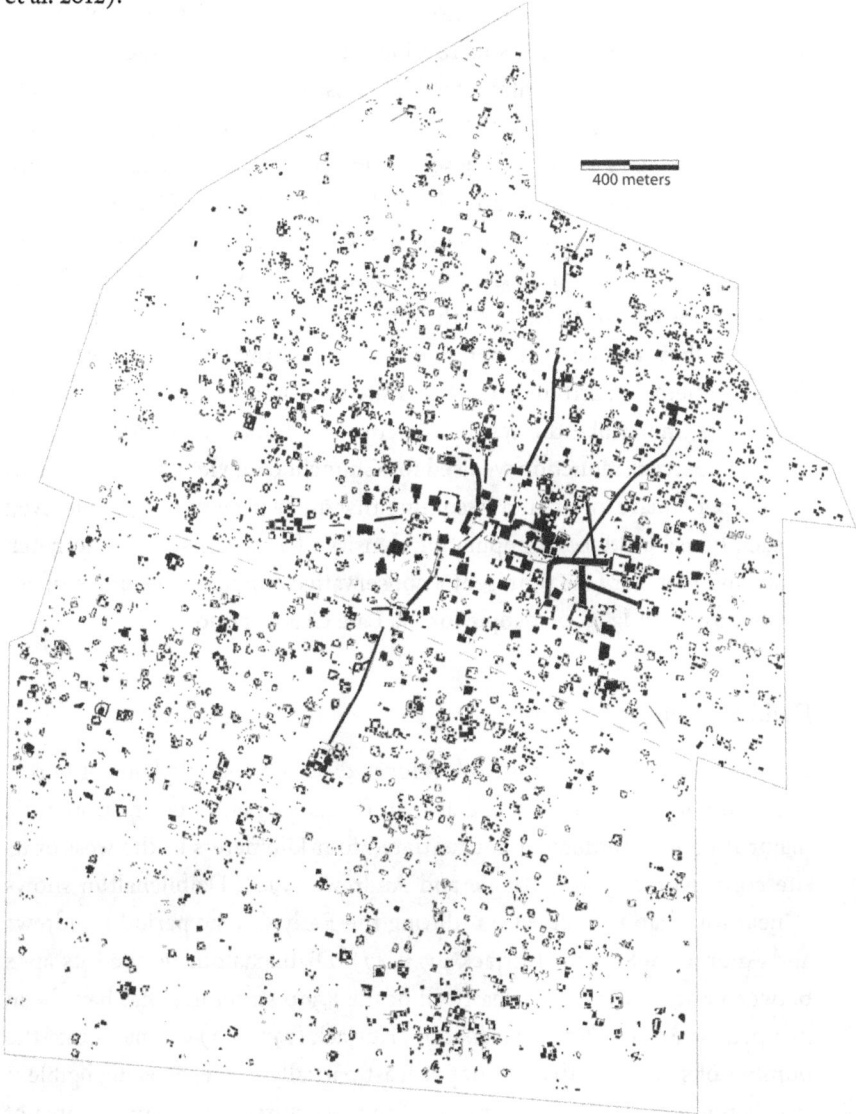

Figure 2.4. Map showing 9.3 square kilometers of the center of Chunchucmil, Yucatan, Mexico; structures shown in black. The dotted line running east to west is a modern road.

Coba

Coba is located on flat terrain in Quintana Roo, Mexico. A team led by William Folan surveyed 21.3 square kilometers of the site. In the published report on this work (Folan et al. 1983), the maps of Zones I and VI, which form a wedge-shaped area extending north from the site core and covering 3.5 square kilometers, show the most detail. Kintz and Fletcher (1983) estimate that the site covered 63 square kilometers and had an average density of 265 structures per square kilometer. The density of the area close to the site core, however, is much higher than that of the edges. For example, in zone I, map sheet 2, an approximately square 27.5-hectare block whose southern boundary is 650 meters north of the Coba Group (one of Coba's two largest architectural compounds) has about 225 structures. This yields a density of 818 structures per square kilometer (figure 2.5). Data from the published maps of zones II (to the east of the site core) and III (to the south of the site core) show equally high settlement densities. Thus, a ring of dense residential settlement surrounds the Coba site center and covers several square kilometers, much like the residential core at Chunchucmil. Applying the same 37.5 percent reduction we used for Chunchucmil yields a density of 511 houses per square kilometer. Assuming that an average of five people lived in each house produces a population density of 2,555 per square kilometer. Kintz and Fletcher (1983) present a conservative population estimate of between 40,000 and 60,000 people for the Late Classic period.

Dzibilchaltun

Dzibilchaltun, like Chunchucmil, is located on the coastal plains of northwest Yucatan. Dzibilchaltun had a small Preclassic period occupation but a major Preclassic settlement concentrated four kilometers to the west of its site core (Kurjack 1974; Ringle and Andrews 1990). Dzibilchaltun shows a "near total gap in occupation" during the Early Classic period (Andrews and Andrews 1980, 272; Kurjack 1974, 47). Dzibilchaltun reached its apex between 600 and 850 CE. Nearly all of the 8,390 structures that have been mapped have Late Classic occupation. Kurjack (1974, 94) estimates that the number of structures that are not at least partially domestic is negligible. I am skeptical about this since many of the structures have a surface area of less than 20 square meters. At the same time, hundreds of structures have quite a large surface area (over 200 square meters) and probably supported

Figure 2.5. Map of a residential portion of Coba, Quintana Roo, Mexico. The gray polygon in the inset map in the lower left corner shows where this portion lies in reference to the site's major causeways. Adapted from Folan 1983, zone 1, sheet 2. Courtesy of William Folan and Elsevier.

more than one perishable house on top. In addition, Kurjack admits that the mapping project probably missed a lot of small structures. These two considerations counterbalance the number of structures that are not houses. Kurjack decreased the number of houses by 10 percent to account for structures that are not Late Classic. I would probably decrease this number by another

5 percent to account for the probability that not all Late Classic structures were occupied throughout the entire Late Classic period. The final estimate of the number of residences per square kilometer comes to 375. Five people per residence yields an average population density of 1,875 per square kilometer (and I emphasize the word average, given the patchiness of settlement within the 19 square kilometer map), which converts to about 35,000 people who lived within the 19 square kilometers shown on the map. Kurjack (1974, 94) estimated a total population of 42,000.

Sayil

Sayil is located in the Puuc hills of Yucatan, Mexico, and the map of it that Sabloff and Tourtellot (1991) produced is one of the best maps of a Maya site made thus far (figure 2.6). Although their map covers a substantially smaller area than the maps that have been produced for Tikal, Dzibilchaltun, Coba, and Calakmul, it surpasses these in detail thanks in part to the excellent preservation of surface features. The Sayil team, which Sabloff and Tourtellot directed, estimated that the site covered 3.45 square kilometers, of which they mapped 2.44 square kilometers. Sayil had a short occupation, from 700 to 900 CE (Tourtellot et al. 1992). Tourtellot et al. (1990) estimate that 10,858 people lived at Sayil during the site's peak. This estimate yields a population density of 3,147 people per square kilometer. However, several factors unnecessarily inflated this estimate. First, Tourtellot et al. presumed that each room in Sayil's buildings could house a family of four. However, the average room on foundation brace buildings covers only 8 square meters and the average room on stone buildings covers only 12 square meters. Most archaeologists agree that a family needs a minimum of 20 square meters of roofed space (Ashmore 1981b, 47). Second, Tourtellot assumed that all chi'ich mounds mapped at the site housed a family of four. Many of the chi'ich mounds on the Sayil maps are under 20 square meters, probably too small to be houses. Third, Tourtellot et al. assumed that all rooms and all platforms served as houses. Most archaeologists presume that at least 15 percent of all structures in residential areas of sites were not houses. Finally, I would assume that 5 percent of the structures were unoccupied even during the Late Classic peak. Taking these points into consideration, we should reduce Sayil's population estimate by perhaps 40 percent, bringing the population density down to 1,888 people per square kilometer.

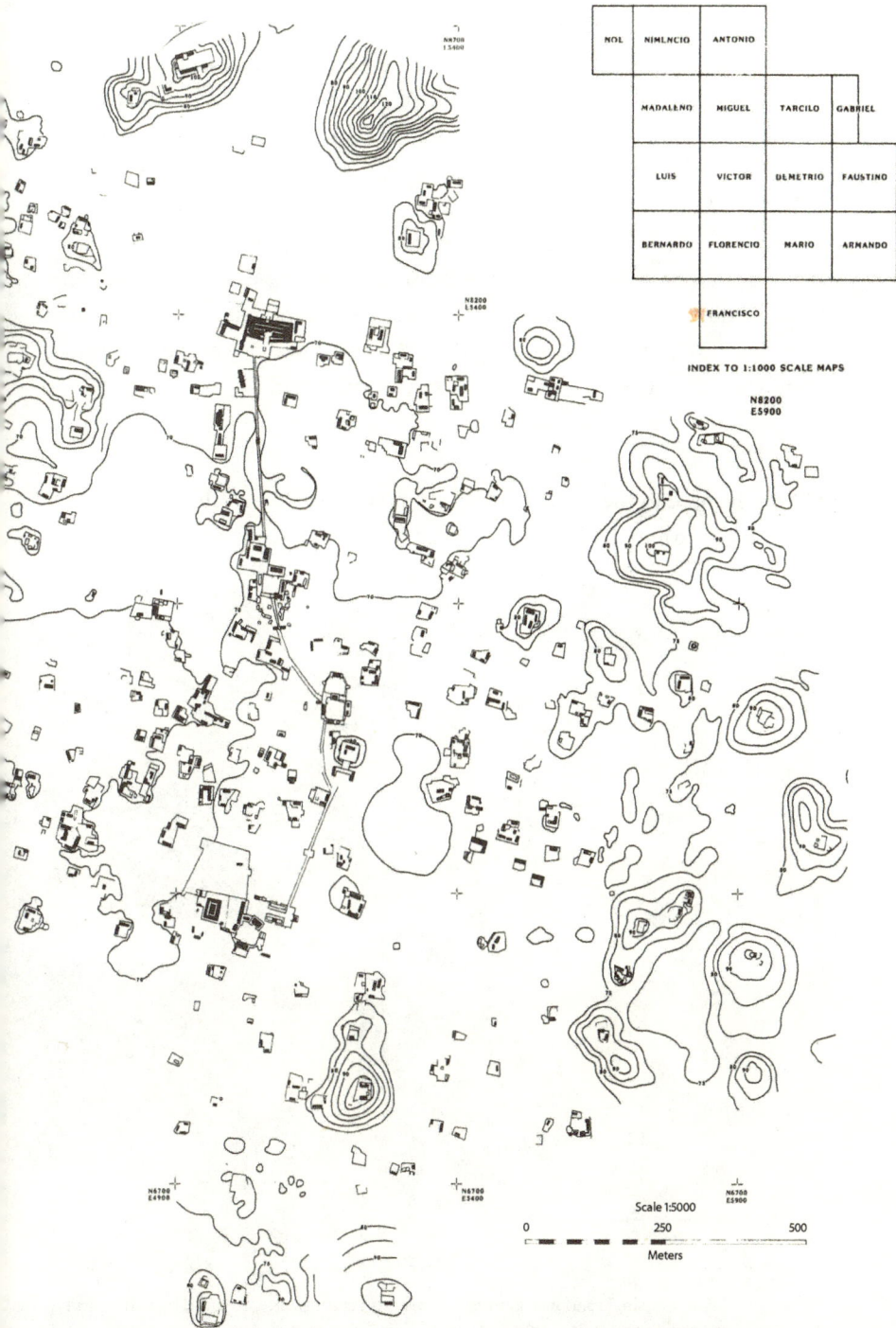

INDEX TO 1:1000 SCALE MAPS

Figure 2.6. Map of Sayil, Yucatan, Mexico. Contour lines represent five-meter intervals; structures are shown in black. Reproduced courtesy of the Sayil Archaeological Project.

El Peru/Waka'

El Peru/Waka' is located in northwest Peten, Guatemala. Damien Marken (2011, 230) and colleagues mapped 303 structures in an area of 0.24 square kilometers of the urban core. Marken estimated that the site core covers 1 square kilometer, for a total of 1,263 structures per square kilometer. Since only 85 percent of this square kilometer is habitable, Marken reduced the structure count to 1,061. To take account of contemporaneity and the fact that many of the structures in the site core are likely to be temples and other kinds of nonresidential structures, I would reduce this number by 40 percent, leaving 637 houses. Assuming that each house had five residents gives a population density of 3,185 people per square kilometer.

Copan

Copan, located in the Copan pocket of the Copan River Valley in Honduras, had an extremely dense residential population in its site core (figure

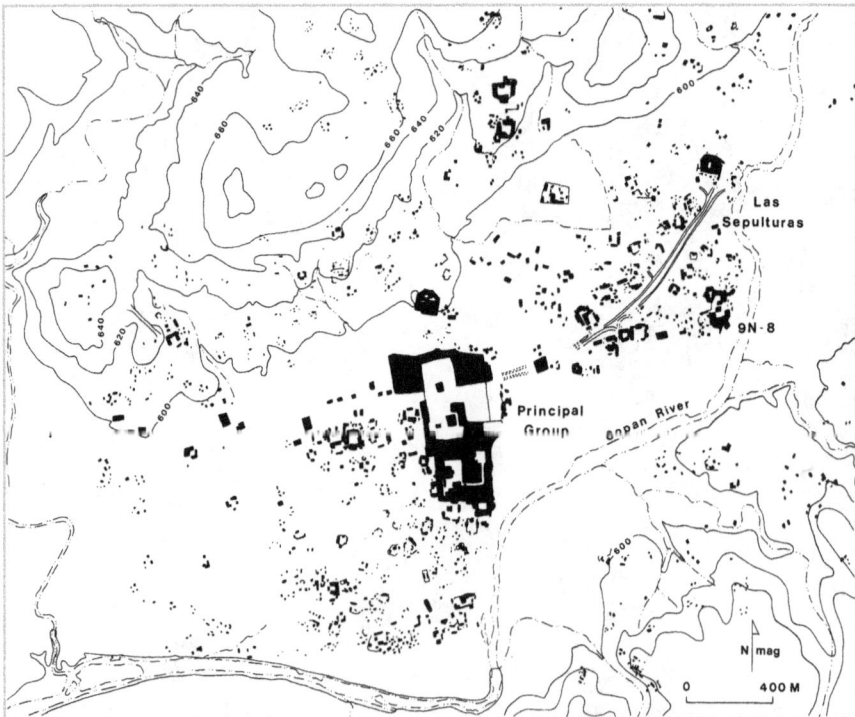

Figure 2.7. Map of Copan, Honduras. Courtesy of Wendy Ashmore. Reproduced by permission of the Society for American Archaeology from *Latin American Antiquity* 2(3), 1991.

2.7). Webster (2008, 241) estimated a density of 12,000 people per square kilometer. Although the area—0.6 square kilometers—that had this density is small, over 7,000 people would have lived within it in the Late Classic period.

⌗

Palenque, Chunchucmil, Dzibilchaltun, Sayil, El Peru/Waka', Copan, and Coba show that several Classic period Maya cities had settlement densities of about 2,000 people per square kilometer or higher. Mayapan, which archaeologists once saw as exceptionally dense, actually fits within the range of settlement densities presented above. The population at Mayapan was concentrated within walls that enclosed 4.2 square kilometers, although additional settlement was found up to 500 meters beyond the walls (Masson and Peraza Lope 2014, 28, Russell 2008). A. Ledyard Smith (1962) estimated a population of between 10,000 and 12,000 people for Mayapan. Since Smith's team missed a significant number of structures, Brown estimates that between 15,000 and 17,000 people lived inside the walls (Brown 1999, 149), giving a density of between 3,500 and 4,000 people per square kilometer.

Although the Maya cities discussed above are much less densely populated than most of the 600 Old World cities analyzed by Storey (1997), they are relatively dense compared to many U.S. cities today. This point may seem overblown, but it is in fact quite important because these are the same U.S. cities from which Wirth and others developed the concept of urbanism defined in chapter 1. Densities such as those seen at Chunchucmil and Chicago are what prompt urbanization. They are what generate attractions (markets, multiplicity), disadvantages (crowding, anomie, health problems), and strategies for coping with those disadvantages (neighborhood formation, technologies of privacy). In sum, several Maya cities were unquestionably urban. They were nucleated in both of the senses that I distinguished earlier: higher population density than what one finds in the rural areas that surround these cities (clustering) and high population density when comparted to settlements from some other part of the world, such as western Mesoamerica in ancient times or the contemporary United States.

Technologies of privacy are easily observable in some of the urban centers just mentioned (and in subsequent chapters I discuss neighborhood formation as a way to cope with crowding). For example, at Coba, Chunchucmil, and Mayapan, three of the five Maya cities with the highest settlement densities, people built stone walls that encircle their domestic spaces. These walls delimited house lots, a pattern of spatial organization seen today in dense Maya settlements across Yucatan. These walls are not high enough to impede vision, but they provide a clear threshold that is closely respected in contemporary and historic house lots (Hanks 1990, 95; Restall 1997, 99). Do such walls count as technologies that help "disregard the needs, interests, and demands of those whom one does not define as relevant to the satisfaction of personal needs" (Milgram 1970, 1462)? Although houselot walls that encircle house compounds are occasionally found at less dense Classic period sites, such as Becan (Thomas 1981), lower proportions of household compounds have such walls at these sites. The arrangement of domestic architecture into plazuela groups, in which houses that are part of the same domestic compound face inward toward each other, can also be seen as a strategy for creating privacy (Hutson 2002). Although plazuela groups are common at many of the urban centers discussed above, they are also common in Maya sites without crowding. Therefore, if the plazuela arrangement does afford privacy, it does not do so as part of urbanization.

Low-Density Cities

As noted above, two misconceptions about population density have hindered better understanding of Maya cities. The second misconception has to do with the argument that low-density settlements should not be considered cities. Following the flexible definition of cities provided in chapter 1, a settlement can qualify as a city if it has three of the following four characteristics: social differentiation, large size, high population density, and specialized functions. Thus, settlements can be considered cities if they have social differentiation, large size, and specialized functions but lack high population density. Considering low-density centers as cities is important because it suggests that insights learned from tropical behemoths such as Tikal and Angkor are relevant to contemporary demographic, social, and ecological challenges (Costanza et al. 2007; Chase and Scarborough 2014). Stated differently, if we dismiss Tikal and Angkor as mere towns or ceremonial centers that were not comparable in any way to contemporary cities, we render potential lessons from the past inapplicable to the city-dominated context of the modern world.

But what contributes to low population density in large settlements that have social differentiation and specialized functions? Let us first clarify the question by returning to the distinction between population density and settlement clustering. As noted above, Tikal, where the density was relatively low compared to cities such as Chunchucmil or Copan, certainly exhibited settlement clustering: its core had higher settlement density than its periphery did (Haviland 1969, 1970; Puleston 1983). Caracol, another low-density site, also exhibits clustering of population. Recent LiDAR data clearly show that the density of residential compounds gradually decreases as distance from the Caracol site center increases (Chase et al. 2011; Figure 11). Although many low-density centers exhibit clustering, not all do. In chapter 6 and elsewhere I provide reasons for such clustering, but here I consider reasons why Maya centers generally had lower population densities than Old World cities did.

Cities with settlement clustering such as Caracol and Tikal may have low densities for a number of reasons. Lower density certainly afforded the Maya more privacy (see Moore 2005, 16–26). Some argue that the ancient Maya chose a low density settlement pattern as an adaptation to the tropical lowland environment, which provides a more fragile subsistence base in which resources are more dispersed (Scarborough 2005, 218). The notion that slash-and-burn agriculture, which requires high amounts of land, some of which must be at great distances from centers, scattered farmers centrifugally away from centers has been refuted (Drennan 1988), in part because the Maya used many other forms of agriculture that were more land and labor intensive (Beach et al. 2015; Dunning and Beach 2010; Fedick 1996). Intensive agricultural plots, such as ridged fields in wetlands and terraced fields in hilly areas, require much attention, and the people who worked them would have had to live near them, and therefore farther away from centers, in order to reduce the cost of traveling to such fields. Low densities may also be the result of a decision to use parcels of land within cities ("infields") for staple crops, gardens, and orchards (Chase and Chase 1998; Dunning 1992; Isendahl and Smith 2013; Sanders 1981). Although urban planners and students of the history of cities equate the phrase "garden city" with Ebenezer Howard's (1902) idea of building dense, small cities in the middle of the countryside, Caracol is an excellent example of a more literal kind of garden city: one in which terraced agricultural plots were interspersed throughout the city's residential zones (Chase and Chase 1998). The confirmed presence of infields is precisely what gave cities such as Caracol and Sayil (Dunning 1992) a lower population density than that of Old World cities.

Whatever the reason for low population density within clustered settlements, and whatever terms (garden city, sprawl) we use to refer to large, clustered, low-density cities, such cities are commonly found elsewhere in the world during a variety of time periods. Other examples include Khmer cities such as Angkor, which, in addition to temple precincts, has an extensive residential zone tied together by waterworks (Evans et al. 2007), Bagan in Myanmar (Hudson 2000), Anuradhapura in Sri Lanka (Fletcher 2009), cities in southeast Asia (Miksic 1999), and some early cities in Africa and South America (Isendahl and Smith 2013). The abundance of such low-density cities has been overlooked because dense cities tend to come to mind more quickly when one thinks of cities. This is unfortunate because ancient and historic cities of this type have proven to be more sustainable than we might assume (Chase et al. 2011; Fletcher 2009; Graham 1999; Isendahl and Smith 2013).

In some areas, settlement did not cluster around centers. This fact vindicates the ideas of Ricketson, Willey, and Bullard to some degree. For example, the Late Classic center of Xunantunich, Belize, did not have much residential settlement surrounding the site core (Yaeger 2010). Yet, in contrast to Tikal, which had strong roots extending back to the Middle Preclassic, Xunantunich appeared rather rapidly in a Late Classic landscape already studded with long-lived settlements such as Actuncan and Chan. Xunantunich's prosperity was short lived, from about 600 to 850 CE (LeCount et al. 2002). Dzibilchaltun, which also did not have a significant early occupation in its site core (see below), had a similar boom during about the same period of time. But, unlike at Xunantunich, people at Dzibilchaltun continued to build a substantial amount of vaulted architecture into the tenth century. In the latter part of Dzibilchaltun's history (the Pure Florescent period of the Copo II ceramic complex), the distribution of vaulted structures contracted toward the site center (Kurjack 1974). Perhaps Xunantunich would have experienced a similar episode of clustering had it survived longer.

In sum, several Maya cities have population densities that are high enough to be considered urban. Maya cities with lower population densities, such as Tikal and Caracol, exhibit nucleation in the sense of clustering. Even when a city exhibits clustering, however, defining the exact edges of the cluster can be difficult. In other words, the existence of clustering does not imply the existence of sharp boundaries between centers and their hinterlands. For example, it was once thought that the earthworks of Tikal marked the boundaries of the site (Puleston and Callendar 1967), but they do not actually do so (Webster et al. 2007). Areas of higher settlement density often grade into areas of lower settlement (Hutson et al. 2008; Trigger 2003, 124). Although Hirth (2003a, 63) proposes that Mesoamerican centers were not "qualitatively distinct" from the countryside, people would certainly have recognized the difference between a center and a small rural site (Webster 2008, 259). However, centers in the Maya area and elsewhere had a variety of bonds with their hinterlands (Joyce 2009, 189; Morley 1997, 54; Pyburn 1997, 157). The complex connections between center and hinterland bring up two concepts: Maya centers as city-states and the complexity of Maya economies.

Maya City-States

The concept of the city-state, which is derived from Classical Greece but is often applied to many other parts of the world (Charlton and Nichols 1997; Hansen 2000a), fits political, economic, and settlement aspects of Maya cities very well (Grube 2000). As Hansen (2000b) defines the concept, city-states are self-governing polities with economies that integrate both farmers and specialists. They contain a center (the city) and a hinterland that usually does not go beyond 30 kilometers from the center. Populations may range from a few thousand to figures in the low six digits. Many city-states are part of "city-state cultures" (Hansen 2000b). City-state cultures develop when several city-states are located close to each other and the people in them speak the same language and share customs and a common world view. Although city-states sometimes go to war against each other, defeated city-states usually retain autonomy in most affairs.

The classic period Maya fit Hansen's description of a city-state culture in many ways. As exploration of the southern lowlands progressed during the twentieth century, several archaeologists recognized that major centers (sites with massive temples pyramids, large palaces and administrative structures, ballcourts, and, often, carved monuments) formed a lattice that spread evenly across the landscape (Bullard 1960, 360; Hammond 1974, 319; Houston 1993, 178–179). Although most people in the northern lowlands spoke a different language (Yukatek) than most people in the southern lowlands (Ch'olti) during the Classic period, scribes in both regions used a written lingua franca that did not vary greatly from north to south. In addition, the spoken languages in the north and south pertain to the same language family, share cognates, and exhibit systematic similarities. Furthermore, intensive language contact between speakers of these related languages brought about extensive borrowing of morphemes that resulted "in syntactic structures and grammatical and syntactical categories that are remarkably alike" (Law 2014, 3). Maya people in different cities also shared customs and world views, such as maize-based subsistence, the ballgame, leadership by holy rulers (k'uhul ajaw), veneration of ancestors, the importance of sacrificial offerings to gods that represent natural forces such as rain, and a cosmology consisting, at its most basic level, of an earthly plane with four corners and a center that had portals to the underworld (Ashmore 2004; Coggins 1980; Freidel et al. 1993; McAnany 1995; Taube 1992; Schele and Freidel 1990; Schele and Miller 1986).

Classic period Maya writing, emblem glyphs in particular, suggests that the Maya envisioned their polities as something akin to city-states. Emblem glyphs are personal titles that usually appear after the names of specific people. Since 1958, Mayanists have known that they consist of three parts: a pair of affixes that are almost always the same (k'uhul, meaning holy, and ajaw, meaning ruler) and a main sign that varies (Berlin 1958). Some writers thought that the main signs referred to a particular site because each specific emblem glyph usually predominates at one particular site. Today most epigraphers see the main sign as a reference to a political unit (Matthews and Justeson 1984; Stuart and Houston 1994; Tokovinine 2013). Thus, emblem glyphs can be read, approximately, as "holy ruler of a particular realm." The main sign is sometimes a toponym that refers to a place within the capital city of the realm or to the city as a whole. In exceptional cases (such as Dos Pilas, Calakmul, and Palenque), the main sign refers to a dynasty whose court has shifted from one place to another, places that often have their own specific toponyms that differ from the main sign of the emblem glyph. Precisely as in Greek city-states, the capital city—that is, the location of the king's court, sometimes referred to in the main sign of the emblem glyph—is the largest settlement within the ruler's realm (Grube 2000, 556). The existence of dozens of emblem glyphs suggests that the Maya recognized dozens of realms, precisely what we would expect of a city-state culture. A map of the Maya area showing sites with emblem glyphs (e.g., Mathews 1991, figure 2.6) is very similar to earlier maps (e.g., Hammond 1974, figure 2) that show the largest centers.

If ancient Maya writing implies that the ancient Maya envisioned their polities as city-states, does it also imply that they had a concept of city? In other words, following a question posed in chapter 1, did the Classic period Maya have specific words for city or city dweller? The answer is no. Research on place names shows that they generally refer to hills, bodies of water, or specific buildings but not to a city in the sense of a large, dense cluster of buildings (Stuart and Houston 1994). Ancient Maya writing classifies places into two major categories, ch'e'n and kab. Ch'e'n, literally a well or cave, refers to dwellings of gods, ancestors, and kings, and kab refers to land, earth, and soil (Tokovinine 2013). Although Tokovinine (2013, 55) occasionally glosses ch'e'n as "city," in this case city merely carries the connotation of a place of dwellings (see also the contact-era term kaj: Tokovinine 2013, 19). A place of dwelling could be a village or even a natural topographic feature (for certain gods and spirits), not necessarily a city as defined in chapter 1.

Maya cities differed from each other in a variety of ways. They had different patron deities and different sacred places. Palenque, for example, had its own local gods—GI, GII, and GIII—who were centered in the Cross Group (Houston 1996). The springs that feed the tributaries running through the site were of such importance, both as ritual loci and as natural resources, that the people of Palenque gave their city the name Lakamha, meaning wide waters (French et al. 2006).

Perhaps the most noted difference between Maya cities is size. Although most people would agree that the Classic period Maya meet the definition of city-state culture in terms of settlement patterns and shared language and customs, differences in site size and, by extension, diplomatic influence, suggest that perhaps most Maya centers were not politically independent. This conjecture challenges the notion of the city-state as the basic unit of Maya political organization. The argument centers on whether each major city was mostly autonomous or ruled by a small number of larger regional centers. This topic is part of a long-running discussion about the strength of Maya polities (Demarest 1996; Chase and Chase 1996; Foias 2013; Fox and Cook 1996).

Eric Thompson (1950, 7) was one of the first to embrace the idea of Maya polities as city-states as opposed to regional states. In contrast, Marcus (1973, 1976), building on Barthel (1968), used epigraphic data to infer as few as four regional states. Adams (Adams and Jones 1981) used data on quantities of monumental plazas to infer seven regional states. However, Mathews (1985; see also Hammond 1974) proposed that each of the dozens of centers with an emblem glyph, which is to say each of the centers whose ruler held the *k'uhul ajaw* title, was economically and politically independent. Mathews's epigraphic work supersedes Marcus's work (Houston 1993, 7–8) and tilted the balance back toward the city-state model of Maya polities. One might object, however, that vast differences in size between cities that are close neighbors imply at least some degree of hierarchy between city-states. For example, in the Late Classic period, Tikal, with a population of 60,000 (Culbert et al. 1990) dwarfed Motul de San Jose, with a population of 1,200 (Foias et al. 2012). Did Tikal, located only 30 kilometers to the northeast, dominate Motul de San Jose even though Motul de San Jose had its own emblem glyph and royal court? The claim that colossal city-states held some sway over small ones finds support in Martin and Grube's (1995) epigraphic study of alliances and conflicts among Maya centers. Their study showed that the largest, most ambitious cities, such as Tikal and Calakmul, exercised diplomatic influence (arranging royal marriages, manipulating the accession of rulers) over several polities but did not go so far as to administer the economies of these polities. Leaders of some cities may have collected tribute from leaders who had been vanquished on the battlefield (McAnany 2010, 273–277; Stuart 1998, 410–416), but such victories in battle did not result in military occupation or imperial economic administration of the kind seen among the Inca (Grube 2000, 550). For example, Tikal was defeated by Calakmul's ally Caracol in 562 CE, resulting in a 130-year lapse of dated inscriptions at Tikal (Martin and Grube 2000). Yet during this time period, referred to as the hiatus, Tikal thrived: long-distance trade peaked, extensive and innovative construction projects proceeded, households prospered, and its population grew (Haviland 2014; Moholy-Nagy 2003). In another example, after Copan was unexpectedly defeated in 738 CE, resulting in the execution of its king, its dynasty was weakened, but it had rebounded by the end of the century.

In sum, Maya polities were not equal, but inequality between polities is an expected part of city-state cultures. And although Maya city-states waged war against each other, resulting in victories and defeats, just as in ancient Greece, in both places, a defeat usually did not result in the dismantling of the defeated polity or of annexation of one polity by another (Grube 2000, 550; Hansen 2000b). Rulers of the largest cities could influence rulers of smaller cities, but smaller cities did not always lack influence of their own. Returning to the question of the relation between Tikal and Motul de San Jose, although Motul de San Jose may have had barely 1,000 occupants, a number of secondary centers (Trinidad, Akte, possibly Tayasal) were under its sway at different times (Foias and Emery 2012) and Foias et al. (2012) estimate that the Motul de San Jose polity as a whole contained between 13,000 and 27,000 people. The polity was quite dynamic (Tokovinine and Zender 2012). At the end of the seventh century CE, White Bird, Motul de San Jose's king, used both the *k'uhul ajaw* title and the *kaloomte* title, suggesting regional prominence that extended beyond the polity. Although White Bird's successor was a vassal of Tikal, later rulers also used the *kaloomte* title and were even acknowledged as *kaloomtes* by *k'uhul ajaws* from other polities. The widespread distribution of fancy vases associated with Motul de San Jose also suggests the broad scale of the polity's geopolitical network (Tokovinine and Zender 2012, 65). Thus, while Tikal, a city with 60,000 people and perhaps double this number in its hinterland, could claim Motul de San Jose as a vassal at certain points in time, it did not simply absorb or colonize its neighbor 30 kilometers to the southwest. Motul de San Jose had its own extensive network of allies and opponents and flourished in a challenging geopolitical context.

Some authors state that Maya city-states "dwarf" Greek city-states (Grube 2000, 556), leading Marcus and Sabloff (2008, 22) to declare that Tikal and Calakmul do not fit Hansen's definition of city-states. I disagree. The population of Greek city-states ranged from a few thousand to well over one hundred thousand. Maya polities also fit this range. In addition, Hansen states that a city-state usually is no larger in size than 3,000 square kilometers. The Tikal polity, which covered 1,963 square kilometers, according to Culbert et al. (1990), clearly fits below this threshold. The important distinction here is between sphere of influence and polity/sphere of control. For example, Tikal could influence, even install, leaders at sites as far away as Copan, but Copan was in no sense part of the Tikal polity. The only centers that were truly part of Tikal's polity were close neighbors (Uolantun, El Encanto, Jimbal, etc.) whose lords were of lesser rank (not *k'uhul ajaws*) and named Tikal's *k'uhul ajaw* as their patron. Grube (2000), who helped work out spheres of influence, is clear about the large degree of autonomy exercised by kings who were influenced by city-states such as Tikal and Calakmul.

Yet calculating the exact population and size in square kilometers of a Maya polity/city-state causes problems because "boundary maintenance and territorial integrity were not of prime importance to the Maya rulers" (Hammond 1991, 277). Who belonged to what polity was based not so much on where someone lived as on "networks of personal, political, and religious authority that radiated from the ruler himself" (Demarest 2004, 216). In some cases, villages and homesteads at the edge of a polity had somewhat tenuous relations to the city center and could be politically independent or shift their allegiance (Inomata 2004; Scarborough and Valdez 2009). Occasionally borders of polities could become fixed and even marked by built features, as seen in the border between Yaxchilan and Piedras Negras at the end of the Classic period (Golden et al. 2008).

In addition to personal linkages between the ruler and settlements beyond the city, Maya cities and their hinterlands were also linked by flows of food. While it is true that the largest Greek city-states, such as Athens, had to import food from other parts of the Mediterranean (Whitby 1998), a very large portion of the people in Greek city-states were farmers (Weber [1921] 1958; see also Childe 1950) and many of them lived outside cities. Hansen (2000a, 159) therefore states that the close link between city and countryside was an important aspect of Greek city-states. This is also true of Maya city-states. The Greeks made no linguistic distinction between people who lived in the city and those that lived in the *chora*, or hinterland of the city-state (Hansen 2000a). This implied blurring of boundaries between city and country in Greek city-states resonates strongly with the situation among the ancient Maya, for whom the geographical boundaries of cities were likely even more blurry (see above). The question of the economic integration of Maya city-states deserves its own section.

Maya Economies

How complex were Maya economies? To what degree were Maya cities economically integrated with their hinterlands? To what degree were Maya economies commercialized? Given that whole books could be written in response to these questions (King and Shaw 2015; McAnany 2010), it may seem cavalier to broach these issues in a handful of pages. However, these questions demand answers for several reasons. First, any overview of Maya cities must discuss the degree of linkage with hinterlands. Second, the degree of commercial development has been a topic of disagreement among those who attempt to characterize the kinds of cities the Maya had. Finally, as discussed in chapter 1, marketplaces attract people to urban centers, potentially allowing such centers to sustain dense populations in the face of a variety of challenges. Marketplaces are in fact just the tip of the iceberg of a complex economy. In a part of the world where poor preservation and lack of economic texts make it difficult to document most nuances of production and consumption, the existence of marketplaces presupposes economic complexities that are normally invisible to archaeologists. I begin with the question of linkages between cities and hinterlands.

Relations between cities and hinterlands went both ways: each depended on the other for goods and services. People living at the core of Maya cities depended on a variety of products from the countryside. For example, potters living beyond the site cores of Palenque and Tikal supplied the residents of their respective centers with the ceramic vessels necessary for everyday life (Fry 1979, 1980; Rands and Bishop 1980). Furthermore, many people who lived in site cores traveled beyond their city to farm, although this was not as common in lower-density garden cities such as Caracol (Chase and Chase 1998), where smallholders lived just meters from their labor-intensive plots. Likewise, people in the hinterlands depended on cities. For example, the villagers of Ceren, El Salvador, went to markets at regional centers to acquire goods such as obsidian and polychrome pottery (Sheets 2000). People who lived in hamlets up to 5 kilometers from Chunchucmil received appreciable amounts of obsidian, but those who lived farther away had less access to Chunchucmil's markets, suggesting that economic bonds with cities were stronger among the nearer hinterlands (Hutson et al. 2010).

Scarborough and Valdez take an approach to regional economies that might be construed as conflicting with these interdependencies of city and hinterland. Their model grows from disagreement, voiced by many others (Graham 2002; Lohse 2004; Lucero 2007; Pyburn 2008; Sheets 2000; Yaeger and Robin 2004), with the idea that Maya centers dominated a single monolithic economic system (Scarborough and Valdez 2009, 211). Scarborough and Valdez argue that sustainable management of the diverse and fragile semi-tropical lowlands required economic decision-making and scheduling by multitudes of geographically dispersed producers and distributors (see also Fedick 1996; Fry 1979; Lohse 2013; Rands and Bishop 1980). Scarborough and Valdez go further and declare that some of these decentralized producers operated in complete independence from (though they were not unaware of) leaders in Maya cities. Scarborough and Valdez thus promote the idea of a dualistic economy: one economy contained cities that were tightly linked to nearby villages and the other contained communities that operated outside the political orbit of cities and secured their economic well-being without interacting with cities. Although Scarborough and Valdez argue that some villages were independent of cities, they do not imply the reverse—that some cities were independent of villages. Therefore, Scarborough and Valdez do not in fact challenge the notion of linkages between city and hinterland.

What about commercial development at Maya cities? Commercial development refers to the degree to which goods are exchanged at marketplaces. Commercial development and markets should not be seen as present or absent in a particular society. Rather, ancient economies should be characterized in terms of the degree of commercialization and market exchange (Masson and Freidel 2013, 221; Smith 2004). The term market has been defined in many different ways. At one point the pioneering economic anthropologist Karl Polanyi (1957, 247) insisted that at markets "all goods and services, including the use of land, labor, and capital, are available for purchase." In this approach, few if any markets existed prior to capitalism. A less restrictive approach defines market transactions as ones in which supply and demand affect prices (Garraty 2010). In this definition, supply and demand need not be the exclusive determinants of prices, since market exchange always takes place within institutions and value systems that can regulate various aspects of exchange. Perhaps the most inclusive approach comes from Hirth (2010), who states that markets need only have balanced and negotiated forms of exchange, a definition that implies some notion of equivalency. A marketplace is different from a market. A marketplace is a physical space where multiple buyers and sellers congregate to exchange a variety of goods. Although a market can exist without a marketplace (a seller, for example, could hawk wares door to door), a marketplace cannot exist without markets (Dahlin et al. 2007). Thus, evidence of a marketplace implies the existence of markets. At the same time, having a market does not imply a market economy—that is, an economy in which market-based exchange dominates all other forms of exchange (redistribution, reciprocity, etc.). For example, markets in Mesoamerica were part of mixed economies in which many nonmarket forms of exchange were important (Hirth and Pillsbury 2013).

Although many Mesoamerican cities had marketplaces, probably none supported themselves exclusively or even predominantly with specialized production and trade of non-agricultural goods. This means that most Mesoamerican cities were not mercantile centers as Fox defined the concept

(Sanders and Webster 1988, 539). Many people in ancient Maya cities still devoted a lot of their time to farming (Haviland 2008, 269). Yet complex commercial activity can certainly occur in cities that are not "mercantile" (Sanders and Webster 1988, 539). Scholars have recognized complex commercial activity in western Mesoamerica for quite some time yet have been slow to recognize the complexity of economies in eastern Mesoamerica, namely the Maya area.

At least four circumstances have delayed the recognition of markets and marketplaces in the Maya area: the timing of Spanish contact, the anti-market legacy of Karl Polanyi, a perceived lack of population nucleation, and a perceived lack of resource diversity. When the Spaniards penetrated central Mexico in 1519, they found the Aztec Empire at full strength and witnessed first-hand the bustling marketplace at Tlatelolco, which famously astounded them with its scale and variety of merchandise (Hutson 2000). In contrast, when the Spaniards at last established a tenuous colonial presence in the Maya lowlands of northern Yucatan in the 1540s, European diseases already had been on the scene for over twenty years, enough time to infect and disrupt local populations. Furthermore, conquest-era Maya society in northern Yucatan was already at a nadir both politically and economically because of the fragmentation of the Mayapan confederacy in the previous century and a variety of droughts and famines (Masson and Freidel 2013). Thus, nothing in the Maya area on the order of the Tlatelolco marketplace survived by the time the Spaniards ensconced themselves in the 1540s. Spanish documents therefore give a clearer picture of commercialization in Central Mexico than they do in the Maya area, resulting in a mistaken tendency of some scholars to assume that little marketing occurred in the Maya lowlands (Farriss 1984, 156).

Turning to the second circumstance that delayed the recognition of marketing among the Maya, Polanyi (1944, 1957) thought that although westerners of the last few centuries adopted the profiteering logic of markets, it was alien to most nonwesterners. He argued that in nonwestern societies, economies were embedded in strong webs of kinship and systems of values that mitigated or made inconceivable the drive to maximize and make a profit. The market mentality that, according to Polanyi, encourages relentless dickering and the search for individual gain at the expense of others, would have threatened community well-being in these societies. Marketplaces could exist only in societies where authorities were strong enough to regulate prices and police transactions, thus reducing the socially destructive aspects of the marketplace. Polanyi argued that states had enough authority to regulate a market, but less complex polities, such as chiefdoms, did not. Anthropologists now recognize that Polanyi's dichotomies between modern and premodern people, westerner and nonwesterner, do not hold: nonwesterners also seek to maximize profits while markets in western societies are embedded in and pervaded by values and institutions (Feinman and Garraty 2010; Garraty 2010). However, in the 1950s and 1960s, the influence of Polanyi's ideas caused researchers to neglect the possibility of markets in the Maya area. Well into the 1960s (e.g., Vogt 1969; Willey et al. 1965) many Mayanists thought that Maya societies were small and lacked strong leaders, precisely the kind of society that, in Polanyi's logic, would not be expected to have markets. As discussed above, work on settlement patterns, excavations, and deciphering of hieroglyphics show that Maya societies were large and complex and were characterized by extensive social differentiation, populous cities, and hereditary rulers who had the economic resources to support a number of administrative functions. Thus, even in Polanyi's terms, the Maya could handle markets. Several researchers have proposed that the supervision and sponsorship of markets was quite important to Maya authorities because this was one of the ways they could collect taxes and gain prestige (Chase and Chase 2004; Masson and Peraza Lope 2004; Shaw 2012).

The third circumstance that delayed the recognition of marketing among the Maya—the lack of population nucleation—needs little comment. Chapter 1 explained how urban centers are excellent locations for markets because a high number of producers and consumers live close to each other. Placing a market in a population center thus reduces travel time for the broadest swath of society. A related proposition is that without population nucleation, one might not expect markets. A lack of population nucleation can no longer be used as a reason to doubt market development among the Maya because, as earlier parts of this chapter have made clear, several Maya cities were substantially nucleated in terms of both high population density and clustering of population. Furthermore, as Freidel (1981a) has made clear, even a dispersed settlement pattern does not necessarily imply a lack of markets because Maya people living in rural areas are known to have visited centers for a variety of ceremonies, and markets often accompany such ceremonies.

Finally, the notion that highland Mesoamerica exhibits significant environmental diversity while the Maya lowlands exhibit resource redundancy

(Sanders 1973, 350; Sanders and Price 1968) has also delayed a clearer understanding of Maya economies. Several studies have shown that resources in the Maya lowlands are not as evenly dispersed as was once thought (Dunning et al. 1988; Fedick 1996; Gómez-Pompa et al. 2003; McAnany 1993a). The availability of lowland resources such as salt (Andrews 1983), chert (Shafer and Hester 1983), and cacao (McAnany et al. 2002) are famously patchy, but even in areas without such assets, other features such as escarpments (Dunning et al. 2003), swamp edges (Kunen 2004), karst depressions (Kepecs and Boucher 1996), rivers (Siemens 1996), hills (Chase and Chase 1998), and fracture zones (Fedick et al. 2000) permit local resource specializations. Resource diversity and community specialization have fueled market-based models of ancient Maya economies: "By combining the variety and abundance of specialized production at a marketplace . . . a greater region of communities obtained the necessary balance of resources for a sustainable harvesting of an otherwise fragile environment" (Scarborough and Valdez 2009, 211).

Mayanists have used four different lines of evidence when researching markets: contextual, distributional, linguistic, and ethnohistorical. The contextual approach refers to research that attempts to locate physical marketplaces among archaeological sites. This approach is difficult because the most important thing that people do at marketplaces—exchange goods—leaves little or no physical signature (Dahlin et al. 2007; Shaw 2012). Yet analysis of chemical residues, architectural remains, pedestrian access patterns, and associated debris have enabled archaeologists to suggest the presence of marketplaces at many sites in Guatemala, including Tikal (Jones 1996), Trinidad de Nosotros (Dahlin et al. 2010) and Motul de San Jose (Bair and Terry 2012); sites in Mexico such as Chunchucmil (Dahlin et al. 2007), Coba (Coronel et al. 2015), Mayapan (Masson and Freidel 2013), Sayil (Wurtzburg 1991), Calakmul (Folan, Fletcher, et al. 2001; Martin 2012), and Chichen Itza (Braswell 2010; Ruppert 1943, 230); and sites in Belize such as Buenavista del Cayo (Cap 2015), Caracol (Chase and Chase 2014; Chase et al. 2015), and Maax Na (Shaw and King 2015). These marketplaces were of course not all the same. Some may have taken place in facilities built specifically for marketing and others appear to have taken place in spaces that also accommodated other events, suggesting that some marketplaces appeared only occasionally. This variation among marketplaces suggests different degrees of commercialization at different sites. Coba and Motul de San Jose provide faint evidence of marketplaces and recall the marketing model Freidel (1981a) proposed in which marketing took place as part of occasional fairs and ceremonies. At the other extreme, Tikal, Calakmul, and Chunchucmil had centrally located plazas with nonperishable architecture in the form of rows of stalls (see chapter 6). These marketplaces approximate the permanent marketplace that the Spaniards witnessed at Tlatelolco.

The marketplace at Calakmul includes a building in its center with multiple murals showing a series of people in roles named by hieroglyphic labels: the pottery person, the tamale person, and so forth. Simon Martin (2012) interprets these scenes as depictions of people offering goods for sale at a marketplace. Although anomalous, this evidence is remarkable because art and hieroglyphic inscriptions generally express little about markets and merchants in Central Mexico (where Spaniards witnessed booming markets) and in the Maya area, likely because most art and writing were the interests of royalty, of which merchants were not a part (Masson and Freidel 2013, 209). Maya artists depicted God L, the Classic period patron of trade and traders, as rich and powerful but constantly humiliated and stripped of his possessions. According to Tokovinine and Balieav (2013), "God L's interactions with the divine patrons of royalty—including the Sun God, the Maize God, the Moon Goddess and the Hero Twins—reflect some ambivalence in the classic Maya attitude toward trade and traders."

The distributional approach to identifying marketplaces assumes that when a good is available at a marketplace, everyone has access to that good (Hirth 1998). Thus, as long as a good is priced in such a way that most people can afford it, archaeologists should find that differences in wealth and/ or power among consumers do not skew the distribution of that good. The distributional approach does not locate a marketplace directly but infers it by looking at the distribution of goods across a site or region. Distributional evidence has been presented for goods such as pottery, obsidian, and figurines at Classic period sites such as Tikal (Masson and Freidel 2012, 2013), Chunchucmil (Hutson et al. 2010), El Peru/Waka' (Eppich and Freidel 2015), and Motul de San Jose (Halperin et al. 2009). Few archaeologists have distributional evidence, however, because getting a representative picture of how goods are distributed requires extensive sampling across a large selection of households.

As for linguistic data about markets, native cognate words for buying (*man*), selling (*chon*), bartering (*k'ex*), trading or profiting (*p'ol*), and market (*k'iwik*; although *k'iwik* can also mean plaza) are found in Maya languages that are known to have split from each other by the end of the first millennium BCE. This means that "market exchange played a significant role in classic Maya society, with all the essential terms for trade-related activities already in place by the first millennium AD" (Tokovinine and Beliaev 2013, 172).

Ethnohistorical evidence for markets and marketplaces among the Maya is mixed. Although Bishop Landa wrote in his 1566 summary of life in northern Yucatan that "the occupation to which [the Maya] had the greatest inclination was trade" (Landa in Tozzer 1941, 94; see also Roys 1943, 51–53), some ethnohistorians believe that most Maya around the time of conquest did not participate in market economies (Farriss 1984, 156). As noted above, political, economic, and demographic downturns at the time of Spanish contact lead us to expect conquest-era markets to be less prominent in northern Yucatan, where many contact-period documents originated. However, ethnohistorical documentation of markets and marketing in the lowlands survives in many forms (King 2015). Evidence from the highlands may be more abundant (Feldman 1985; Tokovinine and Beliaev 2013). Both Landa and native texts discuss merchants embarking on long-distance trade expeditions. Forms of currency such as cacao beans, shell beads, greenstones, and copper axes are mentioned in a variety of documents from northern Yucatan. Landa's major informant discussed pricing systems (Tozzer 1941, 231). Roys (1943, 51) mentioned marketplaces in Yucatecan towns such as Cachi and Chauacha. Yucatecan dictionaries from the colonial era include words for buying, selling, market, itinerant peddlers, shopkeepers, and perhaps wholesalers (King 2015, 48–50).

To summarize, there can be no doubt that the ancient Maya had markets and marketplaces. Although few today would deny the complexity of Maya economies, Blanton (2013; see also Hirth and Pillsbury 2013; Masson and Freidel 2013) argues that the Tenochtitlan market system represents a greater degree of commercial development than that of Maya urban economies, mostly because political integration by the Aztecs allowed a network of interlocking markets to cover a broader area, which brought a greater variety of goods to specific marketplaces and presented both consumers and producers with more choices about which marketplaces to attend (Sheets 2000). However, it should be kept in mind that the degree of integration seen in Aztec Mexico was unusual. Rather than saying that Central Mexico was more commercially developed than the Maya area, it is better to recognize that each region experienced peaks and troughs of commercial development (Braswell 2010). In the Maya area, political integration at Chichen Itza in the Terminal Classic and Mayapan in the Postclassic likely stimulated peaks in commercial development.

The concentration of consumers and producers in cities stimulated commercial development. Markets made Maya cities attractive (Masson and Freidel 2012, 461), although much production took place in rural areas linked to the city. As Hirth and Pillsbury (2013, 16) note, "The development of the marketplace would have been a boon to Maya domestic economy. It would have enhanced household resource procurement, helped convert surplus production into other items, and provided a point of sale and distribution for craft goods made in rural households" (see also Shaw 2012, 121). Marketplaces also have great social appeal, as I discuss in chapter 6. Although economic complexity in the hinterlands should not be underestimated (e.g., Scarborough and Valdez 2009), cities brought great economic potential (Trigger 2003, 121). Households did not need to abandon farming and producers did not need to devote themselves to full-time specialization in order to capitalize on this potential. The fact that the Maya have been called a low-tech, low-energy civilization (no wheel, no beasts of burden, etc.) does not necessarily impede the formation of cities or their urbanization (cf. Arnauld 2008, 3; Sanders and Webster 1988, 541–542).

Conclusion

By the 1970s, the vast majority of researchers could agree that the Maya had cities. Yet Maya cities exhibit great variety. Some were small and qualify as cities only because they serve specialized functions and exhibit social differentiation. Others, such as Tikal, Calakmul, and Caracol, were very large and had extensive political entanglements. Still others (Coba, Chunchucmil, Palenque) had the kind of population density that forces us to label them urban as defined in chapter 1. Although some Maya cities were urban and some were not, they all share enough in common to constitute a city-state culture. Systematic economic research has progressed slowly (McAnany 1993a), but we now have enough data to conclude that many city-states had complex economies that involved marketplace exchange (and other kinds of exchange), occupational specialization, and interdependencies between city and hinterlands.

The relatively new data on marketplaces and high settlement densities in urban areas are quite remarkable. As discussed in chapter 1, people must have seen good reason to live in cities, particularly the denser ones. Marketplaces were attractive to everyone involved. They made exchange more efficient and they helped households provision themselves. As an outlet for exchanging surpluses, they provided an incentive for households to specialize in crafts and increase surplus production. They gave ruling institutions venues for converting tribute and other goods. They brought prestige and potential revenue to rulers who were not powerful enough to control many other aspects of the economy. Although people could access markets without living in cities, the biggest markets would be in cities, and this may have encouraged people to live closer to cities. In addition to these economic considerations, markets were also attractive from a social standpoint, as discussed in chapter 6.

The high settlement density of sites identified as urban centers means that people rubbed shoulders with a diverse mix of strangers. As discussed in chapter 1, this can be psychologically taxing. People do many things to mitigate this kind of situation, and one strategy is creating neighborhoods. Neighborhoods are also common in cities with lower densities. Whether in cities of high or low density, research on neighborhoods is important because it examines units of settlement that are intermediate in size between the household and the city. The following chapter explores these kinds of units and the methods for detecting them in ancient cities.

3

Identifying Neighborhoods and Other Intermediate Social Units

> In the last analysis, each neighborhood
> is what the inhabitants think it is.
>
> National Commission on Neighborhoods (1979, 7)

As described in chapter 1, urbanism—the condition of spatial proximity to people who are socially distant—presents challenges. I follow Beals (1951, 5) in using the term urbanization to refer to the ways that people modify their lives in order to cope with urbanism. One strategy by which people make urban centers livable is to create nooks where they expect to find familiar faces. When people who know each other cluster together, life becomes less isolated and social interactions become more predictable. In providing refuge from the discontinuities, uncertainties, and anonymities of the urban milieu, such clusters appear to restore a remnant of village life within the city (Lewis 1965; Hannerz 1980). Writers from various continents have commented on social clustering for many millennia and continue to do so today. This implies that divisions within a city are a universal characteristic of urban life (Smith 2010, 137; York et al. 2011, 2400). However, the study of divisions within ancient Maya cities has received relatively little attention.

Archaeologists use a number of terms for such clusters, including barrios, wards, neighborhoods, communities, and districts. In the field of Maya studies, the word cluster has the deepest pedigree. I want to clarify nuances in meaning between these terms and use them consistently. Of the five terms— community, ward, district, cluster, and neighborhood—all but the first are names for entities that are always intermediate in size between the household and the city. Research on these kinds of units is important not just because this kind of social clustering is common and helps residents adapt to cities but also because such units might be longer lasting than the political regimes in which they are often embedded (Smith 2006, 98; Ashmore et al. 2004). They endure. I begin by defining the concept of a neighborhood.

Sociologists and urban planners began to discuss neighborhoods explicitly over a century ago (Keith 2003, 57). Definitions of neighborhoods therefore abound. The epigraph that opens this chapter suggests, however, that definitions of "neighborhood" based on the expertise of researchers and professionals offer generalities that cannot capture how actual neighbors use the term. Because ancient Maya texts say very little about neighborhoods, letting ancient inhabitants of Maya cities define the term will not work. Returning, then, to the professionals, specifically those who work with ancient cities, I use Michael Smith's (2010; see also Keith 2003, 58) definition of neighborhood as my point of departure, knowing that any definition that attempts to describe varied but common social phenomena will suffer from the shortcomings inherent in the process of generalization. Smith (2010, 139) defines a neighborhood as "a residential zone that has considerable face-to-face interaction and is distinctive on the basis of physical and/or social characteristics."

Although a neighborhood should have many homes, it may also have shops, shrines, and other kinds of spaces, and a strong argument can be made that such institutions are critical parts of neighborhoods (Jacobs 1961, 8; Ahlbrandt 1984, 191; Downs 1981, 19–20). Although face-to-face interaction creates familiarity, I follow Smith in emphasizing that neighbors are not necessarily friendly. Smith sees neighborhoods as "distinctive on the basis of physical and/or social characteristics." Physical characteristics can refer to barriers around the neighborhood, a peculiar arrangement of the buildings within the neighborhood or some other pattern in the use of space. Social characteristics refer to aspects of identity such as "race, ethnicity, class, religion, occupation, or political affiliation" (Smith 2010, 146). I agree that neighborhoods can be distinctive in either of these senses but maintain that sometimes they are distinctive in neither of these ways. Although a shared identity in terms of race, ethnicity, class, and so forth may cause people to create or join a neighborhood in the first place, a sense of distinctiveness—people's recognition that their space is a distinct place—does not presuppose a shared identity. Nor does it presuppose physical characteristics that would be distinctive to the researcher (Jacobs 1961, 120). Distinctiveness can arise from people who have little in common but interact when sharing the same space and working together to care for that space (Downs 1981, 14; Jacobs 1961, 117). The distinctiveness that makes a space a neighborhood can vary greatly, as the epigraph suggests. A neighborhood, then, is an area that is home to people who interact with each other on a face-to-face basis and come to see their area as distinctive.

A cluster refers to one particular way that a neighborhood might be physically distinctive: spatial integrity. Some kind of boundary separates one cluster of buildings from another cluster. The terms district and ward overlap in the literature; I will try to keep them apart. In discussing social structure in early Mesopotamia, Postgate (1992, 82) distinguishes between administrative wards and socially bonded neighborhoods. Although houses might predominate in wards, just as they do in neighborhoods, wards are usually larger than neighborhoods. Neighborhoods are "bottom up"—that is, formed and transformed by the actions and interactions of the people within them—but wards as Postgate and I use the term are "top down": formed by administrators who need to divide the city into governable units. Smith (2010, 140) identifies two kinds of district: an administrative district, which is identical to what I have been calling a ward, and a social district, a large residential zone that encompasses many neighborhoods, exhibits one or more distinctive characteristics, and is not necessarily an administrative unit. In this chapter and elsewhere, I restrict the use of the term district to the latter of Smith's two uses of the term: a division within a city that is larger than a neighborhood but whose members still share something in common. In any particular city, administrators may borrow already-existing district boundaries (if they are easy to recognize) and use them as ward boundaries.

In terms of scale, the four entities defined thus far (neighborhood, cluster, ward, district) all fall in between the household and the city. The final entity, community, does not always fall in that intermediate range. Archaeologists use the word community in many different ways, and a large literature has developed around the many different valences of this word (Canuto and Yaeger 2000; Hutson et al. 2008; Kolb and Snead 1997; Varien and Potter 2008). Although a small village where everyone knows everyone else's business can be a community (Redfield 1955), so can a mass of strangers who share a mentality cultivated by knowing the same landmarks and reading the same newspapers (Anderson 1991). Ancient neighborhoods usually qualify as communities, but many communities, particularly those not formed around a small place, are not neighborhoods.

Among the terms defined above, neighborhood, which gets at the shared activities and experiences that create nooks of familiarity, is key for understanding urbanization. This chapter focuses on the identification of neighborhoods in ancient cities. It begins by presenting the different methods archaeologists have used in the Maya region to identify neighborhoods and case studies for each of these methods. For any particular city, no single method will be entirely successful and combining multiple methods still fails to find every last neighborhood. As I demonstrate below, this is the case even in one of the best-known cities, Teotihuacan. In the next chapter, I present a case study of the Maya city of Chunchucmil that is exemplary in terms of both the amount of resources devoted to identifying neighborhoods and the built features that aid this identification.

Identifying Neighborhoods

Archeologists use many different criteria to identify neighborhoods within cities (see Smith 2010, 145–147). In this chapter I look at four criteria: 1) spatial clustering; 2) focal nodes; 3) stylistic clustering; and 4) craft specialization. Chapter 5 explores a fifth criterion: levels of wealth. The first two criteria will be broken down minutely because there are many kinds of spatial clusters and focal nodes. Although I have listed them separately, the four criteria can combine in different ways. For instance, excellent examples of neighborhoods emerge when they take the form of spatial clusters anchored by focal nodes.

Spatial Clustering

Spatial clustering was the first criterion Mayanists used to suggest the existence of something like a neighborhood. At least five different kinds of data have been used to identify clusters of settlement that may correspond to social units larger than the household. These include 1) topography; 2) vacant spaces; 3) distance measures; 4) transportation routes; and 5) walls and other built boundary features. This last dataset, which was used to good effect at the site of Xochicalco in central Mexico (Hirth 2003b), will not be discussed in this chapter. Although several Maya cities have walls that encircle the site core, be it for defense or some other purpose, these walls do not divide Maya cities into multiple residential neighborhoods (Dahlin 2000; Webster 1976, 1979). A few Maya cities have low walls that encircle residential groups. At Chunchucmil, such walls create pathways and these transportation routes (specifically which residential groups are linked by particular pathways), as opposed to the walls themselves, help identify clusters (see chapter 4).

Decades ago, Bullard's (1960, 367) reconnaissance in northeast Peten, Guatemala, showed that houses often occurred in clusters of five to twelve within an area of four or more hectares. Bullard used both of the first two kinds of data discussed above to identify boundaries between clusters: 1) topography in the sense of gullies, arroyos, and other dips in the terrain; and 2) vacant spaces 200 meters wide. Bullard suggested that these clusters were hamlets occupied by kinship groups. As more survey data mounted, the participants in a seminar devoted entirely to Maya settlement patterns (Ashmore 1981a) established that the clusters Bullard found in northeast Peten show up in most other parts of the Maya world, although they are probably not universal (Ashmore 1981b, 51). The seminar members disagreed, however, about what these clusters meant in terms of social organization (Fash 1983, 262). Along the Copan River, while surveying the 24-square-kilometer pocket that contains the ruins of Copan, the largest of the five pockets that make up the Copan River Valley, Leventhal (1979) identified clusters separated by natural drainage ditches (*quebradas* or arroyos), which qualify as Bullard's first kind of cluster boundary. Surveyors had difficulty identifying such clusters in other pockets of the Copan valley (Freter 2004, 96). To interpret these clusters, Fash (1983) used an ethnographic analogy to the *sian otot* of the Chorti Maya of mid-twentieth-century Honduras. Wisdom (1940, 216), the ethnographer upon whose work Fash's analogy rests, described the *sian otot* as a "neighborhood, the habitat of kin and family," containing sixty to eighty nuclear families and a population of between 200 and 300. According to Fash's calculations, the twenty Late Classic *sian otot*–like clusters identified in the Copan pocket contained, on average, forty nuclear families (minimum 14, maximum 116) for a population of about 200, which suggests that the ancient clusters at Copan were demographically similar to twentieth-century *sian otot*.

Both the *sian otot* of the twentieth century and most ancient clusters Fash and Bullard discussed were rural villages. Yet clusters also occur in cities. The map of the city of Dzibilchaltun, which contains 8,390 structures in an area of nineteen square kilometers, shows the presence of clusters separated by vacant terrain, although Kurjack admits that the Dzibilchaltun mappers might have missed smaller structures (Kurjack 1974, 80–81). Some of the clusters identified at Dzibilchaltun match the scale of Bullard's clusters (figure 3.1); others are much larger. Although Tikal has vacant terrain in its central 16 square kilometers, it is seasonal swamp: the decision to leave that terrain vacant has more to do with flooding than with maintaining swaths of empty space between social clusters. Other low-density cities around the world, such as nineteenth-century Addis Ababa (Smith 2011, 54), also contain spatial clusters.

Ellen Kintz's (1983, 181) attempt to define neighborhoods at Coba makes the social logic of spatial clustering explicit: "The greater the distance be-

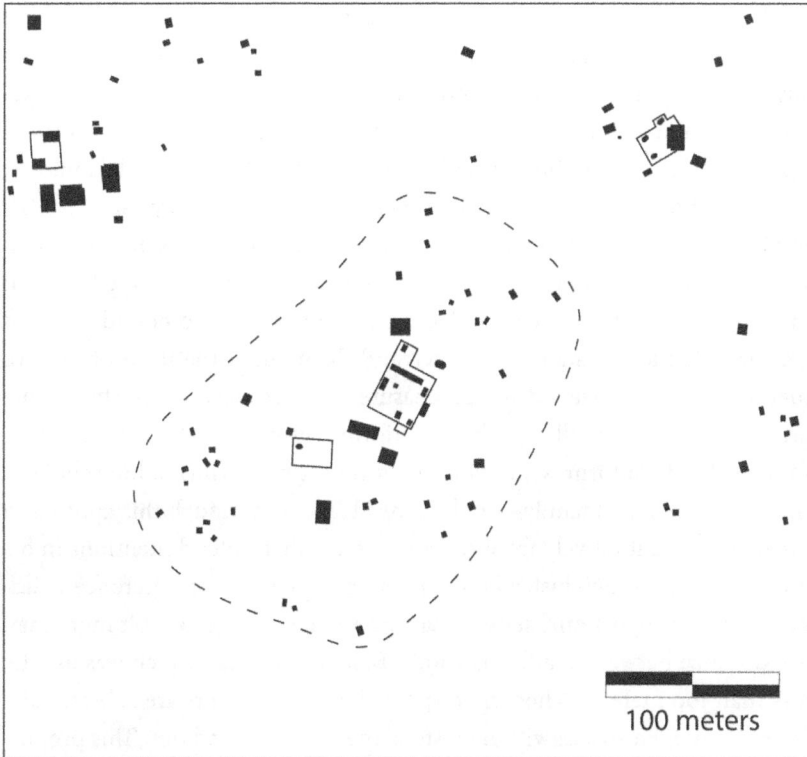

Figure 3.1. Map of a settlement cluster to the southwest of the site core, Dzibilchaltun, Yucatan. Adapted from block I-n of Stuart et al. (1979).

tween household units, the more limited the interaction." Stated differently, households that are spatially close must also be socially close. Although a law named after geographer Waldo Tobler (1970) expresses this same logic—"near things are more related than distant things"—we should treat it not as a law but as a hypothesis. Epigraphic, ethnohistorical, and ethnographic data from the Maya area show that this hypothesis is not always correct. For example, a close look at Vogt's map of lineage-based neighborhoods (called waterhole groups) in the modern town of Paste in the highlands of Chiapas, Mexico (figure 3.2), shows that the occupants of houses that are very close to waterholes 2 and 4 in fact belong to waterholes 1 and 3 (Vogt 1976, 99). Okoshi-Harada (2012, 291), who looked at contact-period alliances between towns in Yucatan, found that the distances between towns did not automatically index the closeness of relations. A town located very close to the lead town of one alliance could in fact belong to a different alliance. Such relations hold for the Classic period as well, when the cities and towns that formed a single political alliance did not always cluster together in space (Martin and Grube 1995; A. Smith 2003). For example, Dos Pilas, which became a strong ally of Calakmul in the late seventh century, is located much closer to Tikal than to Calakmul. It is also located south of Tikal (Calakmul is to the north of Tikal), such that Tikal almost stands in between Dos Pilas and Calakmul.

While the logic of Tobler's law sometimes fails in the Maya area, Kintz's implementation of that law at Coba also presents difficulties. Kintz created clusters using the map of zone 1, which represents a wedge-shaped portion of Coba (figure 3.3). Since Coba lacks both of the first two boundary types (topographic features and vacant terrain), Kintz used the third of the five methods named above—distance measures—for establishing clusters. Kintz grouped into clusters all household platforms within 70 meters of each other (a household platform is a broad platform on top of which a household—usually an extended family—built its residences). Although this appears to differ only quantitatively from the 200 meters that Bullard mentions in his method for creating cluster boundaries, this quantitative difference is important in a proportional sense because 200 meters is quite a bit more than the distance between platforms within Bullard's clusters, which was usually less than 100 meters. When open spaces between clusters are substantially larger than open spaces within clusters, the clusters stand out. This proportion between these two kinds of open spaces makes clusters clearly visible to the naked eye. If the size of the distance measure used to separate clusters

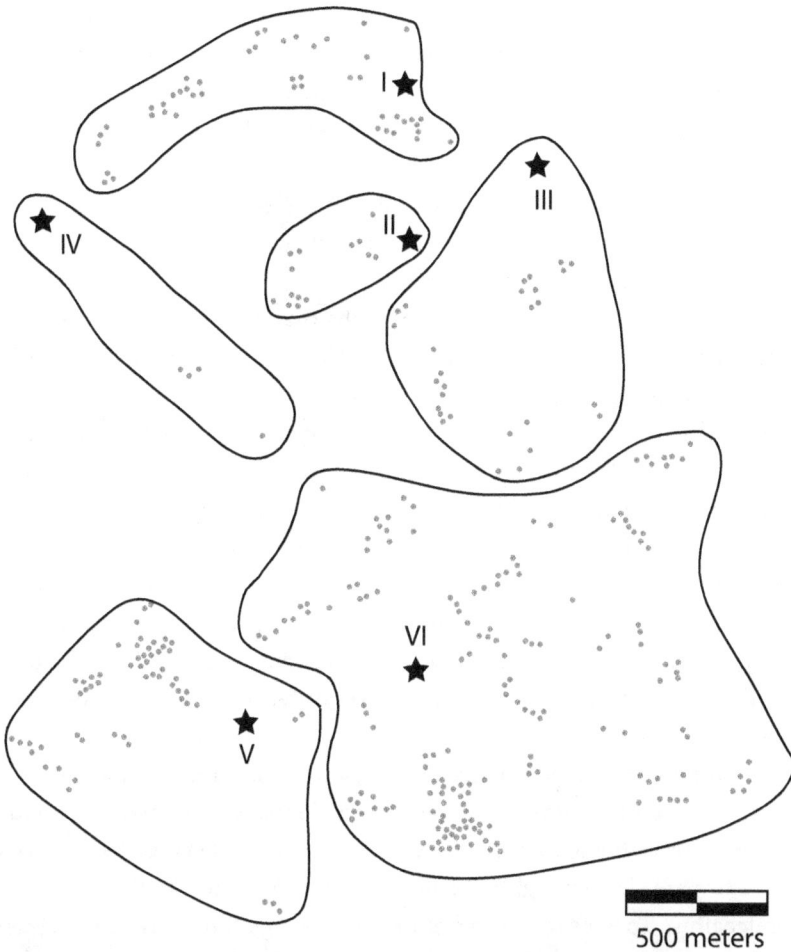

Figure 3.2. Map of twentieth-century Paste, Chiapas, showing houses (small rectangles) and waterholes (stars). Each house is grouped with the water hole the household uses. Adapted from Vogt 1976, figure 25.

is not much larger than the distances between household platforms within the same cluster, the application of such a distance measure runs the risk of producing clusters that are not visually discrete. For example, the naked eye cannot distinguish clusters in the part of Coba depicted in figure 2.5. Applying a distance measure of 70 meters is risky because this measure is very close to the average distance between platforms in this area (about 50 meters). A 70-meter distance measure divides the platforms in figure 2.5 into two clusters. The first cluster includes platforms 221, 259, 260, 261, 266, and 276. The second cluster includes all unlabeled platforms in the figure (platform 271 pertains to a third cluster whose other members are off the map). The naked eye would not be able to replicate such clusters. The fact that the naked eye can distinguish clusters at Dzibilchaltun but not at Coba suggests a different form of neighborhood organization for these two cities.

Furthermore, Kintz's map of the clusters created by the application of a 70-meter distance measure (figure 3.3) shows that a pattern in Coba's settlement density interfered with the process of creating clusters. Since settlement is more dense toward the core of Coba than in the periphery, where distances between structures are larger, most household platforms in the periphery (toward the widest part of the wedge) remain isolated in terms of the 70-meter distance measure: they form their own clusters as opposed to clustering with other platforms. Toward the center of the site, a single cluster encompasses all structures within 600 meters of the tip of the wedge. Clusters get smaller as distance from the site core increases, not necessarily because of the actual configuration of ancient neighborhoods but because settlement density decreases with distance from the site core. Although Kintz did not explain why she used a 70-meter buffer, the settlement density issue would skew the results in the same way if the buffer distance were 60 meters or 80 meters.

The bottom line is that distance measures may not work well for identifying neighborhood boundaries in some cities. In many cases neighborhood edges were probably blurry even to the residents of these cities. When spatial clusters are clear enough to be immediately discernible to the eye, as at Dzibilchaltun, Tobler's law makes more sense. When things are not as clear cut, the distance measure method forces houses into clusters based on an arbitrarily chosen buffer distance and is more likely to yield neighborhood boundaries that are at odds with the boundaries that past people recognized.

A fourth spatial clustering method involves identifying footpaths or streets at a site to see if transportation features funneled people living nearby into the same routes, thus creating clusters of interaction. While mapping the site of Mayapan, the densely settled Postclassic urban center in the northern lowlands, researchers documented pairs of low stone walls that created lanes several meters wide. Although Smith (1962, 210) did not believe that these lanes were part of a carefully organized, city-wide system of transit, Hare and Masson (2012) suggest that Mayapan's inhabitants saw order in their footpaths, which may have defined key routes to water sources and other impor-

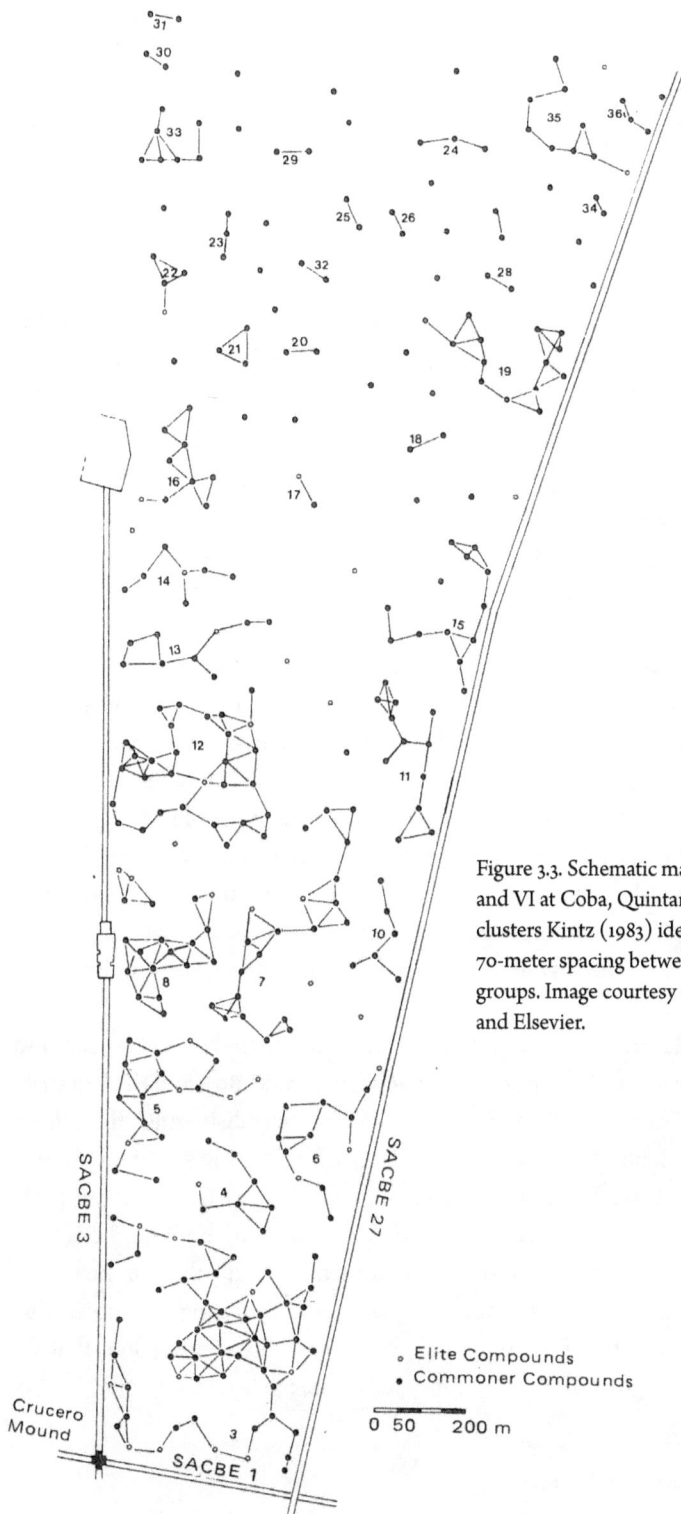

Figure 3.3. Schematic map of zones I and VI at Coba, Quintana Roo, showing clusters Kintz (1983) identified using 70-meter spacing between architectural groups. Image courtesy of William Folan and Elsevier.

SACBE 3

SACBE 27

SACBE 1

Crucero Mound

○ Elite Compounds
● Commoner Compounds

0 50   200 m

tant destinations. The fragmented state of Mayapan's lanes (few run for more than 100 meters) and the lack of systematic mapping of them prevent conclusions about how footpaths zoned people into routes of interaction intense enough to create distinctive neighborhoods. However, the paths at Chunchucmil allow such a study (see chapter 4).

Focal Nodes

Although the Coba study showed the difficulties of using distance measures to identify neighborhoods, it also presented a second method. Kintz (1983) noted that several of her clusters contained elite compounds, a common feature of neighborhoods elsewhere in the world (Keith 2003, 66). Such compounds are an example of a broader category of building referred to as a focal node. Ashmore (1981b, 51), who noted the presence of clusters with focal nodes at Maya sites, wrote that some clusters have a single large building at their core while other clusters focus on a plazuela group containing large buildings. To the extent that people who live near each other participate in ceremonies at the same temple, temples exemplify the kind of building that counts as a focal node. Other kinds of buildings that can serve as focal nodes are the residences of neighborhood leaders, particularly those who use their residence as a place for neighborhood-wide events. Focal nodes do not have to be buildings. They can also be open spaces where people get together or a resource shared by people living nearby, such as a quarry or a well. The key point about focal nodes is that they bring about the kind of face-to-face interactions that bind neighbors. Focal nodes help neighborhoods flourish (Ahlbrandt 1984, 191; Downs 1981, 19–20) and might also make neighborhoods distinctive.

Focal nodes may or may not complement the spatial clustering method. Not all clusters have focal nodes (Kurjack 1974, 80–81, 89), and the fact that a city has focal nodes does not mean that we can easily distinguish the boundaries of the neighborhoods associated with each node. The site of La Joyanca, located in the Peten District of Guatemala, provides an example of this problem. La Joyanca is an excellent candidate for studying neighborhoods because it has eleven spatially discrete monumental groups that can be treated as focal nodes. Lemmonier (2012) assigned the surrounding commoner residences to each of these monumental groups, creating eleven zones that she interprets as neighborhoods. Lemmonier (2012, 194) writes that her "spatial distance analysis points to a nucleation process of commoner households having clustered around each monumental compound." Although it does appear to be the case that commoners moved from rural areas to La Joyanca, the site map (Lemmonier 2012, figure 9.1) shows that commoner houses are interspersed rather evenly among the eleven monumental compounds. In other words, each monumental compound/focal node does not have a tight orbit of houses around it and then a clear ring of empty space separating it from another monumental compound and its respective orbit of houses. This is also the case with the waterhole groups Vogt (1976) documented: since houses do not cluster around the waterholes, an archaeologist with nothing more to work with than house locations would not be able to reproduce the ethnographically documented waterhole group boundaries in figure 3.2. To impose zones on an evenly distributed settlement, Lemmonier resorted to distance measures. As a result, some of the attributions of specific residential groups to zones are counterintuitive. For example, a patio group that is only 30 meters from the Tepescuintli monumental compound but 310 meters away from the Loro Real monumental compound gets assigned to the Loro Real neighborhood. Likewise, a group that is 30 from the Ardilla monumental compound but 220 meters from the Loro Real monumental compound also gets assigned to the Loro Real neighborhood. Such assignments are not necessarily incorrect: ethnographically verified yet counterintuitive groupings that violate Tobler's law also exist in Vogt's waterhole groups. I do not doubt that the monumental compounds served as focal nodes for neighborhoods at La Joyanca: the issue is that the mere existence of focal nodes does not mean that neighborhood boundaries can be easily identified and does not eliminate the problems associated with the distance measure technique. Assigning boundaries that "must have been recognized in the spatial taxonomies of the Maya" is easier at a site such as Dzibilchaltun, where several clusters are both isolated by open space and have nodes consisting of substantial architecture at their center (Kurjack 1974, 80).

The difficulties Kintz and Lemmonier faced in stipulating clear neighborhood boundaries within a settlement highlight a question. When archaeologists struggle to find clear boundaries, is this merely because such boundaries were not marked in ways that would be visible today or is it because clear boundaries never did exist? Both possibilities are plausible. Neighborhood boundaries are often not clear in cities today, especially in parts of cities with grid patterns rather than subdivisions. Fixed boundaries may have been rare among the ancient Maya. Recall that in some Maya city-states, territorial integrity in the sense of clear, stable polity borders did not always exist (see chapter 2). Relations of political allegiance between city and hinterland may have been determined less by proximity to the center than by (unstable) networks of personal authority (Demarest 2004, 216; Hammond 1991, 277). Presuming that clusters with focal nodes within a city represented competing factions or lineages (Fash 2005, 75; Lucero 2007), commitments to these factions and lineages may have wavered over time. Thus, in the same way that rural villages might have shifted from being highly committed to a particular center to being mostly independent of that center, people within a city who were physically or socially distant from the focal nodes of an established district or neighborhood may have strengthened or weakened their commitment to such nodes, depending on local histories.

Variation in focal nodes leads to multiple interpretations of how the neighborhoods that used these nodes were integrated. The key variables that affect interpretation include the size of the cluster associated with the focal node, whether or not the focal node is physically centered in the cluster, and what the focal node is. At Coba, the fact that focal nodes were elite residences led Kintz to believe that elites exercised control over the commoners in the cluster. She hypothesized "that these neighborhood units . . . exercised political, social and economic functions" (Kintz 1983, 188). In a later publication, she and her colleagues (Folan et al. 2009, 68) argued that commoner and elite households in these neighborhoods formed corporate social units. The site of Rio Bec, Campeche, Mexico, provides an excellent example of how clusters with focal nodes can be interpreted as corporate groups (figure 3.4). To begin with, Arnauld and colleagues (2012), unlike Kintz or Lemmonier, had a better opportunity to delimit the edges of neighborhoods because a series of drainage channels created topographic barriers that separated clusters of structures. Arnauld and colleagues (2012, 209) strengthened the hypothesis that these topographically bounded clusters were indeed neighborhoods by noting that each cluster had a high-ranking group: a focal node. Arnauld and colleagues saw these neighborhoods as Levi-Straussian houses, in which the key thing that integrates people of different status is not kinship (although kinship may figure prominently) but the resources, both symbolic and material, held in common (Gillespie 2000; Joyce and Gillespie 2000; Levi-Strauss 1982). People work together to preserve the house's economic interests, and such work is the foremost factor in determining membership. Thus, Arnauld and colleagues argued that sharing the work that went into constructing the largest buildings in the neighborhood (see also Peuramaki-Brown 2013, 585; Smith 2011, 54) integrated the people of that neighborhood just as much as the fact of living close together in a space bounded by drainage channels.

Lemmonier's La Joyanca case study provides another example of how working together might create corporate groups. Each of the neighborhoods Lemmonier identified has a vacant space within it identified as farmable terrain. Although monumental compounds likely served as focal nodes at La Joyanca, as discussed above, farmable plots as nodes also bring about the

Figure 3.4. Map of the core of Río Bec, Campeche, showing marshes and drainage canals that serve as spatial boundaries and large groups that serve as focal nodes. Blocks measure 500 meters by 500 meters. Image courtesy of the Río Bec Project.

kind of face-to-face interaction that neighborhoods require. Lemmonier argues that these farm plots were corporately owned and that everyone in the neighborhood worked together to farm them, thus making the neighborhood "economically meaningful." However, because nearly all the vacant areas were smaller than 2 hectares and most neighborhoods had twenty or more structures, indicating at least fifty or so residents, the corporate farm plots could support only a small fraction of the neighborhood. This means that most agricultural labor would probably have been scattered over a larger area.

In addition to working and living close together, the process of attending events and ceremonies together at a focal node also creates the distinctive interweaving of people and place that qualifies as a neighborhood. Jason Yaeger's (2000) research at San Lorenzo, a settlement cluster located in the low-density city of Xunantunich, Belize, whose ceremonial core lies 1.5 kilometers to the west, provides a good example. San Lorenzo contained seventeen residential groups in an area of about 10 hectares. Yaeger refers to it as a cluster because it is surrounded by mostly vacant terrain (figure 3.5). At the center of the cluster lie its two largest residential compounds (SL-22 and SL-23), both of which show evidence of hosting feasts for the entire cluster. In other words, both are potential focal nodes. Such feasts solidified social ties, making San Lorenzo a community and a neighborhood. Although the focal nodes for neighborhood ceremonies at San Lorenzo were high-status residences, at the nearby site of Buenavista, Megan Peuramaki-Brown (2013) identified focal nodes that are nonresidential. To the south of the Buenavista site core, Peuramaki-Brown identified a cluster of architecture that was surrounded by both natural topographic boundaries and vacant space. At the center of this cluster is a public nonresidential structure (the tallest building in the cluster) fronting a patio. The public building and patio provided both a space for ceremonies that could integrate neighborhood members and "a venue for chance encounters, which serves to strengthen associated community bonds" (2013, 582). Dzibilchaltun also has nonresidential pyramids scattered around the city, but it is not possible to ascertain whether such pyramids were part of focal nodes (Kurjack 1974, 92). In Mesopotamia, at Third Dynasty Ur, Woolley identified a series of what he called "wayside chapels" (Woolley 1976, 30). Dedicated to minor deities, these small spaces that open onto streets were not affiliated with any particular family or funded by royal authorities (A. Smith 2003, 213).

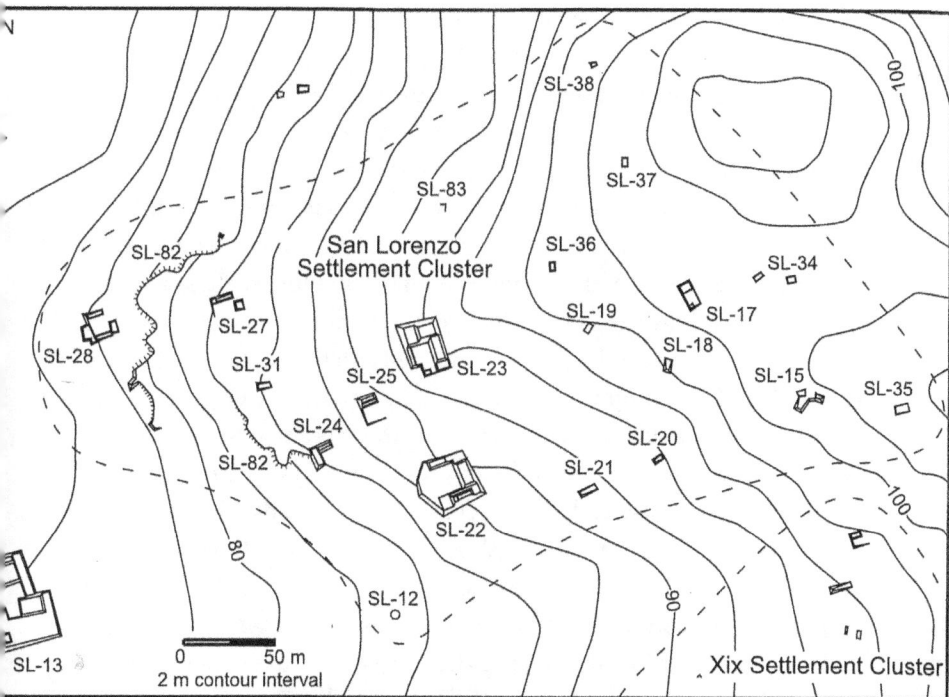

Figure 3.5. The San Lorenzo settlement cluster, located 1.5 kilometers to the east of the Xunantunich site core in Belize. Image courtesy of Jason Yaeger.

Whether the focal node is an elite residence (as at San Lorenzo) or a public space (as at Buenavista) may provide information about how the neighborhood is bound together. Yaeger (2010) argues that in the San Lorenzo case, feasts in residences of elites who had access to much more exotic resources than the rest of the neighborhood may have undercut the rhetoric of community and led to instability on the eve of the Maya collapse. The cluster Peuramaki-Brown studied appears to have had fewer social divisions. There was likely a spectrum in terms of how closely knit each neighborhood was. At Dzibilchaltun, Kurjack (1974, 93) opined that people within the same focal cluster had stronger bonds with each other than they did with people beyond the cluster. However, "haphazard distribution and orientation of buildings within the clusters is the rule" (1974, 81). Thus, Kurjack believed that if kin groups occupied the clusters, there were many divisions within these kin groups. Alternatively, kinship may not have played much of a role in organizing the clusters or determining membership (see also Smith and Novic

2012, 16). For those who see neighborhoods as corporate units, there are multiple models of corporate groups (Hageman 2004; Hayden and Cannon 1982; Joyce and Gillespie 2000; Watanabe 2004). The important point is that people in the group are interacting: venerating a common ancestor, working together on a large labor project, eating together during occasional parties.

When focal nodes are not at the center of clusters, this may indicate the presence of wards rather than neighborhoods. Structure SL-13 lies just beyond the western edge of the neighborhood of San Lorenzo. It is larger than any of the buildings in the neighborhood, was not a residence, lacked an ancestral shrine, and was built and abandoned exactly in sync with the quick rise and fall of Xunantunich. These lines of evidence led Yaeger to suggest that SL-13 was an outpost of the leaders of Xunantunich that was used in top-down efforts to administer the city. Beyond Mayapan's primary civic-ceremonial center, Hare and Masson (2012, 241–242) and earlier researchers (Proskouriakoff 1962, 127–131; Smith 1962, 202–205) identified up to eight conspicuous nonresidential compounds consisting minimally of a temple or a shrine, often combined with a colonnaded hall or other special-purpose building. Hare and Masson believe that Mayapan's ruling elites probably sponsored ceremonies and feasts at these focal nodes. To the extent that the events at each node brought together a subdivision of the city, these subdivisions qualify as wards that were created at the behest of the central authorities. With a maximum of eight subdivisions for a population estimated to be about 15,000, these divisions would have been much larger than the *sian otot* Fash described. Hare and Masson, who used spatial statistics to divide Mayapan into clusters based on settlement density, found that the focal nodes did not fall within the spatial centers of the statistically generated clusters.

Finally, the size of a cluster with a focal node also affects the interpretation of the social group that it integrated. For example, at Dzibilchaltun, the cluster shown in figure 3.1, located 1.9 kilometers to the southwest of the site core, has about fifty structures associated with it, yielding a Late/Terminal Classic population of perhaps 200 people. This cluster resembles the size of neighborhoods at Buenavista, Rio Bec, Copan, La Joyanca, and San Lorenzo. In contrast, a cluster located 1.3 kilometers to the southeast of Dzibilchaltun's main plaza has over 450 structures, yielding a Late/Terminal Classic population of well over 1,000 people. This is probably too many people for face-to-face interaction and should be called a district as I define it above.

Stylistic Clustering

Distinct stylistic assemblages that cluster in space can also be used to identify neighborhoods. Janusek's research on Tiwanaku in Bolivia is a successful case study in this regard (see also Goldstein 2000). Tiwanaku was populated by corporate groups riven internally by status differences but that nevertheless maintained distinct social identities: each group revered the same ancestor, engaged in communal work projects, maintained distinctive cuisines, and favored particular styles of pottery (Janusek 2002, 51–52). As I discuss below, the distinctive styles of pottery, architecture, adornment, and so forth have often been interpreted as manifestations of different ethnic identities, but this is not always the case. Mayanists have rarely looked at spatial clusters of distinctive stylistic assemblages in part because it requires systematic excavations all over a site, not just at the site core and a few outlying houses. At Caracol, spatial clusters of distinctive stylistic assemblages appear to be absent. Instead, Chase and Chase (2004, 141) discuss caching rituals and other practices that helped establish a pan-Caracol identity. At Tikal, Fry (2003, 89) noticed differences in the coarse jars consumed in different parts of the city but he attributes this to localized supply zones of the workshops that produced the jars, not to neighborhood identity. At Mayapan, Brown (1999) noticed that two different clusters of house lots consumed pottery with slightly different slip colors.

In addition to corporate group solidarity, one of the most important causes of variability in stylistic assemblages in cities is migration. As discussed in chapter 1, pathologies associated with crowding and poor sanitation result in high mortality rates, which means that migration into the city, as opposed to an increase in the birth rate, plays a large role in sustaining high populations. Morley (1997, 49) wrote: "It is clear that Rome's massive expansion in the two centuries before Augustus, and its success in maintaining that level of population, could only have been achieved through large scale migration on a regular basis." For Teotihuacan, Cowgill (2003a, 42–43) argues that rural migrants from nearby would have sustained the city's population and that new migrants likely settled in the apartment compounds that housed earlier migrants from the same village or region of origin. Kemper (2002) documented this pattern—migrants from the same place of origin clustering together in the city and building support networks for themselves—in twentieth-century Mexico City.

In the Maya area, archaeologists have discussed migration in a variety of contexts. Tourtellot (1993, 224–225), for example, discussed movements of people out of conquered polities. Building on colonial documentation of Maya villagers moving around to avoid the burdens of the Spanish colonies (Farriss 1984), Inomata (2004) discussed farmers who voted with their feet": they moved from one polity to another in the hope of negotiating lower tribute burdens. Rice and Rice (1990, 134) documented a depopulation of rural hinterlands south of Tikal in the Early Classic period as Tikal grew in population. Piedras Negras shifted quickly from a "sleepy backwater" to a regal-ritual center in the Early Classic, thanks in part to migrants who likely came westward from the central Peten (Webster and Houston 2003, 437; Child and Golden 2008, 77). If cities consist of clusters of people from different places, this might show up archaeologically as a pattern of slightly different proportions of pottery types and/or pottery modes and/or architectural styles in different parts of the city. The next chapter attempts to distinguish neighborhoods on the basis of material culture patterning at Chunchucmil. Since urban-to-rural migration or movement between neighboring polities could be considered examples of short-distance migration, we expect such material culture patterns to be more subtle than what we would observe for an ethnic migration, which I now discuss.

Migration to urban centers may create not only clusters of people from the same village but also clusters of people of the same ethnicity, as Greenshields' (1980) chapter about ethnic neighborhoods in the history of the Middle East makes clear. One of the lines of evidence Janusek and Blom (2006) used to distinguish neighborhoods at Tiwanaku was contrasting styles of cranial deformation, a marker of ethnic identity (see also Goldstein 2000). Among the ancient Maya, cranial deformation was not an ethnic marker. Although Freiwald (2011) and Miller (2015) have used skeletal material to document migrations within the Maya world, these exciting data do not yet allow us to discern ethnic neighborhoods. The phenomenon of people of a particular ethnic group clustering together and forming a neighborhood is well known in contemporary cities around the world, and Sjoberg (1960) listed it as a common characteristic of preindustrial cities. Yet ethnic clustering was not the norm in ancient cities. Emberling (2003, 260) reports that ethnic neighborhoods appear to be absent in Mesopotamia. In contrast to Tiwanaku, Moche, a contemporary urban center on the north coast of Peru, did not have ethnic neighborhoods (Chapdelaine 2009, 192).

Although archaeologists have detected ethnic enclaves within Teotihuacan (see below), archaeologists have not been as successful in Maya cities. In the Postclassic period, ethnic boundaries have been proposed, such as that between the Kowoj and the Itza in northeast Peten (Pugh 2003), but this work does not involve distinguishing different ethnic neighborhoods within the same city. For Late Classic Tikal, Marshall Becker (2003a, 2009) has argued that people occupying architectural compounds in the style of Plaza Plan 2 were ethnically distinct migrants who came from the east. Compounds designated as Plaza Plan 2 stand out because they have an ancestor shrine on their east side. Becker (2003a, 259) suggests that 14 percent of the 690 compounds within Tikal's central 16 square kilometers qualify as Plaza Plan 2. A well-known cluster of Plaza Plan 2 groups occurs on a peninsula 1.5 kilometers east of the Tikal site core (Becker 1999). Since 80 percent of residential compounds at Caracol have shrines on their east side, Becker believes that Tikal's Plaza Plan 2 occupants came from Caracol. However, Chase and Chase (2004, 144), the excavators of Caracol, note that east shrines at Caracol have caches that are distinct from those found in the east shrines of Plaza Plan 2 groups at Tikal.

Perhaps the best-known discussion of ethnic enclaves in the Maya area involves the possibility of non-Maya settlers from Teotihuacan. Since much has been written on this topic (Braswell 2003; Sanders and Michels 1977), I will be brief. In the fourth and fifth centuries CE, elites who adorned themselves with Teotihuacan regalia became kings at cities such as Tikal and Copan, where archaeologists have found inscriptions, pottery, and architecture that also refer to Teotihuacan. Tikal and Copan, however, lack residential neighborhoods in which a high proportion of buildings and ceramics emulate Teotihuacan (Haviland 2008, 271). Becker (2003a, 2009) believes that architectural groups with layouts that conform to Plaza Plan 4 at Tikal (a plaza with an altar in the center of the patio) show evidence of a Teotihuacan connection, but the eight examples do not cluster in space and they date to the Late Classic, after the time of the closest contacts between Teotihuacan and Tikal. Several other sites have less thorough associations with Teotihuacan. Michael Smyth (Smyth and Rogart 2004; Smyth and Ortegón Zapata 2006) argues that Chac 2, located in the Puuc hills of northern Yucatan, contains a Teotihuacan-style apartment compound in association with other Teotihuacan attributes, but others question the reliability of these identifications (Stanton 2005).

Craft Specialization

In some cities, households located next to each other participate in the same specialized craft activities. Sharing a craft probably also resulted in these neighbors interacting with each other more often, perhaps forming associations to manage the procurement of supplies or negotiate access to markets. In addition to having a distinctive social identity, such a cluster of households would leave a distinctive material signature in the form of craft by-products, allowing archaeologists to identify the cluster as a neighborhood. The identification of craft-based neighborhoods combines two criteria: spatial clustering and crafting. Neighborhoods that share a common craft have been identified at Tiwanaku (Janusek 2002, 151–152) and Teotihuacan, as I discuss further below. Yet in many cities, people who practiced the same craft did not cluster together in neighborhoods (Smith and Novic 2012). At Xochicalco, for example, specialists in obsidian were located in different parts of the city (Hirth 2009a, 57–58). Babylonian neighborhoods also lack clusters of craft specialists (Keith 2003, 75; Stone 1987).

In the Maya region, discussions of crafting usually bring the flint knappers of Colha (Shafer and Hester 1983) to mind, but this is not a case of a craft neighborhood because Colha was not an urban center and flint knapping was not localized to one sector of Colha. Tikal provides a better example of a craft-based neighborhood. Becker's (2003b) excavations of nine neighboring patio groups sharing a peninsula that jutted into a seasonal swamp 1.5 kilometers east of the site core revealed that people in most of the groups made polychrome pottery. Each patio group probably housed an extended family consisting of two or three nuclear families. This neighborhood is distinctive not only because of its shared craft and its spatial clustering (which was topographically bounded) but also because most of the groups exhibit Becker's Plaza Plan 2 (see above). Hare and Masson (2012, 242) note a cluster of thirteen domestic groups at Mayapan that produced shell, obsidian, chert, and pottery, although it is not clear whether these varied craft activities led to the kind of increased social interaction and familiarity that typifies a neighborhood.

Assessment: Teotihuacan

As a way of putting all of the criteria discussed above into practice, I present an extended example of the search for neighborhoods at Teotihuacan. Teotihuacan provides an excellent opportunity for highlighting both the successes and failures of neighborhood research because it is an urban center par excellence that has received extremely extensive research. Teotihuacan was an exceptional city for many reasons: its large population (approximately 100,000 people lived there from 150 to 550 CE), its high population density (approximately 6,000 people per square kilometer; Millon 1981), and its orthogonal layout. Teotihuacan's grid, keyed to the 15.5° orientation of its main avenue, the Street of the Dead, made the city more orthogonal than any other ancient center in the Old World or the New (Cowgill 2007, 269).

While other central Mexican cities such as Cholula and Tenochtitlan might have equaled or exceeded Teotihuacan in size, Teotihuacan provides a unique opportunity for researchers because unlike these other two ruins, large portions of the city remain unburdened by historic and modern settlement. In fact, very little of the site was disturbed in the 1960s when René Millon and his team mapped and surface collected 20 square kilometers with great detail and precision (Millon et al. 1973). Since then, dozens of scientific excavations have been conducted, arguably giving us more information about Teotihuacan than any other Mesoamerican city.

Given its large population, high population density, and relatively good preservation, Teotihuacan is an excellent candidate for finding neighborhoods. With so many people living so close to so many strangers, we would expect that people carved out niches of familiarity. More precisely, we would expect that people created neighborhoods—places where people knew they would find friends and family and could take comfort in the predictable. Teotihuacan is also an excellent candidate for identifying wards. Administrators would have needed to divide the city into wards so they could organize and carry out a variety of activities—such as extracting labor and distributing information—that were fundamental to the survival of the city. Teotihuacan's leaders appear to have had the power to create and oversee wards. These leaders succeeded in getting most residents to align the exterior walls of their homes—the famed "apartment compounds"—to the same grid that oriented Teotihuacan's major temples and avenues. Having imposed a spatial plan onto most of the city, these leaders should also have had the influence to incorporate wards into the plan.

However, identifying neighborhoods and wards at Teotihuacan has proven difficult. Walls encompass most of the temples along the Street of the Dead, thus demarcating a civic ceremonial core, but not many of the city's residents lived inside the core. The few boundary walls beyond the core are too incomplete to enable researchers to delineate districts or neighborhoods. Each apartment compound had its own boundary wall, usually with only one entrance. Teotihuacan had about 2,000 apartment compounds, most of which were rectangular with sides averaging between 40 and 50 meters long (Cowgill 2008, 91). Each compound normally contained three or more families, each with their own rooms, and a patio space that all families in the compound shared. Even though the apartment compounds were bounded, they were too small to be considered neighborhoods.

Manzanilla (2012, 66) states that neighborhoods consisting of several apartment compounds are the basic social unit at Teotihuacan. Using the focal node criterion, Manzanilla (1997, 120) suggested that complexes containing three temples around a plaza served as neighborhood centers. Yet Cowgill noted that beyond the site core there are fewer than ten such complexes and almost all of them cluster in one part of the city (to the northwest of the Moon Pyramid; Cowgill 2007, 279).

Ian Robertson's (2004) analyses of the ceramics from surface collections taken across the entire site tested the possible existence of status- or wealth-based neighborhoods. I expand upon this criterion for detecting neighborhoods in chapter 5. Although Robertson's analysis includes only the first half of the period 150–550 CE, the time of Teotihuacan's demographic plateau, it reveals that despite the fact that people of high socioeconomic status tended to locate their compounds closer to the site center, compounds of higher and lower status were interspersed among the city. Robertson did not identify districts composed exclusively of elites for the time period from about 150 to 350 CE.

Teotihuacan's two ethnic enclaves—which have been identified on the basis of stylistic clustering (see above)—serve as excellent examples of neighborhoods (Cowgill 2008, 99). At about 200 CE, people from the Valley of Oaxaca, located 375 kilometers to the south, established what has been called the Oaxaca Barrio on the western edge of the city. Over the next 300 years, a few hundred people, none of whom actually spent much time in Oaxaca, carried on native Oaxacan mortuary customs and made some of their pottery in Oaxacan styles but blended in with the locals in terms of their architecture and the rest of their pottery (Spence 1991). The Merchants' Barrio, located on the eastern edge of the city, housed people who came from lowland Veracruz. Residents imported pottery from Veracruz and initially lived in round structures said to be common in Veracruz. Eventually, they built apartment compounds typical of the rest of the city.

Researchers at Teotihuacan have also identified intermediate social units on the basis of crafts. The strongest example here is the Tlajinga district, a cluster of eighty-nine apartment compounds on the southern edge of the site bounded by mostly vacant space (Figure 3.6; Widmer and Storey 2012). As many as thirty-five compounds show evidence of producing San Martin Orange pottery, although pottery was not the only specialization (see Widmer 1991 for lapidary evidence). Most important, potters from different compounds produced standardized forms, suggesting the presence of officials who helped organize production at the level of the district (Sullivan 2006). Given the scale of the Tlajinga cluster (which probably housed over 1,000 people at its height), Widmer and Storey consider it to have been larger than a neighborhood and called it a district. Their use of the term district matches my own usage. Tlajinga's eighty-nine compounds appear to have shared a single administrative facility. The fact that this facility is at the far edge of

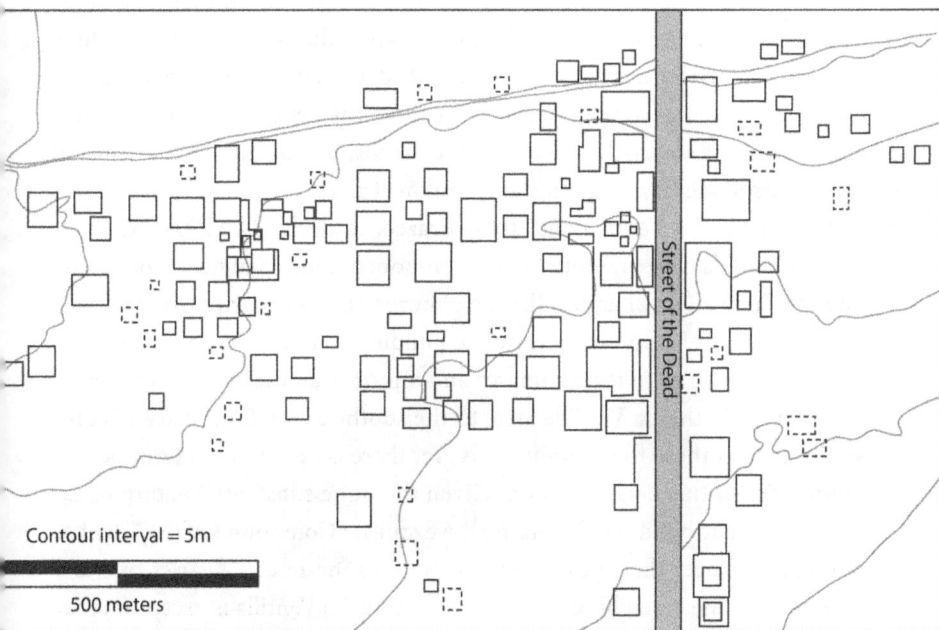

Figure 3.6. Map of the Tlajinga barrio, located on the south edge of Teotihuacan. Rounded gray rectangles represent potential plazas in the Tlajinga barrio. Adapted from Widmer and Storey (2012). Courtesy of Rebecca Storey and Randolph Widmer.

the cluster, adjacent to the state-planned Street of the Dead, suggests a top-down kind of administration, thus making Tlajinga a ward as well as a district. Other potential districts include an area on the northwest edge of Teotihuacan where several contiguous compounds are smaller and more tightly spaced than their neighbors and a group of about thirty-five compounds (one of which is Tepantitla) east of the site core that cluster together spatially (Cowgill 2007; Manzanilla 2009).

Further parsing the Tlajinga district, Widmer and Storey (2012, 105) inferred three neighborhoods by identifying three focal nodes in the form of open plazas (figure 3.6; Cowgill [2008, 93] suggests that open spaces may have been gardens). However, Widmer and Storey (2012, 109) note that the presence of two temple complexes within Tlajinga implies the presence of only two neighborhoods, an analysis that coheres with Gómez Chávez's (2012, 81) argument that each neighborhood must have its own temple complex.

Elsewhere at Teotihuacan, researchers have uncovered evidence for specialized production of other goods, such as obsidian, textiles, and incense burners. However, the data do not yet support the notion that neighborhoods formed around these production locales. The concentration of shell and greenstone workers located on the east edge of city (Turner 1991) stands on good ground as a neighborhood because the six to eight compounds where lapidary debris has been recovered form a distinct spatial cluster nearly surrounded by vacant terrain (Millon et al. 1973).

Working at La Ventilla and Teopancazco, respectively, Gómez Chávez and Manzanilla have presented multi-component models of neighborhoods. Gómez Chávez (2012) argues that neighborhoods consist minimally of residences, spaces of common use, public buildings for administration and ritual, and a public plaza for commerce and information exchange. A cluster of compounds in the La Ventilla area, to the southwest of Teotihuacan's core, shows each of these four components. Yet there is no way to determine the boundaries of this neighborhood. Given the quite substantial nature of La Ventilla's public buildings, including the exquisite Compound of the Glyphs, one might expect that they served as the focal node of a district or ward rather than a mere neighborhood. Furthermore, La Ventilla is exceptional in the sense that it housed very powerful elites (Gómez Chávez uses the phrase "ruling class"). Based on excavations of the Teopancazco compound, Linda Manzanilla (2009) presented a neighborhood model for non-elites. In addition to the four components Gómez Chávez specified, Manzanilla added a craft area, military quarters, and kitchens to feed the warriors and crafters (in some publications Manzanilla [2012] includes medical facilities). While La Ventilla had different components in different compounds, Teopancazco, a single compound, had all of the components Manzanilla identified. Excavations of neighboring compounds would determine if Teopancazco was the only compound in the vicinity with each of the seven (or eight) components or if neighboring compounds also had them; in the latter case, the Teopancazco excavations would not provide grounds for the identification of a neighborhood. As in the case of La Ventilla, we do not know the boundaries of the Teopancazco neighborhood.

In summary, research at Teotihuacan has produced excellent examples of both districts and neighborhoods. The craft, spatial clustering, and focal node criteria helped identify Tlajinga as a combination of two to three neighborhoods forming a district and ward. The spatial clustering and stylistic clustering criteria helped identify ethnic neighborhoods referred to as the Oaxaca Barrio and the Merchants' Barrio. La Ventilla was probably a focal node for a district or ward. However, these examples account for a very small portion of the total population of the city and have required extensive excavation. As George Cowgill (2007, 279) has noted, "Except for a few ethnic enclaves and areas of craft specialization we have not so far been able to identify spatial units."

Conclusion

To be frank, the criteria for identifying neighborhoods presented in this chapter often do not get us very far. This resonates with the sentiment from the epigraph that neighborhoods, rather than being marked by clearly visible traces, are what their inhabitants think they are. The one Maya example discussed above where archaeologists have divided a large portion of the settlement into neighborhoods and succeeded in specifying their boundaries is Rio Bec (Arnauld et al. 2012). Yet Rio Bec, with its dispersed clusters and lack of a single center, is very different from many of the major Maya sites discussed thus far. Identifying neighborhoods is difficult not because entities intermediate in size between the household and the city did not exist (York et al.'s [2011] broad survey shows that while neighborhoods were very common, they were not universal) but because they were messy and complex. Neighborhood boundaries were not always clear to occupants, perhaps because a variety of factors of unequal strength produce neighborhoods in the first place (Hare and Masson 2012, 252; York et al. 2011, 2409–2410). Even when people in the past could recognize neighborhood boundaries clearly, they may be very difficult to detect archaeologically. Probably no city breaks down easily into zones based on a single criterion (Smith 2010, 150). Some of the criteria above may work for one small part of a city while others will work for another small part. The distinctiveness and face-to-face interaction that characterize neighborhoods may never have developed in other parts of cities.

The small number of neighborhoods and districts found thus far at Teotihuacan illustrates the complexity of the problem. I do not deny the existence of additional neighborhoods or districts at Teotihuacan. Rather, in calling attention to problems in identifying neighborhoods and their boundaries at Teotihuacan, Classic period Mesoamerica's preeminent urban center, I foreground the quandary I will face in the following chapter, which attempts to find intermediate social units at Chunchucmil using each of the four criteria presented above. The cases presented above suggest that the attempt will not be 100 percent successful. Nevertheless, the presence of spatial features rarely preserved at other sites has helped us make unusual headway in locating neighborhoods at Chunchucmil. I like to think that this means that neighborhoods were common and distinct at Maya centers that lack the spatial divisions that help archaeologists detect them. Either way, the search for neighborhoods is a valuable pursuit because it is a search for the ways normal people made their everyday experience in cities livable. As such, this research foregrounds urbanization as an active process involving a broader range of agents than have usually been considered in Mesoamerica (Joyce 2009).

4

Neighborhoods at Chunchucmil

SCOTT HUTSON AND JACOB WELCH

> Neighborhood is a word that has come to sound like a
> Valentine. As a sentimental concept, "neighborhood" is
> harmful to city planning. It leads to attempts at warping city
> life into imitations of town or suburban life. Sentimentality
> plays with sweet intentions in place of good sense.
>
> Jacobs (1961, 112)

Chapter 3 showed that those who attempt to identify neighborhoods face many difficulties. As Mike Smith (2010, 150) has noted, "We badly need more cases with quantitative data and better spatial analytical methods to investigate the degree of social clustering in past and present cities." In this chapter my coauthor Jacob Welch and I apply the methods for finding neighborhoods discussed in the previous chapter to the ancient city of Chunchucmil. In particular, we look at Chunchucmil from the perspective of the first criteria presented in the previous chapter for identifying neighborhoods: spatial clustering, focal nodes, stylistic clustering, and crafts. Chapter 5 applies the fifth criterion—wealth—to Chunchucmil and other Maya cities.

Chunchucmil is an excellent test case for identifying neighborhoods and other intermediate-sized social units for four reasons. First, it is an urban center. The site has one of the highest settlement densities of all Maya cities (see chapter 2). High settlement density means a larger number of socially distant people pressed into the same space and thus a greater need for establishing order and familiarity. Neighborhood formation responds to this need. Second, like a few other high-density Maya cities, Chunchucmil has a system of residential fences. The fences, which consist of stone walls and are referred to as *albarradas*, mark the edges of house lots. These fences would not have stood much more than a meter high. In a site with little space to spare, the walls clearly communicate whose space is whose and, as a possible adaptation to crowding, prevent trespass. Most important for the purposes of identifying neighborhoods, these walls demarcate pathways through the site. They thus permit us to determine where people walked and what routes were available from house to house and from houses to the core of the site. As we discuss below in the section on spatial clusters, the circulation patterns these paths enable us to identify suggest neighborhoods and districts.

Third, the visibility of these circulation patterns and the other remains of the site is relatively robust. A large contiguous portion of the city (9.3 square kilometers) has been mapped, and the preservation conditions and architectural characteristics in northern Yucatan favor the visibility of ancient structures. The flat terrain and absence of rivers mean that the forces that typically bury features—the deposition of sediments from flooding and/or slopeside erosion—did not take place here. Thus, the number of buried structures is minimal: of the more than 800 "off-mound" test pits dug at Chunchucmil, only one test pit located a buried structure. In addition, the Maya of Yucatan usually built houses on top of stone platforms, and those platforms have preserved well. However, we still struggle with the problem of the "invisible Maya" (Johnston 2004): although most houses had, at the least, stone foundation braces, thus making their location visible to archaeologists, some may have been built entirely of perishable materials. In sum, the broad swath of the city that was mapped and the high degree of visibility of the built environment enable us to use the map to gather extensive data on stylistic clustering (such as orientation of buildings) and the presence or absence of certain kinds of focal nodes (such as temples and open spaces).

Fourth, a representative sample of house lots at Chunchucmil has been excavated. This means that we have the artifact data necessary to determine whether or not crafting neighborhoods existed and to see if certain areas of the site exhibit distinct stylistic clustering in terms of ceramics.

Before launching into the identification of neighborhoods, we pause to provide more detail about Chunchucmil. It was, and still is, a dry, stony place.

"Yucatan is the country with [the] least earth I have ever seen, since it is all one living rock," declared Bishop Diego de Landa (Tozzer 1941), who arrived from Spain in the sixteenth century. People piled up the ubiquitous limestone into domestic platforms, elevating their houses, although not enough to escape the mosquitos. Although people tended gardens at home, yields of maize from nearby fields were uncertain due to variation in the amount and timing of rain. In the dry months, a warm, brackish breeze comes from the northwest that originates at places such as Celestun, where salt flats drew the ancient city's people at the end of the dry season. Scorched by the summer sun, they bent to collect "white gold" (McKillop 2002) at the bottom of knee-deep briny ponds. They probably gave thanks when summer thunder showers from the east broke as they packed the salt for transport. Merchants peddled the salt far and wide, bringing back obsidian, food, baubles, and valuables.

Chunchucmil consists of a center that covers 0.55 square kilometers surrounded by a dense residential core that covers an estimated 5.85 square kilometers and a residential periphery that covers an estimated 8.7 square kilometers (figure 2.5; Hutson et al. 2008; Hutson et al. 2016a). The boundaries between these three zones are fuzzy. Both the center and the residential core have monumental compounds and residences. However, the center has many more monumental compounds and two things the residential core lacks: a large marketplace and a collection of unbuilt spaces. The residential periphery differs from the residential core mainly in terms of settlement density: the periphery has 392 structures per square kilometer, in contrast to the 1,064 per square kilometer in the core. Beyond the residential periphery, settlement density drops to about 60 structures per square kilometer in most directions. Excavations at Chunchucmil have been both extensive and intensive (Hutson 2010; Hutson et al. 2010; Magnoni 2008). Ceramics from the Maxcanu, Hunabchen, and Oxil groups, which have been radiocarbon dated to between 400 and 700 CE, dominate most assemblages from the site. The population of the site at the end of the Early Classic was somewhere between 30,000 and 45,000. Only 4 percent of the pottery is Preclassic. Although a larger amount of pottery dates to the Late and Terminal classic periods (9.4 percent), these sherds come from a limited set of architectural contexts because the site was mostly abandoned by 700 CE (Magnoni 2008).

A total of 1,476 architectural groups have been mapped at Chunchucmil. These have been classified into a variety of types, depending on the number of structures per compound, the presence of monumental structures or resources such as *sascab* quarries, and whether or not they have house lot walls. The vast majority of architectural compounds are domestic and most have fewer than ten structures, at least one preserved house lot wall, and no monumental structures. Most of these domestic compounds are patio groups (much like in the southern lowlands; Ashmore 1981b) with structures arranged around the sides of a central patio that is usually artificially raised above the natural ground surface.

Spatial Clustering

The previous chapter presented four spatial clustering methods that have been used to identify intermediate units in cities. The first two methods— looking at how topographic features such as arroyos create spatial divisions and looking for clusters of buildings surrounded by open space—are not applicable to Chunchucmil because the terrain is flat and because, as figure 2.5 shows, few clusters are clear to the naked eye. In such a context, the third method, spatial distance measures (creating clusters by lumping together all structures separated by less than a certain distance), would produce clusters that are constructs of the archaeologist and have little meaning to ancient people. Luckily, at Chunchucmil we can use the fourth method, which looks at whether transportation routes within the city create nooks in which some of the same people repeatedly come across each other, resulting in clusters of regularized social interaction. With the exception of raised stone avenues (*sacbes*), which are usually restricted to city centers, transportation routes in residential areas are usually invisible at Maya ruins. Because the people of Chunchucmil built paths and *sacbes* throughout the city, we have the luxury of evaluating the patterning in these circulation features to see whether they encouraged the formation of neighborhoods.

But first, what arrangements of paths help delineate neighborhoods? Two sorts of arrangements come immediately to mind: the grid pattern, as seen in figure 4.1a, and the hub-and-spoke pattern, as seen in figure 4.1b. Note that these idealized maps present space schematically and neutrally, as if people did not have affinities for or aversions toward specific places. In other words, the maps are just heuristic devices to suggest possibilities. In either idealized pattern, neighborhoods can form easily. In the grid pattern, we ask the reader to consider one block of a street with dwellings on both sides. Suttles (1972,

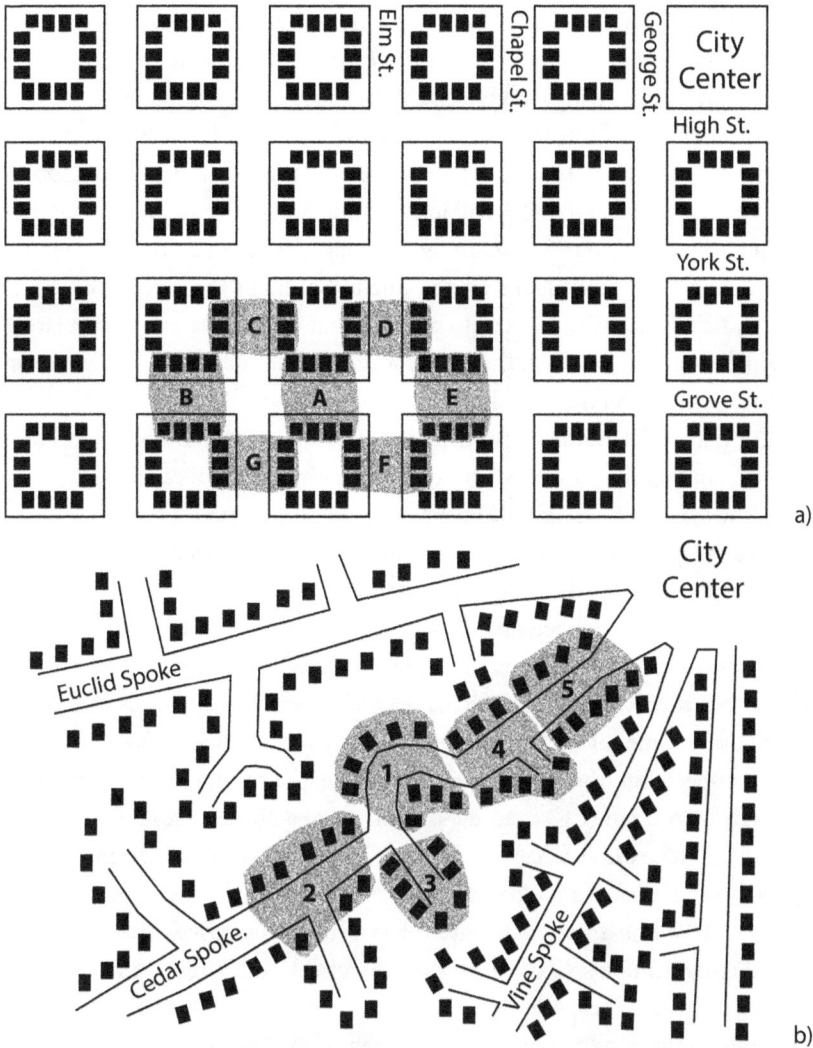

Figure 4.1. Two models of circulation patterns within cities: a) grid pattern; b) hub-and-spoke pattern.

56) calls this a face-block. Residents of the same face-block will see a lot of each other, thus making neighborhood formation likely, though such neighborhoods might be small. Moving to a scale above the face-block, it is difficult to identify larger neighborhoods in the grid pattern based on the layout of the streets alone because we have no way of knowing which face-blocks might have been grouped together. We might assume, probably wrongly,

that the residents of face-blocks that are close together in space knew each other better, but in the absence of arroyos or other kinds of boundaries, we have no way of knowing which face-blocks might have grouped into a larger unit (or how many larger units there should be). The hub-and-spoke pattern poses less difficulty in this regard. In figure 4.1b, the layout of streets dictates that a resident of face-block 1 will interact much more frequently with other residents of the Cedar Spoke, in face-blocks 2, 3, and 4, than they would with residents of face-blocks on the Euclid Spoke or the Vine Spoke. The hub-and-spoke layout allows us to propose that each spoke might be a larger neighborhood. In contrast, the grid layout provides us with no mechanism for specifying larger neighborhoods.

The paths at Chunchucmil articulate to form a layout that resembles the hub-and-spoke pattern. This is quite exciting to us because such a layout shows clear divisions within the city. These divisions serve as heuristic devices for grouping Chunchucmil's house lots into a series of intermediate scale social units. Further below (see figure 4.2) we discuss these hypothetical units and add evidence that strengthens the case that these units were socially salient to the people who lived in them. Before doing so, we continue to contrast the two idealized city plans (grid versus hub-and-spoke) in order to expose additional social features of the hub-and-spoke layout. Paths can fall on a spectrum from accessible and busy (e.g., a throughway) to secluded and lightly trodden (e.g., a cul-de-sac). Areas of a city that contain many accessible paths exhibit what we might call an open circulation pattern. The grid pattern serves as a good example of a relatively open circulation pattern. In contrast, a hub-and-spoke pattern has a relatively closed circulation pattern. Figure 4.1 helps visualize this. In the grid layout (figure 4.1a), when a resident of face-block A leaves the block, they have six possible directions available to them, all within a block of their home. This means they have six possible face-blocks, not counting their own, to pass through (B, C, D, E, F, and G). In the hub-and-spoke pattern in figure 4.1b, residents have fewer options. For example, someone living in face-block 1, which is the same size as face-block A, has only three directions available to them and one of them is a dead end. Thus, this resident has at best three other immediately adjacent face-blocks (2, 3, and 4) and only two (2 and 4) that they are likely to pass through. The result is that in the hub-and-spoke pattern, the limited number of paths immediately accessible to a resident forces more frequent interaction with a smaller set of neighbors.

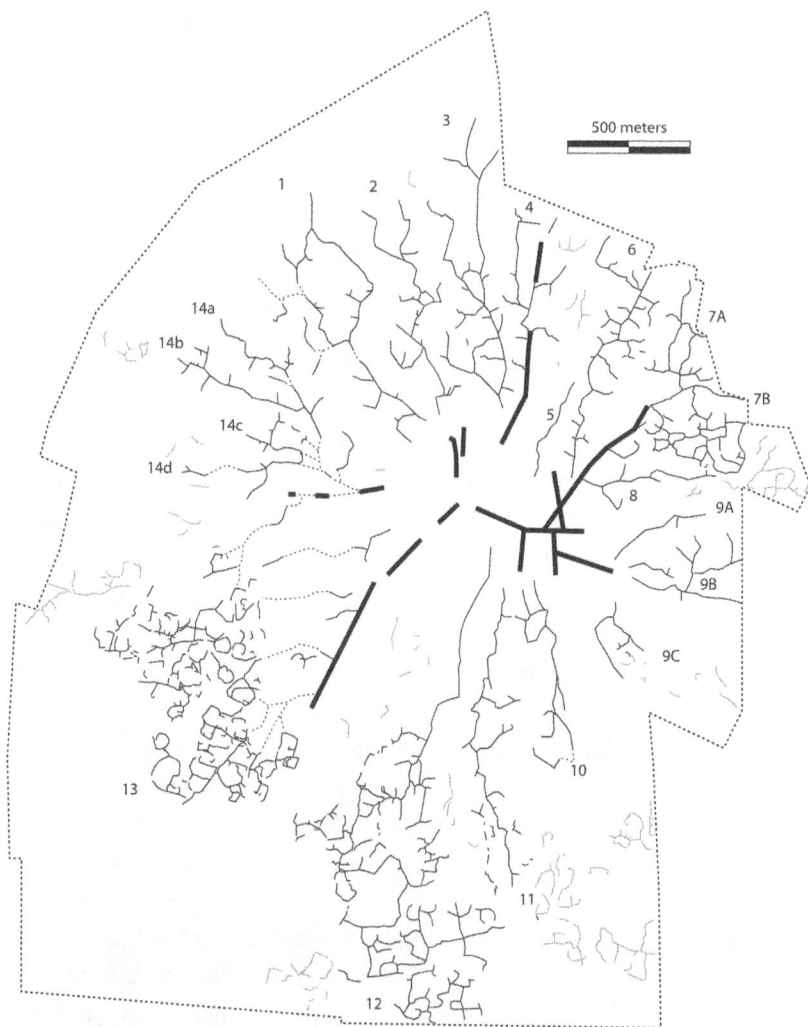

Figure 4.2. Map of paths (thin, wavy, black lines; gray lines are paths not connected to a network that reaches the site core) and causeways (thick, straight, black lines) at Chunchucmil, Yucatan. All buildings have been removed for ease of viewing (see figure 2.5 for Chunchucmil's buildings).

The hub-and-spoke pattern also has a more limited number of walking routes through the city. In contrast, in a city grid, people can chart multiple pathways to a destination, thus creating choices about which face-blocks to enter. For example, a resident in face-block A of the city grid can get to the city center by taking a left on Elm St. and then a right on High St. Or they can take Grove St. and then a left on George St. Or they can use Elm, York, and George or Grove, Chapel, and High or two other possible combinations. All six combinations are the same distance and these six combinations allow them to pass through a choice of twelve different face-blocks. In contrast, a person living in neighborhood 1 of the hub-and-spoke-pattern has only one route (the Cedar Spoke) to the city center, which means that they have no choice but to interact with people in face-blocks 4 and 5 every time. Thus, for a hub-and-spoke city, which has fewer routes, it is easier to predict who will take what route. In addition, there will be more people per route.

To the extent that one can predict who will be using what routes, a hub-and-spoke layout produces the kind of interpersonal familiarity that is a hallmark of a neighborhood. Yet, as Jane Jacobs's quote in the epigraph stresses, too much predictability and familiarity results in neighborhoods that are sterile islands turned inward toward themselves. This may decrease the appeal of cities. Unlike villages and towns, cities bring many different people, institutions, and enterprises into a small space, making a great variety of social, commercial, and other relations accessible to its residents (Jacobs 1961, 116). Thus, people may settle in cities because they offer the opportunity of different kinds of friends or vendors, to give two examples. This is one of the foremost critiques of Howard's Garden City idea (1902), which proposed to take people out of large cities and resettle them into small, village-like units. Although a hub-and-spoke layout contains the kinds of channeling mechanisms/bottlenecks that make pedestrian traffic flow more predictable, such a layout does not discourage circulation. The hub-and-spoke layout does not lock people into the same inward-looking places with the same acquaintances because more people are using each possible route to the center or edge of the city. Also, the hub-and-spoke pattern simplifies access to the central plazas and marketplaces that promote the chance encounters—the multiplicity—that make cities attractive. Thus, although hub-and-spoke layouts are more "closed" than grid layouts, they do not dampen mobility or stifle the allure of cities.

The map in figure 4.2 shows only the circulation features (paths and *sacbes*) of Chunchucmil. The similarity to a hub-and-spoke circulation pattern is clear. Most of the paths form a sinuous spoke pattern. We use the term spoke cluster to refer to each set of architectural groups linked to a particular spoke. These clusters take the approximate shape of pizza slices. We have given each spoke cluster a number for ease of reference. Circulation patterns sharply bound these clusters, giving them an impressive integrity. For example, people living in the middle of cluster 3 cannot easily walk westward to cluster 2 because there are no paths in that direction. To get to cluster 2, they have to walk south on their spoke to the site center/hub and then walk outward on the cluster 2 spoke. Or they can follow either of the two spoke 3 tributaries northward toward the edge of the city, traverse the open space in the residential periphery to get to one of the two Spoke 2 endpoints, and then walk south on the spoke. The only other option is to abandon the paths/spokes, climb over other peoples' house lot walls, and cross their yards. This may have happened in some parts of the site, since a small number of house lots in densely settled areas do not have a path leading to them (see below). On the other hand, there may have been paths for these residents that we simply cannot see archaeologically. In some cases relations between neighbors could have been good enough for someone to consistently scale their neighbor's wall and cross their house lot (see Stanton and Hutson 2010 on kinship relations between members of neighboring house lots). Given the fact that in contemporary Yucatan, house lot space is considered to be inviolably private, as was the case in historic Yucatan (Hanks 1990, 95; Restall 1997, 99), we argue that in most cases people at ancient Chunchucmil stayed on the paths, only occasionally scaling someone else's walls and cutting across their house lot.

At a closer scale, some of the spoke clusters—12 and 13 to the south and southwest of the site center and 7A and 7B to the northeast of the site center—do not fully conform to the hub-and-spoke layout. For example, cluster 13 has no single central spoke. Cluster 12 has a central spoke in its north portion. Cluster 12 contains a total of 148 house lots, the majority of which are located in the warren of paths on the south side of the spoke cluster. In this southern area, the network of paths has a very open circulation pattern: paths go in all directions, a bit like a windy, curvy grid. Yet as people moved northward from the southern part of the cluster, which holds most of the house lots, a bottleneck would have occurred about 800 meters south of the Chunchucmil site core. At this bottleneck, the warren of paths to the south narrows to a single path going northward. This bottleneck thus forced people into predictable and familiar social interactions: they likely saw people mostly from their own cluster when they headed to or from the site core. However, the degree of familiarity was diffuse because we estimate that the 148 house lots in this cluster contained over 2,000 people. Returning to Jane Jacobs's point that vibrant city neighborhoods should not be too homey and village-like, we think a neighborhood of 2,000 people can be quite lively, probably too big to be a single neighborhood.

The estimate of 2,000 people (and other estimates in table 4.1) is based on the following data and considerations. On average, the house lots mapped at Chunchucmil contain 5.14 structures (Magnoni et al. 2012), of which 3.5 are residences (the others are kitchens and/or shrines). Assuming that each residence housed a nuclear family, the social unit that occupied a house lot was probably an extended family. Using the standard estimate of 5 people per residence, the average houselot with its three or four residences would have housed between 15 and 20 people; 17.5 people in short. Assuming that only 90 percent of the 148 house lots in the cluster were occupied at the same time, we multiply 17.5 by 133 house lots, yielding approximately 2,300 people. Cluster 12 therefore qualifies more as a district than a neighborhood. Later we discuss whether or not it could have been a ward. Cluster 13, directly to the west of cluster 12, probably also contained too many people to be a neighborhood; it had 138 house lots. Cluster 13 is also the most open of Chunchucmil's clusters because it has no single bottleneck for those moving toward the site core. The people of cluster 13 could have chosen three different routes to the site center that did not overlap with each other. Clusters 7A and 7B exhibit an open path pattern. We believe that clusters 7A and 7B are smaller than clusters 12 and 13, but we have not mapped them fully; they extend northeast beyond the boundaries of our map.

The other spoke clusters (1, 2, 3, 4, 5, 6, 8, 9A, 9B, 9C, 10, 11, 14a, 14b, 14c, and 14d) are smaller, implying a demographic unit at the scale of the neighborhood. The number of house lots on these spokes ranges from 7 to 74; the mean is 29 and the median is 19 (table 4.1). With the 10 percent reduction for contemporaneity, 29 house lots/extended families converts to about 450 people. In comparison, the *sian otot* Wisdom identified and the clusters in the Copan pocket that Fash (1983) interpreted as *sian otot* (see chapter 3) each contained about 25 extended families, which they believe is equivalent to between 200 and 300 people. In sum, the number of extended families in Chunhcucmil's neighborhoods is about the same as the number of extended families in the *sian otot* near Copan, while the number of people in Chunchucmil's neighborhoods may have been higher

In total, 846 of the 1,405 architectural groups in the 9.3-square-kilometer polygon shown in figure 4.2 pertain to the clusters discussed above. The remainder of the groups can be classified in four different ways: 1) house lots in

Table 4.1. Population estimates for each spoke cluster and estimates of the amount of patio space in the large monumental compounds that pertain to spoke clusters

Spoke cluster #	Hectares/ cluster	# House lots	Estimated population	Associated monumental compound(s)	Patio length (m)	Patio width (m)	Patio area (m²)	Patio capacity at 0.46m²/ person	Patio capacity at 1.0 m²/ person	Patio capacity at 3.1 m²/ person
1	36	74	1,166	Katsin	65	60	3,900	8,478	3,900	1,258
2	22	55	866	Chi'ik	30	25	750	1,630	750	242
3	30	66	1,040	Chakah	65	50	3,250	7,065	3,250	1,048
4	19	32	504	N5E1-F	40	32.5	1,300	2,826	1,300	419
5	6	8	126	Pich	25	25	625	1,359	625	202
6	22	18	284	Pomoche	60	55	3,300	7,174	3,300	1,065
7	26	64	1,008	N3E3-M	35	32.5	1,137	2,473	1,137	367
8	8	19	299	Pomoche	60	55	3,300	7,174	3,300	1,065
9	32	41	646	Chukum	45	35	1,575	3,424	1,575	508
10	19	30	473	Picholte	62.5	50	3,125	6,793	3,125	1,008
11	28	53	835	Copo	50	45	2,250	4,891	2,250	726
12	89	148	2,331	Guaje	45	37	1,665	3,620	1,665	537
13	100	138	2,174	Kakaltun	40	32.5	1,300	2,826	1,300	419
				S4W4-A	35	30	1,050	2,283	1,050	339
				Chimay	90	70	6,300	13,696	6,300	2,032
				N1W4-d	37.5	32.5	1,218.75	2,649	1,218	393
14	41	100	1,575	Xpim	80	75	6,000	13,043	6,000	1,935

Note: Patio dimensions pertain to the main patio of the monumental compound.

areas with paths that are not clearly linked with a single spoke cluster (there are several hundred of these, many in the southeast part of the mapped polygon); 2) house lots located farther out from the site center than the paths, usually in the residential periphery where terrain not bounded by house lot walls is abundant and paths are not necessary (there are several hundred of these); 3) house lots or monumental groups in one of the areas closer to the site center without paths (there are perhaps sixty of these); and 4) "landlocked" house lots that are close to paths but have no path access, forcing people to pass through a neighbor's house lot (there are thirty of these).

Some of the clusters can be combined to form districts. For example, the spokes of clusters 14A, 14B, 14C, and 14D all eventually combine into a single spoke near the site center. Clusters 7A and 7B also feed into the same spoke. Finally, the spokes of clusters 9A, 9B, and 9C all feed to a single monumental compound. The notion that clusters share a monumental compound brings up the focal node criterion, which we will discuss shortly. As noted in chapter 3, districts can be the same size as wards. The two are distinguished by the fact that a ward is an administrative unit created by centralized leaders while a district forms more organically, usually as a cluster of neighborhoods that share something in common. In the case of spokes that more than one cluster shares, such as the two examples presented in this paragraph, the shared spoke itself is not likely to have been arranged by a central authority, since the paths at Chunchucmil were built so easily and informally. That is not to say that an authority could not have made convenient use of the fact that 14A, 14B, 14C, and 14D all feed to a shared spoke and thus made this district into a ward. Likewise, spoke clusters 12 and 13, which we believe are districts but not neighborhoods, could also have been administered as wards.

Focal Nodes

Stronger identifications of neighborhoods (and districts) result when archaeologists combine the criterion of spatial clustering with that of focal nodes. For Chunchucmil, we examine five candidates for focal nodes: large buildings that presumably served special purposes, monumental architectural compounds connected to *sacbes*, open spaces, wells, and *sascaberas*. We begin with large buildings, which can be focal nodes in two ways. They might be part of a house lot of a high-ranking individual who served as the leader of the neighborhood (as Kintz [1983] argues for Coba) or they might be a temple belonging to the neighborhood as a whole and independent of any particular residence (as A. Smith [2003, 213] argues for Ur in the Third Dynasty). At Chunchucmil, large buildings found outside the site core are almost always found within the house lots of high-ranking households. What counts as a "large" building is open to interpretation, so we will look at two categories: all buildings whose ruins today stand 4 meters or taller and all buildings whose ruins today stand 5.5 meters or taller (the second category is a subset of the first). We do not place in either of these categories Chunchucmil's largest buildings, which were usually over 10 meters high and are, with one exception, connected to the site core by *sacbes*. We discuss these as a separate kind of focal node below. Since we have not excavated buildings higher than 4 meters within house lots, we are not certain what functions such buildings served, though on the basis of mapping data some appear to have been vaulted residences built on solid platforms and others appear to have been pyramidal shrines/temples.

Figure 4.3 shows the distribution of all buildings taller than 4 meters. It overlays these buildings onto the pathway map and highlights alternating spoke clusters to make cluster boundaries more clear. The map shows that buildings 4 meters high or taller are distributed relatively evenly across the site. However, not all neighborhoods identified above contain such a building; for example, clusters 2, 10, and 14D lack one and clusters 9A and 9B share one. Furthermore, several spoke clusters contain multiple buildings of this size. While we would expect the larger clusters that seem to be districts (clusters 12 and 13, for example) to have multiple focal nodes because there may have been multiple neighborhoods within these districts, cluster 6, which has only eighteen house lots (perhaps 300 people) and is a good candidate for a neighborhood, has three buildings higher than 4 meters. These considerations lead us to conclude that house lots with buildings 4 meters or higher may not tell us about focal nodes. Chapter 5 explores what they may tell us about heterogeneity among house lots.

The site contains eighteen buildings 5.5 meters high or taller in the residential zones (figure 4.4), not counting the *sacbe*-linked monumental compounds also visible in the figure. Since there are twenty spoke clusters, we come close to a one-to-one correspondence between clusters and large buildings. However, half of the clusters (2, 3, 4, 7A, 7B, 8, 9A, 9B, 10, and 11) lack a building of this size. In addition, these buildings are not spread evenly across the site; they are very rare on the north, northeast, east, and southeast

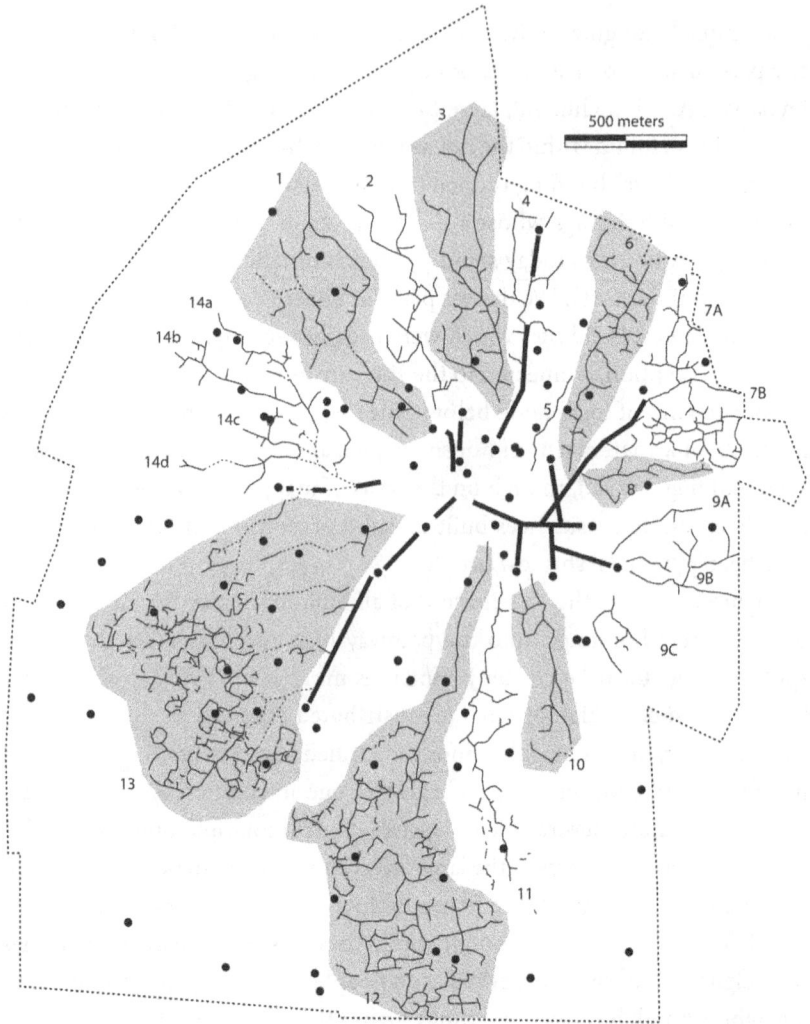

Figure 4.3. Map of all buildings taller than 4 meters (represented as circles) overlaid onto the map of circulation features. Alternating spoke clusters are highlighted to make cluster boundaries more clear.

sides. This latter fact strongly suggests that buildings of this size were not focal nodes.

We now turn to the second type of focal node: monumental compounds connected to *sacbes*. Of the sixteen compounds shown in figure 4.4, fourteen are quadrangles and two (the ones in gray) are not. A quadrangle consists of a quadrilateral patio with a pyramid (ranging between 8 and 17.5 meters tall) usually on the east side, long platforms on the other three sides, and a low

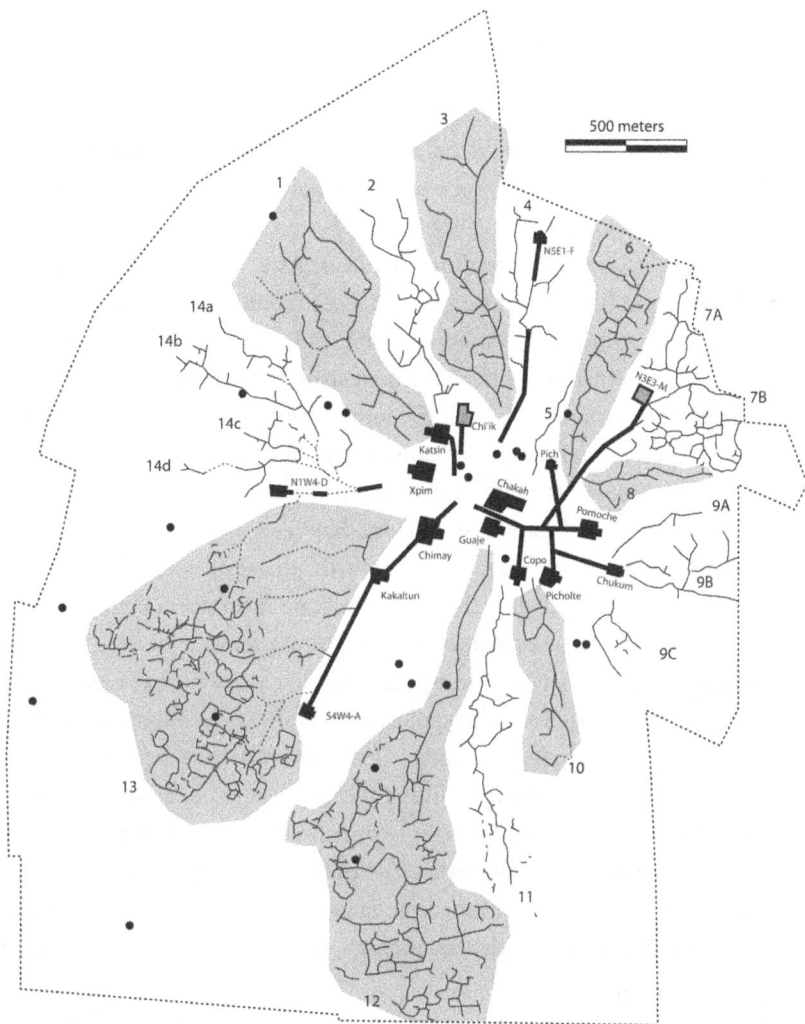

Figure 4.4. Distribution of buildings 5.5 meters high or taller. Quadrangles (solid black) and monumental groups (gray) linked to causeways are named and represented with polygons showing correctly scaled surface area. Other tall buildings are represented with circles.

square platform in the middle (Dahlin and Ardren 2002, 268). Excavations in the Pich quadrangle (Group N1E1-C) suggest that the long platforms on the side of the patio were stepped viewing stands. For example, structure N1E1-23, an 18-meter-long structure that lines over half of the north side of the Pich quadrangle patio, had a 14-meter-wide staircase leading from the patio floor to the top of the structure (Blackmore and Ardren 2001). Patios lined with steps in other parts of the Maya area were designed as venues for spectacles

(Fash 2005, 97). We believe the patios in Chunchucmil's quadrangles served the same purpose.

None of the patios of the quadrangles could hold the entire site's population, but it is possible that they could host the members of a neighborhood or district. The idea here is that for a monumental compound to serve as a focal node, it should host feasts, rallies, meetings, ceremonies, and other neighborhood/district events throughout the year. As a way of testing this, we suggest two expectations that monumental compounds should meet if they served as focal nodes in this manner. First, did each spoke-like neighborhood or district have a clear and convenient spatial connection to a particular monumental compound? Second, if Chunchucmil meets the first expectation, could each monumental compound have accommodated the number of people in its associated neighborhood or district?

Figure 4.4 suggests many connections between specific spoke clusters and monumental compounds. In other words, the spokes of most clusters channel their pedestrians directly toward a single monumental compound: cluster 1's spoke feeds to the Katsin quadrangle, cluster 2's spoke feeds to the Chi'ik quadrangle, and so on. At the same time, in cases where an entrance to a quadrangle can be inferred, the spokes do not always terminate directly at the entrances. For example, in figure 4.5 the entrance to the Copo quadrangle would appear to be on the north side of the quadrangle, since *sacbe* 5 enters the group from this side and the temple pyramid faces north. Yet the cluster 11 spoke terminates on the southwest side of the quadrangle. Directly to the east, the cluster 10 spoke terminates at the southwest edge of the Picholte quadrangle: the entrance to that quadrangle would likely be on the west or north side of the quadrangle.

In some cases the spokes of more than one cluster feed to a single monumental compound (table 4.1 shows the correspondence between clusters and monumental compounds). For example, clusters 9A, 9B, and 9C form a district that pertains to the Chukum quadrangle. Likewise, clusters 14a, 14b, 14c, and 14d form a single district that pertains to the Xpim quadrangle. Cluster 13 feeds to multiple monumental quadrangles, but this is to be expected because cluster 13 is a large district that probably contained many neighborhoods. Each quadrangle near cluster 13 may have served a neighborhood within the cluster that has not been detected yet. Two clusters—6 and 8—do not feed directly to a monumental compound. The spokes of these two clusters feed directly to *sacbe* 1, which terminates at compound N3E3-M to the

Figure 4.5. Portion of the Chunchucmil map showing how spokes 10 and 11 articulate with the Picholte and Copo quadrangles, respectively. Dotted lines show suggested continuation of pedestrian flow.

north, but the spots where these spokes join with the *sacbe* are in fact closer to quadrangles such as Pomoche and Pich. In Table 4.1, we have assigned both of them to Pomoche, which has no other spoke cluster feeding to it. This suggests that cluster 8, a rather small one, may in fact have combined with cluster 6 to make a district. We admit that the focal node connections for clusters 6 and 8 are questionable, but since all the other clusters match well with monumental compounds, we consider that Chunchucmil satisfies the expectation that spoke-like neighborhoods and districts had a ceremonial focal node.

What about the second expectation? Could all the people from a particular neighborhood or district have fit into the performance space of the monumental compound to which they belonged? Although a performance space could have succeeded in integrating a target group of households even if every last household member may not have been able to fit, showing a correlation between the amount of people in a spoke cluster and the size of the associated plaza would strengthen the argument that quadrangles served as effective focal nodes for intermediate scale social units, giving them the distinctiveness that is part of the definition of a neighborhood and a district.

Inomata (2006a) uses three measures for discussing the number of people that plazas could accommodate: one person per 0.46 square meters, one person per 1 square meter, and one person per 3.1 square meters. Table 4.1 provides data on the size of each of the monumental compounds and how many people could fit in them presuming 0.46 square meters, 1 square meter, and 3.1 square meters per person. These calculations are conservative in that they assume that all the people had to fit just in the patio, not the range structures that line the patio or the stairways leading up to the range structures. The table also shows the number of people presumed to have lived in each spoke cluster, but in this case we have combined Spokes 14a, b, c, and d into a single cluster; Spokes 9a, b, and c into a single cluster; and Spokes 7a and b into a single cluster. The table reveals which monumental compounds would have had sufficient patio space to host the full population of the affiliated neighborhood or district.

At 0.46 square meters per person, all of the monumental compounds could successfully have held the population of their affiliated clusters. However, the figure of 0.46 square meters per person, which Inomata takes from Moore (2005), strikes us as too crowded for anything but a short event (no more than an hour or so) during which people would have had no choice but to stand in place. We believe that the figure of 1.0 square meter per person is more plausible. Table 4.1 reveals that the people of all but two of the fourteen clusters could have fit into the patios of their monumental compounds, assuming 1.0 square meter per person. The two clusters that do not fit—spoke clusters 2 and 12—are close calls and these possible misfits both have more than one solution. The first solution is to propose that the relatively small amount of people that could not have fit in the patio at 1 square meter per person could have occupied the stairs of the range structures or the range structures themselves, as Inomata (2006b, 198) suggests. The other solutions are specific to each cluster. When Chunchucmil was at its height, over 2,000 people probably lived in spoke cluster 12, making it a district. The Guaje patio that the cluster 12 spoke arrives at could have held only 1,665 people at 1 square meter per person. Yet Chimay, the quadrangle 200 meters to the east of Guaje, has the largest patio at Chunchucmil and could easily have accommodated all of the people of cluster 12. Although in table 4.1 we list Chimay as one of the four quadrangles pertaining to cluster 13, Chimay is the most distant from the cluster 13 house lots. In addition, the other three monumental compounds associated with cluster 13 could have accommodated the entire population of that district. Thus, if the Guaje patio was too small for cluster 12, Chimay could have accommodated all the people in that district.

The other spoke cluster with too many people for its monumental compound is cluster 2, which had an estimated population of over 800. Its spoke feeds to the Chi'ik compound, which could have held 750. This is a rather small difference: if necessary, the extra people could probably have been accommodated on the stairs of one of the two low structures that border the Chi'ik patio. Though the explanations for the two misfit clusters—2 and 12—may seem like special pleading, we reiterate that in both cases, the discrepancy between how many people pertain to each cluster and how many people can fit in the monumental compound at 1 square meter per person is small to begin with. The fact that there aren't more misfits is remarkable, given the dynamic nature of settlement growth at Chunchucmil. As residential neighborhoods expanded at the end of the Early Classic period, they might have outgrown a performance space built to serve a smaller group. Overall, there is a statistically positive correlation between the estimated population of the spoke cluster and the size of the plaza in the corresponding monumental group (Pearson's $r = 0.534$, $p = 0.049$). If we presume that each person needed 3.1 square meters, there are five misfits, though we feel that 3.1 square meters per person is overly generous.

Did open spaces serve as focal nodes? At Chunchucmil, open spaces with no ostensible architecture do exist in the densely packed residential core, but it is not clear whether they served as focal nodes. They could have hosted marketplaces, but with the exception of a few open spaces in the site center we have no data to assess this. Unbuilt open spaces in the center of the site do not show soil chemical patterns associated with ancient marketplaces (Dahlin et al. 2010). Open spaces in the residential core range in size from a tenth of a hectare to a hectare. They are difficult to quantify since it is difficult to establish a size limit at the low end (e.g., it is difficult to know just how big a space must be in order to qualify as a communal open space) and since it is possible to argue that some of these spaces were in fact not open and public but were rather affiliated with a private house lot. We count roughly thirty open spaces in the residential core (table 4.2). With the exception of clusters 9A and 10, all clusters have at least one open space. Clusters 12 and 13, the two largest, have the most open spaces, each with four or five. These spaces fall into two categories: spaces that the paths cross right through (figure 4.6) and spaces alongside paths that the paths do not enter (figure 4.7). Figure 4.6 shows that some of the spaces in the first category do not look like excellent candidates for focal nodes: house lots protrude into the space. However, such spaces would have worked just fine for informal gatherings. Perhaps twenty spaces fall into this category. Spaces in the second category are walled off. They look a bit like house lots that lack houses. Perhaps fully

Table 4.2. Open spaces and wells per spoke cluster at Chunchcumil

Spoke cluster	House lots per spoke cluster	Open spaces	Enclosed open spaces	Wells	Wells inside houselots
1	74	2			
2	55	3		2	2
3	66	0 or 1			
4	32	0	2		
5	8	1			
6	18	0	2	2	2
7	15				
7A	20		1	1	1
7B	29	1	1		
8	19	0		1	
9A	7				
9B	19	2			
9C	15	1		1	
10	30	0			
11	53	1	1	1	1
12	148	0 or 1	2 or 3	3	2
13	138	4 or 5		1	1
14	100	2	2		
No affiliation				6	2

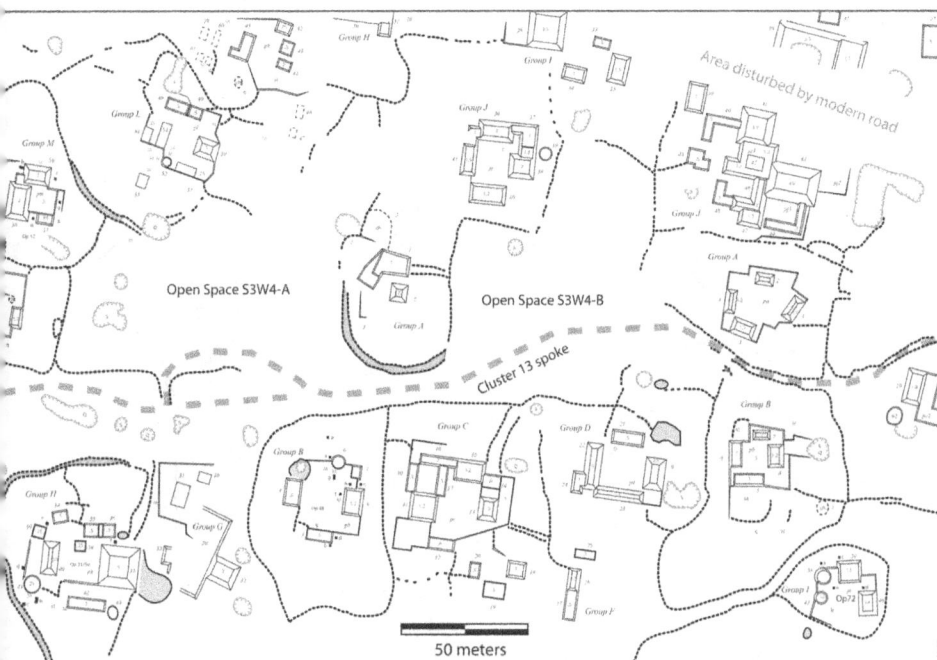

Figure 4.6. Portion of the Chunchucmil map showing an example of a pair of open spaces in cluster 13 crossed by the cluster 13 spoke.

perishable structures once stood inside, which would mean that they were neither public nor open and therefore could not have served as focal nodes. There are perhaps ten of these spaces.

Two other shared resources, wells and *sascaberas*, might count as focal nodes at Chunchucmil. We mapped eighteen wells in the central 9.3 square kilometers of Chunchucmil, although we may have missed several (see below). When the same people repeatedly use the same wells, they will likely get to know each other. Since the eighteen wells we found would have to serve at least the 18,000 or so people living in the central 9.3 square kilometers, people would have to wait to take a turn filling their water jars, thus encouraging interaction while waiting in line. Waterholes in twentieth-century Maya communities in highland Chiapas anchor intermediate-scale social groups (Vogt 1969) and facilitate gossip and socializing (Groark 2008). In these cases, fewer people share a well than would have been the case at Chunchucmil. The eighteen wells at Chunchucmil are not distributed evenly enough across the site to suggest that they served focal nodes. Most of the

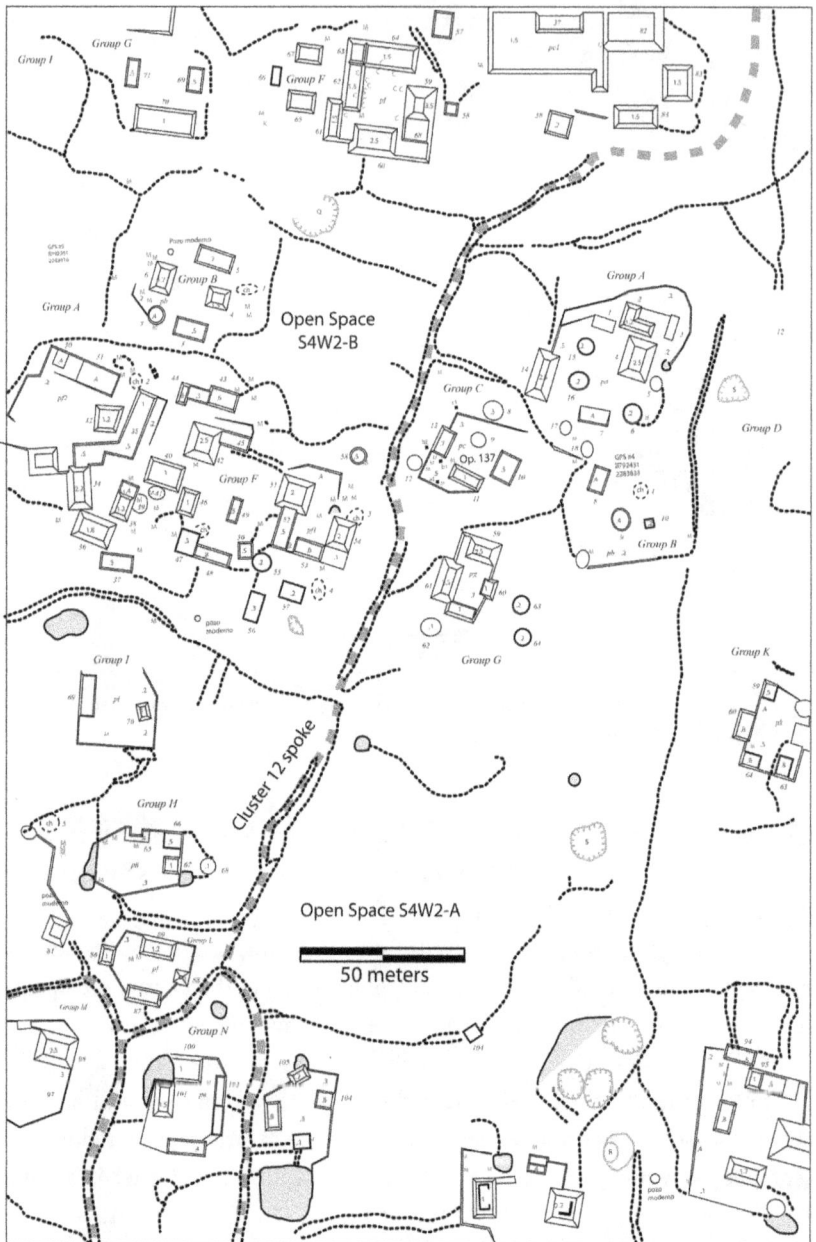

Figure 4.7. Portion of the Chunchucmil map showing an example of a pair of open spaces next to the cluster 12 spoke but not entered by any paths.

house lots on the western side of the site are located far away from a well, whereas there are clusters of three and four wells in the southern and northeastern parts of the site. Of the eighteen wells, only six are located in what we consider public space: the others are located within house lots. Table 4.2 shows that the wells are not evenly distributed across the spoke clusters (clusters 1, 3, 4, 7B, 9A, 9B, 10, 14a, 14b, 14c, and 14d each lack wells). In addition to wells, perhaps a dozen small caves called *sascaberas* located within the walls of ancient house lots have water in the wet season, but we do not have systematic data on this. Ancient wells can fill with vegetation and sediment once they are abandoned, which makes them very difficult for archaeologists to find. It is probably easier to assume that we have missed some wells than to assume that all of the people on the west side of the site lacked a nearby water source. Thus, we probably cannot trust our data on the distribution of wells as a line of evidence for analyzing focal nodes of intermediate spatial units.

Two hundred fifty-six *sascaberas* are spread very evenly across the central 9.3-square-kilometer map of Chunchucmil. *Sascaberas* are quarries from which the ancient Maya extracted *sascab*, a soft limestone gravel (Littman 1958) used to make plaster and other construction mortars. *Sascab* might also have been used as a mulch for gardens or as a source of lime to add to water for soaking corn. Fewer than 10 percent of the *sascaberas* were mined deeply enough to create caves that could have provided a climate humid enough for weaving baskets and processing other cordage products. In one case at Chunchucmil, the ancient Maya dug into the base of a *sascabera* to get to the water table. We know that other *sascaberas* had water in the wet season, but we do not know how many. Since we mapped 1,406 architectural groups and 256 *sascaberas*, there would have been one *sascabera* for every five or six groups. With about three nuclear families, or fifteen people per group, this means that fewer than 100 people shared a *sascabera*. This is a small but not unreasonable number of people for a neighborhood. However, *sascaberas* were not used as often as other resources, such as wells or communal farm plots. If *sascaberas* were used only for construction material, people would not have used them that often, and the infrequency of use would not have stimulated much face-to-face interactions among neighbors.

Stylistic Clustering

Chapter 3 suggested the possibility of spatial clusters of distinctive stylistic assemblages. While we know of no studies that have successfully used this criterion to discover neighborhoods in ancient Maya cities, the Oaxaca Barrio at Teotihuacan (see chapter 3) stands as an excellent example. In the third century CE, Migrants from the Valley of Oaxaca, 350 kilometers away as the crow flies, settled at the far western edge of Teotihuacan, where archaeologists found Oaxacan-style pottery and burials. At Chunchucmil, although the possibility of finding a neighborhood of migrants from far away is not out of the question, given that Chunchucmil participated actively in long-distance trade, we have failed to find such an enclave. However, migration probably played a large role in explaining Chunchucmil's rapid growth from perhaps 1,000 people around the third century CE to at least 30,000 people by the end of the sixth century CE. These migrants probably came from nearby areas, and they likely would not have brought with them wildly different pottery styles, building practices, or mortuary customs. But they may have maintained subtle preferences in the pottery they consumed and they may have built their houses and house lot walls in slightly different ways. This presumes that migrants from the same place of origin clustered together in the same part of the city and built support networks based on their shared place of origin (Kemper 2002; Lewis 1965). This would result in neighborhoods marked by subtle patterns in pottery or architecture. In addition, other forms of social organization aside from shared place of origin outside the city could account for such patterns in material culture. For example, a group of people who lived near each other and claimed descent from the same distant ancestor (a maximal lineage) or each anchored their identity around a corporate estate (a house society) might also have used pottery or lived in houses of a similar type.

Does the city of Chunchucmil contain spatial clusters of people with stylistically distinct material culture? We address the question with three different categories of evidence: pathways, architecture, and pottery.

Pathway Style

Most of the pathways discussed in this chapter consist of parallel stone walls that create an alley that was usually two to six meters wide. In some cases, however, the surface of the alley has been modified by adding a layer of rubble that gives the pathway a slight elevation. We call these *chichbes*. They are usually a bit narrower than other pathways. Figure 4.8 shows that *chichbes* dominate in the south and southwest part of the site, particularly in spoke clusters 11, 12, and 13. *Chichbes* also dominate in cluster 7B, a neighborhood east of the site center. There are 36.072 kilometers of *chichbes* in the central 9.3 square kilometers of Chunchucmil. Of these 36 kilometers, 90.4 percent (32.627 kilometers) pertain to clusters 11, 12, 13, and 7b and an area to the southwest of cluster 13 that is probably part of cluster 13 but is not technically linked by specific pathways. However, these clusters account for only 37.7 percent of the total land in our map (3.56 square kilometers of 9.3 square

Figure 4.8. Map of Chunchucmil showing *chichbes*, causeways, and monumental compounds and the four spoke clusters in which *chichbes* are most common.

kilometers). Perhaps the most striking feature of the *chichbes* is how closely the boundaries of the areas with dense *chichbes* match the boundaries of the area covered by clusters 11, 12, and 13. The preference for building pathways in the form of *chichbes* in this area suggests a kind of megadistrict because clusters 12 and 13 are probably districts in themselves, since they are too large to be neighborhoods. Though it is difficult to even speculate about why the people in the south part of the site chose to build *chichbes*, the fact that they did so while most other people did not suggests some sort of meaningful and shared group identity.

Orientation of Architecture

Buildings are difficult to analyze systematically because of the small sample of architectural groups that received broad-scale excavations. However, the map gives us easy access to at least one variable regarding house style: the dominant orientation of the architecture of each group. We measured orientations in 843 of the 846 architectural groups that were affiliated with a spoke at Chunchucmil. In most of the house lots with more than one structure, ancient Chunchucmileños oriented each structure in the same direction. In cases where different buildings within the same house lot had different orientations or where a single building had multiple orientations we used one of two methods for assigning an orientation. When one structure was much larger than all the others in terms of volume, we measured the orientation of that structure (usually several other buildings also follow the alignment of the large structure, which often appears to be a temple). If there was no dominant structure, we measured the orientation that occurred in a majority of the group's buildings. Since most buildings at Chunchucmil are rectangular, the orientation could be given in two ways: for example 10°/190° or 100°/280°. We present the orientation that is closest to north. In the example above, we would say that the group's orientation is 10° east of north.

Over two-thirds (68 percent) of Chunchucmil house lots have orientations that fall between 0.3° west of north and 19.1° east of north. While the inhabitants of Teotihuacan followed strict city planning rules and aligned their structures at 15.5°, the orientations of Chunchucmil dwellings varied widely. However, interesting patterns stand out, some of which help pinpoint social divisions of space within the city. We specifically look at spoke clusters 12, 7B, and 3.

With 147 households, cluster 12 is the largest at Chunchucmil. In this cluster, orientations range from 12° west of north to 40° east of north, and the orientations of over two-thirds of the groups lie between 4° west of north and 16.7° east of north. Observing the cluster as a whole was no help in pinpointing an overarching pattern that favors a single orientation. However, when we looked at variability within this spoke cluster, a different story emerged. The most common orientation, which occurred in thirty-two house lots, is 4° west of north. Most (n = 26) of the house lots oriented at 4° west of north are found in an area 500 meters by 500 meters at the southern end of the cluster. Of the forty-six total house lots in this area, 26 (56.5 percent) have this orientation. Seven of the remaining twenty house lots have an orientation of 3° west of north. Thus, 71.3 percent of the house lots in this area have nearly identical orientations. In this case, ancient Chunchucmileños appear to have followed a specific convention. Although this is not the heavily structured and expansive urban planning of Teotihuacan, this closely shared pattern could not have come about without explicit communication and coordination between the members of the house lots that share that orientation. This implies the two key components of a neighborhood: close interactions between people in a shared space.

District 7 contains 64 house lots linked to a spoke that runs northeast of the site center and eventually forks into two paths, 7A and 7B. Fork 7A consists of twenty house lots that exhibit a broad range of orientations between 10° west of north and 40° east of north. However, within this broad range there are some consistencies in alignment. For example, seven house lots have alignments between 10° and 3° west of north, and these are all located in the north part of the 7A spoke. Six house lots have alignments between 17° and 19° east of north, and these are all located in the south part of the 7A spoke. No house lots on spoke 7A have alignments between 17° east of north and 3° west of north. So there seems to have been two conventions for orienting buildings in alleyway 7A with no middle ground between them. In spokes 7A and 7B, most house lots have an orientation between 1° and 27° east of north. The orientation of the monumental group associated with spoke 7 (N3E3-M) has an orientation of 15°, close to the middle of the range between 1° and 27° east of north. Some other monumental nodes have orientations that are close to the midpoints of the range of orientations of their associated house lots, but this is not a clear pattern at Chunchucmil.

In spoke clusters 12 and 7A, subdivisions share conventions for laying out buildings. However, in other spoke clusters there do not seem to have been any trends in the way people oriented the structures in their house lot. We observed this in spoke cluster 3, which has sixty-six house lots. In this spoke cluster, the most common orientation (5° east of north) appears at only five house lots (8 percent of the sample) and these are dispersed throughout the spoke cluster. Even more noteworthy, in only a few circumstances do two or three adjacent house lots have the same orientation. Although orientations are usually coordinated within the house lot, among adjacent house lots there is no shared preference for aligning structures. Similar disorder occurs in clusters 5, 6, and 8. With the exception of two house lots in cluster 8, no two adjacent house lots share the same orientation in these three clusters. Cluster 5, however, is the smallest of districts with only 8 associated groups, and the sample size may not be sufficient for orientation studies.

Pottery

To get at differences in pottery across the site, we consulted data from a systematic test-pitting program that sought to provide chronological, economic, and social data from a representative sample of architectural contexts at Chunchucmil (see Hutson, Magnoni, and Dahlin 2016). To carry out this strategy, the universe of architectural contexts at Chunchucmil was stratified with respect to location and group type. The site was divided into blocks of 1 square kilometer. Each architectural context was assigned to one of fifteen types, based on whether or not it had monumental architecture, the number of structures in the group, presence or absence of *sascaberas* and *albarradas*, and proximity to other architectural groups. Table 4.3 presents exhaustive detail about the total number of groups per type and per one-square-kilometer block and the number that received excavations. Groups to be excavated were randomly selected for a particular group type within a particular square-kilometer block.

In theory, the stratified random sampling strategy ensures that some examples of every group type in every one-square-kilometer block would be excavated. In practice, we fell short of this ideal; table 4.3 shows that some particular group types in a particular block did not receive excavations. However, we maintain that our sample is representative at certain scales.

By the end of the project, excavations had been done in 174 areas, about 40 of which had been chosen opportunistically before the representative sampling strategy was implemented. The number of excavations accounted for in table 4.3 (159) is less than the total number of excavations because five excavations were located on transects (Ops. 139 [a type 15 group], 156 [a type

8 group], 157, 158, and 159 [type 13 groups]) and ten excavations consisted of soil pits that were not executed with the intention of producing chronological or socioeconomic data about a particular group. These 159 excavations represent 11.3 percent of the 1,405 groups in the central 9.3 square kilometers (figure 4.9). Of these 159 groups, eleven date mostly to the Late and Terminal Classic platforms (Magnoni 2008) and were therefore dropped from the cur-

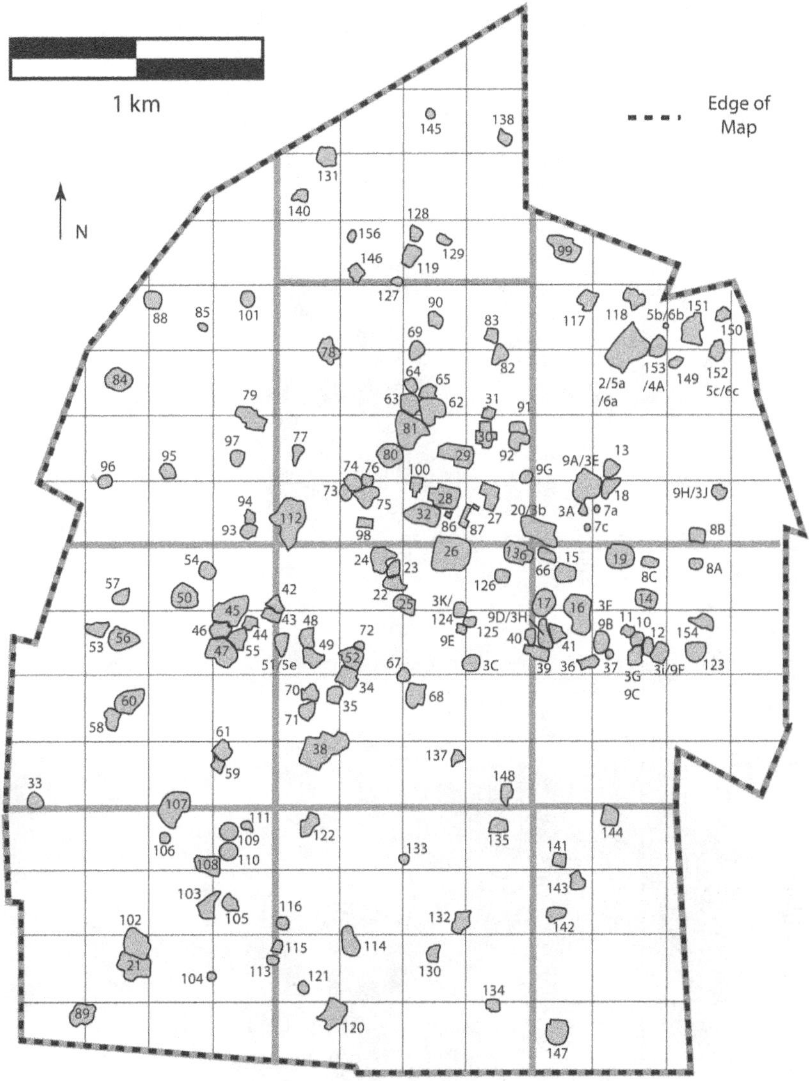

Figure 4.9. Map showing the locations of the 159 architecturally focused excavation operations in the central 9.3 square kilometers of Chunchucmil. Gridded squares are 250 meters by 250 meters.

Table 4.3. Total architectural groups at Chunchucmil and number of excavated architectural groups sorted by group type and by the one-square-kilometer block within which they are located

Type	Block 1			Block 2			Block 3			Block 4			Block 5		
	N1	N2	%	N1	N2	%	N1	N2	%	N1	N2	%	N1	N2	%
Type 1	3	3	100.0	1	1	100.0	1	1	100.0	3	3	100.0			
Type 2	1	1	100.0	2	2	100.0	2	2	100.0	1	1	100.0			
Type 3	3		0.0	1		0.0	3		0.0	1		0.0	2	1	50.0
Type 4				2	1	50									
Type 5	1		0.0	2	1	50	3		0.0						
Type 6	8	5	62.5	7	5	71.4	1	1	100.0	7	4	57.1			
Type 8	97	7	7.2	116	8	6.9	127	5	3.9	89	8	9.0	28	1	3.5
Type 9	32	4	12.5	46	6	13.0	41	2	4.9	25	2	.08	12	1	8.3
Type 10	9	3	33.3	12	2	16.7	14	3	21.4	2		0.0	1		0.0
Type 12	21	2	9.5	21	3	14.3	23	1	4.3	13	1	7.7	5	1	20.0
Type 13													2	1	50.0
Type 14a															
Type 14b															
Type 15	4		0.0	6		0.0	1		0.0	7	3	42.8	1		0.0
Type 16	3		0.0	3	1	33.3	1	1	100.0				1		0.0
Unknown										4					
Totals	182	25	33	219	30	13.7	217	16	7.4	152	22	14.5	52	5	9.6

Type	Block 6			Block 7			Block 8			Block 9			Block 0			Totals		
	N1	N2	%	N1	N2	%	N1	N2	%	N1	N2	%	N1	N2	%	N1	N2	%
Type 1				1	1	100.0										8	8	100.0
Type 2																7	7	1
Type 3	8	1	12.5	1		0.0	6	2	33.3	2	1	50.0	1		0.0	28	5	17.8
Type 4																2	1	50.0
Type 5																6	1	16.6
Type 6							1	1	100.0							24	16	66.6
Type 8	97	4	4.1	29	3	10.3	79	4	5.1	54	2	3.7	67	4	6.0	783	46	5.8
Type 9	30	2	6.7	4	4	100.0	34	5	14.7	21	2	9.5	17	1	5.9	262	29	11.0
Type 10	3	1	33.3	1		0.0	2	1	50.0	1		0.0	2	1	50.0	47	11	23.4
Type 12	15		0.0	3		0.0	11	3	27.3	6		0.0	8	1	12.5	126	12	9.5
Type 13	1	1	100.0	8	2	25.0				1	1	100.0	4		0.0	16	5	31.2
Type 14a				6	1	16.7				4		0.0	2	1	50.0	12	2	16.6
Type 14b	9			9		0				5	1	20.0				14	1	7.1
Type 15	3	1	33.3	4	2	50.0	5	1	20.0	21	3	14.3	4	2	50.0	56	12	21.4
Type 16	1	1	100.0							1		0.0				10	3	30.0
Unknown																4		
Totals	158	11	7.0	66	13	19.7	138	17	12.3	116	10	8.6	105	10	9.5	1,405	159	11.3

Notes: N1 = number of groups.

N2 = number of excavated groups.

% = percent block sample.

rent study to ensure contemporaneity of the contexts (these eleven are type 6 groups). The excavations done in 128 of the 148 contemporaneous groups were substantial enough to be included in the analysis below. By substantial, we mean that either at least six 1-meter-by-1-meter test pits were dug or excavations yielded large amounts of sherds (always over 4 kilograms). We thus draw on a large set of excavations spread broadly across the site and across the different kinds of architecture.

Our goal in the pottery analysis was to see if people in particular areas of the site preferred certain styles of pottery or certain vessel forms. We should note before beginning that excavations failed to discover the kind of evidence—such as kilns or wasters—that would indicate ceramic production locales. The fact that we found evidence for household specialization in crafts other than pottery within Chunchucmil leads us to believe that some people in the city may have produced pottery, but we have not found them. It is also possible that people in Chunchucmil's rural hinterland supplied the city with a large proportion of its pottery, as has been observed in other parts of the Maya area (see chapter 2; Fry 1979, 1980; Rands and Bishop 1980). The excavations also show that no specific parts of the site consumed substantially more pottery on the whole than other parts of the site. Though some domestic groups owned greater quantities of ceramics overall, these consumers do not cluster in any specific part of the site. Furthermore, distributional analysis (Hirth 1998) of Oxkintok thinwares and Early Classic polychromes (Varela Torrecilla 1998) suggests that these fancier pots were exchanged via markets. Indeed, Chunchucmil has yielded some of the strongest evidence for market exchange and a large central marketplace has been found (Dahlin et al. 2007, 2010; Hutson et al. 2010).

We looked at whether certain parts of the site preferred pottery with particular paste and slip combinations. Using the type variety system, the dominant system for classifying pottery in the Maya area (Sabloff and Smith 1969), we looked mostly at the level of the pottery group. Since there is variation in the slipped groups during the period of Chunchucmil's apogee, we focused on five common slipped groups: Batres, Chuburna, Hunabchen, Kanachen, and Maxcanu. Maxcanu and Hunabchen, the most common groups, showed up in 98 percent of the assemblages. We noticed no spatial clustering among any of these five styles of pottery. Visual analysis of site maps that highlight the amount of each pottery group found in the 128 excavation operations revealed no areas with a heavy preference for one particular pottery group or combination of groups. Although different house lots can have widely different amounts of, say, Hunabchen red pottery, there is no clear spatial pattern to this variation.

We also looked at the distribution of fancier and less common Early Classic ceramic groups—Acu, Aguila, Chencoh, and Kochol—across the site. We consider these groups fancy because of their thin walls or elegant decoration. In exceptional cases, sherds from these groups comprise 13 percent of an architectural compound's entire ceramic inventory. However, in a majority of excavations, pottery from these groups makes up less than 1 percent of the assemblage. Much like our results with the more common pottery groups, there are no areas within the site where all architectural compounds (or no architectural compounds) show high access to these fancier styles.

Thus, no sector of the site had a preference for or special access to one or multiple ceramic groups. If restricted redistribution networks existed, we did not pinpoint them synchronically using pottery styles, but we concede that they may still exist.

The results of an attribute analysis of 815 rim sherds enable a finer-grained look at stylistic variation within the site. The sherds came from three intensively excavated compounds: Pich (n = 285), Aak (n = 275), and Chiwol (n = 255). Aak and Chiwol are middle-sized *albarrada* groups in the 9C spoke cluster that are located only 50 meters from each other (Hutson et al. 2006). The Pich group is a monumental quadrangle group that is located closer to the center of the site and affiliated with spoke cluster 5. For each sherd, a suite of qualitative and quantitative measurements was taken, though only the data on paste color suggest material culture patterning at the neighborhood level.

The most prominent paste color (2.5 YR 5/6, red; n = 222) is found in nearly equal portions among the three groups. At Aak, this color constitutes 32.9 percent of the pottery; at Chiwool, 36.9 percent; and at Pich, 30.2 percent. Certain less common paste colors are used predominantly in the Pich group. These colors include 2.5 YR 6/4 (light reddish brown), 2.5 YR 6/6 (light red), and 2.5 YR 5/4 (reddish brown). Other paste colors are more commonly found in the Aak and Chiwool groups, such as 5 YR 5/4 (reddish brown), and 5 YR 6/6 (reddish yellow). We believe that these differences are not an artifact of measurement error or some other chance process because the common Pich paste colors are all from the 2.5 YR hue while the Aak and Chiwool colors are from the 5 YR hue. The most common hue in a fourth intensively investigated group, Kaab, which is located in spoke cluster 10, about 250 meters from Aak and Chiwol, was 2.5 YR, reminiscent of what was found at Pich (Magnoni 2008, 301). In other words, the major difference between Pich and Kaab, on the one hand, and Aak and Chiwool, on the other, is that Aak and Chiwol pottery has browner paste colors and Pich and Kaab pottery has redder paste colors. We believe that these differences are not coinciden-tal. They may reflect differences in pottery preferences or perhaps differences in pottery distribution. It may be that consumers in Aak and Chiwool got pots from potters with slightly different clay sources, paste recipes, or firing techniques. It bears repeating that Aak and Chiwool are part of the same spoke cluster. Brown (1999) has argued that similar differences at Mayapan reflect neighborhood identity. We believe these differences are suggestive of neighborhoods at Chunchucmil, but the sample size (four architectural com-pounds) is far too small to be conclusive.

Finally, we hoped to determine whether certain vessel forms were more common in certain parts of the site. Such a pattern could be interpreted in several ways, each of which could relate to neighborhood identity. For ex-ample, a preference for a particular vessel form could indicate differences in the kinds of food consumed; a differences in how people stored, prepared, or served the same foods; or perhaps an economic specialization in a particular food-based activity or some other type of activity that requires specific vessel forms. The forms that appeared most were plates (*cajetes*); large, unrestricted vessels for cooking (*cazuelas*); cylindrical vases; unrestricted semispherical bowls (*cuencos*); restricted semispherical vessels (*tecomates*); and restricted orifice jars (*ollas*). Of these forms, *ollas* were most common: they occurred in all of the 128 assemblages and almost always constituted more than 20 per-cent of the sample. *Tecomates* were the least common; they were present in only 11 percent of the assemblages. Visual analysis of site maps that highlight the proportion of each vessel form in the 128 excavation operations revealed no areas with a heavy preference for one particular vessel form or combina-tion of forms.

In sum, the ceramic analysis shows that neighborhoods and districts, ei-ther of the kind identified by pathway and focal node analysis or some other kind of analysis, did not demonstrate distinct preferences for pottery styles or forms. The one possible exception to this statement relates to a prefer-ence for pots with particular paste colors in spoke cluster 9c. The fact that no particular area at the site systematically preferred particular kinds of pottery does not suggest that the neighborhoods identified on the basis of the spokes were meaningless. On the contrary, neighborhoods worked together to maintain the pathway spokes that helped define their boundaries (see chapter 6), and these same pathways may have helped to ensure that anyone in the neighborhood who wanted access to a particular kind of pottery could easily get to Chunchucmil's central market or potential rural producers to procure it.

Craft Neighborhoods

Can we identify craft-based neighborhoods at Chunchucmil? Our goal is to see if particular kinds of craft workers clustered in particular areas of the site. We have data on three kinds of activities that might count as craft specializations: grinding, quarrying, and cutting with obsidian blades. As noted above, we have no data on pottery production locales. In addition, although obsidian is abundant at the site, little chert and no chert workshops have been found. We begin with grinding. Metates (stone basins) are direct evidence of grinding, and some compounds at Chunchucmil have a dozen or more. The compounds with the most grinding stones date to the Late/Terminal Classic, when few people lived at Chunchucmil, so they are not included in this analysis. Grinding stones certainly would have been used to grind corn, but they were probably also used to grind salt (a major commodity at Chunchucmil; Dahlin and Ardren 2002), pigments, calcite, cacao, herbs, other plant foods, insects, bones, meat, and fish (Horsfall 1987; Watanabe 2000). They could also have been used for washing clothes and fermenting or storing liquids. To get a sense of whether or not metates were more abundant in certain parts of the site, we split the site into quads measuring 250 meters by 250 meters and calculated the number of metates per structure for each quad. Figure 4.10 shows the results. Perhaps the clearest pattern that emerges from the figure is that there are more metates per structure toward the center of the map than at the peripheries. The center of the map, which consists of the site center and the residential core, is also the area with highest settlement density. There is a strong positive correlation (Pearson's $r = 0.708$, $p = {<}0.001$) between metates per structure and settlement density. Since we measured metates as a ratio to structures, this correlation cannot be explained by the tautology that there are more structures in areas with higher settlement density. The higher amount of metates per structure probably has less to do with settlement density and more to do with chronology: the center of the site, where settlement happens to be more dense, was occupied from the Middle Preclassic, whereas the areas on the periphery date exclusively to the relatively short time period of Chunchucmil's apogee.

Five of the seven quads with the highest metate densities are contiguous and thus may have been a neighborhood where grinding specialists clustered. These quads are marked with dots in figure 4.10. This potential neighborhood of grinding specialists is not very discrete, however, for three reasons. First, the map shows that to the north and west of these five quads there is no sharp drop-off in the number of metates per structure. In other words, this is not a tightly bounded area. Second, within the five quads with the highest numbers of metates, over a third of the architectural groups (22 of 64) have two or fewer metates, and these groups are dispersed somewhat evenly through these quads. In other words, residents of the 64 architectural groups in this cluster were not uniformly doing a lot of grinding. This should not disqualify the area as a neighborhood or district, however, since in the Tlajinga potting barrio at Teotihuacan (see chapter 3), a very good example of a district, not all of the apartment compounds produced pottery. Finally, the architectural groups in these five quads are associated with three different spoke/focal node clusters, 9c, 10, and 11. The quad at the far west of the site in figure 4.10 seems to stand out as a candidate for a grinding neighborhood, but a closer look at the site map reveals that this quad has few architectural compounds and that a high number of metates in just two compounds skews the quantity for the quad as a whole.

What about quarrying? We have identified two kinds of quarries at Chunchucmil: *sascaberas* and quarries for construction stone. As we did with our research on metates, we split the site into quads measuring 250 meters by 250 meters and calculated the number of quarries and *sascaberas* per structure for each quad. Figure 4.11 shows the combined number of quarries and *sascaberas* per quad across the site and suggests four promising locations, labeled A through D, for neighborhood specialization in quarrying. Two of these— A and C—are dead ends, since an examination of the site map reveals that the quarries in these two areas are not affiliated with any residential groups and there are few residential groups in these two quads. Locations B and D are much more promising because they include quarries located close to architectural compounds (figure 4.12). Furthermore, all of the architectural compounds in location B pertain to spoke cluster 3 and those in location

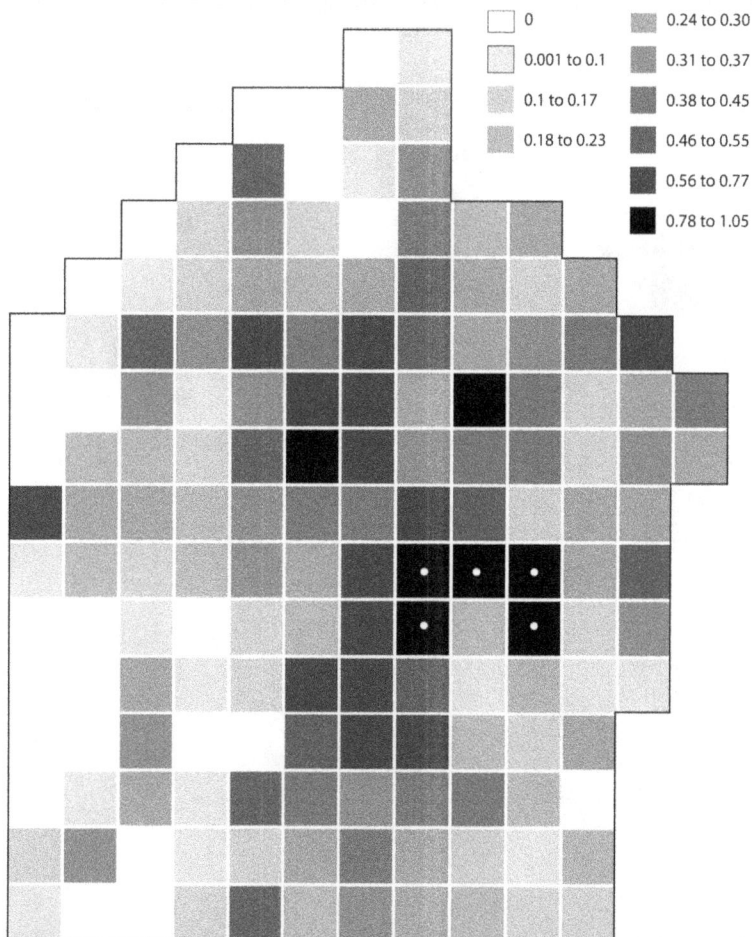

Figure 4.10. Schematic representation of the central 9.3 square kilometers of Chunchucmil, divided into 250-meter-by-250-meter blocks, showing the number of metates per structure for each block. Blocks with white dots show a potential but unlikely neighborhood characterized by households specializing in grinding.

D pertain to spoke cluster 13. This means that circulation features at Chunchucmil facilitated interaction among the people in each of these locations, thus strengthening opportunities for neighborhood identity formation. The quarries in location D are larger than those in location B, indicating a greater likelihood that the residents of location D specialized in quarrying. Earlier in this chapter we argued that spoke cluster 13 is a district as opposed to a

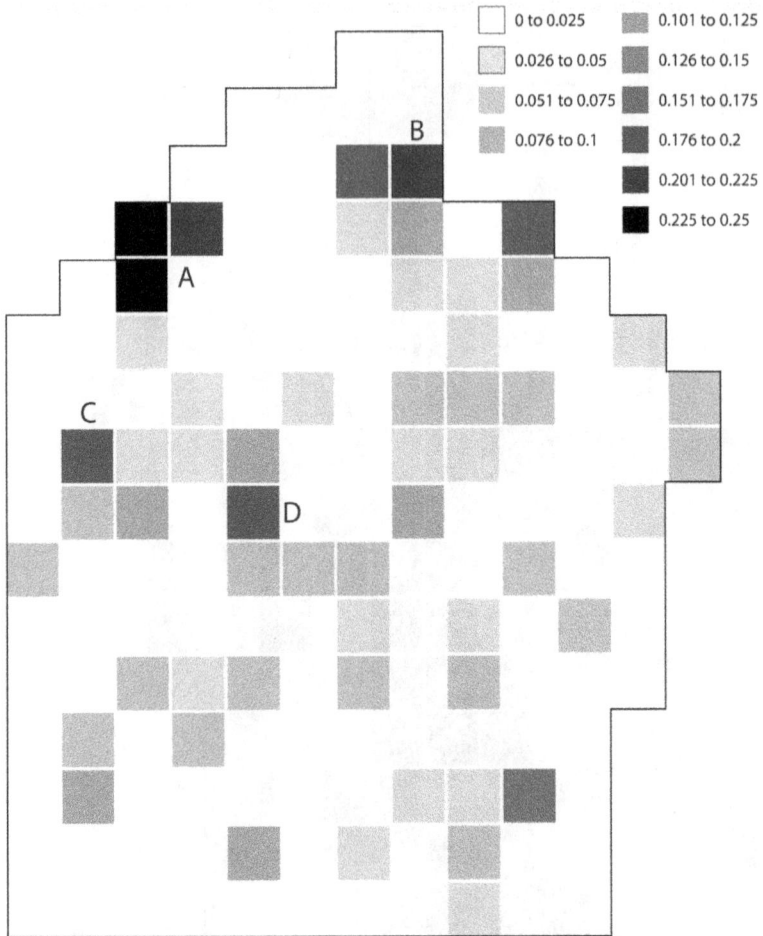

Figure 4.11. Schematic representation of the central 9.3 square kilometers of Chunchucmil, divided into 250-meter-by-250-meter blocks, showing the number of quarries and *sascaberas* per structure for each block.

neighborhood and that there were probably neighborhoods within the district. The households in location D would count as a neighborhood within district 13.

Finally, we considered craft specializations that involve cutting with obsidian blades. What we had in mind were potential areas of the site that consumed large quantities of obsidian. Locations where obsidian blades were produced are limited at Chunchucmil and the data do not allow us to talk of lithic production neighborhoods (Hutson et al. 2010). Instead, we refer to households that may have specialized in activities that required obsidian

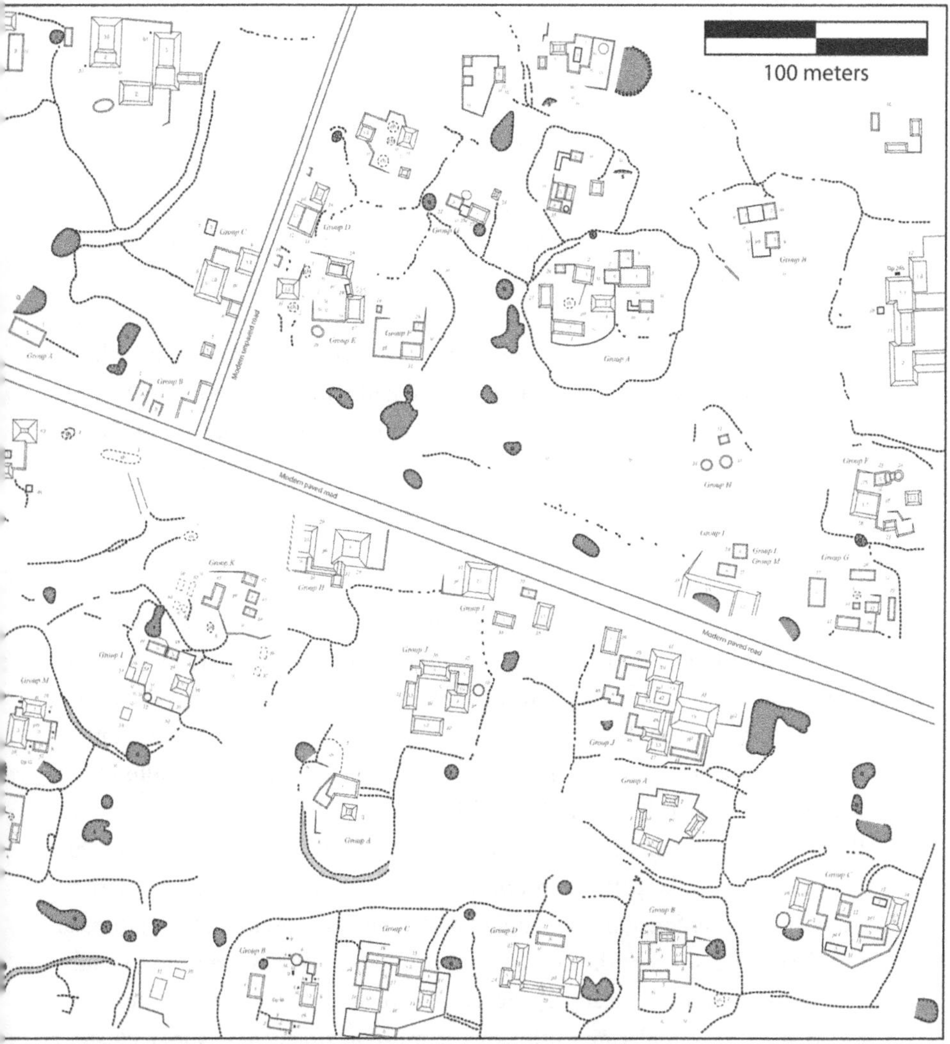

Figure 4.12. Map of a portion of Chunchucmil showing Area D from figure 4.11. Dark gray shapes are quarries and *sascaberas*.

blades. Microscopic use-wear has helped specify the ways ancient people used obsidian blades in only one household at Chunchucmil (Hutson et al. 2007). A study of obsidian blades recovered from the 128 architectural groups mentioned in the ceramic analysis above revealed one area, in the northeast corner of the Chunchucmil site map, with a cluster of four house lots whose obsidian blade consumption placed them in the topmost quartile. The four house lots (Ops 150, 151, 152, and 153) are located within an area of about four hectares. Two of them are part of spoke cluster 7A, one is part of spoke cluster 6, and the other is connected to both clusters. Other house lots are interspersed between these four house lots, but since we have not excavated in them, we do not know whether they also consumed relatively large amounts of obsidian.

In summary, our exploration of craft-based neighborhoods produced mixed results. Data on the spatial distribution of metates suggests that there do not appear to have been groups of people who lived near each other and bonded over the production of a surplus of items that required grinding. In spoke cluster 13, there does appear to have been a neighborhood whose members were all involved in quarrying. Finally, we tentatively identified a neighborhood where people engaged in a craft requiring a large number of obsidian blades.

Conclusion

In this chapter we have used a number of strategies to search for social units that are intermediate in size between households and the city as a whole. Chunchucmil is ideally suited to this undertaking because it has a network of paths that created circulation patterns in which members of some households would encounter and interact with each other much more often than with members of other households. This kind of interaction is at the core of the concept of neighborhood. The layout of paths at Chunchucmil conforms to a hub-and-spoke pattern and household members usually had access to only one spoke. Since most people had to travel on their spoke for several hundred meters before they could get to another spoke, we refer to the hub-and-spoke pattern as relatively closed. However, within some of the larger spoke clusters, circulation options were more flexible; these spoke clusters were thus relatively open. The closed nature of some of the spokes does not, however, mean that Chunchucmil's intermediate social units were turned inward toward themselves, as in certain rural villages. Most people needed to walk no more than 15 minutes to get to other spoke clusters or spaces at the site core that were accessible to a wide variety of people (see chapter 6). Some of the spoke clusters (12 and 13, for example) were quite large (with more than 2,000 residents) and should be considered districts as opposed to the cozy kind of neighborhood Jacobs spoke of in the epigraph.

Once we had classified spoke clusters as hypothetical neighborhoods or districts, additional data allowed us to strengthen these tentative classifications. For example, a distinctive manner of constructing paths at Chunchucmil (the *chichbe*) is very common in four spoke clusters (12, 13, 7A, and 7B) but rare in the others. Those same four clusters also exhibit relatively open circulation patterns. This contributes to the notion that these clusters were distinct from the others. Probably the strongest line of evidence supporting the notion that each spoke cluster was indeed a distinct social unit comes from the distribution of monumental architectural compounds. The main thoroughfare of each spoke cluster usually connects with a single monumental compound and the main patio of each of these compounds is generally large enough to host all the people living in the spoke cluster. The exceptions to this pattern can be accommodated, as we noted in the section on focal nodes. Our search for other nodes—wells, open spaces, *sascaberas*, or midsized temples—around which neighborhoods could form was not as successful.

Extensive test pitting produced a large and representative sample of ceramics from across the site. Our analysis of the distribution of fancy ceramics, particular ceramic groups, and particular vessel forms did not identify any areas where neighboring households shared a marked preference for certain kinds of pottery. Analysis of the chief orientation of the buildings in 843 architectural groups did uncover a few areas where members of neighboring households lived in buildings with very similar orientations. One of these areas is at the south side of spoke cluster 12 and the other two are in spoke cluster 7A. Finally, some data suggest the existence of crafting neighborhoods: two focused on quarrying and the other focused on obsidian. Although the evidence for the neighborhood of obsidian workers is not strong, the evidence for one of the two quarrying neighborhoods is strong.

Chunchucmil is a special test case for neighborhoods and other social units intermediate in size between the household and the city because of the visibility of its pathways. We do not think, however, that the kinds of social units we found exist only at Chunchucmil. The same kinds of neighborhoods and districts might have existed in other densely occupied cities where pathway boundaries might have been made of materials that do not preserve. One important distinction between Chunchucmil and many other large Maya cities is that Chunchucmil lacks a single large monumental plaza for ceremonial performances. Instead, as this chapter showed, monumental architectural compounds were embedded in intermediate scale social units. This suggests a different kind of political organization for Chunchucmil (Dahlin 2009, 347). In stark contrast to the regal-ritual city model (see chapter 2), Chunchucmil appears to have lacked the kind of holy ruler that presumably held some other polities together (Houston et al. 2003). Chapters 5 and 6 suggest additional processes and attractions that lured people to large cities such as Chunchucmil and kept them there.

5

The Spatial Experience of Inequality

The city itself is a boiling, roiling cauldron for the
brewing of newly invented corporate belonging.

McIntosh (2005, 18)

Chapters 3 and 4 omitted discussion of wealth and inequality. This chapter tackles both of these issues in Classic period Maya cities, focusing on the following questions: How can we define and quantify wealth and other aspects of social inequality in ancient cities? How unequal were ancient Maya cities? Did wealthy people cluster at the center of cities? Did wealth-based neighborhoods exist? Did people of different wealth levels live adjacent to each other, creating opportunities for co-presence? Finally, could an integrated mix of wealth levels make Maya cities attractive?

This chapter begins by defining key terms such as wealth, status, rank, elite, and class as they pertain to social inequality among the ancient Maya. It then discusses how wealth in a city can be measured in a systematic and standardized way that allows for comparison across cities. Such a measure would place the degree of inequality in Maya cities in the context of other cities and societies. From the perspective of how people experience cities and what makes them want to stay in cities, the degree of inequality looms large for many reasons. On the one hand, wealth enchants. People may find cities attractive because of the possibility of getting a share of wealth. On the other hand, greater inequality results in more social dysfunction (Wilkinson and Pickett 2009). The city loses stability as poor people may question why they are participating in a social system that benefits other people much more than them.

The chapter then explores the spatial distribution of wealth within Maya cities. Sjoberg (1960) argued that elites separated themselves from the masses in preindustrial cities. Diego de Landa, a sixteenth-century bishop who collected testimony about the northern Maya lowlands, identified a similar pattern for Maya towns: "In the middle of the town were their temples with beautiful plazas, and all around the temples stood the houses of the lords and priests, and then [those of] the most important people. Thus came the houses of the richest and those who were held in the highest estimation nearest to these, and at the outskirts of town were the houses of the lower class" (quoted in Tozzer 1941, 62). Archaeologists continue to debate whether or not wealthy people lived near the center of cities. In this chapter I cover this debate and present new data on this topic from several cities.

If one thing is clear from the various Maya case studies on the location of wealthy people, it is that people of different wealth levels were interspersed throughout cities. This is precisely the situation that produces multiplicity, or the co-presence of diverse people in a single place. Multiplicity makes contact with strangers possible. From the perspective of social capital and social networks, multiplicity is an attraction because opportunities for interaction with different kinds of people expose one to novelty, variety, and the possibility of making contacts that could lead to economic, social, political, or other opportunities. Also, like people-watching, being able to see people from different walks of life can be amusing. Multiplicity is a challenge, however, because rich people may find unstructured interaction with the poor uncomfortable and the poor may resent their lot when they witness the situations of the rich. This kind of discomfort and resentment grows when wealth differences are more extreme and provides a motivation for the creation of exclusive wealth-based enclaves/neighborhoods. Thus, the question of the precise degree of wealth inequality in cities beckons, as does the question of whether or not wealthy people secluded themselves, as Sjoberg (1960) maintained.

Defining Social Inequality in Maya Cities

Inequality is present in all human societies, even egalitarian ones, and takes many different forms. The position that the Maya were relatively egalitarian survived into the 1960s (see Becker's 1979 review). For example, proponents of the vacant ceremonial center model (see chapter 2) saw very little inequality among the ancient Maya: the wealth of those who began to get ahead would be decreased when they took public office and assumed the financial burdens that went with it. Archaeologists such as Bullard (1964) and Willey (Willey and Bullard 1965, 375) took this idea of rotating public office as a leveling mechanism from Mesoamerican ethnographic sources (Vogt 1961; Wolf 1955). Yet other ethnographic cases show that individuals could also use public office to aggrandize and enrich themselves (Flannery 1972, 414–415; Hayden and Gargett 1990). Since we now know that Maya centers were cities brimming with difference—their residents included kings, courtiers, clerics, carvers, farmers, fishmongers, flint knappers, and fiber workers—I will not belabor the notion of egalitarian societies except to repeat Fried's (1967) dictum that within specific age and gender categories the number of prestigious positions in an egalitarian society might be equal to the number of people with the ability to fill them. Inequalities between genders and age grades may exist. Although several authors have discussed gender- and age-based inequalities for the classic Maya (Hutson et al. 2013; Joyce 1993, 1996; Pyburn 2004), this chapter examines wealth inequalities. Status inequality also structured ancient Maya societies, so it is important to get clear about terms such as wealth and status and how the nature of the archaeological record of Maya cities limits discussions of inequality to wealth.

A number of writers have clarified the difference between wealth and status (Chase and Chase 1992, 7; McAnany 1993b). Wealth generally refers to the amount of labor and physical resources (land, portable goods) at one's disposal. Smith (2015) has recently noted that wealth is one of two components of quality of life, an emerging theme in research on social inequality. The other component of quality of life is capabilities, which refers to the ability of members of a household to choose between a wide array of activities and goals and is grounded in the knowledge of those household members and the size of their social networks.

Status generally refers to genealogical pedigree, access to supernatural forces, and control of knowledge. One example of the difference between wealth and status is that titled aristocrats have high status but not necessarily much wealth. In contrast, nouveau riches have wealth but not necessarily high status. Landa's quote in the previous section, which distinguishes merely wealthy people from lords and priests, may faintly echo this same distinction.

The relation between wealth and status can be complex, as the two concepts often overlap in practice and can be highly correlated. For example, ancient Maya leaders who made compelling cases about their exalted status—about their control of esoteric knowledge and privileged contact with the supernatural world—did so with the help of something that, following the definitions above, would be considered an aspect of wealth: control of the labor necessary to build the elaborate temples used in rituals that reinforced status. Thus, status can depend on wealth. Another area of overlap between status and wealth has to do with wealth as a portable good. Although durable and portable goods might initially be seen as wealth (Smith 1987), McAnany (1993b, 71; see also LeCount 1999, 240) notes that some portable goods, such as jade, should not be considered fungible wealth because their value might depend on status: "High status Maya individuals pictured on polychrome vases and stelae as dripping with jade and shell ornaments symbolize all the social power, political authority and esoteric knowledge of the dominant class, but ironically and perhaps counterintuitively, those jade ornaments may not be convertible into anything else and so, strictly speaking, have little direct economic value."

In this quote, the concept of status—"social power, political authority and esoteric knowledge"—merges with another common term in discussions of social inequality: "class." The concept of class has been used in different ways within the Maya area. Some authors equate class with occupation. For example, Adams (1970) presented four social classes, graded from top to bottom according to occupational categories: 1) kings, priests, and administrators; 2) skilled artisans (sculptors, scribes); 3) semi-skilled workers (masons, potters); and, 4) farmers. Others define class on the basis of birthright. For example, Joyce Marcus (1992) argued that a person's ability to claim descent from supernatural beings exclusively and unequivocally determines class membership. In this view, the Maya had only two social classes: elite and commoners (see also Sanders 1992; cf. A. Chase 1992). For Marcus, classes are endogamous social strata. The notion of social strata calls to mind Fried's distinction between ranked societies and stratified societies. Although Fried (1967) saw a ranked society as one in which social inequality is less extreme and more negotiable than in stratified societies, I avoid this use of the term rank and instead use it in the broader sense of a person or a thing's relative place on a hierarchical scale (see Webster 1992, 135). The endogamous social strata Marcus (1992) perceived for the ancient Maya prevent mobility. A commoner could never become elite. However, Marcus argued that a great deal of variety and ranking existed within each of these two classes and that people could move up and down within their class. Hammond (1991), who also sees two general categories of status—members of the governing apparatus and commoners—provided just such a model of the multiple levels existing within each class. On the basis of extensive residential excavations across Tikal, Haviland (2014, 157–158) argued that the Classic Maya were stratified by class.

It is important to point out that the amount of inequality that existed within classes may have been so large that a low-ranking member in the upper class may have been less wealthy than someone born into the lower class. The Penn State excavations in Las Sepulturas, a dense residential zone of Copan located to the east of the Main Group (figure 2.7), illustrate the vast amount of inequality within classes. The surveyors of Copan assigned groups of mounds into a ranked typology (types 1, 2, 3, or 4) based on the number of buildings, the size of buildings, and construction techniques and materials (Willey and Leventhal 1979). According to Willey and Leventhal, the occupants of a type 4 group, which may have dozens of buildings, some with dressed blocks and vaulted roofs, outranked people who occupied mound groups assigned to types 1, 2, or 3. Nearly complete excavation of group 9N-8, a type 4 group with about fifty buildings—the largest elite establishment in the Copan Valley, not counting the Principal Group (Webster 1992, 142)—revealed extreme ranking of the households within the group. Of nineteen residences Abrams (1994) analyzed, the most elaborate—9N-82c—required over 10,000 person-days of labor to construct. Hieroglyphic inscriptions carved on a bench mark 9N-82c as the residence of a titled lord who was perhaps second in rank only to Yax Pasaj, Copan's king at the end of the eighth century. The two least elaborate residences Abrams studied in the 9N-8 group lacked decorative flourishes and required only about 250 person-days to construct. The quality of mortuary offerings and access to imported pottery also varied strongly among the patios within group 9N-8 (Hendon 1991). However, following project director William Sanders's segmentary lineage model for Copan, Penn State project members saw everyone living in group 9N-8 as members of the same maximal lineage and part of the same descent group. This means that the people living in the group's shoddiest houses could not be seen as servants or commoners but rather as low-ranking members of the same descent group. In Marcus's two-class system, this makes them elites, even though "they may have functioned essentially as servants" (Hendon 1991, 912) and even though non-elite people in some type 2 groups lived in better houses than the lowest-ranking members in 9N-8 (Abrams 1994, figures 18 and 20). These elites' low rank within 9N-8 may have been determined by birth order or individual genealogy.

Given anthropology's heritage as a social science, no discussion of class would be complete without a consideration of Marxism. Neither of the two models of class in the Maya literature—class as a gradation of occupations and class as an immutable birthright—align with Marxist understandings of class. Since Marx's analysis of class was confined mostly to industrial societies, a Marxist understanding of class applied to the ancient Maya would come from structural Marxists who see class as a person's position in the process of surplus extraction (Bloch 1983). Class in this sense depends on whether a person gives up surplus, collects surplus, or receives surplus from those who collect it (Saitta 1994). The class-as-birthright approach can overlap with the Marxist approach, since people of noble birth and political and ritual authority tend to extract surplus from others.

Several archaeologists (Sanders 1992; Marcus 1992) use elite as another name for those of the upper classes, and nearly all Mayanists would agree that people of high status are elites. But elite has more than one definition. On the one hand, if we define elite as "rich, powerful, and privileged" (G. Marcus 1983, 3), then people of high status in the sense of birthright, access to supernatural forces, and control of knowledge do indeed qualify as elites. On the other hand, if we define elite as those who run society's institutions and make decisions that affect a wide swath of people (Chase and Chase 1992, 3; G. Marcus 1983), then not all elites are of high status. In addition, not all elites are wealthy, as is demonstrated by several modern-day politicians who come from modest backgrounds (see Kowalewski et al. 1992, 259). While these distinctions bring up the concept of power, perhaps the most debated concept in the social sciences, this is not the space to enter that debate.

Having explored wealth, status, and class, I now turn to the question of which one is most easily inferred and measured in Maya cities. Although wealth is often associated with elites, high-status people, and membership in the upper class, membership in these categories, regardless of the nuances of how they are defined, requires something more than wealth. It may require a privileged genealogy, ritual knowledge, or the authority to make decisions with broad impact. In the Maya area, the archaeological signatures of these things include, but are not limited to, hieroglyphic statements of parentage, the tools of ritual specialists, or personal adornments that distinguish the status of the wearer. Uncovering these kinds of evidence requires extensive excavation, as they are unlikely to be found in test-pit middens. Because such excavations are cost- and time-intensive, archaeologists can conduct them only as a sample of architectural compounds.

Thus, systematically studying social inequality in cities poses many challenges (A. Chase 1992, 33; Haviland 1982). Since cities are large, getting a representative sample requires broad excavations in scores of architectural compounds distributed across all zones of a site. Predictably, no Maya city has received this kind of coverage, although work at Tikal and Caracol comes close. Several years of well-funded research, can, however, yield a massive site map and minor excavations at a representative sample of mapped architectural groups. These data permit quantification of wealth based on the cost of architecture and the quantity of fancy portable goods. When a large sample of residences or architectural groups from a single site are arrayed in histograms according to these variables (see Figures 5.1, 5.2, and 5.3), it is sometimes difficult to find a clear cutoff point that distinguishes elites/the upper class/high-status people from the hoi polloi (see also A. Chase 1992; Tourtellot et al. 1992). However, the example of group 9N-8 at Copan suggests that some people who are elite in terms of birthright might live in very modest

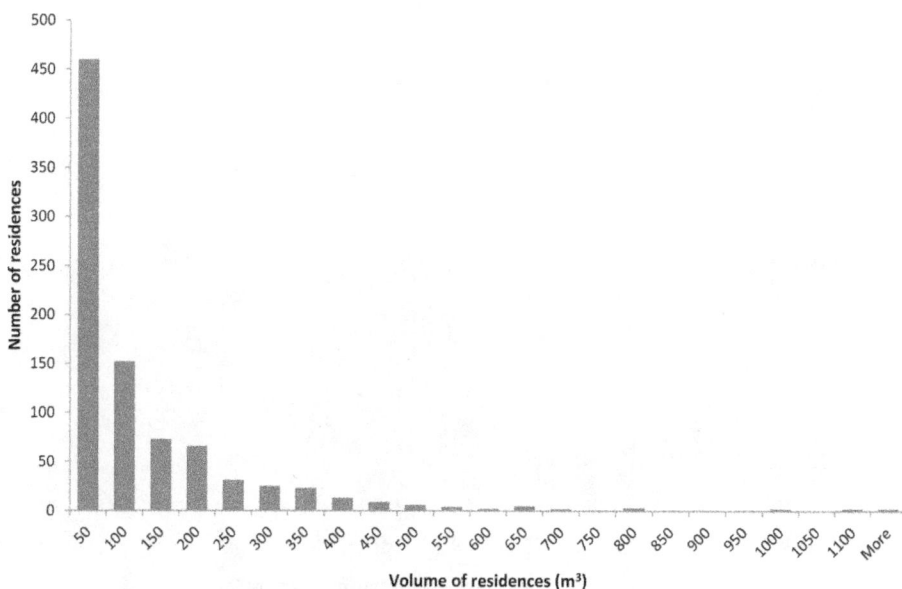

Figure 5.1. Histogram of volume of residences at Chunchucmil (n = 884).

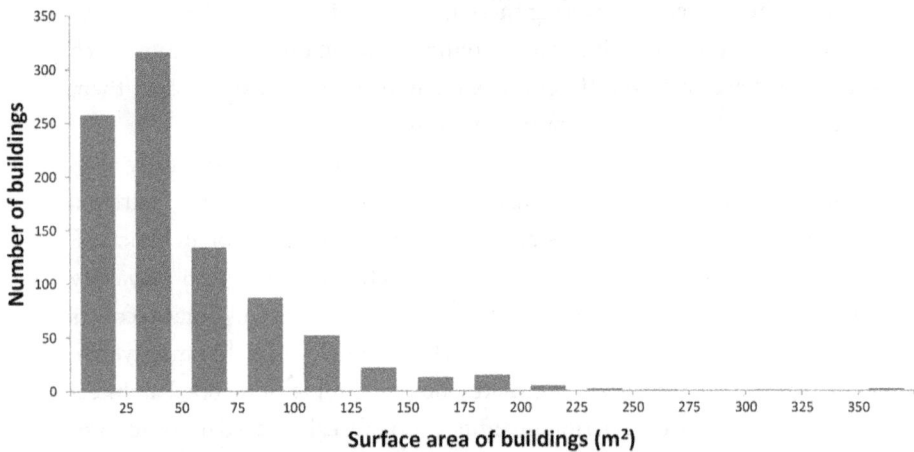

Figure 5.2. Histogram of surface area of buildings at Chunchucmil (n = 128).

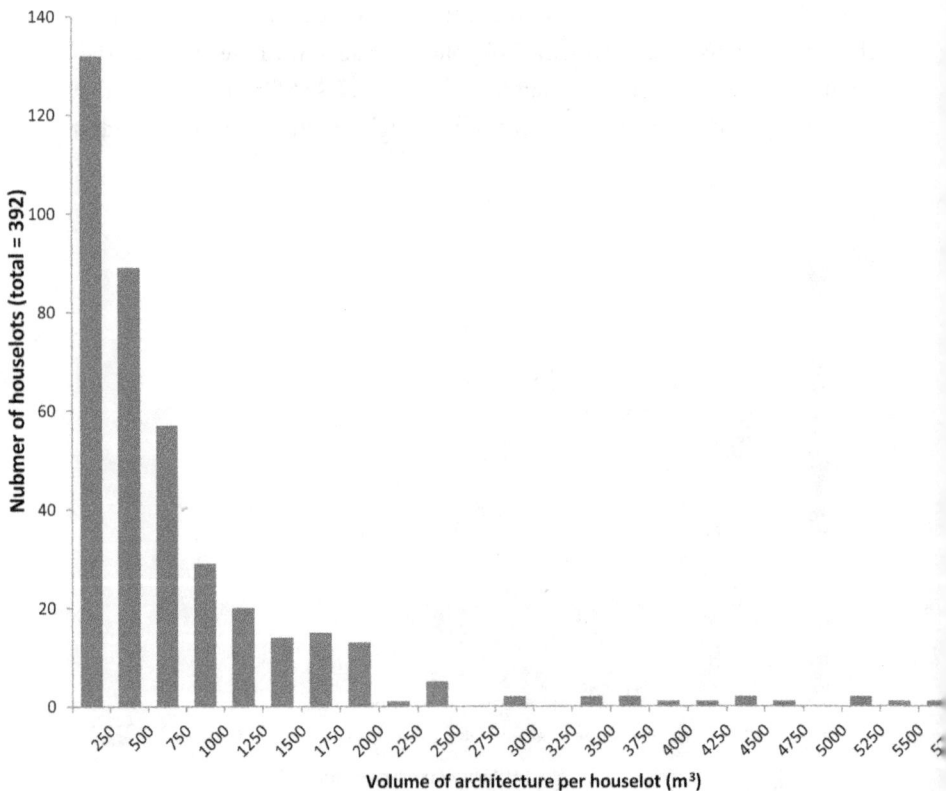

Figure 5.3. Histogram of volume of architecture of house lots at Chunchucmil (n = 392).

houses. These realizations mean that we can get at status and class across an entire site only to the extent that they overlap with something more tangible, such as wealth. Status and wealth certainly overlap among the Classic Maya, but measuring wealth without presuming that we are also capturing status would be a more parsimonious way of approaching social inequality across large cities. Thus my approach to social inequality, which focuses on architecture and portable goods, gets at wealth inequality as opposed to inequality in terms of status or class. However, since neither architecture nor portable goods are unequivocal indicators of wealth, they both require some discussion. Before getting to these two variables, however, I discuss the different scales of social unit that could be scored using these variables.

Social Units to Be Measured

Exactly which socially meaningful unit should be ranked according to wealth? The discussion of group 9N-8 at Copan introduced the concept of nested hierarchy: ranking within a group that is itself ranked (Hendon 1991). For example, we could rank units within 9N-8 at two different levels in addition to the level of the entire group. The first level focuses on residences within a courtyard: residences that share the same patio can exhibit large differences in terms of access to labor and portable goods. The social unit that pertains to the residence is most often the nuclear family. The second level is the structures that share a courtyard/patio. Many patios have multiple residences and thus multiple nuclear families. For 9N-8, families that shared the same courtyard have been called lineages. For several reasons, including the fact that ritual activities were shared by all residents of the same patio, Hendon (1991) used the term household to refer not to each nuclear family but to all the residents of the same patio; that is, the lineage. More recently, several archaeologists have come to see the extended family households that share a patio as "houses" in the sense of Levi-Strauss's house society model (Gillespie 2000; Hutson et al. 2004; Joyce 2000a). In the parlance of the Penn State project, each of the lineages in the 9N-8 group combined to form a single maximal lineage.

All of these three levels (residence, courtyard, and group) can be ranked in terms of architecture. However, archaeologists customarily rank the smallest unit (the residence) or the largest unit (the architectural group). Since many architectural groups have just one patio, the second and third levels (courtyard and group) are often the same. Although it would be a mistake to assume that groups with many patios, such as 9N-8, housed the same social unit as a group with just one patio, extremely large groups such as 9N-8 are rare exceptions. Most multi-patio groups have only two or three patios. The difference between a group with one patio and a group with two or three patios might be quantitative rather than qualitative; that is, they may be different sizes of similar kinds of social units. Thus, I see making comparisons at the level of the group rather than at the level of the patio as minimally troublesome. Making comparisons at the level of the nuclear family can be attempted to the extent that each nuclear family has a discrete residence that can be assessed in terms of construction labor and resources invested in the residence. However, in the Maya area, where residences usually group together in the form of patio groups, formation processes get in the way of assessing individual residences according to portable wealth: the products that the members of a residence consume often get discarded in locations that pertain to the group as a whole. Thus, a test-pitted midden may contain residues of wealth that are not easily attributable to one particular residence. Portable wealth is therefore best measured at the level of the group. This is unfortunate because ranking at the level of the group flattens the heterogeneity within the group (McAnany 1993b, 80).

Variables of Wealth

Architecture as Wealth

Archaeologists use residential architecture as a measure of household wealth because different buildings can exhibit a wide range in the amount of labor and resources needed to construct them. Since control of labor and resources are aspects of wealth, people living in the costliest houses are likely to be the wealthiest. Most archaeologists accept some sort of relation between architecture and wealth (Arnold and Ford 1980; Becker 1973; Carmean 1991; Carmean et al. 2011; Folan et al. 2009; Hammond 1972; Haviland and Moholy-Nagy 1992; Kurjack 1974; Tourtellot et al. 1992; Willey et al. 1978), and many state that architecture is the clearest indicator of wealth (Abrams 1994, 77; Ashmore 1988, 161; Brown et al. 2012; Smith 1987). Housing is "probably the strongest and most consistent expression of wealth levels in agrarian states" (Smith 1987, 301) because it is "relatively permanent, functional and not merely symbolic and furthermore not subject to the vagaries of gift, offering, payment, loan, accident, and disposal that conceivably explain the recovered distributions of portable items" (Tourtellot et al. 1992, 81). At several cities, the costliest houses also have artifacts of greater quality and broader variety (Haviland and Moholy-Nagy 1992; Hendon 1991; Webster and Gonlin 1988) than other houses. Such variety might index the kinds of networks and capabilities that accompany wealth in the determination of quality of life (Smith 2015).

Wilk's ethnographic work in southern Belize clarifies one of the ways that wealth correlates positively with house cost. In the relatively egalitarian Kekchi villages Wilk (1983) studied, newlyweds often choose to build their own house in one of their parents' compounds because this gives them access to the compound's land and they benefit from the pooling of labor and risk within the compound. In return for such access and security, newlyweds contribute more labor to the compound as a whole and the compound leader draws on this labor to build himself a bigger house and increase his wealth (measured in terms of ownership of pigs). The variation in the costliness of houses is not extreme among the Kekchi, but it is much larger among the Mopan Maya, who have a deeper exposure to cash cropping and a higher degree of social inequality. Wealthier Mopan people pour their wealth directly into costlier houses.

One of the challenges to the relation between wealth and architecture arises from the methods used to calculate the cost of architecture. Archaeologists have used three methods to quantify the cost of houses. In order of descending accuracy, these methods are energetics, mound volume, and surface area. The latter two measures are not so much calculations of cost as proxies for cost. Energetics, the most detailed method, involves dividing the construction process into the full suite of required tasks (quarrying stone, shaping blocks, transporting materials, making plaster, applying plaster, assembling walls, etc.); determining how much time each task required, given the specific construction features of the building in question; and totaling this construction time in the form of person-days of labor. Since these calculations require very precise knowledge of each structure, they are best applied to excavated buildings, as Abrams (1994) has done at Copan. Because energetics requires fully excavated buildings and because no Maya city has a large, representative sample of fully excavated buildings, energetics cannot be used for city-wide studies. However, archaeologists have applied simplified energetics calculations to structures that have not been excavated. The simplified version works best when architectural details are highly visible and have been recorded systematically, as at Sayil (Carmean 1991; Sabloff and Tourtellot 1991). It works less well when architectural details are not as visible, as at Tikal (Arnold and Ford 1980; Folan et al. 1982; Haviland 1982). In the latter case, where most buildings appear simply as mounds of rubble, the second method for quantifying cost of architecture—measuring volume of architecture (Hutson et al. 2006)—must be used. Although calculating the volume of architecture is rather straightforward, it requires maps that supply the height of every structure. Unfortunately, most maps of large cities (e.g. Tikal, Coba, Mayapan, Calakmul, Dzibilchaltun) provide height for only a small fraction of the buildings. In such cases, calculating the surface area of buildings, though the least accurate of the three methods, is the only option.

Because I was unable to use energetics for the examples below, I used volume when possible and surface area when forced to do so by the lack of detail in maps. Volume and surface area as proxies for cost of architecture each have problems that deserve exploration. The most serious problem has to do with measuring the volume or surface area of buildings that have not been excavated. In cases where a structure was built on a hillock, it is often difficult to determine what part of the fill is natural and what part was human-made (Masson et al. 2014). In addition, people may have expanded buildings over many generations. If a large mound was built incrementally with small enlargements every few years or decades, the builders would have needed to control only small amounts of labor and materials at any one time, indicating a low level of wealth. But when it is not possible to note that a building's final size is the result of multiple, periodic additions, the cumulative volume and surface area would be attributed to a single construction effort that would have required much more labor and materials and thus more wealth. In such a case, calculating cost on the basis of maps alone will inflate the wealth calculations for structures that have undergone multiple expansions (Hendon 1992). This could be called the dynamic architecture problem. Maps represent only the final snapshot in what was likely a series of dynamic, intergenerational cycles in the reproduction of households, as Haviland's musical hammocks model for Tikal has documented (Haviland 1982, 1988; see also Evans 1993; Tourtellot 1988). Ford and Arnold (1982, 437) reply to this concern by noting that for buildings that were gradually enlarged, "all preexisting labor investments would continue to lend value to residences, reflecting wealth and status." Although Arnold and Ford may be correct in claiming that living in a large building enhanced an individual's status even if the person living in that building had not built much of it, status is different from wealth and merely living in a building does not necessarily reflect wealth.

In sum, using volume and/or surface area as measures of wealth can create problems. Nevertheless, these problems are not as troublesome at sites where the architecture in question was occupied for a short time or where excavations have shown that when households expanded, they did so not by enlarging individual buildings but by adding new buildings to the compound (Tourtellot 1988).

Another problem with wealth inferences based on measurements of what is left of stone architecture is that they do not take into account the cost of perishable constructions or "hidden housemounds"—low platforms now covered in humus and invisible without excavation (Hammond 1991, 265–266; Johnston 2004). There are several ways to address this problem. First, some sites have fewer invisible structures in the first place. Across much of the northern lowlands, thin soils, flat topography, lack of alluviation, and minimal leaf litter combine to make it unlikely that small platforms will be buried (Hutson et al. 2008). Second, hidden housemounds are small, which means that their exclusion has a predictable effect on wealth calculations: the poorest people will be underrepresented. Finally, perishable structures are low cost and do not add significantly to the cost of the stone platforms they once stood upon (Abrams 1994, 64)

Working with surface area alone brings up two additional considerations. First, precisely what determines the surface area of a house? Some ethnographic studies show that the surface area of a house depends on the number of people living in it (Kramer 1979; Narroll 1962). Although this correlation seems reasonable, it does not always exist. Wilk's (1983) study of Kekchi villages in southern Belize did not find a significant correlation between number of residents and the surface area of houses. Although Kramer showed a positive correlation between these two variables in one twentieth-century Iranian village, Jacobs (1979) failed to find such a correlation in another twentieth-century Iranian village. Kramer's case study is very informative, however, because she found a positive correlation between household wealth and household size (the number of people in the household). Netting's (1982) cross-cultural study of positive correlations between household wealth and household size suggests that household size is not an independent variable that determines the surface area of the house. Instead, household size depends on household wealth because wealthy households gain dependents from poor households. Thus, the ultimate cause of variation in house surface area is not household size but household wealth.

The second consideration with surface area as a proxy for cost of architecture is that looking at surface area alone fails to take into consideration other costly aspects of a building such as the type of walls and roof. In other words, when surface area is used as a proxy for cost, the analyst would give the same cost score to a 40-square-meter perishable house and a 40-square-meter stone house with a vaulted roof. In reality, the latter house could easily cost ten times as much as the former (Abrams 1994); cost per square meter can vary widely from one building to the next. Since there is no resolution to this problem, calculations made on the basis of surface area should be used with great caution if at all. This problem is not as bad when using mound volume as a proxy for cost since the remains of a vaulted building will have a larger volume than the remains of a nonvaulted one.

Portable Goods as Wealth

The most common portable good excavations in Maya household middens have turned up is pottery. Serving ware functions as a strong communicator of household wealth to the extent that households use it to convey messages to people beyond the household in the process of serving food and drink. Smith (1987, 312) states that serving ware is "the most useful class of archaeological artifact for assessing wealth." Large-scale excavations bear this out at places such as Copan, where residents of courtyards with more impressive burial goods and costlier architecture also had more access to polychrome pottery and the most prestigious types of polychrome (Abrams 1994; Hendon 1991; Sanders 1989; Webster and Gonlin 1988). In the examples that Smith used to correlate portable household possessions with wealth, most possessions were purchased. More and more evidence has come to light about ancient Maya marketplaces that suggests that fancy serving wares could have been bought and sold there, but LeCount (1999) makes a strong case that at the site of Xunantunich, elites gave polychrome pots as gifts to lower-status people in order to solidify alliances. In such a case, polychrome pots qualify as prestige goods whose presence in a household marks that household's social networks (obligations to and affiliations with powerful patrons) as much as or more than it marks wealth. However, to the extent that social networks, in addition to wealth, factor into measures of inequality

(Smith 2015), the means by which a household acquired a valuable portable good should not distort indices of urban inequality.

Another issue has to do with lack of correlation between costliness of architecture and access to fancy portable goods. Some families with modest houses had access to impressive portable goods (Hutson 2004; Masson et al. 2014, 237). Other families might have been poor in terms of access to fancy portable goods (for instance, the land the family farmed might have had the lowest productivity, thus providing little or no surplus to exchange for other resources) but might have been rich in terms of labor if they had many off-spring. This would lead to a situation in which a family could have a large house with few wealth goods inside it. Such a situation is unusual since there is normally a positive correlation between household size and household wealth, but it has been documented in the Maya area (Hutson and Davies 2015; Stockton 2013). Either way, such a situation does not invalidate the use of architecture or portable goods as wealth indicators; it merely highlights that there is more than one kind of wealth and that as many measures of wealth as possible should be consulted.

Calculating Wealth Inequality

How severe was inequality in ancient Maya cities? Some degree of inequality can be positive because it provides the diversity and heterogeneity that make cities socially and economically attractive. Yet too much inequality can be dysfunctional. Although many people who have written about inequality within Maya cities ("classics" include Abrams 1994; Carmean 1991; Haviland 1967; and Hendon 1991), there is still room to expand on this work. Specifically, it would be useful to have a synthetic measure of inequality across a city as a whole that is standardized to allow comparisons between cities, both Maya and otherwise. Economists have developed a widely used and relatively simple method—the Gini coefficient—for quantifying the magnitude of inequality in the distribution of a measurable resource, be it land, income, or volume of residential architecture (Brown et al. 2012, 305–306). The Gini coefficient determines how much the distribution of a resource differs from a situation of total equality (in which everyone has the same amount of the resource) or total inequality (in which one person monopolizes the resource). The Gini coefficient ranges from 0 (total equality) to 100 (total inequality). In 2010, a special section of the journal *Current Anthropology* that focused on wealth inequality in premodern societies provided ranges of Gini coefficients for premodern hunter gatherers, pastoralists, horticulturalists, and intensive agriculturalists. A sample of hunter gatherers exhibited a mean Gini coefficient of 25; the range was 6 to 47. The mean indicates a rather even distribution of wealth (Smith et al. 2010). A sample of mostly non-urban, intensive agriculturalists exhibited a mean Gini coefficient of 57 with a range of 45 to 71 (Shenk et al. 2010). Gini coefficients for the largest modern cities exhibit a wide range: Johannesburg 75, Mexico City 56, New York 50; Guatemala City 50, Los Angeles 48, Manila 40, Beijing 22 (United Nations Human Settlement Programme 2010; Kurtzleben 2011; for Gini coefficients of countries, see Ortiz and Cummins 2011; World Bank 2014). The estimated Gini index for the entire world was 43 in 1820 and is now 70 (Milanovic 2009). The fact that the range of Gini coefficients in contemporary cities is wider than that for contemporary, non-urban, intensive agriculturalists suggests that economic life in cities is quite variable. Some of this variability likely is the result of the range of non-farming occupations found in cities.

Clifford Brown and colleagues (2012) have used the Gini coefficient to get a sense of the degree of inequality in ancient Maya cities, focusing on house size in particular. I follow this lead, and also use ceramic data, when possible, since portable goods may tell a different story than architecture. Of the many conditions that must be met to ensure useful results, the sample of houses or architectural groups or pottery included in the Gini calculation for a city should be representative of the city as a whole and should date to the same time period. Cities that were occupied for a relatively short period of time—three centuries or less—work best. A short occupation period also mitigates the dynamic architecture problem. Chunchucmil and Palenque meet this criterion. In addition, mound heights on their maps make it possible to use mound volume measurements. At Chunchucmil, a representative sample of excavations across the site makes possible the calculation of a Gini coefficient for portable wealth as well. I also present Gini coefficients for residential surface area at Dzibilchaltun, Sayil and Mayapan. Most of the architecture at each of these sites was built within a relatively short period of time. I now discuss sampling, chronology, and results for all five sites.

For each of these sites, structures with less than 20 square meters of surface area are more likely to be auxiliary structures, such as kitchens or storage sheds, than houses (Ashmore 1981b). Thus, at all five sites, structures had to be 20 meters square or greater to be included in the sample. Structures that take the form of temple pyramids were also excluded since they were probably not residences. However, when comparing architectural groups (as opposed to individual residences), domestic shrines should be included in inequality calculations because they represent an investment of resources by the group and they suggest a degree of social integration that provides information about the capabilities and social networks side of quality of life.

At Chunchucmil, the ancient Maya built most structures as parts of groups. A representative sample of 159 groups of the 1,405 groups in the central 9.3 square kilometers was chosen for excavations. Chapter 4 presents additional details about the sampling strategy. With the exceptions enumerated below, the architecture in these groups forms the basis of the sample I used to calculate Chunchucmil's Gini coefficients. Approximately 75 percent of Chunchucmil's pottery dates to the fifth and sixth centuries CE. After Chunchucmil declined, a small population built new platforms in the Late and Terminal Classic period. The sample of 159 excavated groups contains eleven of these platforms, all of which were dropped from the Gini calculations to ensure chronological contemporaneity. Within these 148 groups, all of which were principally occupied in the fifth and sixth centuries, 884 structures qualify as residences; the other 660 structures were temples, structures too small to be houses, or basal platforms on top of which many of the group's structures were built. The Gini coefficient for mound volume for this sample of 884 residences is 63 (table 5.1). This is probably a bit too high since some of the large, nontemple structures in the monumental groups may be observation stands or storehouses as opposed to residences. Figure 5.1 presents a histogram of the 884 variates in this sample. I also calculated the Gini coefficient at the level of the group. To do this, I looked at 128 of the 148 fifth- and sixth-century groups; the twenty groups I excluded from this sample have monumental temples. I believe these temples served broader social groups, such as the neighborhoods and districts discussed in chapter 4, and therefore should not be counted as part of the wealth any particular household. For each of the 128 groups, I combined the mound volume of all buildings in the group, both residential and otherwise, using the logic that nonresidential buildings also require an investment of resources. The resulting Gini coefficient—60—is close to that for individual residences. Another sample of 392 residential groups (Magnoni et al. 2012) is also available for a Gini calculation. This sample includes all the groups within the 9.3-square-kilometer mapped polygon that are completely or nearly completely encir-

Table 5.1. Measures of wealth inequality for a sample of Maya cities

Site	Approximate chronology	Item measured	Gini co-efficient	Sample size	Source
Chunchucmil	400–600 CE	Volume of individual residences	63	884	This study
Chunchucmil	400–600 CE	Volume of residences per group	60	128	This study
Chunchucmil	400–600 CE	Proportion of fancy pottery per group	52	128	This study
Chunchucmil	400–600 CE	Volume of all buildings per group	57	392	This study using data in Magnoni et al. 2012
Palenque	600–800 CE	Volume of individual buildings	63	1,135	Brown et al. 2012
Dzibilichaltun	700–900 CE	Surface area of probable residences	39	908	This study using data in Stuart et al. 1979
Sayil	700–900 CE	Surface area of structures	59	57	This study using data in Carmean 1991
Sayil	700–900 CE	Surface area of structures	71	767	Brown et al. 2012
Mayapan	1200–1400 CE	Surface area of structures	32	1,214	Brown et al. 2012

cled by house lot walls. This sample is not representative, as it clearly favors groups with walls. Although most of these groups have not been excavated, the representative sample of excavations across the site suggests that these other groups also date to the fifth and sixth centuries. From Magnoni et al.'s calculations of the total mound volume for each of these 392 groups, I derived a Gini coefficient of 57. Figure 5.2 presents a histogram of the 392 variates in this sample.

Of the 148 contemporaneous excavated groups, 128 yielded a decent amount of ceramics (see chapter 4). For each of these groups, I calculated the ratio of fancy ceramics (polychrome sherds and sherds from the Chencoh, Acu, and Kochol groups; Varela Torrecilla 1998) to total potsherds by mass. The Gini coefficient for fancy pottery is 52, which suggests that wealth in terms of portable goods was distributed more evenly than wealth in terms of architecture. There is no correlation between architectural wealth and pottery wealth ($r = 0.056$) or between architectural wealth and access to obsidian ($r = -0.131$) or between pottery wealth and access to obsidian ($r = -0.117$). Access to fancy pottery certainly contributes to quality of life, although such pottery might say less about wealth and more about social networks (see also LeCount 1999; Mills et al. 2013).

Most of Palenque's residential occupation dates to the Late Classic (Barnhart 2001, 75; Gonzalez Cruz 1993; Miller 1999, 35–43). Brown et al. (2012) used Barnhart's site map to produce Gini coefficients for both volume and surface area of residences. Barnhart mapped 1,481 structures in a 2.2-square-kilometer area. Although Palenque's settlement continues to the west on a 0.8-square-kilometer plateau beyond the 2.2-square-kilometer map, Barnhart (2001, 108–110) states that settlement density appears to decrease in that direction. Thus, the 1,481 structures Barnhart mapped represent most, though not all, of Palenque. Brown and colleagues considered 1,135 of these structures to be residential. They calculated the Gini coefficient for mound volume as 63, identical to that for Chunchucmil (table 5.1).

At Dzibilchaltun, I collected data on structures in an east-west transect measuring 6,800 meters long and 500 meters wide. This represents one-sixth of the total area mapped at Dzibilchaltun (Stuart et al. 1979). This transect cuts right through the site center, using *sacbes* 1 and 2 as its south border, and extends to the eastern and western edges of the Dzibilchaltun map. The north border of the transect is the north boundary of all of the one-kilometer-square blocks in row J. I consider this sample to be representative because it crosses the entire site map from the center to the east and west edges. Dzibilchaltun reached its demographic apex between during the Copo ceramic phase (700 to 1000 CE), and most of its vaulted buildings were constructed between 700 and 850 CE. Preclassic period pottery was found in 103 of the 392 nonvaulted structures that received test pits (Kurjack 1974, 47). Kurjack's (1974) maps, which give chronological information for 715 structures, can be used to identify Preclassic buildings so they can be removed from the sample, but there is no chronological data for some structures. Thankfully, many of the Preclassic period structures in the sample transect are part of a cluster at the far west that did not have any later occupation. Thus, I assumed that other structures without chronological data in this cluster probably also date to the Preclassic period and could be removed from the sample. From a total of about 1,350 structures in this transect (which represent almost exactly one-sixth of the total buildings at Dzibilchaltun), 908 were considered residential. Surface area measurements for these 908 structures yielded a Gini coefficient of 39 (table 5.1). Using surface area is problematic because, as noted above, surface area as a proxy for cost does not recognize that the construction costs of buildings with the same surface area may vary because of the presence or absence of, for example, a vaulted roof. The data from Dzibilchaltun are also problematic because it is often not easy to distinguish the remains of a house from the remains of a platform that supported perishable houses.

Sayil is a good candidate for the Gini coefficient because it was occupied for a short time. Tourtellot et al. (1992) state that Sayil was occupied for two centuries. Although nearly all of the pottery comes from the Cehpech sphere, these data alone do not pin the site down to a particular 200-year span since some Cehpech types, such as Muna Slate, were produced both in the Late Classic and the Terminal Classic. Thus, the occupation of Sayil potentially spanned from 600 to 1100 CE. However, Tourtellot et al. (1990) used Andrews's (1985) architectural seriation to place Sayil firmly in the eighth and ninth centuries. Using energetics calculations based on mapped structures, Carmean (1991) produced person-day estimates for 57 residences in a north-west-to-southeast swath of the site. The Gini coefficient for this sample is 59, but, as Carmean has acknowledged, the sample is not representative: there are too many "middle rank" houses and not enough high- and low-ranked houses. The actual Gini coefficient should be higher. Brown et al. (2012) calculated a Gini coefficient of 71 based on the surface area of 767 structures (table 5.1), but, as is the case with Dzibilchaltun, this method fails to account for the great variability in the cost of construction of buildings that range from perishable structures to vaulted structures and everything in between. In addition, many structures at Sayil have five or more rooms, suggesting that more than one family lived in them.

Based on radiocarbon dates, Mayapan reached its peak population between 1200 and 1450 CE, though it had a significant occupation dating back to 1000 CE (Peraza Lope and Masson 2014; Milbrath and Peraza Lope 2003; Smith 1971). Using surface-area calculations from a random sample of 1,214 residences (extracted from a total of 4,000+ structures mapped at Mayapan; Pollock et al. 1962), Brown and colleagues calculated a Gini coefficient of 32 (table 5.1). Hare et al. (2014, 170) note, however, that the map Brown used, the Carnegie map produced in the 1950s, is often inaccurate with regard to the size and details of architecture.

In summary, the Gini coefficients of Palenque, Sayil, Dzibilchaltun, Chunchucmil, and Mayapan range from 32 to 71. This mirrors the range of Gini coefficients of modern cities and suggests that in terms of wealth inequality, ancient Maya cities do not differ vastly from today's cities. As noted above, some of the coefficients from the Maya cities are not as trustworthy as others, yet this same uncertainty pervades the calculation of contemporary Gini coefficients: various authors, for example, list New York City's Gini as 46 (Adomaitis 2013), 50 (Kurtzleben 2011), and 60 (Glaeser et al. 2008). Although the data Brown and colleagues presented suggest a trend of increasing inequality toward the end of the Classic period, the Gini coefficients presented here do not substantiate this: the Gini coefficients from the early Classic (e.g., Chunchucmil) are about the same as those from the Late Classic (e.g., Palenque).

The substantial amount of wealth inequality in Maya cities suggests that walking through a city may indeed have involved chance encounters between people of widely different wealth levels. But were Maya cities organized in such a way that these encounters could occur on a day-to-day basis? Although the Gini calculations reaffirm the data from scores of other studies that document inequality in Maya cities, did rich people live in the same area as poor people, passing each other on public pathways? The following section addresses these questions. But first, precisely who would be walking through a city? Children as well as adults? Men as well as women? Rich as well as poor? Rosemary Joyce's (1993, 1996) research on the roles of men and women, as inferred from Classic period Maya imagery and ethnohistorical sources, suggests that both men and women would have been out and about. Although these sources emphasize activities that women performed at home, such as food preparation and tending animals, several activities would have sent them out into the city and beyond. As curers, women would have visited households across cities. As vendors, women would have visited marketplaces (see chapter 6). As cooks and weavers, they would have brought their products to feasts and other ceremonies that took place beyond the household. As key players in the economic self-sufficiency of the household, they would have gone to the market, to other parts of the city, and beyond the city to procure critical raw materials and tools for cooking, making clothes, and more. To the extent that children participated actively in household production among the ancient Maya (Ardren 2006; Lopiparo 2006), they probably also left the house on errands to get raw materials such as fuel, water, clay, and reeds. Men also circulated in Maya cities while on their way to hunt, fish, or farm (women may have farmed beyond the house lot as well; Robin 2006); participate in rituals and ceremonies; play the ballgame; or do battle, to name just a few activities. Although some of these reasons for circulating within cities (going out to farm or fetching water) are better suited to people on the lower levels of the social pyramid, the rich would also have circulated as they left their houses for rituals, meetings, and other activities. The most exalted members of society may have appeared in public only on special, scripted occasions, and, when mobile, perhaps on litters such as those seen in Maya graffiti (Houston 1998a, 340).

Did Maya Cities Have Wealth-Based Neighborhoods?

In the Maya area, many archaeologists have discussed a pattern in which the wealthiest and most important people lived close to the civic/ceremonial cores of Maya cities (Arnold and Ford 1980; Folan et al. 2009; Haviland 1966, 1970; Kurjack 1974). As noted in the introduction, the pattern, often referred to as concentric zonation, finds a precedent in Landa's description of towns in northern Yucatan, though Landa may have taken his description from earlier Spanish sources that described non-Maya towns in lower Central America (Chase 1986, 362–363). Concentric zonation implies multiple rings around the core, each ring homogeneous in terms of wealth. Sjoberg (1960, 98–99) argued that concentric zonation consisting of upper-class people at the core, middle-class people surrounding them, and poor people on the outskirts was universal in the nonindustrial world. Although Sjoberg envisioned neighborhoods beyond the elite core forming along ethnic or occupational lines, the homogeneity of wealth in the upper-class core fulfills an important condition for the formation of neighborhoods: the distinctiveness of the people living close to each other.

It is important to note, however, that the situation of wealthy people living close to the civic/ceremonial core can exist in the absence of concentric rings. For example, wealthy households close to the center of the city may be interspersed with less wealthy households that also are located near the center. There are no rings in this example because the area around the city center is not homogeneous: it does not exclude people of particular wealth levels.

We have, then, two models in which wealthy people might be distributed across a city: 1) concentric zonation, in which people of relatively homogeneous levels of wealth live in rings around the core and the degree of wealth in each ring declines with distance from the core; and, 2) "centering of wealth," in which wealthy people tend to live closer to the core but there are no rings. Of course, people of different wealth levels might be distributed evenly across the site, leading to a third model: even dispersion of wealth. Finally, cities may also have enclaves that include only wealthy households but not in the form of rings (and not necessarily located in the site center). Only the first and fourth patterns imply neighborhoods based on wealth. In this section, I evaluate the spatial patterning of wealth in a variety of Maya cities and discuss the social consequences of different patterns. Because Maya cities are diverse, we should not expect one pattern to dominate. In what follows, I am looking at the spatial patterning of wealth, not of density (or something else). Although sites such as Chunchucmil (Huston et al. 2008) and El Peru/Waka (Marken 2011) exhibit concentric spatial patterning in terms of density (dense residential areas close to the center, less dense areas further away), this says nothing about spatial patterning in terms of wealth.

Arnold and Ford's (1980) pathbreaking article on Tikal presented the first systematic study of the spatial distribution of wealth in a Maya city. Arnold and Ford used energetics estimates for unexcavated structures (both residential and ritual) to calculate the labor costs for the construction of 630 groups in the central 9 square kilometers of the Tikal map (Carr and Hazard 1961) and then measured the distance of these groups from the center. They then computed a non-parametric correlation coefficient that showed no relationship between costliness of architecture and distance from the site center (Kendall's tau = 0.03). Arnold and Ford claimed that their results "cast doubt on the assumption that Classic period Maya centers manifested a pattern of concentric zonation" in terms of the wealth of the residents. However, Haviland (1982) and Folan and colleagues (1982) responded that several issues undermine Arnold and Ford's conclusions. Arnold and Ford did not successfully refute some of these issues in their reply (Ford and Arnold 1982). First, Arnold and Ford did not include palaces at the site core. Since Harrison (1999) has demonstrated that many of Tikal's palaces were residential, Arnold and Ford's study left the richest people out of the analysis. Second, the Tikal maps lack building heights. Arnold and Ford classified all buildings as either low or high, thus eliminating much of the variation in cost per building. Third, the map did not enable Arnold and Ford to distinguish between vaulted and unvaulted buildings, again minimizing variation in cost. Fourth, Arnold and Ford presumed that all residential shrines were the same size. Fifth, instead of measuring length and width of buildings, Arnold and Ford measured the diagonal, which has the effect of overrepresenting the size of long rectangular buildings. Sixth, Arnold and Ford ran into the dynamic architecture problem (see above): since Tikal had substantial occupation in the Preclassic, the Early Classic, and the Late Classic, the size of a building may represent the cumulative result of labor additions from multiple time periods. A size measurement might therefore not reflect the degree of inequality that pertained only to the final time period.

Because most palaces are located in Tikal's two-square-kilometer epicenter, Haviland (2008, 269; see also Haviland and Moholy-Nagy 1992) recently declared that "a degree of concentric zonation is clearly evident." Yet he noted that small houses are interspersed among these palaces. Haviland did not identify any concentric rings on the basis of wealth. Tikal therefore does not exhibit concentric zonation as Landa described it or as I have defined it in this chapter. Haviland's point about the clustering of palaces suggests instead a centering of wealth. To the extent that Arnold and Ford's measurements can be trusted, the next 7 square kilometers of Tikal (beyond the two-square-kilometer epicenter) exhibit an even dispersion of wealth. The city of Copan clearly shows a centering of wealth. Although the wealthiest residences are found throughout the Copan Valley, most of them concentrate near Copan's Principal Group (Webster 2008, 245), where they are interspersed among less wealthy residences.

At other cities, using maps with building heights and using different methods for selecting and measuring structures will eliminate the first five difficulties with Arnold and Ford's study and permit a more direct test of the relationship between cost and distance (cf. Haviland 2008, 429). Folan and colleagues (2009) resolved the first, third, fourth, and fifth difficulties with the 1980 study in their analysis of Coba. They focused on a nine-square-kilometer swath to the north of the site core that extended over four kilometers out from Coba's centrally located Iglesia group and included zones I, VI, and XIII of the Coba map (Folan et al. 1983). Folan and colleagues (2009, 63) state that the "largest and highest basal platforms and those with the most superstructures and the highest frequency of vaulted buildings were closest to the urban center." However, platforms of all sizes are close to the center. This may explain why Folan and colleagues' data yielded the same results that Arnold and Ford found for Tikal: no statistically significant correlation between costliness of structures and distance from the site core. Although Folan and colleagues claim that alternative manipulations of their data using Geographic Information Systems (GIS) support a positive correlation between cost of structure and distance from center, they do not provide a clear explanation of these methods in their article. Furthermore, the map of zone XIII shows extremely even spacing between structures when compared to zones I and VI, suggesting that zone XIII was one of the zones that Folan's team mapped with less detail and accuracy (Folan 1983, 8). Thus, zone XIII should not be used in the analysis. In any case, Folan and colleagues (2009) noted several times that massive compounds at Coba are interspersed within a sea of meager compounds. Wealthy households did not cluster at the site core. I return to the significance of this finding later.

Chunchucmil is an excellent city for testing the relationship between costliness of architecture and distance from the site center because nearly all of the residential groups were built in a relatively short time span thus addressing the dynamic architecture problem (the sixth issue with Arnold and Ford's study). Additionally, the map contains critical details for calculating not just the volume of individual structures but also the volume of the basal platforms on which so many structures stand (thus eliminating other issues discussed above). My colleagues and I have tested the relationship between costliness of architecture and distance from the site center multiple times (Hutson et al. 2006; Magnoni et al. 2012), each time using a different sample of architectural groups, and we have never found significant correlations. The largest sample contains 392 groups spread throughout the 9.3-square-kilometer map. This sample does not include monumental temples at the site core. The correlation coefficient between mound volume and distance demonstrates a perfectly even dispersion of wealthier households across the site (Pearson's $r = -0.0028$). In the smaller sample of 128 house lots mentioned above, there are also no significant correlations between distance from the site center and quantities of obsidian or fancy pottery per group at Chunchucmil (see also Hutson et al. 2010). Needless to say, there is neither concentric zonation nor centering of wealth at Chunchucmil, and the map shows no other kind of clustering that would suggest wealthy neighborhoods.

Diane Chase (1992, 128–130) makes a similar case for Mayapan. She shows that neither elaborate residences nor high-status burial contexts clustered at the site core. The maps Chase provided suggest an even dispersion of costly residences and high-status burials. Chase therefore argues that Mayapan does not accord with the concentric model, a conclusion that may come as a surprise given that Landa's concentric description was based on towns in this same area. At Sayil, Smyth and colleagues (1995, 329–321) do not find concentric zonation with regard to architecture. Instead, the most costly architecture is arranged linearly along Sayil's north-south causeway. Maintaining that architecture alone is not sufficient to test concentric zonation, they used data from systematic surface collections across the entire mapped portion of the site to see whether fine ceramics clustered in any particular area. They found no clustering of fine ceramics.

Data from the extensively mapped city of Caracol also permit an assessment of the distribution of wealth. Chase and Chase (2004, 142) note that the wealthiest residences are located at Caracol's central architectural node—the Caana Acropolis—and at causeway termini located anywhere from 500 meters to 3 or more kilometers away. Dietary data indicate that people living in the immediate area surrounding the wealthiest residences had the lowest intake of maize and protein (Chase and Chase 2004, 142). People living beyond the residences of those with low-quality diets had better diets. Chase and Chase believe Caracol offers an example of Burgess's (1923) concentric model. In this model, which was based on Chicago, the inner circle—zone I—is the central business district. Zone II, which encircles zone I, has two rings within it: an inner ring of factories and an outer ring of slums that teem with crime, vice, poverty, and vagrants. Zone III encircles zone II and contains low-income employees of factories and shops. Zone IV encircles zone III and contains "high-class" apartments and "exclusive" residences (Burgess 1925, 50). Beyond zone IV is the commuter zone. The discrepancies between Caracol and Chicago (Caracol's richest people are in the center whereas Chicago's richest people are further out; Caracol lacks factories and a commuter zone) make Burgess's model a rough fit, but Chase and Chase's point that poor people are close to the center is well taken.

Although the map of Dzibilchaltun is not detailed enough to systematically test the correlation between costliness of architecture and distance from the center, Kurjack's (1974, 86) data on the distribution of vaulted structures reveal the same pattern as at Caracol. Vault construction at Dzibilchaltun occurred from 700 to 1000 CE. Of the 237 vaulted buildings, two-thirds (n = 155) are located within 100 meters of the causeways and the large plazas these causeways connected. The other one-third is dispersed evenly across the 19-square-kilometer map. Within the area that contains two-thirds of the vaulted buildings, Kurjack notes an area of about 28 hectares where a quarter of the site's vaulted buildings cluster. This area also has small nonvaulted buildings, but a four-hectare swath within it located south of the Cenote Xlacah contains almost exclusively vaulted residential buildings, suggesting a very wealthy neighborhood. On its northwest edge, this neighborhood connects to another two-hectare cluster of exclusively vaulted buildings, although many of these buildings were probably ceremonial and administrative, given that they face the South Plaza, Dzibilchaltun's third largest paved plaza. Vaulted buildings that stylistically date to the late ninth and tenth centuries cluster even more closely to the causeways and central plazas. This phenomenon led Kurjack to suggest that toward the end of the city's history, elites wanted to have easier access to each other, something that was more difficult to achieve in earlier periods, when a larger number of vaulted buildings were embedded in spatial clusters that featured less wealthy households.

The pattern at Caracol and Dzibilchaltun of wealthy residences near large plazas and the causeways that connect them does not quite represent concentric zonation because the wealthy residences do not huddle in a central circle or in a ring around such a circle (see also A. Chase 1992, 31). Rather, each plaza (including those at the center and those at the termini of causeways) could be considered a nucleus. This pattern differs from J. Marcus's (1983, 202–204) usage of the multiple nuclei model because not all nuclei are equal: at both Dzibilchaltun and Caracol, the most costly houses are located at the plazas where the causeways converge. Because the main focus of causeway termini at Caracol and Dzibilchaltun was ceremonial, commercial, and/or administrative, such termini should not be considered neighborhoods, even though they include residences.

Discussion

Gini coefficients show that the degree of inequality in ancient Maya cities was substantial, mirroring the degree of inequality seen in many cities today. How was this inequality experienced on a day-to-day basis? Did people of different wealth levels live near each other, thus creating a mosaic of difference? Or were cities zoned according to wealth, thus keeping different people apart? The review of wealth-based spatial patterning at Tikal, Copan, Coba, Chunchucmil, Sayil, Mayapan, Caracol, and Dzibilchaltun permits several responses to these questions. First, no large Maya cities exhibit concentric zonation in the sense of extremely rich people living in the center, surrounded by rings of progressively less wealthy people, with the poor living furthest out from the center. In addition, there were few exclusively wealthy neighborhoods at large Maya cities (see also Freidel 1981a, 376). The four-hectare swath of twenty-five vaulted residences south of the Cenote Xlacah at Dzibilchaltun stands as the clearest example. It is true that many large Maya cities have massive and exclusive royal compounds that contained wealthy residences, such as the Central Acropolis at Tikal, Group B at Coba, the Principal Group at Copan, and the Caana Acropolis at Caracol. Yet I do not consider these neighborhoods as defined in chapter 3 because they are not primarily residential: the administrative and ceremonial functions of these compounds equaled or exceeded their residential functions.

Neighborhoods may also form around shared poverty as opposed to wealth. Anne Pyburn and colleagues (1998) have interpreted dense clusters of small houses on Albion Island, Belize, as the remains of the homes of landless laborers at the bottom of the social hierarchy. Masson and colleagues (2006, 205) have discussed possible dwellings of laborers at Mayapan and Dzibilchaltun. These studies suggest promising avenues for future research.

Areas of mixed wealth are much more common in Maya cities than exclusively wealthy neighborhoods. Mixed areas occur in cities in which wealth is evenly dispersed, such as Chunchucmil. In cities such as Copan, many of the wealthiest households were located close to the site core. The areas with these high densities of wealthy households should still be considered mixed because less wealthy people lived there as well. Understanding the social organization of these mixed areas is critical for understanding the experience of urban life. The archaeologists who have studied mixed-wealth areas at Coba and Copan argue that the rich people and the poor people in these areas were related to each other. For example, researchers argue that within Copan's Group 9N-8 the people living in cheaply built perishable houses were descended from the same known ancestor as the people living next to them in elaborate stone houses (Hendon 1991, 912; Webster 2008, 245). Although the people who lived in the shoddy houses were subservient to the others, they were all part of the same lineage and were therefore equally entitled to certain rights. Likewise, Folan and colleagues (2009, 64) argue that the people who lived in cheap dwellings close to the vaulted houses of elites near the center of Coba were related to those elites by kinship or affinity. Folan and colleagues see heterogeneous collections of patio groups as broad, corporate households that performed political, social, and economic functions. Poor households joined corporate groups centered on rich households (and likely accepted subordinate roles) not necessarily because they were genealogically related but because they could gain access to land and other economic resources (Folan et al. 2009). In contrast, Haviland (2008, 269) has argued that poor dwellings located near rich ones at Tikal housed the servants of the rich and that these servants did not have a close connection, kin or otherwise, to the neighbors they served. Trigger (2003, 122) comments more generally that servants' quarters blur distinctions between rich and poor areas. At Dzibilchaltun, large numbers of poor dwellings, too many for them all to be the homes of house servants, frequently clustered around the vaulted dwellings of richer residents (see figures 3.1 and 3.2). Kurjack (1974, 81, 93) believed that each cluster represented some kind of social group, but since the poor dwellings were oriented and distributed haphazardly within these clusters, he thought that the divisions within the social unit that occupied the cluster were numerous.

In sum, there is no agreement about the kinds of social relations among people of different wealth levels who lived near each other, and it is probably impossible to resolve this question. If we agree that within a particular area, such as group 9N-8 at Copan, people in inexpensive dwellings were part of the same lineage or Levi-Straussian house as people living nearby in costly dwellings, then the potential for multiplicity was decreased. In other words, encounters between rich and poor people *within this group* may have lacked the kind of excitement and tension that accompany encounters between people who do not know each other well because the people of 9N-8 were members of a carefully and internally ranked kin group. Their interactions with each other probably lacked any of the enticing elements of unpredictably because kinship rules and knowledge of each other's position in the group hierarchy regimented and circumscribed face-to-face encounters. Yet even if this kind of kinship organization existed at Copan and elsewhere, it is likely that multiplicity still abounded because of inequality at a higher level: that between groups. For example, the residents of group 9M-24, a modest group in terms of wealth, lived only 50 meters away from group 9N-8. Since the residents of these two groups were not part of the same lineage or corporate group, they probably did not know each other very well. This means that a degree of unpredictability might have characterized encounters between residents of the different groups. Poor people and rich people who lived near each other were not necessarily part of the same kin group. We also cannot conclude that modest houses located near elite houses must in all cases be servants' quarters because at cities such as Coba, Dzibilchaltun, and Chunchucmil, the number of low-wealth households is too high for all of them to be the homes of servants.

Is there a relation between gross wealth inequality and settlement patterns within cities? In other words, is the spatial distribution of wealthy households different in cities with high Gini coefficients as opposed to the distribution in cities with low Gini coefficients? I can only address this in a preliminary way given the small number of Maya cities for which Gini coefficients and systematic measures of the spatial distribution of wealth are available. Sayil and Chunchucmil have higher Gini coefficients while Mayapan and Dzibilichaltun have lower Gini coefficients. Of these four cities, only Dzibilichaltun exhibits both centering of wealth and an exclusively wealthy neighborhood. This should not lead to the conclusion that wealthy households cluster in cities with less overall social equality (such as Dzibilichaltun) because Dzibilchaltun's Gini coefficient is artificially low: it was created only on the basis of structure size and did not take into account the presence or absence of vaulted roofs. Wealthy households were dispersed relatively evenly across the cities of Sayil and Mayapan and absolutely evenly at Chunchucmil. The only conclusion I will draw from this sample is that in cities with higher degrees of inequality, the homes of the wealthy are not necessarily clustered. I encourage others to expand the sample and explore this relationship in other regions of the world and for other time periods.

Conclusion

Histograms show that one cannot find an objective cut-off point to differentiate classes based on wealth. Although Gini coefficients show that wealth inequality was high in Maya cities, exclusively rich neighborhoods were very rare in the Maya world and truly concentric zonation of wealth did not exist. Thus, people at different ends of the wealth spectrum did indeed live near each other. In these situations, wealth differences could not always be softened by kinship and affiliation. Furthermore, not all of the less wealthy people living near richer people were servants. To the extent that people left their house lots and patio groups and walked in public spaces, there were opportunities for people of diverse wealth levels to bump into each other. Gated communities basically did not exist. Instead, we find both centering of wealth and dispersion of wealth, and both of these settlement patterns permit multiplicity: the co-presence of diverse people. Chance encounters between rich and poor may have caused tension but they may also have provided excitement and other desirable results (Hannerz 1980, 112–113; Mumford 1961, 96). Unstructured contact between people of very different wealth levels can be intriguing because of the potentially contrasting styles of dress, adornment, and comportment on display. Schele and Freidel (1990, 365) have noted that each of the hundreds of people depicted on the columns of the temple of the warriors at Chichen Itza is distinctive in terms of clothing and adornments. This suggests that there was indeed great diversity to be seen. Chance encounters between strangers also create the possibility of making acquaintances that could lead to a variety of empowering economic, social, or even political opportunities. These unpredicted opportunities are one of the things that make cities dynamic. If the city is a boiling, roiling cauldron for the brewing of novelties, as McIntosh maintains in the epigraph of this chapter, encounters between people of different wealth levels give the brew a zest and piquancy not found elsewhere.

Wealthy and less wealthy people who lived near each other would presumably have come to know each other well enough that encounters between them no longer generated excitement. They may simply have become familiar faces in the neighborhood. Yet beyond the neighborhood, there are settings in large cities where who one might bump into remained unpredictable. I discuss these settings—central plazas and marketplaces—in chapter 6.

6

The Allure of Maya Cities

In the city, even the humblest could vicariously
participate in greatness and claim it for his own.

Mumford (1961, 68)

For the most part, the Maya exhibited a dispersed settlement pattern (Freidel 1981a). If living in small towns and dispersed hamlets was common and perhaps normal, why did some people buck the pattern and leave the countryside? What brought people to cities? Given that many Maya cities grew quickly—four of the cities discussed in chapters 2 and 5 (Chunchucmil, Sayil, Dzibilchaltun, and Palenque) had population explosions reminiscent of those seen in premodern cities in other parts of the world (Fletcher 1986)—and that urbanites faced high mortality rates, the demographic growth and maintenance of cities required in-migration. Some people must have moved from rural areas to cities. Urban neighborhoods helped people adapt to urbanism but are not necessarily an improvement over the strong, familiar social networks found in rural areas. The encounters made possible by the dispersion of wealth discussed in chapter 5 might have been attractive but this is just a small part of what cities offer. What other factors lured people to cities?

Whereas other chapters have looked at various spatial forms and relations within Maya cities, this chapter pays close attention to what first comes to mind when people think of Maya cities: the massive buildings that rose above the canopy and loomed large on the horizon. This chapter looks at monumental buildings and the broader spatial plans in which they were rooted. I argue that these forms featured both compelling symbolism and attractive aesthetics. I then turn to spectacles and markets and the plazas and other locales where they took place. Continuing the emphasis on built form, the chapter concludes with a consideration of how people in Maya cities had the opportunity to shape parts of their own built environment. This chapter begins, however, by addressing two hypotheses that I find unlikely. First is the idea that deficiencies of rural life pushed people to cities. Second is the idea that leaders could force people in the countryside to move to cities.

Country Life and Oppressive Force

Elements of life in the hinterlands can push people into cities, just as elements of city life can pull people toward them. The shortage of archaeological projects focused on rural areas limits our ability to discuss push factors, but from what we know thus far, people lived well in the countryside. I do not mean to romanticize rural life (Williams 1973); agricultural catastrophes and political insecurities likely pushed people to cities on occasion. Yet there do not seem to have been any predictable or systemic shortcomings of rural life. Scarborough and Valdez (2009) demonstrate that heterogeneous rural communities near La Milpa, Belize, satisfied social, ritual, and economic needs through complex webs of interaction that did not require cities. Innovative farmers at Chan, a small rural center in Belize, conserved forests better than cities and outlasted their short-lived sovereigns at nearby Xunantunich (Lentz et al. 2012; Robin 2012). Pull factors thus seem more compelling.

Factors that pull people to cities can be arrayed on a continuum between voluntary and involuntary. Olivier de Montmollin (1989, 93) argues that "much variation in settlement nucleation may be profitably interpreted in terms of the degree to which forced settlement was being used as an instrument of political control." He argues that involuntary resettlement produced nucleation in urban areas. In contrast, others have argued that leaders did not use force alone, even in the most extreme cases of resettlement from country to city. These researchers maintain that leaders also relied on persuasion and incentives. For example, at Teotihuacan, 80 to 90 percent of the population of the Valley of Mexico relocated to the city, which meant that many farmers had to walk long distances to and from their fields (see also Adams 1974 for the depopulation of Early Dynastic Uruk's countryside). Although "some involvement by the state seems probable" in the case of settlement relocation at Teotihuacan (Millon 1976, 228), brute force was not the primary cause of relocation. Cowgill (2003a) strongly argues that Teotihuacan offered attractions that made life in the city desirable to migrants.

Authorities had much to gain from nucleation because political control is easier when political subjects are nearby. Leaders can collect tribute, communicate messages, organize corvee labor, and mobilize armies much more efficiently when everyone lives close together (Sanders and Price 1968, 201). Nucleation can certainly occur by force, as it did in Yucatan under Spanish rule in the sixteenth century, yet even in such an oppressive colonial situation, Maya farmers exhibited considerable mobility (Restall 1997, 174–175; Okoshi-Harada 2012). Ethnohistorical documentation confirms that pre-contact leaders attempted to attract settlers to their towns (de Montmollin 1989, 91–92; Roys 1957; Scholes and Roys 1948), but there is no clear statement that coercive force was used (Inomata 2004, 183). In the Postclassic period, leaders compelled provincial nobles to move to Mayapan (Freidel 1981b), possibly as a strategy for limiting factionalism (Louis XIV's court at Versailles comes to mind). It is not clear, however, whether the threat of force was the only incentive Mayapan's rulers used (Freidel 1981b, 314).

Did some of the strongest Classic period rulers relocate potentially fractious subordinates, perhaps establishing a precedent for what happened at Mayapan? Evidence does not speak as directly to this issue as we might like, but we have some leads. While cities such as Calakmul and Tikal exercised diplomatic influence over their allies, the rulers/*k'uhul ajaws* of these allied but less powerful kingdoms did not move to Calakmul. Instead, Calakmul and Tikal's rulers visited the courts of their allies (Marcus 1976; Martin and Grube 2000). The *k'uhul ajaw* titles of these lesser rulers—"holy ruler" of a particular realm—root them within their polity (see chapter 2 for a fuller discussion of place names for realms).

The status of those who held the office of *sajal*, a title for lords below the level of the *k'uhul ajaw* that was used most commonly in the Usumacinta region, sheds more light on the question. In the eighth century AD, Tiloom, a *sajal* loyal to King Yaxun B'alam IV ("Bird Jaguar") of Yaxchilan, governed the site of La Pasadita, located approximately 17 kilometers north of Yaxchilan. Golden's (2003) research at La Pasadita shows that the site played an important role in regulating trade and defending Yaxchilan's frontier against its rival to the north, Piedras Negras. Yaxun B'alam needed Tiloom at La Pasadita to manage these roles. Yaxun B'alam probably dispersed other *sajals* to Yaxchilan's various frontier sites, such as Tecolote (Golden and Scherer 2013). The case of Tiloom shows that kings could relocate certain *sajals*. Yet Tiloom was not a potentially fractious subordinate; he was closely attached to and supportive of the king. Unlike Yaxchilan *sajals* at La Pasadita and Tecolote, frontier allies of Piedras Negras at sites such as El Cayo and La Mar were less strongly attached to their king (Golden and Scherer 2013). El Cayo and La Mar predated the Late Classic antagonism between Yaxchilan and Piedras Negras, whereas sites such as La Pasadita and Tecolote seem to originate in the context of that conflict (Golden and Scherer 2013). It is thus unlikely that the kings of Piedras Negras could have shuffled around *sajals* at El Cayo and La Mar as easily as Yaxun B'alam did with his *sajals*. The *sajals* of Piedras Negras had stronger attachments to their own centers, which were more deeply entrenched in the landscape than Yaxchilan's frontier outposts.

What about commoners? Did kings have the authority to relocate settlers by the hundreds? In the Classic period, leaders did not have enough control of their economies to be able to withhold critical resources from their subjects as a way of compelling obedience (Graham 2002; Masson 2002; McAnany 2010; Pyburn 2008). Although Lucero (2003, 546) has argued that leaders could force people to pay tribute in the dry season by threatening to withhold water reserves from royal reservoirs, water was not in short supply at many sites (Demarest 2003) and at sites where it was more restricted, such as in the Puuc hills, there is evidence that common households had their own stores of water independent of central reservoirs (Dunning et al. 2014). Access to water could not have been used to force people to move from country to city. Household investments in immobile goods (landesque capital, ancestor shrines, houses) probably figured more heavily than leaders' decrees when it came to mobility of subject populations (Gillespie 2000; Gilman 1981; Inomata 2004).

If leaders could not *force* people to come to their cities, they nevertheless sought to *convince* people to do so. The magnetic attraction demonstrated by the court at Piedras Negras in the Early Classic stands as a successful example (Child and Golden 2008; Houston et al. 2003). Because a decision to settle in a city likely was influenced by some combination of incentives provided by leaders and followers' calculations of self-interest, a study of what makes a city attractive must look at both bottom-up and top-down factors, as stated in chapter 1. Elites certainly "pursue their personal and collective goals in cities" (Trigger 2003, 121), but so do others. Non-elites are also agents who can choose to vote with their feet and move to cities. What perceived benefits may have motivated such choices? I now turn to symbolic meanings as a perceived benefit/attraction of Maya cities.

Meaning as an Attraction of Built Space

The structures at the core of Maya cities were planned and built with foresight and strategic intention. In this section I discuss the kinds of meanings that builders likely hoped these structures would convey. I also consider unintended meanings that were associated with these structures. I argue that some of these meanings were a pull factor that attracted people to cities. While smaller-scale buildings at the core of smaller settlements may have had similar meanings, the monumentality of the massive ones in the major cities gave them greater pull and were enhanced by their involvement in larger and more elaborate ceremonies, which I discuss in a later section. To be sure, getting at meaning is difficult because single buildings could have been multivalent, the meanings themselves could have been incredibly diverse, and different parts of the same building could have evoked different meanings. For example, a stairway may have evoked the notion of warfare (Miller 1998), while the superstructure of the same building could have been a microcosm (Taube 1998). This is not the place to systematically categorize buildings into broad types or to enumerate the full range of potential meanings communicated (see Houston 1998b). Instead, I present just a sample of potential meanings embedded in the cityscape.

Peter Harrison (1999, 187–191) has found that at Tikal, the placement of certain buildings was loaded with meaning. In some cases, rulers placed the center point of a new building in a location that forms a right triangle with the center points of two other buildings. Calling to mind a rectangular building with a doorway in the middle of one of the long sides, Harrison defines a building's center point as the spot where the building's central axis (the line that bisects the building's central door) intersects the line formed by the front wall of the building (the wall with the doorway). Admittedly, not all of Tikal's important buildings are part of right triangles, and, given how many buildings there are at Tikal, some right triangles will likely show up only by chance. However, a right triangle like that formed by the center points of Temples I, IV, and V at Tikal was unquestionably planned (figure 6.1). King Jasaw Chan K'awiil built temple I in the Great Plaza, and his son, King Yik'in

Chan K'awiil, built temple IV to the west. Yik'in's son, King Yax Nuun Ayiin II, placed the center point of his own major construction, temple V, in a spot that would form a right triangle with the center points of the temples of his father and grandfather. Thus, Yax Nuun Ayiin II planned the location of his temple in a way that would respect his direct ancestors and reiterate his legitimacy as heir to the throne. Temples I, IV, and V are not a random assemblage of buildings. They are politically and genealogically related in obvious ways. The fact that the triangle connecting these temples is a perfect 5-12-13 right triangle makes it even more unlikely that Yax Nuun Ayiin II chose the location of temple V at random.

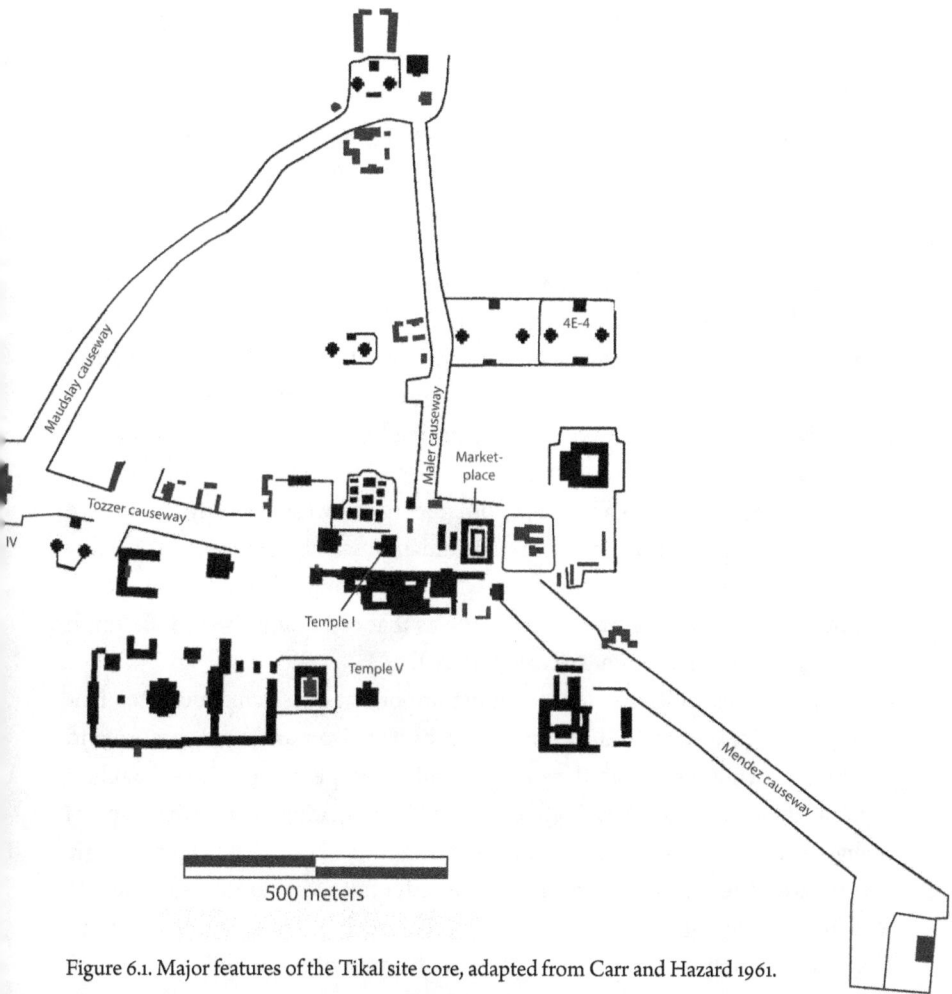

Figure 6.1. Major features of the Tikal site core, adapted from Carr and Hazard 1961.

Harrison (1994) has also shown that builders at Palenque used the right triangle planning principal. For example, nearly all of the most important buildings at the site form a perfect 3-4-5 Pythagorean triangle. The vertices of this triangle are the center points of the Temple of the Inscriptions, the Temple of the Foliated Cross, and the west structure of the North Group (structure VIII). The sides of this triangle pass through the long axis of the ballcourt, the northeast corner of the palace and the center points of the Temple of the Sun and the Temple of the Cross. Harrison has identified several other architectural arrangements at both Palenque and Tikal that could not have come together by chance. People at Chunchucmil may also have used this principal of site planning; I have identified eleven right triangles there using the center points of the temples in the eleven quadrangles closest to the site core. Each of these eleven temples is part of at least two right triangles. However, 165 triangles can be made from these eleven temples: is it merely coincidence that eleven of the 165 are right triangles? Without a clear understanding of the temporal and genealogical relationships between the builders of these temples, I cannot pursue such a planning principal any further for Chunchucmil.

The relations between the three kings and their temples (I, IV, and V) at Tikal highlight political relations in site planning. Ashmore and Sabloff (2002, 202) make the reasonable case that political relations among sites, along with ideational, social, environmental, economic, engineering, and historical factors, influenced planning principles. For example, the civic ceremonial core of Xunantunich has a north-south alignment that resembles that of Naranjo, located about 15 kilometers to the west. Since Naranjo's site core took shape slightly before that of Xunantunich and since one of the few texts from Xunantunich mentions the king of Naranjo, Ashmore and Sabloff conclude that Xunantunich's core emulates that of Naranjo (see M. E. Smith 2003 and 2005 for a critique of this pattern).

For the present discussion, the most important question about site planning principals such as those proposed by Harrison and by Ashmore and Sabloff is whether or not they actually attracted people to cities. Would a plaza aligned north-to-south appeal more to a migrating villager than a plaza aligned east-to-west? The fact that one temple makes a 3-4-5 right triangle with two others was important to the builder but were residents of the city aware of such a geometric relationship, especially if they were not present when the siting, construction, and/or dedication of the building occurred?

Although most vantage points in a city offer a view of at least one large pyramid, fewer vantage points allow a person to see each of the three temples that form a right triangle and it would have been almost impossible for a person to notice that they did so. If the esoteric details of city plans remained obscure to a visitor, the major built features of a city could have enticed people to stay if they reminded them of religious precincts at their home but on a larger scale. Expanding on this notion, Cynthia Robin has noted the similarities between stepped pyramids in city centers and the hillsides terraced by farmers (Robin 2013, 94).

Several other aspects of ancient Maya built environments may have been both attractive and perceptible to a pedestrian on the ground. The ways the Maya adorned temple pyramids and referred to them in texts made them significant places that people would desire to be near. Temple pyramids may have attracted people because the Maya built them as visually stunning god houses, places of creation, and world centers. Some temples could embody all three of these concepts at once. Several authors have recognized similarities between ancient Maya houses and the superstructures of pyramids, leading to the proposal that temples are the houses of gods (Andrews 1975, 12; Taube 1998; Wauchope 1938, 149–151). Classic and Postclassic period Maya texts use both the general term for dwelling—*nah*—and the more specific term for an occupied, possessed home—*otoot*—to refer to temples. Inscriptions at several cities list the specific gods that possessed particular houses or temples (Plank 2004; Stuart 1987, 33–39). Palenque again provides an excellent example: texts refer to the three temples of the Cross Group (the Temple of the Sun, the Temple of the Cross, and the Temple of the Foliated Cross) as the birthplaces and homes of the three gods of the Palenque Triad, gods GI, GII, and GIII (Houston 1996). Because these temples house gods, they serve as "pivotal links between the living and the divine" (Taube 1998, 427). Because of the nature of the relations of ancient Maya with gods, such pivotal linkages could have anchored dense populations. In other words, people stood to gain by living close to temples, and it is no surprise that large temples are almost always found at city centers. In addition, people who did not live in cities could visit temples as part of pilgrimages, an indication of the prestige temples gave to cities.

The Maya did not see supernatural entities—be they revered ancestors or the gods of the Palenque triad—as abstractions removed from daily life but as hungry, tangible beings entangled in the affairs of the community

(Houston 2013; Monaghan 2000; McAnany 2010). The Maya and their gods entered into covenants of mutual indebtedness and interdependency (Monaghan 2000). Based on their ethnographic work in Yucatan, Redfield and Villa Rojas (1962, 127) summarize this concept: "What man wins from nature, he takes from the gods." The gods give sustenance to humans, who in turn fed and cared for the gods (Becker 1993; Chuchiak 2009; Hutson 2015; Tedlock 1985). Gods who resided in a city's temples were important partners in the most basic undertakings and were therefore petitioned and pampered. At Palenque, people chose to crowd onto a terrace on the side of the mountain near the site core as opposed to settling on the ample plains that the city overlooked to the north. Did they do so because the temples on the terrace housed their most prominent gods?

Freidel, Schele, and Parker (1993; Schele 1998) and others (Taube 1998) elaborate on the notion that particular buildings in city centers were analogs of important places from Maya creation mythology. We know about Maya creation from a number of sources, including texts from the Classic period that describe the activities that took place on the first day of the calendrical cycle (August 13th, 3114 BC), oral histories that survived into the Spanish Colonial period (e.g. the Popol Vuh: Tedlock 1985), and Classic and Postclassic period depictions of creation myths, some of which are clearly related to known oral histories. One of the key places in creation mythology is the three-stone hearth. This is the first place the gods established on the first day of the Long Count calendar, and it symbolically marks the center of the world. Architectural compounds with three prominent buildings (e.g. triadic groups) and hearth-like censers placed at the center of temples have been identified as analogs of three-stone hearths and thus as spaces for the reenactment of creation. Schele (1998) argued that the most pervasive image from creation mythology is the creation mountain, a place where the first maize crop emerged. Iconography and epigraphy identify many temples in the Maya area as sacred mountains (Stuart 1987). These have been interpreted as places of both emergence and abundance (Taube 2004).

Researchers have interpreted buildings with quadripartite arrangements as both places of creation and as world centers. In the Maya creation myth from the Popol Vuh, the Maize God completes the creation of the universe by staking out the four corners and sides of a house. The Postclassic Madrid Codex depicts the world as having four directions and a center. The Maya understood the sky to be held up by a kind of cosmic house with four corner posts and a central axis created by a ceiba tree (Ashmore 1991; Coggins 1980; Freidel et al. 1993; Mathews and Garber 2004; Taube 1998). The ceiba tree in fact serves as a world tree, an axis mundi (Wheatley 1971) that connects all three of the major planes of the Maya cosmos: the underworld, the heavens, and, in the middle world, the earthly plain of the living. The notion of the four-cornered house as a model of the cosmos helps explain why the ancient Maya saw their houses as microcosms (Gillespie 2000) and why building and dedicating ancient houses reenacted creation and renewed the cosmos (Stuart 1998).

Quadripartite representations have been found in nearly all imaginable media (codices, pottery, carvings, stucco facades), at all scales (individual artifacts, arrangements of multiple artifacts, single buildings, layouts of multiple buildings), and in both elite and common contexts. In most cases, archaeologists have argued that the feature in question serves as a microcosmic image of a world with four corners and a center (Ashmore 1991; Coggins 1980; Estrada-Belli 2006; Fedick et al. 2012; Hutson and Welch 2014; Maca 2006; Mathews and Garber 2004; McAnany 1995; Rice 2006, 270–271; Robin 2002; Schele and Freidel 1990; Taube 1998; Tourtellot et al. 2002; Zaro and Lohse 2005). Group 4E-4 at Tikal is an exemplary quadripartite architectural compound (Ashmore 1991; Coggins 1980). Twin temples to the east and west mark the passage of the sun. The building to the north, which contains portraits of deceased kings, symbolizes the heavens, the place of ancestors. The building to the south, which has nine doorways, symbolizes the underworld, which has nine levels. One could go further: the north-south axis could be interpreted as the world tree conduit between underworld and heaven and the intersection of the north-south world tree axis with the east/west solar axis could invoke creation, though this specific interpretation has been discredited (Aveni 2009, 58). However, a more basic point is that leaders in the Maya area and throughout Mesoamerica built temples and other features in a way that would get people to see them as axes mundi and thus recognize the city where they were located as a holy space at the center of the world. Such a city would attract both settlers and visitors on pilgrimage. In cities with more settlers and visitors, kings had increased opportunities for gaining power and resources. People in small settlements also built/appropriated their own axes mundi, setting up the kinds of competition that are typical in weaker states (Demarest 2004, 216).

Freidel and Schele (1988; Schele and Freidel 1990) and others (Ashmore and Sabloff 2002; Demarest 1992; Taube 1998) have argued that Maya kings used temples and other aspects of the built environment to attempt to place themselves in the center of the world and become axes mundi. For example, Structure 5C-2nd, the earliest temple at Cerros, Belize, contains four massive posts at its summit and an iconographic program that represents the orbit of the sun and Venus. Freidel and Schele hypothesize that during ceremonies, the king, adorned with jewels that symbolized the three hearthstones of creation, would stand in the center of the four posts, which is also in the center of the celestial orbits; in that location, the king would become the axis mundi (Taube 1998). As Taube (1998) notes, the symbolic center of most houses could be a three-stone hearth, a substitute for the world tree. Taube's (1998, 466) study of temples in the southern Maya lowlands revealed that the hearth was a central motif of temple architecture: "As the vitalizing centers of temples, censers symbolized the basic three-stone hearth of the Maya household. Through the ritual process of focusing, censers constituted the house and seat of conjured gods." Taube's line of thought combines each of the three meanings of temples—god houses, places of creation, and world centers—that might have attracted people to Maya cities.

In sum, the spiritual freight of temple pyramids helped Maya kings give their cities a cosmic coherence. Much like what A. Smith (2003, 210) has documented for Mesopotamian cities, the interplay of gods, leaders, and temples made the urban landscape transcendent. It is clear that many non-elite households throughout Maya cities sanctified their own houses, performed their own centering rites, and revered their own ancestors (Blackmore 2011; Hutson et al. 2004; McAnany 1995). Leaders of small, non-urban centers also built sanctified spaces for interacting with the gods (Hutson and Welch 2014; Robin et al. 2012), and this fact goes some distance, I believe, in explaining why many people continued to live in smaller settlements, choosing only to visit cities instead of moving to them. However, the ability to live close to a much more elaborate god house and a much more elaborate axis mundi—hedging one's bets, so to speak—may have motivated some people to move to or stay in a city. Massive temples in ancient Maya cities attract tourists today. In the past, did these temples attract people who wanted to live near spaces that were so lofty that they enticed powerful gods to uphold their end of the covenants?

Beyond their allure as god houses, places of creation, and world centers, massive buildings may have attracted people because their lives intertwined with them (Joyce and Barber 2015; Hutson 2002, 66). Thousands of people provided the labor that built Maya temples, and because Maya leaders were not strong enough to coerce them, these laborers could decide not to contribute their time and resources (Pauketat 2000). In return for their labor, people may have received a variety of things: a feast or the comfort of knowing that their work went toward something that touted the strength of their own community or satisfied covenants with the gods. The important point is that the laborers may have felt a sense of ownership of the buildings because they helped build them (Hutson 2002; Lohse 2007, 16; McAnany 2010, 149–153). Parker Pearson and Richards (1994, 3) suggest that commoners may have recognized monumental constructions as products of their own labor or the labor of their ancestors and thus may have read the mounds as a celebration of their strength and collective will. The epigraph by Mumford at the top of this chapter conveys a sense of the satisfaction that may have been involved in making such claims to the grand landmarks of the city. From this perspective, monumental architecture welcomes its viewers, emphasizing a sense of unity and community integration (Burger 1992, 38) rather than merely exerting and maintaining authority (Trigger 1990). Living near such temples did not necessarily alienate people: it could have reminded them of their agency and kept them in the city.

Form as an Attraction of Built Space

Several art historians have commented on the attractiveness of the built form of ancient Maya cities. George Kubler (1961, 515) argued that Maya builders placed plazas in front of massive pyramids to create a "valuable experience" of place. Tatiana Proskouriakoff (1963, xvii) wrote that the Maya "produced architectural forms which can evoke in us an aesthetic response and which share with other, more familiar styles certain qualities of design and composition which seem to have universal validity." Adding to Kubler's comments on the conjuncture of pyramid and plaza, Andrews (1975, 7) argued that the combination of pyramid and plaza created "a suitable place for man to express his ideas of humanness and godliness in a setting apart from the jungle which surrounds and sustains him." He added, "this contrast between solid and void, or mass and plane, sets up a configuration that is truly monumental, a heroic form that dominates both man and nature alike." Kubler, Proskouriakoff, and Andrews (see also Miller 1999) all agree that builders planned Maya architecture in ways that would contribute positively to the allure of the city. More recent analysis examines how particular features such as symmetry, sharply cut moldings, recessed doorways, and negative batters (façades whose tops lean outward gently from the base) give specific buildings a visual effect that makes them aesthetically engaging (Kowalski 1987, 132–146).

These writers get at how people perceive and experience places without any reference to specific cultural meanings. When Andrews talks of "man," he seems to refer to a transcultural agent whose experiences are not shaped by a life embedded in any particular place. Likewise, Proskouriakoff's notion of universal validity suggests that architecture can evoke responses that have universal validity. Such an approach to architecture is not limited to those who study the ancient Maya. For instance, the internationally esteemed architect Le Corbusier suggested that people can respond emotionally to a setting without considering the meaning of that setting. Le Corbusier's (1986, 211) comments about the Parthenon exemplify this perspective: "Here is something to rouse the emotions. There are no symbols attached to these forms; they provoke definite sensation. There is no need of a key or order to understand them—brutality, intensity, the utmost sweetness, delicacy and great strength." In archaeology, phenomenological approaches (e.g. Tilley 1994) sometimes embrace a similar principle: a contemporary archaeologist's physical experience of Neolithic landscapes and monuments purportedly teaches us about the lived experience of people from many thousands of years ago. This statement implies that perception and emotion are universal things that are not affected by local customs, moralities, and world views. As I discuss below, there are some senses in which this sentiment rings true and can be leveraged for archaeological analysis. Yet it would be a mistake to use the bodily experience of a single archaeologist to support a conclusion about past experience.

There are other reasons to quarrel with universalist claims about experience. While sensation, experience, and emotion are critical for understanding cityscapes, they cannot be bracketed off from symbol, understanding, and meaning (Hodder 1999). Lewis Mumford (1961, 69) voiced this objection well: if we deprive buildings and monuments of the symbolism and sacred power discussed in the previous section, "the ancient city would have been only a heap of baked mud or stones, formless, purposeless, meaningless; since without such cosmic magnifications, the common man could live an equally good or even far better life in the village." Another potential problem with looking at built form in the absence of meaning is that it separates understanding from sensation, implying a Cartesian split between mind and body. Others have stressed that selfhood comes not just from thought (the mind) but also from a melding of mind, body, other objects, and other people (Heidegger [1927] 1996; Bourdieu 1977). Thus, understanding and sensation should go hand in hand.

Responding in part to critiques of universalist approaches to built environments, the social sciences took what has been called a "spatial turn" in the 1990s. As part of the spatial turn, anthropologists utilized and produced canonical texts about space and place (e.g., Lawrence and Low 1990; Lefebvre 1991; Tuan 1977) and began to recognize the importance of looking at built environments from localized perspectives of experience (A. Smith 2003). Archaeologists have begun to look at how ancient Maya people may have experienced their built environments (Houston and Taube 2000; Hutson 2010, 151; Meskell and Joyce 2003; Robin 2002), but few have systematically explored the question of how the form of ancient Maya cities might have struck their inhabitants as attractive, perhaps even drawing people to live in cities.

What other methods aid a study of how the ancient Maya experienced/ sensed/perceived the physical forms of their ancient cities? One possibility is to look at how the ancient Maya represented their built environments.

The Maya represented their built environments in a small corpus of paintings, graffiti, and sculptures that have survived and they wrote about certain kinds of buildings in hieroglyphic texts (Houston 1998a). However, these data do not provide much help in answering the question of whether cities were built to attract a broad range of people. Palace scenes dominate the corpus of ancient Maya representations of built space, in part because palaces were critical institutions in the eyes of the royals and nobles who commissioned and produced these representations. The most commonly depicted locales within the palace are inner recesses (for example, throne rooms) as opposed to stairways fronting a broad plaza. As Houston (1998a, 361) writes, "These are the most intimate views of all, for the location is inherently exclusive and the numbers of participants are few." The events, people, and regalia depicted in these scenes must have fascinated observers at the time just as they fascinate scholars, museum-goers, and collectors today. Although attractive, the scenes that the ancient Maya depicted in throne rooms would not have been accessible to most people in the city (cf. Inomata 2006b, 203).

Furthermore, the architectural details in palace scenes tell us little about the place of the palace in the cityscape or perceptions of the city at large. Nevertheless, a large corpus of colonial manuscripts, Classic period texts, and ethnographic material can aid our interpretation of ancient Maya sight, sound, and smell (Houston et al. 2006). Furthermore, the surveying and excavation of dozens of ruins has told us a quite a bit about the daily contexts that shaped the perceptions and habitus of the ancient Maya (Hendon 2010; Hutson 2010; Robin 2004). Because of this, we understand some of the dispositions that conditioned ancient Maya engagements with built environments. I will draw upon some of these dispositions in the analysis that follows.

A second approach to studying how ancient people experienced cities is to reconsider how the perception of form evokes affective response. When writers claim that a certain built form evokes a specific feeling, they often do not provide much support for the claim. For example, when Andrews writes that the conjuncture of pyramid and plaza evokes heroism and domination, it is not clear what data he has used to draw this conclusion. Andrews's claim reads like speculation. Yet there is now a wide body of research in the neurosciences and ecological psychology that suggests strong links between certain perceptual experiences and particular types of affective responses. Physical sensation and affective response are intertwined in such a way that built form can evoke meaningful responses without presuming a split between meaning/mind and sensation/body (Gibson 1966, 1979; Bermudez 1995; Butterworth 1995). Neuroscientists have produced empirical data that can help justify a claim for how the conjuncture of pyramid and plaza, for example, might have made an ancient person feel (Betz 2002; Moore 1996, 2005).

Virginia Betz (2002) has synthesized psychological research about how humans perceive built environments and converted this into a set of five characteristics that make cities inviting: salience, permeability, centricity, subordination, and ambiguity. The first three are relatively easy to discuss in the context of Maya cities and align well with three of the principles—landmarks, paths, and nodes—that, according to Lynch (1960), people use to understand their surroundings. Lynch's study offered two other principals: 1) districts, which are like neighborhoods and the other intermediate social units discussed in chapters 3 and 4; and, 2) edges, which, like shorelines, help establish easily perceived boundaries. Furthermore, Betz's principles of permeability and centricity are at the core of what has come to be known as

New Urban Design Theory, which attempts to harness the potential of public spaces "as integrative forces: locations where people can join together and create an atmosphere and identity of community beyond the home" (Peura-maki-Brown 2013, 579).

The approach I take in this section combines the concepts of salience, permeability, and centricity with native Maya understandings of space, as gleaned from archeology, epigraphy, ethnohistory, and ethnography. I hope to show not only that Maya cities exhibited these three attractive formal properties but that these properties would have resonated with the ancient Maya. Salience refers to features that are recognizably different from other settlement architecture. Contrasts created by salient features arouse perception and are therefore pleasurable (Betz 2002, 206; Lynch 2006). Monumental architecture is undeniably salient. Childe (1950, 12) included monumental architecture as one of the ten criteria that distinguish cities from other settlements (see also Trigger 1990). Maya temple pyramids certainly count as salient because they rise well above the surroundings and their solid mass greatly exceeds that of other buildings. Furthermore, as discussed in the previous section, the ancient Maya certainly saw temples as symbolically salient landmarks; as sacred mountains, homes of gods, and places of abundance. In flat parts of the Maya area, such as the northern Maya plains, home to Chichen Itza, Dzibilchaltun, Coba, and Chunchucmil, the natural ground surface is relatively flat, which means that high pyramids are prominent on the horizon and can be seen for kilometers. Maya pyramids therefore serve as landmarks in Lynch's (1960) sense: they help residents build an image of the city, which helps them orient themselves and feel more rooted in place.

Yet features can be salient without towering over the horizon. Causeways are good examples since walking on them would have been very different from walking on regular neighborhood pathways. For example, the pathways at Chunchucmil meander from side to side, whereas causeways run straight for hundreds of meters. In addition, most pathways were not built up: walking on them meant walking on the natural ground surface or, at most, a low surface of *chi'ich*. Walking on a causeway, however, elevated the pedestrian onto a level, smooth plaster surface. Thus, walking on a causeway contrasted sharply with the embodied dispositions inculcated by the much more common experience of walking along pathways.

Permeability refers to the impression that a built environment is accessible, that it is easy to get around the city. Permeability is less specific than

Hillier and Hanson's (1984) concept of accessibility, which focuses on comparing which particular spaces, such as rooms in a house, require an individual to cross the smallest number of intervening spaces to get to. The distinction between permeability and accessibility is slight but important. A very open city plan with few distinct paths is very accessible but might have too much freedom to create a sense of comfort. The kind of plan that is inviting and arousing should have clear-cut paths that simplify the choices available to a pedestrian (Betz 2002, 217–231; Lynch 1960). The paths should also be bounded, thus keeping a person on the path and making the choice between paths clear. Paths that align with a landmark at the end, such as a temple pyramid, create a sense of directionality that can heighten the impression of the path space. In the Yucatec Maya language, the root *b'eh*, which means road or path, has extensive associations, ranging from the physical paths underfoot to one's general state of being (Hanks 1990, 312). One of the first expressions that native speakers learn is "how is your road?," which is equivalent to "how are you doing?" Hieroglyphic texts from the Classic period reveal that this same root had the same set of valences (path/road in both physical and metaphorical senses) for the ancient Maya (Stuart 2006). Thus, the notion that clear paths make a city inviting does in fact resonate with Maya senses of self and place.

Causeways found at the largest Maya cities appear to have made those cities exceptionally permeable. More than one archaeologist has expressed the point that leaders designed Maya cities to "facilitate traffic and permit gatherings of large groups, thereby embracing and encompassing populations at an experiential level" (Lohse 2007, 17–18; see also Ashmore 1991). For example, Chunchucmil, Dzibilchaltun, Coba, Caracol, and Chichen Itza each had a system of causeways that gave their residents clearly defined pathways into and out of the site core (figures 4.4, 6.2). Large pyramids often stand at the termini of these causeways, punctuating the view and enhancing communicative potential (Moore 1996, 101). At Coba, Chunchucmil, and Chichen Itza, causeways intersect and connect with each other in ways that give pedestrians choices (but not more than three at a time) of where to proceed. On special occasions, causeways served as sacred avenues for ritual processions (Freidel et al. 1993). At other times they served as conduits for everyday foot traffic (Folan 1991; Shaw 2008, 107). At Chunchucmil, pathways bounded by stone alignments fed to causeways. Although many of the major pathways are like spokes on a wheel, these paths afforded pedestrians a variety of choices:

they had many spurs that branched off them, and in some areas (such as spoke cluster 14) they split into subsidiary spokes. At a site such as Tikal or Palenque we have no way of identifying path networks beyond the site core, but there must have been distinct paths, marked by perishable materials or simply worn into the ground surface, that directed people to common destinations. Colonial manuscripts from across the Maya area describe a variety of pathways, both within settlements and between settlements, that were not built of stone and are therefore invisible to archaeologists (Bolles and Folan 2001; Shaw 2008, 82–83).

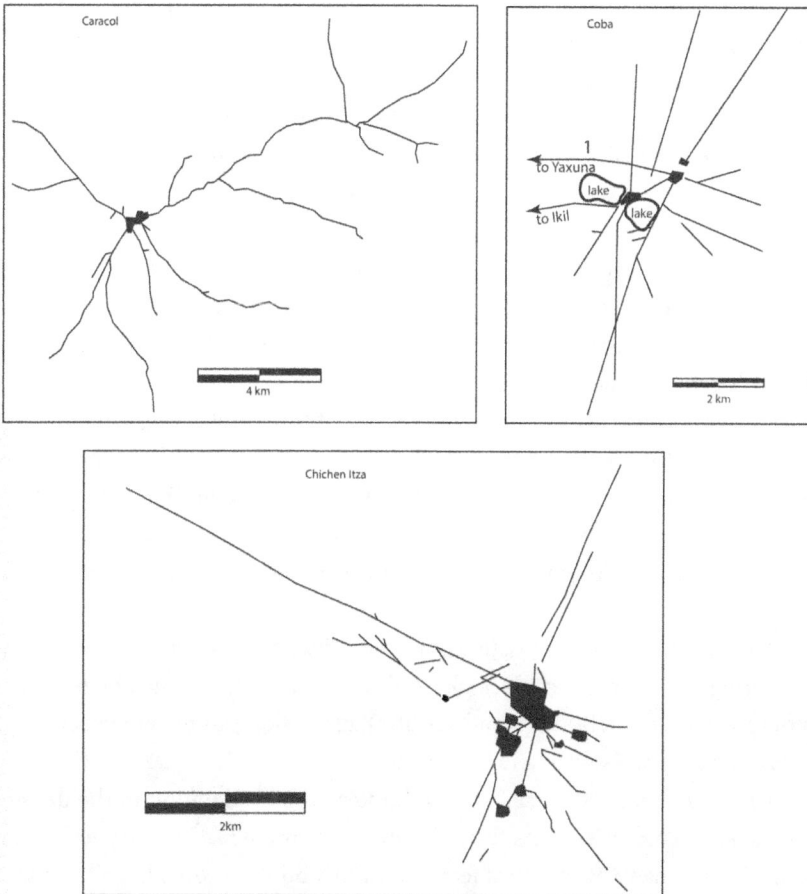

Figure 6.2. Causeway systems extending out from the site cores of Caracol, Coba, and Chichen Itza. Black polygons represent plazas and/or major architecture. Adapted from Chase et al. 2011, Folan 1983, Folan et al. 2009, and Cobos and Winemiller 2001.

Centricity means having nodes that accommodate many people and are easy to get to (Lynch 1960). Locations where people can congregate and see thousands of others can give people a sense of being part of a larger community and provide opportunities for cultivating an esprit de corps. Spaces where large crowds can gather and mingle may also make urban centers attractive. For plazas to succeed as desirable nodes, they should be big enough that a large portion of the city's residents can fit in them (Betz 2002, 252–262). Yet plazas should not be too big (Betz 2002, 223). For the Classic Maya, the scope of vision coincided with the human eye's natural field of view (Houston 2006, 140–141). Plazas should therefore be bounded and not extend beyond what is visible from a single vantage point, usually that of a high-status person on the plaza's edge. On the basis of an analysis of plazas at Copan, Tikal, and Aguateca, Inomata (2006a, 818) has argued that "securing sufficient spaces for public events was a primary concern in the design of Maya cities." He demonstrates that the main plazas of Copan and Aguateca were built large enough to fit the entire population of these cities. For example, Aguateca's main plaza, which covers 1.15 hectares, could have hosted all of the site's estimated 8,000 residents, presuming one square meter of space per person. As a city grew, what was once a centrally located plaza may no longer have been able to serve the entire population. In these cases, we might find several plazas that, taken together, could have accommodated the entire population of the city plus visitors. Tikal fits this pattern. The size of the Great Plaza, bounded on the north by the North Acropolis and on the south by Central Acropolis, was significantly reduced when ruler Jasaw Chan K'awiil built Temples I and II. However, when the next ruler built temples IV and VI, he included substantial paved open spaces in front of them. Inomata's (2006a, 818) point is that when a large portion of a city's population has the space to assemble, they can "witness and sense the bodily existence and participation of other members." This gathering and witnessing gives physical reality to a community, helping the polity see itself as a body (a body politic) and making an imagined community real (see also Golden and Scherer 2013).

The notion that centricity was an important consideration in the design of ancient Maya cities gains further support from the fact that beyond Tikal and Copan, many other cities featured in this book—Coba, Dzibilchaltun, Caracol, Chunchucmil, and Palenque—have plaza spaces that were large enough to fit most residents (figure 6.3). Cities such as Chunchucmil and Dzibilchaltun resemble Tikal in the sense that they lacked a single space large

enough to hold their entire respective populations but had several intercon-
nected spaces that, taken together, could have accommodated everyone. As
discussed in chapter 4, even though all of Chunchucmil's ceremonial plazas
are smaller than 1 hectare, taken together these plazas could have accommodated everyone in the city. At Dzibilchaltun (figure 6.3), the interlinked

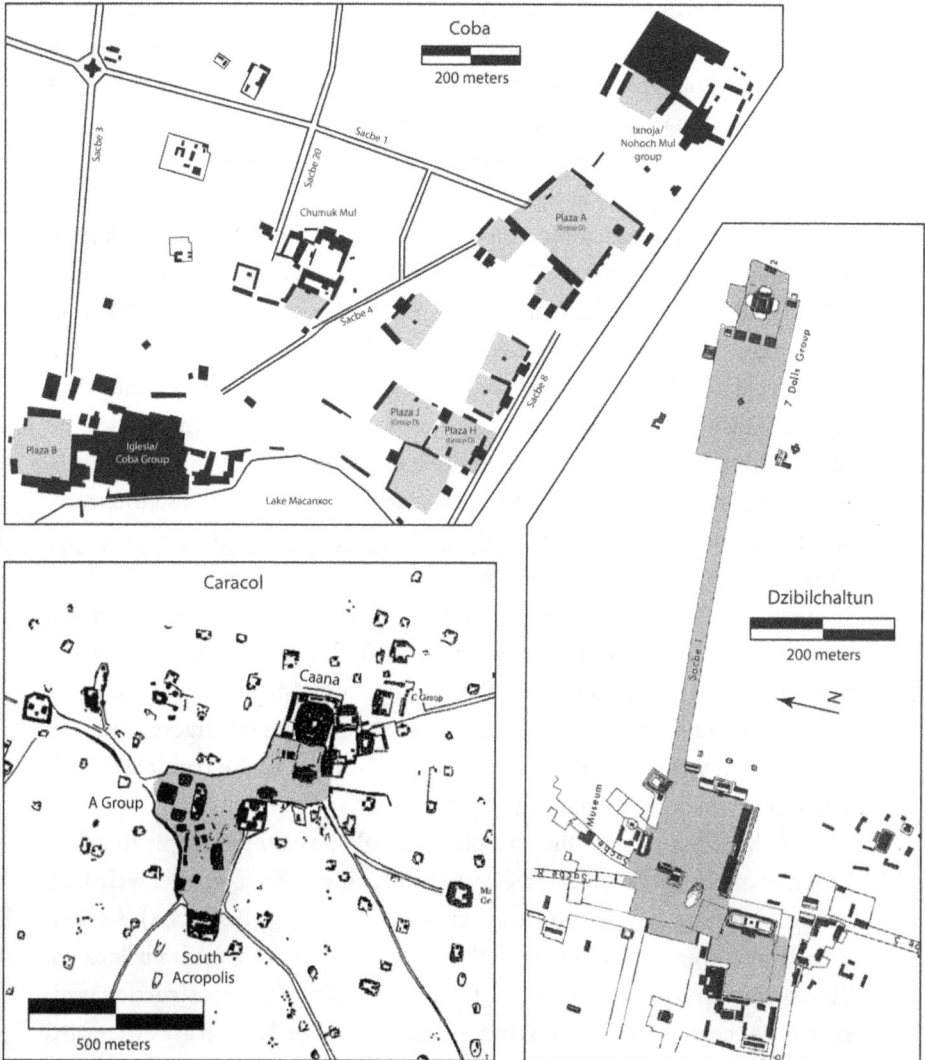

Figure 6.3. Plazas (in gray) at the sites of Coba (*top*; adapted from Graham and von Euw 2004), Caracol (*lower left*; reproduced with permission from Chase and Chase 2001), and Dzibilchaltun (*lower right*; adapted from Stuart et al. 1979).

central and south plazas cover 3 hectares and are linked by a 400-meter-long causeway to the 2-hectare plaza in front of the Temple of the Seven Dolls. Everyone at Dzibilchaltun could have fit in these three spaces. Palenque (figure 2.4) resembles Copan in that it has a single, albeit complex, space that could have held most people. In the hilly terrain at Caracol, builders created a level terrace that integrated the site's central Late Classic architectural nodes (Caana, the South Acropolis, the A Group, etc.) and has about 5 hectares of plaza space. The terrace is irregular in shape and should be conceived of as a series of overlapping plazas rather than a single plaza. Although Caracol's central terrace may have been too small to hold the entire population (estimated at over 100,000), the site has many other spaces where people could gather, such as the plazas at the ends of the causeways.

Coba appears to resemble Copan in the sense that it has an artificially flattened terrace—the Gran Nivelación—that could hold everyone. But on closer examination, Coba is more like Tikal and Chunchucmil. The Gran Nivelación covers at least 64 hectares (Graham and von Euw 2004; Navarrete et al. 1979). This terrace is by far the largest in the Maya area and is not bounded by walls or buildings. From most vantage points on the terrace the edges cannot be seen. Though centrally located, the terrace fails to cultivate a desirable sense of centricity. An open space with little focus and too many choices for movement, it would not have been attractive (Betz 2002:223) and was out of line with the ancient Maya preference for plazas that could be fully scanned from a single vantage point (Houston 2006, 140). Yet the terrace supports a dozen plazas, five of which range from 1 to 3 hectares in size and therefore could have hosted tens of thousands of people. Not all plazas were built at the same time (Navarrete et al. 1979), and the two largest groups of monumental architecture (the Iglesia/Coba Group and the Ixnoja/Nohoch Mul group) do not have the largest plazas.

To enhance the lure of the city, plazas should be easy for people to get to. When plazas are accessible and easy to reach, cities offer a warmer welcome, giving the feeling that people are integrated with the city (Betz 2002). Ancient Maya plazas were easy to get to in the sense that they were centrally located. They were purposefully planned as components of massive construction projects in site cores (Ringle and Bey 2001, 279). Ancient Maya plazas were also easy to get to in the sense that they had many clear routes leading to them and multiple entrances. Axial analysis can be used to quantify these routes (Hillier 2002). Morton and coauthors (2012, 2014) have applied this type of analysis to cities such as Copan and Teotihuacan, but the results—that the Principal Group at Copan and the Street of the Dead at Teotihuacan are well integrated with their respective cities—do not add much to what could be inferred by a glance at site maps. The site maps of Coba, Chichen Itza, and Caracol show that causeway systems integrated central plazas with the rest of these cities. The combination of spokes and causeways accomplished the same task at Chunchucmil. Copan's Principal Group has broad entrances on the east and west sides and the causeway in the densely settled Sepulturas area to the east of the plaza feeds directly to the plaza's east entrance. Tikal is an interesting case because unlike Coba or Caracol, only one of its causeways (the Mendez Causeway to the southeast) extends well beyond the site core. Nevertheless, the nearly equilateral triangle formed by the Maler, Maudslay, and Tozzer causeways creates spatial order and integration just as much as it creates a viable transportation loop (Pollock 1965, 412). Betz (2002, 320) argues that although the topography of hills and *bajos* provided a challenge for the city's planners, the site layout and reservoir network show that "the administrators of Tikal were surely interested in making all inhabitants feel a part of the urban fabric" (see also Peuramaki-Brown 2013, 578–579).

In sum, temple-pyramids, plazas, causeways, and other paths gave Maya cities salience, permeability, and centricity. Palaces are another important component of Maya cities (Inomata and Houston 2000; see below). Though the activities that took place in them (presentation of tribute, reception of important visitors) were important to the city-state as a whole, many palaces, such as the palace at Palenque (Miller 1998), highlight the power of the ruler. To the extent that a ruler served as a barometer of the vitality of the city and to the extent that the city's success was based in part on relations of trust between sovereign and subject (Golden and Scherer 2013), that ruler and, by association, the palace, could have been a magnet that attracted people to the city (Houston et al. 2003). Alternatively, some people may have been put off by palaces like that of Palenque, whose inner courtyard contains sculptures portraying the ruler's brutal domination of cowering captives (Joyce and Winter 1996). Palaces do not figure in my discussion of salience, permeability, and centricity simply because the rooms inside them would normally have been off limits to most of the people that a city might attract. However, some palaces did have a more public face. At Palenque and Tikal, broad palace stairways spilled onto large plazas. I now turn to the spectacles, some of which were orchestrated from the palace steps, observed by those who filled these plazas.

Ceremonies

If the size and position of plazas helped integrate city dwellers into a community, what transpired in plazas may have attracted people to cities in the first place. Several Mayanists have argued that elaborate ceremonies that were performed for large audiences were held in plazas (Demarest 1992; Fash 1998; Looper 2001; Lucero 2007). Inomata (2006a) summarizes several lines of evidence that back these claims. Many contact-era manuscripts document the use of plazas for mass spectacles, and data from the Classic period also support this usage (see also Houston 2006). For example, the murals of Bonampak depict, among other things, dance, music, and presentations of captives on a wide stairway that Miller (1986, 15) identifies as the stairway fronting Bonampak's main plaza. Many plazas in the southern lowlands contain carved stela that depict rulers sumptuously adorned in jade, shell, and feathers, dancing and celebrating a variety of rites. Grube (1992) makes the case that these stelae commemorate rites that took place in the plazas that host the stelae, and Inomata (2006a) points to Tokovinine's identification of a glyph that suggests these rites were meant to be viewed. Furthermore, the large size of headdresses, staffs, and other accoutrements of office worn/ wielded in stela and murals rule out the possibility that such ceremonies took place in other important venues such as the insides of palaces or caves. These rites and ceremonies celebrated and or/sanctified a broad variety of events, none of which were mutually exclusive: the completion of calendrical cycles, the dedication of buildings and other objects, the veneration of ancestors, the reenactment of creation myths, milestones in the lives of leaders (accession, marriage, warfare, death), and more.

Who was in the audience for the ceremonies that took place in broad plazas? Crowds of thousands gathered for ceremonies in Colonial period plazas (Inomata 2006b, 192–3). The Bonampak murals depict dozens of people attending ceremonies in the main plaza. Many of the people depicted (rulers, dancers, musicians, captives) were performers. If the identities of the people participating in ceremonies depicted in images are any indication of the composition of the audience, then the participation of women in ceremonies at places such as Bonampak and Yaxchilan (see also Joyce 1996) suggests that both men and women were in the audience. Landa (Tozzer 1941, 152) wrote that young women were excluded from some ceremonies. I find no compelling reason to suggest that children were not present. According to Landa, some ceremonies explicitly featured boys and girls. Insofar as authorities were invested in indoctrinating children with state ideologies (Ardren 2006; Joyce 2000b), youths would have been a critical and impressionable audience whose attendance was likely encouraged. Who would have cared for young children at home if so many people were at the plaza?

The exquisite details and diversity in costumes, the accompaniment of a variety of musicians, the riveting actions performed during rites (dance, ballgames, bloodletting, human sacrifice), and the staging on or in front of massive buildings abutting the plazas highlighted the theatricality of these ceremonies. Master builders planned these stages in a way that manipulated acoustics to the greatest effect (Houston and Taube 2000, 281). The symbolic meanings of the temple pyramids that formed the stage likely further contributed to the ideological message of the performance

Ceremonies in cities often left the plazas and pyramids, taking the form of processions along causeways. Based on evidence from ethnohistorical documents, we know that at least some pre-Hispanic Maya processions involved priests and nobles moving deity images and other sacred substances from city centers to peripheral areas and back (Ardren 2014; M. Coe 1965; Shaw 2008; Vail and Hernandez 2013). Other processions involved scores of warriors, each of whom was dressed and adorned distinctively, parading their captives, who were often naked but occasionally were arrayed in dazzling attire (as at Chichen Itza) in visually rich ceremonies (Schele and Freidel 1990, 365–371). While causeways in Preclassic and Classic period sites usually connected different temples, they also connected temples with noble and/or royal residences (Ringle 1999; Shaw 2008). Processions put elaborate costumes and items on display, creating spectacles that enriched the experience of city life. Processions likely occurred in smaller settlements beyond cities, but these settlements usually lack causeways. Causeways provide an elevated stage for processions, adding to the theatricality of performances in cities.

A final attraction of large performances in cities is that people may have enjoyed the sense of community that comes from assembling with others en masse. Prior to devices of mass communication such as newspapers, large gatherings were some of the only opportunities for city dwellers to see that they were a part of a group that was much larger than the network of people they knew personally. Assemblies of thousands allowed people to imagine and cultivate a broader urban identity (Anderson 1991; Ardren 2015). Yet this was not the only attraction of large crowds. Ceremonies in plazas are places of multiplicity, of loosely structured and chance interactions between both strangers and friends. People at ceremonies could share information, catch up on gossip, find mates, gaze at distinctive others, and exchange goods. Such interactions were not merely entertaining. They also allowed for the expansion of social networks, which could then have resulted in access to a variety of resources (Kadushin 2012, 6, 162; Putnam 2000). Thus, multiplicity promotes the expansion of social capital. Unexpected encounters and juxtapositions that come from the assembly of crowds can be the stimulus for innovations and other kinds of change (Hannerz 1980; Mumford 1961, 96). Although it is difficult to measure such transformations in ancient cities, commentators on modern cities note the positive scaling of productivity and other measures in urban centers (Bettencourt 2007; Glaeser 2011; Jacobs 1969). Research in cities of pre-Hispanic of the Basin of Mexico suggests the same positive scaling of productivity for ancient Mesoamerica (Ortman et al. 2014, 2015).

Demarest (1992) has argued that theatrical performances were the principal means by which Classic period leaders recruited supporters. But did all people accept such carefully choreographed and impressively delivered messages? Spectators might have recognized that the state drew its power precisely from these spectacles and may therefore have not been enchanted by the pageantry. The exotic attire of the rulers might have reminded some spectators of the massive gulf in wealth and power between the ruler and themselves (Geertz 1980, 123; Joyce et al. 2001). Mayanists have recognized the important role the audience plays in political theater (Houston 2006; Inomata 2006a, 2006b; Lucero 2007). How an audience reacts to a spectacle could lead performers to change aspects of the ceremony. Because the audience can make judgements about the quality or effectiveness of a performance, spectacles are risky; they may fail to convince everyone in the audience of the legitimacy of authority. In the Maya context, the result in such a case would have been a loss of support for the state. People who were skeptical about state ceremonies may nevertheless have been lured by the sheer theatricality of the performance and the possibility of critiquing it.

When state-sponsored spectacles are also holy matters, not all people participate skeptically. Many participants in rituals in the Maya world today sincerely believe in the religious efficacy of ritual performances, whether such performances seek to revere an ancestor; sanctify a person, thing, or relation; petition for good health or good fortune; or feed a sacred being. People take away something meaningful from the experience. Did common farmers among the ancient Maya understand the theological details of religious performances? Finds from Classic period sites in Belize suggest that modest farmers not only understood details of Maya cosmology but created sacred microcosms on their own (Lohse 2007). For example, Robin (2002) has excavated a quadripartite cache of cobbles in a modest rural residence at Chan, Belize, and Zaro and Lohse (2005) have excavated a non-elite architectural group with a quadripartite layout that marks the solstice and zenith passages near Blue creek, Belize.

The religious practices documented at Chan and Blue Creek not only reiterate the cosmological sophistication of people outside of cities (Lucero 2003; McAnany 1995), they also remind us that rural life could be completely independent of cities. My argument about city ceremonies is not that they satisfied a basic need that could not be fulfilled elsewhere but that they satisfied this need quite differently, offering a spiritual and social life that was more striking and attractive. Built form was a huge part of this. Stages in cities placed theatrical performances on the grandest of scales and drew crowds large enough to be a part of the attraction. The only other venue that drew such crowds in Mesoamerican cities was the marketplace.

Marketplaces

Chapters 1 and 2 presented some of the economic attractions of marketplaces. They make exchange more efficient by providing a space where buyers can find a diverse array of goods and where sellers can find a critical mass of buyers. This obviates the need for buyers and sellers to travel very far to complete their transactions. Marketplaces also help people provision their households. In addition, as an outlet for exchanging surpluses, marketplaces provide an incentive for household members to specialize in crafts and increase surplus production. The best-documented marketplaces are at large cities such as Tikal, Calakmul, and Chunchucmil. Although people living beyond these cities could access these marketplaces, living within the city increased efficiency for both producers and consumers, buyers and sellers. Thus, marketplaces draw people to cities (Ardren 2015, chapter 2). Whereas these attractions of marketplaces tend toward the economic, in this section I approach marketplaces from a social standpoint. In particular, I will argue that marketplaces provided those who visited them with a socially and sensually attractive experience.

When the Spaniards finally established control over parts of the Maya lowlands, they encountered Maya society at a nadir both politically and economically, given the fragmentation of the Mayapan confederacy in the previous century and a variety of droughts and famines (Masson and Freidel 2013). There were no large marketplaces such as the ones that the Spaniards found in Tenochtitlan/Tlatelolco, the thriving Aztec capital, and they left few details about Maya marketplaces in the ethnohistorical sources. The scene was quite different during the Classic period. The marketplace at Tikal, located in the East Plaza in the heart of the city, consisted of a complex of long, low gallery buildings. Jones (1996), who excavated the galleries, estimates a total of 310 doorways and argues that each doorway served as the front of a marketplace stall. The complex was built at the beginning of the eighth century during the reign of Jasaw Chan K'awiil, when Tikal was at its political and demographic zenith. When complete, the marketplace covered approximately 1 hectare. The marketplace at Calakmul, the Chiik Nahb complex, was twice as large as the Tikal market, covering slightly over 2 hectares (Carrasco et al. 2009). Murals on Structure 1 in the marketplace depict assorted vendors. These murals date to the seventh century though the structure's three subsequent remodelings and associated ceramics suggest that the complex was in use at least until the middle of the ninth century. Like Tikal's marketplace, Calakmul's marketplace is located in the very center of the city, about 100 meters north of the central plaza. It consists of a roughly square elevated plaza (the Chiik Nahb Acropolis) and over 100 low buildings arranged in ten north-south rows plus a row running east-west from Structure 1. Chunchucmil's marketplace, which dates to the fifth and sixth centuries AD, consists of an artificially raised plaza covering 1.5 hectares (Dahlin et al. 2007). Dahlin, who identified rock alignments on the plaza, argued that they were vending stalls. He supported this argument with soil chemistry data and distributional and contextual evidence (Dahlin et al. 2010; Hutson et al. 2010). Over 500 stalls could have fit in Chunchucmil's marketplace, which is located in the heart of the site center at a confluence of causeways.

Although data from these three sites say little about what it would have been like to experience a large, central marketplace, ethnohistorical descriptions of the Tlatelolco marketplace by Spanish observers can fill us in (see Hutson 2000 and citations therein regarding the veracity of the ethnohistorical sources). Tlatelolco and its neighbor Tenochtitlan were bustling cities when Cortes and the Spanish conquistadors first set foot in them in 1519.

The Tlatelolco marketplace astounded Bernal Diaz del Castillo (1956, 217), one of Cortes' soldiers, not only by its size but also by the variety of goods for sale. Many people went to the market just to see what was sold. Others went to the market not so much for the goods but for the people. Clendinnen (1991, 147–148) drew attention to the possibility that the social excitement of the market was its main draw: like any other "large, promiscuous social gathering" the Aztec market "exercised a powerful attraction over its habitués." There was gossip, socializing, strolling. Spaniards recorded natives finding great pleasure, gratification, and contentment in a visit to the market (Durán 1951, 2:216–217; Torquemada 1943, 556). Authorities at marketplaces helped ensure the fairness of transactions, yet social norms were not policed, lending the marketplace the flavor of a carnival, a world upside down. A variety of spectacles took place at the marketplace: slaves performing, slaves attempting to escape, executions of thieves, foreigners with distinctive clothing, and buffoonery with bodily humor. Young men and women caroused and flirted (Durán 1951, 1:256). Durán (1951, 2:216–217) suspected that if a Nahua woman were given the choice of going straight to heaven or to the market, she would go to the market first simply to stroll around and satisfy her appetite for ribaldry.

Ethnohistorical sources suggest that people of different status approached each other on the same footing at marketplaces (Hutson 2002). As Simmel (1950) has noted, markets are democratic in the sense that they allow the relaxation of hierarchical status differences (Poggi 1993); currency and established standards of value rather than relations of kinship or patronage govern the exchange of goods. To the extent that official Aztec state ideologies downplayed the status of women (Brumfiel 1996), the marketplace was an arena where such gender inequalities could be contested. Among commercial guilds, men did long distance-trading while women worked in the market as vendors and administrators. Although it is sometimes remarked that women who worked in markets were poor (Brumfiel 1991), women could become prosperous in the market (Sahagún 1950–1982, book 4, 2), and as administrators, they could control some aspects of its development.

The Tlatelolco marketplace, in sum, was an exemplary site of multiplicity. People of diverse walks of life intermingled among diverse products for sale, creating an exciting space that drew large crowds. I cannot say whether or not the Classic period Maya markets were as entertaining, stimulating, and liberating as the ones described for Central Mexico, but they certainly could have been (see also Houston 2014). Like the Tlatelolco marketplace, which handled thousands of people at a time, the marketplaces at Tikal, Calakmul, and Chunchucmil were each quite large and could easily have accommodated 1,000 people. The murals in the Calakmul marketplace depict both women and men selling various goods, implying that the marketplace featured social diversity. Wurtzburg (2015) argues that like Aztec women, Maya women played important roles at marketplaces.

Markets were also attractive to elites. Maya leaders would have wanted to attract as many people as possible to their marketplaces. Although marketplaces may have been unruly in a social sense, they served as locales in which authorities could "communicate to the population a great variety of state values and goals" (Kurtz 1974, 696). Authorities could also use markets as a place to convert tribute into other desired goods (Masson and Freidel 2012). Large markets in central Mexico also brought prestige to city leaders (Blanton 1996). Elites likely benefited from sponsoring markets in many ways and may have sought to improve them by making them safe, policing against dishonesty, recruiting vendors, and having trash removed (Pyburn 2008; Hirth 2010, 238).

Centers Accommodate People

In this chapter I have touched on how people shape cities by electing to help build monuments. I have also discussed how people shape cities less literally by participating in large performances. These possibilities for seeing that one's own input can make a difference are part of the lure of cities. In considering the city's appeal to ordinary inhabitants, M. L. Smith (2006, 109) has proposed "that the workings of urban centers were the product of negotiation, compromise, and consensus among many different individuals and groups." Joyce and Weller (2007, 160) note that at the end of the Classic period, ceremonial precincts at cities such as Caracol and Xunantunich became less accessible to common people. The negotiations and compromises that led to these spatial restrictions likely endangered a broader sense of integration and community. In contrast, Hammond (1972, 88) notes that key ceremonial features at Lubaantun, such as the ballcourt, became more accessible to the populace over time. At Tikal, new spaces emerged as older ones shrank (Inomata 2006a). These transformations underscore a point that was central to the school of urban sociologists headed by Robert Park at the University of Chicago: cities are in process, always shifting (Hannerz 1980, 55). Archaeologically, this means that cities will be palimpsests. In this section, I discuss some of the ways that people from different social spheres worked together to shape residential areas.

Admittedly, some residential areas in ancient Maya cities look disorderly. This has given some writers the notion that builders in ancient Maya cities such as Tikal followed a plan only in the epicenter (Smith 2007, 27). The archaeological record as palimpsest might partially explain the disorder: ancient streets shifted over time in places such as Babylon (Keith 2003, 63). I contend, however, that even when the evidence of planning looks blurry, people in dense cities such as Palenque must have cooperated quite a bit in order to successfully and sustainably share limited resources such as land and water (Barnhart 2001, 106). The point to keep in mind is that only some kinds of planning, specifically those that feature repetitive patterns, such as a grid, are easy to detect (Betz 2002, 38). Moving away from the planned/ unplanned dichotomy (Smith 2007, 4–5), we need to search for other kinds of planning: the kind of decentralized, bottom-up processes that Smith (2011, 179) refers to as generative planning. Chunchucmil presents an excellent example of this kind of planning.

At Chunchucmil, the stone walls that served as the boundaries of the pathways through the city also served as the edges of house lots. Having a clearly marked path to the site core was in everyone's interests in a particular spoke cluster, but delineating that path also meant impinging on the land of some households. For example, widening a path by moving each of the path's two parallel boundary walls a meter further from each other meant taking away a meter-wide strip of land from the house lots on either side of the path. Settling such an issue required negotiation and compromise between neighbors (Magnoni et al. 2012, 328). Research on house lots at Chunchucmil (Hutson et al. 2007) shows that occupants used the spaces along the edges of the lots for gardening, among other things. Robin (2006) has built a compelling case that ancient Maya women participated in house lot gardening. This means that neighborhood negotiations about which spaces should be sacrificed for the common good likely involved both women and men. Thus, a large swath of society was impacted by planning decisions. If broader impact implies broader involvement, households could have had a high degree of commitment to neighborhood affairs and a significant investment in the welfare of the city.

High settlement density makes these issues of spatial planning, including questions of where to excrete human waste and what to do with garbage, much more common in cities than in villages. Although such matters can be delicate, working through them promotes a sense of identity and attachment (Peuramaki-Brown 2013). We can imagine other projects (the construction of a causeway, for example) that cut across neighborhoods and engaged central authorities requiring bottom-up and top-down initiatives in order to reach agreement. In addition to planning, life in cities required communal maintenance projects. The pathways at Chunchucmil, for example, had dirt surfaces upon which weeds grew every year and needed to be cut. Big storms would have required cleanup. This would also have been the case at other cities as well. Contact-era dictionaries from a variety of Maya languages contain several terms for sweeping and pathways, suggesting that such maintenance was also common in earlier Maya cities (Bolles and Folan 2001). Such matters probably invited coordination and cooperation across households. Although challenging, these kinds of enterprises likely gave city residents a sense of being part of something much larger than themselves, and in this manner, they participated in city life in ways that are similar to the ways the quote in the epigraph describes.

Conclusion

This chapter has focused on why ancient Maya chose to live in cities. In addition, many of the themes in this chapter touched on how Maya rulers acquired and maintained power. The two processes were closely related: rulers could govern more efficiently when more people moved to cities or when a large portion of the city-state lived in the city. The major buildings of a city helped Maya rulers gain renown. By linking themselves with these god houses and places of creation, rulers attempted to embody core cosmological principles (Demarest 1992).

I have argued that the symbolism of architecture plays a key role in attracting people to cities. Given the close, tangible relations the ancient Maya felt with their deities, living closer to the major buildings of the site core would have been desirable, since these structures were built as god houses and places of creation. Rural residents could have visited these temples and derived benefit from them without necessarily living in the city. The fact that so many Maya people remained in the countryside substantiates the view that rural life was viable, attractive, and complex in its own ways (Yaeger and Robin 2004).

I have also argued that the form and configuration of the built features— pyramids, plazas, and causeways—within cities also made cities inviting. When these features were arrayed in ways that promoted salience, permeability, and centricity, they promoted a positive image of the city that many residents likely shared. They also make cities stimulating environments and help cultivate a sense of belonging and community. Although the concepts of salience, permeability, and centricity were derived independently of details from the ancient Maya world, they align with Maya understandings of built features such as pathways, plazas, and temples.

One of the most attractive features of plazas is that when mass spectacles took place in them, there was great potential for chance encounters between people of widely different backgrounds. Marketplaces also provided an excellent venue for these kinds of encounters. Thus, when successfully designed, cities could bring out the potential for multiplicity, the fortuitous rendezvous that enlarge social networks and add zest to life. Villages lack this. If the diversity in dress and adornment seen in the murals of Bonampak or the carvings at the Temple of the Warriors at Chichen Itza (Schele and Freidel 1990, 365, 371) are fair indications of the variety in styles of dress within a city, such variety would have made events where large crowds gather (ceremonies, markets) even more alluring. In many ways, then, cities pulled people in from the countryside. Cities, of course, were not unaffected by the people that moved to them. I have argued that people played active roles in shaping cities, both in generating spatial organization and disorganization in residential areas and in providing labor and resources for the largest constructions at the site core. These buildings, and the broader city of which they are a part, exist only because of compromises between leaders and followers.

7

Conclusions and Contributions

> Given the lack of resources to compel residence in a center
> of concentrated population and the potential disadvantages
> of city life, the key to success of cities must lie in the social
> aspects and the way in which they are configured by different
> and often competing groups.
>
> M. L. Smith (2003, 2)

Inspired by this epigraph, this book builds on the premise that ancient Maya people chose whether or not to live in cities. Only in quite limited circumstances could ancient Maya rulers compel people to move away from the countryside. That many people lived in rural settlements indicates that living beyond cities was a choice many favored. Those who lived in cities must have thought the attractions of city life outweighed the disadvantages. Although leaders may have lacked the power to compel people to move to cities, it was in their interest to expend effort to convince people to do so. Because city residents could vote with their feet and move back to the countryside (Inomata 2004), leaders had to invest in the city continuously. Cities do more than serve people from across the social spectrum; they exist because of the choices that humble farmers, exalted lords, and others in between make.

A broad group of authors have laid claim to social archaeology (Meskell and Preucel 2004; Renfrew 1973). Despite the debates that have emerged among these researchers, social archaeology does not lack enduring principles. My take on cities conforms to what I believe is a central principle of social archaeology: that past events (construction episodes, ceremonies, crafting, migration) were the outcome of decisions made by people who, using substantial but imperfect knowledge of their interests and the consequences of following those interests, had some degree of choice in the face of demands other actors and tradition imposed on them.

A significant part of this book has focused on the social aspects of cities. These aspects encompass a wide array of attractions, ranging from the prospects of social relations with familiar people in neighborhoods (chapters 3 and 4) to the lure of unfamiliar social relations—multiplicity—in markets and city streets (chapters 5 and 6). Urbanism often comes in a package with social inequality, state organization, occupational specialization, and other social processes (Childe 1950). It is tempting for an observer of cities to get sidetracked by bodies of theory that address these processes (Hannerz 1980, 99). Much can be gained, however, by keeping focus on the cities themselves, be they ancient Maya, Medieval European, or modern American, and attending to the specifics of form, symbolism, and history: the intricacies of place. Thus, in addition to looking at inequality, exchange, and other factors, I have looked at questions such as how the physical arrangement of space contributed to the appeal of ancient Maya cities (chapter 6).

A second enduring point of social archaeology is that the material world can never be fully severed from social relations. Leaders may have used massive, mountain-like temples to naturalize inequality but those temples did not exist on their own, in the same way that a geologically formed mountain might. The universalizing themes that temples communicated iconically and symbolically did not completely obscure the traces of the laborers that produced them. Though these traces may index inequality between laborer and leader, they also index the agency of those laborers and can be a point of pride for the descendants of those laborers.

If readers believe that the approaches discussed above position this book as a contribution to social archaeology, I hope they will also consider other ways the book contributes to ongoing discussions about ancient cities. These discussions touch on demographics, neighborhoods, the distribution of wealth in cities, and the allure of cities.

Chapter 2 presented a genealogy of the concept of the city in scholarship on the ancient Maya. By the 1960s, most scholars agreed that the ancient Maya had cities. Several Maya cities had populations in the tens of thousands, clustered around a site core that contained administrative buildings, marketplaces, palaces, ceremonial plazas, temples, and ballcourts. These features unambiguously indicate that these sites served as regional centers that were equipped to perform specialized functions not found in the hinterlands. A very strong argument can be made that the largest cities, such as Caracol, Calakmul, Tikal, and Coba, were more than regal-ritual centers; the dozens of massive buildings and other features (plazas, causeways) at the cores of these sites represent more than just the king's extended household. As is the case with many other ancient cities, such as Teotihuacan, Mesopotamian cities of the third millennium BCE, and capitals of Greek city-states of the first millennium BCE, although most residents farmed, many were craft producers and there was a marked degree of inequality within the populace.

To the charge that Maya cities exhibit settlement densities much lower than cities of the Old World or Teotihuacan, archaeologists have begun to respond that Maya cities are part of a widespread phenomenon called low-density urbanism. In two ways, this book responds quite differently to the foregoing charge. First, although low-density cities certainly existed, "low-density urbanism" is a contradiction in terms. In the definition of urban I have adopted from the Chicago school of sociology, an urban center must have a high density. Second, settlement density in many Maya cities is in fact quite high. Mayanists have known for quite some time about high settlement densities at Mayapan and Copan, but they saw these two cities as exceptional: Mayapan was said to be dense because of influence from beyond the Maya area, and Copan's dense zone covered less than one square kilometer. However, new maps from Palenque, El Peru/Waka', and Chunchucmil reveal settlement densities that approach that of modern U.S. cities, albeit not as high as Teotihuacan or most Old World ancient cities. This kind of density— around 3,000 people per square kilometer—produces a situation in which people who are socially distant are physically close. According to a well-established tradition of scholarship (Beals 1951; Wirth 1940, 752), this is urbanism. All Maya cities had enough people that one person could not know all the others, but at the denser, urban cities—Chunchucmil, Palenque, Coba, Mayapan, Copan, and El Peru/Waka', among others—people who did not know each other lived quite near each other. Encounters with strangers were common enough to be unremarkable.

This study thus claims that high-density Maya cities were not just rare outliers among a predominant pattern of low-density cities. Rather, high-density Maya cities occupied the urban end of a settlement density spectrum, if they did not form a pattern of their own. Such urban centers were not confined to a single area of the Maya lowlands. Although these findings may seem interesting only to Mayanists, I would add that they have broader significance for the study of ancient cities in the tropics. Such cities, whether they be in Africa, Asia, or the Americas, are said to be low density. The data from the Maya lowlands suggests we have to alter this point of view. The high settlement density of an ancient Maya city such as Chunchucmil, which has fragile soils, no rivers, no beasts of burden or wheeled transport, and slim prospects for agricultural intensification, should be seen as an achievement that prompts new questions for lowland tropical cities. For example, how did long-distance trade contribute to the growth of major cities? How did subsistence strategies beyond a reliance on corn or other cereal crops sustain a dense population?

Because high-density cities have social and physical disadvantages that are not found in lower-density settlements, the existence of these cities naturally shifts our attention to the identification of features that offset these disadvantages. Neighborhoods are an excellent example of these features. They are one of a variety of social units that are intermediate in size between the household and the city as a whole. Chapter 3 defines these units and discusses how they might be identified in the Maya area and elsewhere. Neighborhoods foster a mutual familiarity among people that begets networks of trust. In urban contexts, such networks mitigate the kinds of anomie and danger that might appear when socially distant people are physically close. Of course, while neighborhoods and other intermediate social units are not restricted to urban contexts, they can often be more difficult to identify in cities. Chapter 3 presented four methods for identifying neighborhoods—spatial clustering, focal nodes, stylistic clustering, and craft specialization. Chapter 5 discussed another method: clustering of wealth. Of these methods, spatial clustering is easiest to use because spatial clusters often take the form of groups of buildings surrounded by open spaces, which show clearly on maps. But in urban contexts, high settlement density often means a scarcity of open spaces. Other features used to identify spatial clusters (boundary walls, streets, gullies) are not common in Maya cities, though focal nodes (neighborhood temples, water sources) are. Methods other than analysis of spatial clustering, such as excavations that document special clusters of distinctive ceramics, can be useful, and these are costly when done at the scale of the city as a whole.

Beyond systematizing methods for identifying intermediate social units, one of the main contributions of this book is its presentation of a case study that used multiple methods and lines of evidence in the search for such units. The case study comes from Chunchucmil, where a large detailed map and test pitting in a representative sample of domestic contexts throughout the site made it possible to identify neighborhoods and districts on the basis of spatial clustering of residences, focal nodes, stylistic patterning, and craft specialization (chapter 4). At Chunchucmil, the presence of pathways bounded by low stone walls was indispensable for identifying spatial clusters and linking these clusters with focal nodes. The fact that Chunchucmil was subdivided into a relatively discrete set of districts and neighborhoods shows that intermediate units were important. Such pathways did not preserve at most other sites. However, the findings at Chunchucmil emboldened me to speculate that intermediate units might also have been important in cities where details of spatial clustering are no longer visible.

The results of the Chunchucmil case study and those reviewed in chapter 3 (particularly the evidence from Mayapan; Hare and Masson 2012) indicate that combining multiple methods and lines of data may still not be enough to reveal intermediate social units across the entire extent of an ancient city. For example, at Chunchucmil, building orientation and craft specialization suggested just a few neighborhoods and there was no concordance between these two methods. In other words, the residential compounds in proposed crafting neighborhoods did not share a building orientation. We also found no spatial clusters with distinctive styles of pottery. These shortcomings should not dissuade future research because so many key questions about ancient societies involve neighborhoods and other intermediate social units (Yaeger and Canuto 2000). For example, such units are fertile grounds for the construction of corporate identity. They are also a missing link in discussions of political and social organization. We know a great deal about households and polities, but at places such as Tikal or Caracol, households probably engaged with the polity and vice versa through an intermediate level of organization such as the neighborhood or the ward (Yaeger 2000).

Chapter 5 covered a variety of themes related to the distribution of wealth in cities: forms of inequality among the ancient Maya, methods of and pitfalls related to measuring wealth, the degree of imbalance in the distribution of wealth in Maya cities, and the degree to which wealth clustered spatially in these cities. At a bare minimum this chapter demonstrates that the degree of inequality in the distribution of wealth in ancient Maya cities resembles that of many modern cities. This suggests, once again, that ancient cities are not incommensurably different from modern cities. Also, the chapter shows that Maya cites followed no distinct pattern regarding where the wealthiest people lived. In some cities (Chunchucmil) wealth was evenly dispersed. In other cities (Copan, Dzibilchaltun) wealthy people tended to live closer to the center of the site. The latter pattern differs from concentric zonation of wealth, in which all of a site's wealthy people (and nobody else) lived in a ring-shaped area surrounding the site core (Sjoberg 1960). No Maya cities precisely match concentric zonation. Even at sites where wealthy people tended to live closer to the center, less wealthy people also lived close to the center and some wealthy people lived far from it. Neighborhoods composed exclusively of wealthy people are quite rare.

These contributions about wealth imbalance and the spatial distribution of wealth clear the ground, I believe, for a different kind of contribution that relates to a central theme of the book: the reasons why people chose to live in cities. The facts that wealth inequality was substantial at Maya cities and that people of varied wealth levels lived near each other and shared the same footpaths create the potential for multiplicity. Chapter 5 argues that men, women, and children of various wealth levels would have circulated through cities. Multiplicity, which I defined in chapter 1 as unstructured contact between people of diverse backgrounds (banker and bum, ragpicker and retailer), can be a nuisance to the wealthy, but it can be an attraction for many others. Unexpected encounters give cities a zest that is lacking in villages. Chance interactions and transactions can also lead to innovations and opportunities of various kinds, thus providing opportunities for expanding social networks and social capital. For these reasons, the fact that most wealthy people did not seal themselves off from the rest of the city suggests that the lived experience of walking in the city could have been vibrant and attractive. The absence of exclusive enclaves would have engendered dynamism. The perspective of lived experience encourages researchers to move beyond generalized spatial patterns and examine smaller-scale questions of exactly who was living next to whom.

When modern people think of Maya cities, outstanding features of the built environment—temples, palaces, plazas—come to mind. Archaeologists have noted that leaders used these features as tools for maintaining or increasing their power. For example, the iconography of temples helped frame leaders as chief mediators between the sacred and the rest of the populace. Plazas gave leaders a space for performances that enchanted and thus justified inequality. Chapter 6 presented these well-known arguments while also contributing the point that the people who were the targets of these messages and performances found cities attractive for a broader variety of reasons, some of which leaders did not intend. In other words, cities attracted people because they offered enticements that aligned with people's well-informed but imperfect calculations. Leaders of course benefited from people moving to cities and thus presented incentives to bring this about, but these incentives did not dupe people and are not the entire story of what made cities attractive. Along these lines, the chapter made several suggestions. For example, people came to marketplaces in part because of the exciting social opportunities that accompanied the multiplicity there. These social possibilities may not have figured in the intentions of the leaders who sponsored the marketplaces. The chapter offered three more suggestions about city life: 1) people enjoyed royal performances in plazas without necessarily accepting the ideologies communicated therein; 2) people in cities engaged in bottom-up cooperation and governance and this engagement furnished them with a sense of investment in and commitment to their city and its well-being; and 3) people stayed near temple pyramids in part because they were the dwellings of the gods but also because the labor that their ancestors committed to the pyramids gave them a sense of connection to the city, or even a sense of possession, entitlement, or rootedness that anchored them in place. Alternatively, temple pyramids attracted people because, as salient landmarks, they helped people build intelligible images of the city that made navigation easier and a sense of place better grounded.

In sum, Maya cities attracted people from the countryside for multiple reasons, some originating from the top down, others from the bottom up. Together, different and competing groups forged centers that offset the disadvantages of city life. Different cities take different paths toward this result, but all cities, Mesoamerican and otherwise, must achieve it. For cities that are dense enough to be considered urban, this achievement is more critical. There is no prototypical Maya city: they differ widely in size, density, and plan. This book presents a set of tools—analysis of neighborhoods, built form, multiplicity, and economy—that can be used widely. It is hoped that, as part of a broader anthropological project, these tools can help make sense of the variability.

References

Abrams, Elliott
1994   *How the Maya Built Their World*. University of Texas Press, Austin.
Adams, Richard, E. W.
1970   Suggested Classic Period Occupational Specialization in the Southern Maya Low-
       lands. In *Monographs and Papers in Maya Archaeology*, edited by William R. Bullard,
       489–502. Peabody Museum Papers 61. Peabody Museum of Anthropology and Eth-
       nology, Harvard University, Cambridge, MA.
Adams, Richard E. W., and Richard C. Jones
1981   Spatial Patterns and Regional Growth among Maya Cities. *American Anthropologist*
       46:301–22.
Adams, Robert M.
1974   Patterns of Urbanization in Southern Mesopotamia. In *Man, Settlement, and Urban-
       ism*, edited by Peter T. Ucko, Ruth Tringham and George W. Dimbleby, 735–749.
       Duckworth, London.
Adomaitis, Kasparas
2013   The World's Largest Cities Are the Most Unequal. Euromonitor International. http://
       blog.euromonitor.com/2013/03/the-worlds-largest-cities-are-the-most-unequal
       .html. Accessed March 2014.
Ahlbrandt, Roger S.
1984   *Neighborhoods, People, and Community*. Plenum Press, New York.
Alston, Richard
1998   Trade and the City in Roman Egypt. In *Trade, Traders and the Ancient City*, edited by
       Helen M. Parkins and Christopher Smith, 168–202. Routledge, London.
Anderson, Benedict
1991   *Imagined Communities*. 2nd ed. Verso, London.
Andrews, Anthony P.
1983   *Maya Salt Production and Trade*. University of Arizona Press, Tucson.
Andrews, E. Wyllys, IV
1965   Progress Report on the 1960–1964 Field Seasons, National Geographic Society-
       Tulane University Dzibilchaltun Program: Summary of Nine Seasons' Work at Dzi-
       bilchaltun. In *Archaeological Investigations on the Yucatan Peninsula*, edited by E. W.

Andrews IV, 23–67. Middle American Research Institute Publication 31. Middle American Research Institute, New Orleans, LA.

Andrews, E. Wyllys, IV, and E. Wyllys Andrews V
1980   *Excavations at Dzibilchaltun, Yucatan, Mexico*. Middle American Research Institute Publication 48. Middle American Research Institute, New Orleans, LA.

Andrews, George F.
1975   *Maya Cities: Placemaking and Urbanization*. University of Oklahoma Press, Norman.
1985   Chenes-Puuc Architecture: Chronology and Cultural Interaction. In Mission archéologique et ethnologique francaise au Mexique, *Arquitectura y Arqueologia: Metodologias en la Cronologia de Yucatan*, 11–40. Etudes Mesoamericaines, serie II-8. Centre D'etudes Mexicaines et Centramericaines, Mexico City.

Ardren, Traci
2006   Setting the Table: Why Children and Childhood Are Important in an Understanding of Ancient Mesoamerica. In *The Social Experience of Childhood in Mesoamerica*, edited by Traci Ardren and Scott R. Hutson, 3–24. University Press of Colorado, Boulder.
2014   Sacbe Processions and Classic Maya Urban Culture. Paper presented at the "Processions in the Ancient Americas: Approaches and Perspectives" symposium, Dumbarton Oaks Research Library and Collection, Washington, DC.
2015   *Gender and Identity in the Northern Maya Lowlands*. University of Texas Press, Austin.

Arnauld, M. Charlotte
2008   Maya Urbanization: Agrarian Cities in a Preindustrial World. In *El Urbanismo en Mesoamérica/Urbanism in Mesoamerica*, edited by Alba G. Mastache, Robert H. Cobean, Ángel García Cook, and Kenneth G. Hirth, 1–36. Pennsylvania State University, University Park, and Instituto Nacional de Antropología e Historia, Mexico City.

Arnauld, M. Charlotte, Dominique Michelet, Boris Vannière, Philippe Nondédéo, and Eva Lemmonier
2012   Houses, Emulation, and Cooperation among the Río Bec Groups. In *The Neighborhood as a Social and Spatial Unit in Mesoamerican Cities*, edited by M. Charlotte Arnauld, Linda Manzanilla, and Michael E. Smith, 202–229. University of Arizona Press, Tucson.

Arnold, Dean
1985   *Ceramic Theory and Cultural Process*. Cambridge University Press, Cambridge.

Arnold, Jeanne, and Anabel Ford
1980   A Statistical Examination of Settlement Patterns at Tikal, Guatemala. *American Antiquity* 45(4):713–726.

Ashmore, Wendy (editor)
1981a   *Lowland Maya Settlement Patterns*. University of New Mexico Press, Albuquerque.

Ashmore, Wendy
1981b   Some Issues of Method and Theory in Lowland Maya Settlement Archaeology. In *Lowland Maya Settlement Patterns*, edited by Wendy Ashmore, 37–70. University of New Mexico Press, Albuquerque.
1988   Household and Community at Classic Quirigua. In *Household and Community in the*

Mesoamerican Past, edited by Richard Wilk and Wendy Ashmore, 153–171. University of New Mexico Press, Albuquerque.

1991   Site-Planning Principles and Concepts of Directionality among the Ancient Maya. *Latin American Antiquity* 2:199–226.

2004   Classic Maya Landscapes and Settlement. In *Mesoamerican Archaeology,* edited by Julia A. Hendon and Rosemary A. Joyce, 169–191. Blackwell, Oxford.

Ashmore, Wendy, and Jeremy A. Sabloff

2002   Spatial Orders in Maya Civic Plans. *Latin American Antiquity* 13(2):201–216.

Ashmore, Wendy, and Gordon R. Willey

1981   A Historical Introduction to the Study of Lowland Maya Settlement Patterns. In *Lowland Maya Settlement Patterns,* edited by Wendy Ashmore, 3–18. University of New Mexico Press, Albuquerque.

Ashmore, Wendy, Jason Yaeger, and Cynthia Robin

2004   Commoner Sense: Late and Terminal Classic Social Strategies in the Xunantunich Area. In *The Terminal Classic in the Maya Lowlands: Collapse, Transition and Transformation,* edited by Arthur A. Demarest, Prudence M. Rice, and Don S. Rice, 302–323. University Press of Colorado, Boulder.

Aveni, Anthony

2009   *The End of Time: The Maya Mystery of 2012.* University Press of Colorado, Boulder.

Bailey Glasco, Sharon

2010   *Constructing Mexico City: Colonial Conflicts over Culture, Space, and Authority.* Palgrave Macmillan, New York.

Bair, Daniel A., and Richard E. Terry

2012   In Search of Markets and Fields: Soil Chemical Investigations at Motul de San Jose. In *Motul de San Jose: Politics, History and Economy in a Classic Maya Polity,* edited by Antonia E. Foias and Kitty F. Emery, 357–385. University Press of Florida, Gainesville.

Barnhart, Edward

2001   The Palenque Mapping Project: Settlement and Urbanism at an Ancient Maya City. Ph.D. dissertation, Department of Latin American Studies, University of Texas, Austin.

Barthel, Thomas S.

1968   El Complejo "Emblema." *Estudios de Cultura Maya* 7:159–193.

Beach, Timothy, Sheryl Luzzadder-Beach, Thomas Guderjan, and Samantha Krause

2015   The Floating Gardens of Chan Cahal: Soils, Water, and Human Interactions. *Catena* 132(September): 151–64.

Beals, Ralph L.

1951   Urbanism, Urbanization and Acculturation. *American Anthropologist* 53:1–10.

Becker, Marshall J.

1973   Archaeological Evidence for Occupational Specialization among the Classic Period Maya at Tikal, Guatemala. *American Antiquity* 38(4):396–406.

1979   Priests, Peasants, and Ceremonial Centers: The Intellectual History of a Model. In *Maya Archaeology and Ethnohistory,* edited by Norman Hammond and Gordon R. Willey, 3–20. University of Texas Press, Austin.

1993   Earth Offering among the Classic Period Lowland Maya: Burials and Caches as

Ritual Deposits. In *Perspectivas Antropológicas en el Mundo Maya*, edited by Maria J. Iglesias and Josep Ligorred, 45–74. Sociedad Espanola de Estudios Mayas, Madrid.

1999 *Excavations in Residential Areas of Tikal: Groups with Shrines*. Tikal Reports 21. University Museum, University of Pennsylvania, Philadelphia.

2003a Plaza Plans at Tikal: A Research Strategy for Inferring Social Organization and Processes of Cultural Change at Lowland Maya Sites. In *Tikal: Dynasties, Foreigners and Affairs of State*, edited by Jeremy A. Sabloff, 253–280. School of American Research Press, Santa Fe.

2003b A Classic-Period Barrio Producing Fine Quality Ceramics at Tikal Guatemala. *Ancient Mesoamerica* 14:95–112.

2009 Tikal: Evidence for Ethnic Diversity in a Prehispanic Lowland Maya State Capital. In *Domestic Life in Prehispanic Capitals: A Study of Specialization, Hierarchy, and Ethnicity*, edited by Linda R. Manzanilla and Claude Chapdelaine, 89–104. Museum of Anthropology, University of Michigan, Ann Arbor.

Berlin, Heinrich

1958 El Glifo "Emblema" en las Inscripciones Mayas. *Journal de la Société des Américanistes* 47:111–119.

Bermudez, Jose L.

1995 Ecological Perception and the Notion of a Nonconceptual Point of View. In *The Body and the Self*, edited by Jose L. Bermudez, Anthony Marcel, and Naomi Eilan, 153–174. MIT Press, Cambridge, MA.

Bettencourt, Luís M. A.

2007 Growth Innovation, Scaling and the Pace of Life in Cities. *PNAS* 104(17):7301–7306.

2013 The Origins of Scaling in Cities. *Science* 340:1438–1441.

Bettencourt, Luís M. A., and Geoffrey West

2010 A Unified Theory of Urban Living. *Nature* 467:912–913.

Betz, Virginia Marie

2002 The City as Invention: An Environmental Psychological Approach to the Origins of Urban Life. Ph.D. dissertation, Department of Anthropology, Arizona State University, Tempe.

Binford, Lewis R.

1964 A Consideration of Archaeological Research Design. *American Antiquity* 29:425–441.

Blackmore, Chelsea

2011 Ritual among the Masses: Deconstructing Identity and Class in an Ancient Maya Neighborhood. *Latin American Antiquity* 22(2):159–177.

Blackmore, Chelsea, and Traci Ardren

2001 Excavations at the Pich Group. In *Pakbeh Regional Economy Program: Report of the 2001 Field Season*, edited by Bruce H. Dahlin and Daniel E. Mazeau, 58–68. Howard University Department of Sociology and Anthropology, Washington DC.

Blanton, Richard E.

1976 The Anthropological Study of Cities. *Annual Review of Anthropology* 5:249–265.

1978 *Monte Albán: Settlement Patterns at the Ancient Zapotec Capital*. Academic Press, New York.

1996   The Basin of Mexico Market System and the Growth of Empire. In *Aztec Imperial Strategies*, edited by Frances Berdan, Richard E. Blanton, Elizabeth H. Boone, Mary G. Hodge, Michael E. Smith, and Emily Umberger, 47–84. Dumbarton Oaks Research Library and Collection, Washington, DC.

2013   Cooperation and the Moral Economy of the Marketplace. In *Merchants, Markets and Exchange in the Pre-Colombian World*, edited by K. G. Hirth and J. Pillsbury, 23–48. Dumbarton Oaks Research Library and Collection, Washington, DC.

Bloch, Maurice

1983   *Marxism in Anthropology: The History of a Relationship*. Clarendon Press, Oxford.

Bolles, David, and William Folan

2001   An Analysis of Roads Listed in Colonial Dictionaries and their Relevance to Pre-Hispanic Linear Features in the Yucatan Peninsula. *Ancient Mesoamerica* 12(2):299–314.

Boone, James L., and Charles Redman

1982   Alternative Pathways to Urbanism in the Medieval Maghreb. *Comparative Urban Research* 9(1):28–38.

Bourdieu, Pierre

1977   *Outline of a Theory of Practice*. Cambridge University Press, Cambridge.

Braswell, Geoffrey E. (editor)

2003   *The Maya and Teotihuacan: Reinterpreting Early Classic Interaction*. University of Texas Press, Austin.

Braswell, Geoffrey E.

2010   The Rise and Fall of Market Exchange: A Dynamic Approach to Ancient Maya Economy. In *Archaeological Approaches to Market Exchange in Ancient Societies*, edited by Chris P. Garraty and Barbara L. Stark, 3–32. University Press of Colorado, Boulder.

Brown, Clifford T.

1999   Mayapan Society and Ancient Social Organization. Ph.D. dissertation, Department of Anthropology, Tulane University, New Orleans, LA.

Brown, Clifford T., April A. Watson, Ashley Gravlin-Beman, and Larry Liebovitch

2012   Poor Mayapan. In *The Ancient Maya of Mexico: Reinterpreting the Past of the Northern Maya Lowlands*, edited by Geoffrey E. Braswell, 306–324. Equinox Publishing, Bristol, CT.

Brumfiel, Elizabeth M.

1991   Weaving and Cooking: Women's Production in Aztec Mexico. In *Engendering Archaeology: Women in Prehistory*, edited by Joan M. Gero, and Margaret Conkey, 224–251. Blackwell, Oxford.

1996   Figurines and the Aztec State: Testing the Effectiveness of Ideological Domination. In *Gender and Archaeology*, edited by R. P. Wright, 143–166. University of Pennsylvania Press, Philadelphia.

Bullard, William R. Jr

1960   Maya Settlement Pattern in Northeastern Peten, Guatemala. *American Antiquity* 25:355–372.

1964   Settlement Pattern and Social Structure in the Southern Maya Lowlands during the

Classic Period. In *XXXV Congreso Internacional de Americanistas, Mexico, 1962*, vol. 1, pp. 279–287. Editorial Libros de México, Mexico City.

Burger, Richard

1992   The Sacred Center of Chavin de Huantar. In *The Ancient Americas: Art from Sacred Landscapes*, edited by Richard F. Townsend, 265–277. Art Institute of Chicago, Chicago, and Prestel Verlag, Munich.

Burgess, Ernest W.

1925   The Growth of the City: An Introduction to a Research Project. In *The City*, edited by R. E. Park, E. W. Burgess, and R. D. McKenzie, 47–62. University of Chicago Press, Chicago.

Burgess, Ernest W.

1926   *The Urban Community*. University of Chicago Press, Chicago.

Butterworth, George

1995   An Ecological Perspective on the Origins of the Self. In *The Body and the Self*, edited by Jose L. Bermudez, Anthony Marcel, and Naomi Eilan, 87–106. MIT Press, Cambridge, MA.

Canuto, Marcello A., and Jason Yaeger (editors)

2000   *The Archaeology of Communities: A New World Perspective*. Routledge, London.

Cap, Bernadette

2015   How to Know It When We See It: Marketplace Identification at the Classic Maya Site of Buenavista del Cayo, Belize. In *Ancient Maya Marketplaces: The Archaeology of Transient Space*, edited by Eleanor M. King and Leslie C. Shaw. University of Arizona Press, Tucson.

Carmean, Kelli

1991   Architectural Labor Investment and Social Stratification at Sayil, Yucatan, Mexico. *Latin American Antiquity* 2(2):151–165.

Carmean, Kelli, Patricia A. McAnany, and Jeremy A. Sabloff

2011   People Who Lived in Stone Houses: Local Knowledge and Social Difference in the Classic Maya Puuc Region. *Latin American Antiquity* 22:143–158.

Carr, Robert F., and James E. Hazard

1961   *Map of the Ruins of Tikal, El Peten, Guatemala*. Tikal Reports No. 11. The University Museum, University of Pennsylvania, Philadelphia.

Carrasco Vargas, Ramón, Verónica A. Vásquez López, and Simon Martin

2009   Daily Life of the Ancient Maya Recorded in Murals. *Proceedings of the National Academy of Science* 106(46):19245–19249.

Chapdelaine, Claude

2009   Domestic Life in and around the Urban Sector of the Huacas of Moche Site, Northern Peru. In *Domestic Life in Prehispanic Capitals: A Study of Specialization, Hierarchy, and Ethnicity*, edited by Linda Manzanilla and Claude Chapdelaine, 181–196. Museum of Anthropology, University of Michigan, Ann Arbor.

Charlton, Thomas H., and Deborah Nichols (editors)

1997   *The Archaeology of City-States: Cross-Cultural Perspectives*. Smithsonian Institution Press, Washington

Chase, Arlen F.

1992   Elites and the Changing Organization of Classic Maya Society. In *Mesoamerican*

Elites, edited by Diane Z. Chase and Arlen F. Chase, 30–49. University of Oklahoma Press, Norman.

Chase, Arlen F., and Diane Z. Chase

1992 Mesoamerican Elites: Assumptions, Definitions, and Models. In *Mesoamerican Elites: An Archaeological Assessment*, edited by Diane Z. Chase and Arlen F. Chase, 3–17. University of Oklahoma Press, Norman.

1996 More than Kin and King: Centralized Political Organization among the Late Classic Maya. *Current Anthropology* 37(5):803–810.

1998 Scale and Intensity in Classic Period Maya Agriculture: Terracing and Settlement at the "Garden City" of Caracol, Belize. *Culture and Agriculture* 20:60–77.

Chase, Arlen F., Diane Z. Chase, and William A. Haviland

1990 The Classic Maya City: Reconsidering the Mesoamerican Urban Tradition. *American Anthropologist* 92(2):499–506.

Chase, Arlen F., Diane Z. Chase, Richard E. Terry, Jacob M. Horlacher, and Adrian S. Z. Chase

2015 Markets among the Ancient Maya: The Case of Caracol, Belize. In *Ancient Maya Marketplaces: The Archaeology of Transient Space*, edited by Eleanor M. King and Leslie C. Shaw. University of Arizona Press, Tucson.

Chase, Arlen F., Diane Z. Chase, John F. Weishampel, Jason B. Drake, Ramesh L. Shrestha, K. Clint Slatton, Jaime Awe, and William E. Carter

2011 Airborne LiDAR, Archaeology, and the Ancient Maya Landscape at Caracol, Belize. *Journal of Archaeological Science* 38:387–398.

Chase, Arlen F., and Vernon L. Scarborough

2014 Diversity, Resilience, and IHOPE-Maya: Using the Past to Inform the Present. In *The Resilience, and Vulnerability of Ancient Landscapes: Transforming Maya Archaeology through IHOPE*, edited by Arlen F. Chase and Vernon L. Scarborough, 1–10. Archaeological Papers of the American Anthropological Association, American Anthropological Association, Washington, DC.

Chase, Diane Z.

1986 Social and Political Organization in the Land of Cacao and Honey: Correlating the Archaeology and Ethnohistory of the Postclassic Lowland Maya. In *Late Lowland Maya Civilization*, edited by Jeremy Sabloff and E. Wyllys Andrews V, 347–377. University of New Mexico Press, Albuquerque.

1992 Postclassic Maya Elites: Ethnohistory and Archaeology. In *Mesoamerican Elites*, edited by Diane Z. Chase, and Arlen F. Chase, 118–134. University of Oklahoma Press, Norman.

Chase, Diane Z., and Arlen F. Chase

2004 Archaeological Perspectives on Classic Maya Social Organization from Caracol, Belize. *Ancient Mesoamerica* 15:139–147.

2014 Ancient Maya Markets and the Economic Integration of Caracol, Belize. *Ancient Mesoamerica* 25:239–250.

Child, Mark B., and Charles W. Golden

2008 The Transformation of Abandoned Architecture at Piedras Negras. In *Ruins of the Past: The Use and Perception of Abandoned Structures in the Maya Lowlands*, edited by Travis W. Stanton and Aline Magnoni, 65–89. University Press of Colorado, Boulder.

Childe, V. Gordon

1950 The Urban Revolution. *Town Planning Review* 21:3–17.

Chuchiak, John F. I.

2009 De Descriptio Idolorum: An Ethnohistorical Examination of the Production, Imagery, and Functions of Colonial Yucatec Maya Idols and Effigy Censers, 1540–1700. In *Maya Worldviews at Conquest*, edited by Leslie Cecil and Timothy Pugh, 135–158. University Press of Colorado, Boulder.

Clendinnen, Inga

1991 *The Aztecs.* Cambridge University Press, Cambridge.

Cobos, Rafael, and Terrence L. Winemiller

2001 The Late and Terminal Classic Period Causeway Systems of Chichen Itza, Yucatan, Mexico. *Ancient Mesoamerica* 12:283–291.

Coe, Michael D.

1965 A Model of Ancient Community Structure in the Maya Lowlands. *Southwestern Journal of Anthropology* 21(2):97–114.

1973 *The Maya Scribe and His World.* The Grolier Club, New York.

Coe, William R.

1965 Tikal: Ten Years of Study of a Maya Ruin in the Lowlands of Guatemala. *Expedition* 1:5–56.

Coggins, Clemency C.

1980 The Shape of Time: Some Political Implications of a Four-Part Figure. *American Antiquity* 45(4):727–739.

Coronel, Eric G., Scott R. Hutson, Aline M. Magnoni, Chris Balzotti, Austin Ulmer, and Richard E. Terry

2015 Geochemical Analysis of Late Classic and Post Classic Maya Marketplace Activities at the Plazas of Cobá, Mexico. *Journal of Field Archaeology* 40(1): 89–109.

Costanza, Robert, Lisa J. Graumlich, and Will L. Steffen (editors)

2007 *Sustainability of Collapse: An Integrated History and Future of People on Earth.* MIT Press, Cambridge, MA.

Cowgill, George L.

2003a Teotihuacan: Cosmic Glories and Mundane Needs. In *The Social Construction of Ancient Cities*, edited by Monica L. Smith, 37–55. Smithsonian Institution Press, Washington, DC.

2003b Some Recent Data and Concepts about Ancient Urbanism. In *El Urbanismo en Mesoamerica*, edited by William T. Sanders, Alba G. Mastache, and Robert H. Cobean, 427–449. Instituto Nacional de Antropología e Historia, Mexico City.

2004 Origins and Development of Urbanism: Archaeological Perspectives. *Annual Review of Anthropology* 33:525–549.

2007 The Urban Organization of Teotihuacan, Mexico. In *Settlement and Society: Essays Dedicated to Robert McCormick Adams*, edited by Elizabeth C. Stone, 261–295. Cotsen Institute of Archaeology, University of California, Los Angeles.

2008 Teotihuacan as an Urban Place. In *El Urbanismo en Mesoamérica/Urbanism in Mesoamerica*, edited by Alba G. Mastache, Robert H. Cobean, Ángel García Cook, and Kenneth G. Hirth, 85–112. Pennsylvania State University, University Park, and Instituto Nacional de Antropología e Historia, Mexico City.

Culbert, T. Patrick, Laura J. Kosakowsky, Robert E. Fry, and William A. Haviland

1990 The Population of Tikal, Guatemala. In *Precolumbian Population History in the Maya Lowlands*, edited by T. Patrick Culbert and Don S. Rice, 103–122. University of New Mexico Press, Albuquerque.

Dahlin, Bruce

2000 The Barricade and Abandonment of Chunchucmil: Implications for Northern Maya Warfare. *Latin American Antiquity* 11:283–298.

Dahlin, Bruce H., and T. Ardren

2002 Modes of Exchange and Regional Patterns: Chunchucmil, Yucatan, Mexico. In *Ancient Maya Political Economies*, edited by Marilyn Masson and David Freidel, 249–284. Altamira Press, Walnut Creek, CA.

Dahlin, Bruce H., Daniel A. Bair, Timothy Beach, Matthew Moriarty, and Richard E. Terry

2010 The Dirt on Food: Ancient Feasts and Markets among the Lowland Maya. In *Pre-Columbian Foodways: Interdisciplinary Approaches to Food, Culture, and Markets in Ancient Mesoamerica*, edited by J. E. Staller and M. Carrasco, 191–232. Springer, New York.

Dahlin, Bruce H., Timothy Beach, Sheryl Luzzadder-Beach, David Hixson, Scott R. Hutson, Aline Magnoni, Eugenia B. Mansell, and Daniel Mazeau

2005 Reconstructing Agricultural Self-Sufficiency at Chunchucmil, Yucatan, Mexico. *Ancient Mesoamerica* 16(2):229–247.

Dahlin, Bruce H., Chris T. Jensen, Richard E. Terry, D. R. Wright, and Timothy Beach

2007 In Search of an Ancient Maya Market. *Latin American Antiquity* 18(4):363–384.

Del Río, Antonio

1822 *Description of the Ruins of an Ancient City Discovered near Palenque*. Henry Berthoud, London.

Demarest, Arthur A.

1992 Ideology in Ancient Maya Cultural Evolution: The Dynamics of Galactic Polities. In *Ideology and Precolumbian Civilizations*, edited by A. Demarest, and Geoffrey Conrad, 135–158. School of American Research Press, Santa Fe.

1996 Closing Comment: The Maya State: Centralized or Segmentary? *Current Anthropology* 37(5):821–824.

2003 Comment. *Current Anthropology* 44(4):546.

2004 *Ancient Maya: The Rise and Fall of a Rainforest Civilization*. Cambridge University Press, Cambridge.

de Montmollin, Olivier

1989 *Settlement and Politics in Three Classic Maya Polities*. Cambridge University Press, Cambridge.

de Vries, Jan

1984 *European Urbanization, 1500–1800*. Harvard University Press, Cambridge, MA.

Diaz del Castillo, Bernal

1956 *The Discovery and Conquest of Mexico*. Translated by A. P. Maudslay. Farrar, Strauss and Caduhy, New York.

Dobres, Marcia-Anne, and John Robb

2000 Agency in Archaeology: Paradigm or Platitude? In *Agency in Archaeology*, edited by Marcia-Anne Dobres and John Robb, 3–18. Routledge, London.

Downs, Anthony

1981   *Neighborhoods and Urban Development.* The Brookings Institution, Washington, DC.

Drennan, Robert D.

1988   Household Location and Compact versus Dispersed Settlement in Prehispanic Mesoamerica. In *Household and Community in the Mesoamerican Past,* edited by Richard
Wilk and Wendy Ashmore, 273–293. University of New Mexico Press, Albuquerque.

Dunning, Nicholas P.

1992   *Lords of the Hills: Ancient Maya Settlement in the Puuc Region, Yucatan, Mexico.* Monographs in World Archaeology 15. Prehistory Press, Madison, WI.

Dunning, Nicholas P., and Timothy Beach

2010   Farms and Forests: Spatial and Temporal Perspectives on Ancient Maya Landscapes.
In *Landscapes and Societies,* edited by I. Peter Martini and Ward Chesworth, 369–389.
Springer, Dordecht

Dunning, Nicholas P., Timothy Beach, Patrice Farrell, and Sheryl Luzzadder-Beach

1998   Prehispanic Agrosystems and Adaptive Regions in the Maya Lowlands. *Culture and
Agriculture* 20:87–101.

Dunning, Nicholas P., John G. Jones, Timothy Beach, and Sheryl Luzzadder-Beach

2003   Physiography, Habitats, and Landscapes of the Three Rivers Region. In *Heterarchy,
Political Economy, and the Ancient Maya,* edited by Vernon Scarborough, Fred Valdez,
and Nicholas R. Dunning, 14–24. University of Arizona Press, Tucson.

Dunning, Nicholas P., Eric Weaver, Michael P. Smyth, and David Ortegon Zapata

2014   Xcoch: Home of the Ancient Maya Rain Gods and Water Managers. In *The Archaeology of Yucatan,* edited by Travis Stanton, 45–64. Archaeopress, Oxford.

Durán, Francisco D.

1951   *Historia de las Indias de Nueva España y Islas de Tierra Firme.* 2 vols. Editora Nacional,
Mexico City.

Emberling, Geoffrey

2003   Urban Social Transformations and the Problem of the "First City": New Research
from Mesopotamia. In *The Social Construction of Ancient Cities,* edited by Monica L.
Smith, 254–268. Smithsonian Institution Press, Washington, DC.

Eppich, Keith, and David A. Freidel

2015   Markets and Marketing in the Classic Maya Lowlands: A Case Study from El Perú-
Waka'. In *Ancient Maya Marketplaces: The Archaeology of Transient Space,* edited by E.
M. King and L. C. Shaw. University of Arizona Press, Tucson.

Estrada-Belli, Francisco

2006   Lightning, Sky, Rain and the Maize God: The Ideology of Preclassic Maya Rulers at
Cival, Peten, Guatemala. *Ancient Mesoamerica* 17:57–78.

Evans, Damian, Christophe Pottier, Roland Fletcher, Scott Hensley, Ian M. Tapley, Anthony Milne, and Michael Barbetti

2007   A New Archaeological Map of the World's Largest Pre-Industrial Settlement Complex at Angkor, Cambodia. *Proceedings of the National Academy of Sciences* 104:14277–
14282.

Evans, Susan

1993   Aztec Household Organization and Village Administration. In *Prehispanic Domestic*

Units in Western Mesoamerica, edited by Robert S. Santley and Kenneth G. Hirth, 173–190. CRC Press, Boca Raton.

Farriss, Nancy M.

1984   *Maya Society under Colonial Rule: The Collective Enterprise of Survival.* Princeton University Press, Princeton, N.J.

Fash, William L.

1983   Deducing Social Organization from Classic Maya Settlement Patterns: A Case Study from the Copan Valley. In *Civilization in the Ancient Americas: Essays in Honor of Gordon R. Willey,* edited by Richard Leventhal, and Alan L. Kolata, 261–288. University of New Mexico Press, Albuquerque.

1998   Dynastic Architectural Programs: Intention and Design in Classic Maya Buildings at Copan and Other Sites. In *Function and Meaning in Classic Maya Architecture,* edited by Stephen D. Houston, 223–270. Dumbarton Oaks Research Library and Collection, Washington, DC.

2005   Toward a Social History of the Copan Valley. In *Copan: The History of an Ancient Maya Kingdom,* edited by E. W. Andrews IV and W. L. Fash, 73–102. School of American Research, Santa Fe.

Fedick, Scott L. (editor)

1996   *The Managed Mosaic: Ancient Maya Agriculture and Resource Use.* University of Utah Press, Salt Lake City.

Fedick, Scott L., Jennifer P. Mathews, and Kathy Sorenson

2012   Cenotes as Conceptual Boundary Markers at the Ancient Maya Site of T'isil, Quintana Roo, Mexico. *Mexicon* 34(5):118–123.

Fedick, Scott L., Bethany A. Morrison, Bente J. Anderson, Sylviane Boucher, Jorge C. Acosta, and Jennifer P. Mathews

2000   Wetland Manipulation in the Yalahau Region of the Northern Maya Lowlands. *Journal of Field Archaeology* 27:131–152.

Feinman, Gary M., and Chris P. Garraty

2010   Preindustrial Markets and Marketing: Archaeological Perspectives. *Annual Review of Anthropology* 39:167–191.

Feldman, Lawrence H.

1985   *A Tumpline Economy: Production and Distribution Systems in Sixteenth-Century Eastern Guatemala.* Labyrinthos, Culver City, CA.

Finlay, Roger

1981   *Population and Metropolis: The Demography of London: 1580–1650.* Cambridge University Press, Cambridge.

Finley, Moses

1963   *The Ancient Greeks: An Introduction to their Life and Thought.* Viking, New York.

Flannery, Kent V.

1972   The Cultural Evolution of Civilizations. *Annual Review of Ecology and Systematics* 3:399–425.

Fletcher, Roland

1986   Settlement Archaeology: Worldwide Comparisons. *World Archaeology* 18:59–83.

1995   *The Limits of Settlement Growth: A Theoretical Outline.* Cambridge University Press, New York.

2009   Low-Density, Agrarian-Based Urbanism: A Comparative View. *Insights (University of Durham)* 4(2). Electronic document, https://www.dur.ac.uk/ias/insights/volume2/article4/. Accessed August 19, 2015.

Foias, Antonia E.

2013   *Ancient Maya Political Dynamics.* University Press of Florida, Gainesville.

Foias, Antonia E., and Kitty F. Emery (editors)

2012   *Motul de San Jose: Politics, History and Economy in a Classic Maya Polity.* University Press of Florida, Gainesville, FL.

Foias, Antonia E., Christina T. Halperin, Ellen Spensley Moriarty, and Jeannette Castellanos

2012   Architecture, Volumetrics, and Social Stratification at Motul de San Jose during the Late and Terminal Classic. In *Motul de San Jose: Politics, History and Economy in a Classic Maya Polity,* edited by A. E. Foias and K. F. Emery, 94–138. University Press of Florida, Gainesville.

Folan, William

1983   Archaeological Investigations of Coba: A Summary. In *Coba a Classic Maya Metropolis,* edited by William Folan, Ellen Kintz, and Larraine Fletcher, 1–10. Academic Press, New York.

1991   Sacbes of the Northern Maya. In *Ancient Road Networks and Settlement Hierarchies in the New World,* edited by Charles Trombold, 222–229. Cambridge University Press, Cambridge.

Folan, William J., Armando Anaya Hernandez, Ellen R. Kintz, Larraine A. Fletcher, R. G. Heredia, Jacinto M. Hau, and Nicolas C. Canche

2009   Coba, Quintana Roo, Mexico: A Recent Analysis of the Social, Economic and Political Organization of a Major Maya Urban Center. *Ancient Mesoamerica* 20:59–70.

Folan, William, Laraine Fletcher, Jacinto May Hau, and L Florey Folan

2001   *Las ruinas de Calakmul, Campeche, México: un lugar central y su paisaje cultural.* Universidad Autonoma de Campeche, Campeche.

Folan, William J., Joel D. Gunn, and Maria del Rosario Dominguez Carrasco

2001   Triadic Temples, Central Places and Dynastic Palaces. In *Royal Courts of the Ancient Maya.* Vol. 2, *Data and Case Studies,* edited by Takeshi Inomata and Stephen D. Houston, 223–265. Westview Press, Boulder, CO.

Folan, William J., Ellen R. Kintz, and Larraine A. Fletcher

1983   *Coba: A Classic Maya Metropolis.* Academic Press, New York.

Folan, William J., Ellen R. Kintz, Larraine Fletcher, and Burma H. Hyde

1982   An Examination of Settlement Patterns at Coba, Quintana Roo, Mexico, and Tikal, Guatemala A Reply to Arnold and Ford. *American Antiquity* 47(2):430–436.

Ford, Anabel

1986   *Population Growth and Social Complexity: An Examination of Settlement and Environment in the Central Maya Lowlands.* Anthropological Research Papers no. 35. Arizona State University, Tucson.

Ford, Anabel, and Jeanne Arnold

1982   A Re-Examination of Labor Estimates at Tikal: Reply to Haviland and Folan, Kintz, Fletcher and Hyde. *American Antiquity* 47(2):436–440.

Ford, Anabel, and Scott L. Fedick

1992   Prehistoric Maya Settlement Patterns in the Upper Belize River Area: Initial Results of the Belize River Archaeological Settlement Survey. *Journal of Field Archaeology* 19:35–49.

Fox, Richard

1977   *Urban Anthropology: Cities in their Cultural Setting.* Prentice Hall, Englewood Cliffs, NJ.

Fox, John W., and G. W. Cook

1996   Constructing Maya Communities: Ethnography for Archaeology. *Current Anthropology* 37(5):811–821.

Freidel, David A.

1981a   The Political Economies of Residential Dispersion among the Lowland Maya. In *Lowland Maya Settlement Patterns*, edited by Wendy Ashmore, 371–382. University of New Mexico Press, Albuquerque.

1981b   Continuity and Disjunction: Late Postclassic Settlement Patterns in Northern Yucatan. In *Lowland Maya Settlement Patterns*, edited by Wendy Ashmore, 311–321. University of New Mexico Press, Albuquerque.

Freidel, David A., and Linda Schele

1988   Kingship in the Late Preclassic Maya Lowlands: The Instruments and Places of Ritual Power. *American Antiquity* 90:547–567.

Freidel, David A., Linda Schele, and Joy Parker

1993   *The Maya Cosmos: Three Thousand Years on the Shaman's Path.* Quill, New York.

Freiwald, Carolyn

2011   Maya Migration Networks: Reconstructing Population Movement in the Belize River Valley during the Late and Terminal Classic. Ph.D. dissertation, Department of Anthropology, University of Wisconsin, Madison.

French, Kirk D., David S. Stuart, and Alfonso Morales

2006   Archaeological and Epigraphic Evidence for Water management and Ritual at Palenque. In *Precolumbian Water Management: Ideology, Ritual and Power*, edited by Lisa J. Lucero and Barbara L. Fash, 144–154. Tucson, University of Arizona Press.

Freter, AnnCorinne

2004   Multiscalar Model of Rural Households and Communities in Late Classic Copan Maya Society. *Ancient Mesoamerica* 15(1):93–106.

Fried, Morton H.

1967   *The Evolution of Political Society.* Random House, New York.

Fry, Robert E.

1979   The Economics of Pottery at Tikal, Guatemala: Models of Exchange for Serving Vessels. *American Antiquity* 44(3):494–512.

1980   Models of Exchange for Major Shape Classes of Lowland Maya Pottery. In *Models and Methods in Regional Exchange*, edited by R. E. Fry, 3–18. Society for American Archaeology, Washington, DC.

2003   Social Dynamics in Ceramic Analysis: A Case Study from Peripheral Tikal. *Ancient Mesoamerica* 14:85–93.

Garraty, Christopher P.

2010   Investigating Market Exchange in Ancient Societies: A Theoretical Review. In *Ar-*

chaeological Approaches to Market Exchange in Ancient Societies, edited by Chris P. Garraty and Barbara L. Stark, 3–32. University Press of Colorado, Boulder.

Geertz, Clifford

1980 *Negara: The Theatre State in Nineteenth-Century Bali.* Princeton University Press, Princeton, NJ.

Gibson, James J.

1966 *The Senses Considered as Perceptual Systems.* Houghton Mifflin, Boston.

1979 *The Ecological Approach to Visual Perception.* Houghton Mifflin, Boston.

Giddens, Anthony

1984 *The Constitution of Society.* University of California Press, Berkeley.

Gillespie, Susan D.

2000 Lévi-Strauss: Maison and Société a Maison. In *Beyond Kinship: Social and Material Reproduction in House Societies,* edited by Rosemary A. Joyce and Susan D. Gillespie, 22–52. University of Pennsylvania Press, Philadelphia.

Gilman, Antonio

1981 The Development of Social Stratification in Bronze Age Europe. *Current Anthropology* 22(1):1–23.

Glaeser, Edward L.

2011 *Triumph of the City.* Penguin, New York.

Glaeser, Edward, Matt Resseger, and Kristina Tobio

2008 *Urban Inequality.* NBER Working Paper No. 14419. National Bureau of Economic Research, Cambridge, MA.

Goffman, Erving

1963 *Behavior in Public Places: Notes on the Social Organization of Gatherings.* Free Press, New York.

Golden, Charles

2003 The Politics of Warfare in the Usumacinta Basin: La Pasadita and the Realm of Bird Jaguar. In *Ancient Mesoamerican Warfare,* edited by Travis W. Stanton and M. Kathryn Brown. Altamira Press, Walnut Creek.

Golden, Charles, and Andrew Scherer

2013 Territory, Trust, Growth, and Collapse in Classic Period Maya Kingdoms. *Current Anthropology* 54(4):397–435.

Golden, Charles W., Andrew K. Scherer, A. René Muñoz and Rosaura Vasquez

2008 Piedras Negras and Yaxchilan: Divergent Political Trajectories in Adjacent Maya Polities. *Latin American Antiquity* 19(3):249–274.

Goldstein, Paul S.

2000 Communities without Borders: The Vertical Archipelago and Diaspora Communities in the Southern Andes. In *The Archaeology of Communities: A New World Perspective,* edited by M. A. Canuto and J. Yaeger, 182–209. Routledge, London.

Gómez Chávez, Sergio

2012 Structure and Organization of Neighborhoods in the Ancient City of Teotihuacan. In *The Neighborhood as a Social and Spatial Unit in Mesoamerican Cities,* edited by M.-Charlotte Arnauld, Linda Manzanilla, and Michael E. Smith, 74–101. University of Arizona Press, Tucson.

Gómez-Pompa, Arturo, Michael F. Allen, Scott L. Fedick, and Juan J. Jimenez-Osornio (editors)

2003 *The Lowland Maya Area: Three Millennia at the Human-Wildland Interface*. Haworth Press, Binghamton, NY.

Gonzalez Cruz, Arnoldo

1993 *Trabajos Arqueológicos En Palenque, Chiapas. Informe de Campo, VI Temporada*. Vol 8. Consejo Nacional Para La Cultura y Las Artes, Instituto Nacional de Antropologia e Historia, Mexico City.

Graham, Elizabeth

1999 Stone Cities, Green Cities. In *Complex Polities in the Ancient Tropical World*, edited by Elizabeth A. Bacus and Lisa J. Lucero, 185–194. Archaeological Papers of the American Anthropological Association 9. Washington, DC.

2002 Perspectives on Economy and Theory. In *Ancient Maya Political Economies*, edited by Marilyn A. Masson and David A. Freidel, 398–418. Altamira Press, Walnut Creek, CA.

Graham, Ian, and Eric von Euw

2004 *Coba*. Vol. 8, Part 1 of *Corpus of Maya Hieroglyphic Inscriptions*. Harvard University Press, Cambridge, MA.

Greenshields, Thomas H.

1980 Quarters and Ethnicity. In *The Changing Middle Eastern City*, edited by Gerald H. Blake and Richard I. Lawless, 120–140. Croom Helm, London.

Groark, Kevin P.

2008 Social Opacity and the Dynamics of Empathic In-Sight among the Tzotzil Maya of Chiapas, Mexico. *Ethos* 36:427–448.

Grove, David

1972 Development and Characteristics of Urbanism. In *Man, Settlement, and Urbanism*, edited by Peter J. Ucko, Ruth Tringham, and George W. Dimbleby, 559–566. Duckworth, London.

Grube, Nikolai

1992. Classic Maya Dance: Evidence from Hieroglyphs and Iconography. *Ancient Mesoamerica* 3: 201–18.

2000 The City-States of the Maya. In *A Comparative Study of Thirty City-State Cultures*, edited by Mogens H. Hansen, 547–566. The Royal Danish Academy of Sciences and Letters, Copenhagen.

Hageman, Jon B.

2004 The Lineage Model and Archaeological Data in Late Classic Northwestern Belize. *Ancient Mesoamerica* 15:63–74.

Halperin, Christina T., Ronald L. Bishop, Ellen Spensley, and M. James Blackman

2009 Late Classic (A.D. 600–900) Maya Market Exchange: Analysis of Figurines from the Motul de San José Region, Guatemala. *Journal of Field Archaeology* 34(4):457–480.

Hammond, Norman

1972 The Planning of a Maya Ceremonial Center. *Scientific American* 226(5):82–91.

1974 The Distribution of Late Classic Maya Major Centers in the Central Area. In *Meso-*

american Archaeology: New Approaches, edited by N. Hammond, 313–344. University of Texas Press, Austin.

1991   Inside the Black Box: Defining Maya Polity. In *Classic Maya Political History,* edited by T. P. Culbert, 253–284. Cambridge University Press, New York.

Hanks, William

1990   *Referential Practice: Language and Lived Space among the Maya.* University of Chicago Press, Chicago.

Hannerz, Ulf

1980   *Exploring the City: Inquiries toward an Urban Anthropology.* Columbia University Press, New York.

Hansen, Mogens Herman

2000a The Hellenic Polis. In *A Comparative Study of Thirty City-State Cultures: An Investigation,* edited by Mogens H. Hansen, 141–187. Kongelige Danske Videnskabernes Selskab, Copenhagen.

2000b Introduction: The Concepts of City-State and City-State Culture. In *A Comparative Study of Thirty City-State Cultures: An Investigation,* edited by Mogens H. Hansen, 11–34. Kongelige Danske Videnskabernes Selskab, Copenhagen.

Hansen, Richard

2001   The First Cities: The Beginnings of Urbanization and State Formation in the Maya Lowlands. In *Maya: Divine Kings of the Rain Forest,* edited by Nikolai Grube, 50–65. Konemann Press, Verlag.

Hare, Timothy S., and Marilyn Masson

2012   Intermediate-Scale Patterns in the Urban Environment of Postclassic Mayapan. In *The Neighborhood as a Social and Spatial Unit in Mesoamerican Cities,* edited by M.-C. Arnauld, L. Manzanilla, and M. E. Smith, 229–260. University of Arizona Press, Tucson.

Hare, Timothy S., Marilyn A. Masson, and Carlos Peraza Lope

2014   The Urban Cityscape. In *Kukulcan's Realm: Urban Life at Ancient Mayapan,* edited by M. Masson and C. Peraza Lope, 149–192. University Press of Colorado, Boulder.

Harrison, Peter D.

1994   Spatial Geometry and Logic in the Ancient Maya Mind: Part 2, Architecture. In *Seventh Palenque Round Table, 1989,* edited by Merle G. Robertson and Virginia M. Fields, 243–252. Pre-Columbian Art Research Institute, San Francisco.

Harrison, Peter D.

1999   *The Lords of Tikal: The Rulers of an Ancient Maya City.* Thames and Hudson, London.

Harvey, David

1985   *Consciousness and the Urban Experience.* Blackwell, Oxford.

Haviland, William A.

1966   Maya Settlement Patterns: A Critical Review. In *Middle American Research Institute Publication 26,* 21–47. Middle American Research Institute, New Orleans, LA.

1967   Stature at Tikal, Guatemala: Implications for Ancient Maya Demography and Social Organization. *American Antiquity* 32(3):316–325.

1969   A New Population Estimate for Tikal, Guatemala. *American Antiquity* 34(4):429–433.

1970   Tikal, Guatemala, and Mesoamerican Urbanism. *World Archaeology* 2:186–198.

1972   Estimates of Maya Population: Comments on Thompson's Comments. *American Antiquity* 37:261–262.

1974   Occupational Specialization at Tikal, Guatemala: Stone Working and Monument Carving. *American Antiquity* 39:494–496.

1982   Where the Rich Folks Lived: Deranging Factors in the Statistical Analysis of Tikal Settlement. *American Antiquity* 47(2):427–429.

1988   Musical Hammocks at Tikal: Problems with Reconstructing Household Composition. In *Household and Community in the Mesoamerican Past*, edited by Richard Wilk and Wendy Ashmore, 121–134. University of New Mexico Press, Albuquerque.

2008   Tikal, Guatemala: A Maya Way to Urbanism. In *El Urbanismo en Mesoamérica/ Urbanism in Mesoamerica*, edited by Alba G. Mastache, Robert H. Cobean, Ángel García Cook, and Kenneth G. Hirth. Pennsylvania State University and Instituto Nacional de Antropología e Historia, University Park and Mexico City.

2014   *Excavations in Residential Areas of Tikal: Non-elite Groups without Shrines: Analysis and Conclusions*. Tikal Report No. 20B. University of Pennsylvania Museum of Archaeology and Anthropology, Philadelphia.

Haviland, William A., and Hattula Moholy-Nagy

1992   Distinguishing the High and Mighty from the Hoi Polloi at Tikal, Guatemala. In *Mesoamerican Elites*, edited by Diane Z. Chase and Arlen F. Chase, 50–60. University of Oklahoma Press, Norman.

Hayden, Brian D., and Aubrey Cannon

1982   The Corporate Group as an Archaeological Unit. *Journal of Anthropological Archaeology* 1:132–158.

Hayden, Brian, and Rob Gargett

1990   Big Man, Big Heart? A Mesoamerican View of the Emergence of Complex Society. *Ancient Mesoamerica* 1(1):3–20.

Healy, Paul F., Christophe G. B. Helmke, Jaime J. Awe, and Kay S. Sunahara

2007   Survey, Settlement, and Population History at the Ancient Maya Site of Pacbitun, Belize. *Journal of Field Archaeology* 32(1):17–39.

Heidegger, Martin

(1927) 1996   *Being and Time*. Translated by J. Stambaugh. State University of New York Press, Albany.

Hendon, Julia A.

1991   Status and Power in Classic Maya Society: An Archaeological Study. *American Anthropologist* 93:894–918.

1992   The Interpretation of Survey Data: Two Case Studies from the Maya Area. *Latin American Antiquity* 3(1):22–42.

2010   *Houses in a Landscape: Memory and Everyday Life in Mesoamerica*. Duke University Press, Durham, N.C.

Hillier, Bill

2002   A Theory of the City as Object: or, How Spatial Laws Mediate the Social Construction of Urban Space. *Urban Design: International* 7(3–4):153–179.

Hillier, Bill, and Julienne Hanson

1984   *The Social Logic of Space*. Cambridge University Press, Cambridge.

Hirth, Kenneth G.

1998   The Distributional Approach: A New Way to Identify Marketplace Exchange in the Archaeological Record. *Current Anthropology* 39(4):451–476.

2003a   The Altepetl and Urban Structure in Prehispanic Mesoamerica. In *El Urbanismo en Mesoamerica*, edited by William Sanders, Alba G. Mastache, and Robert Cobean, 57–84. Instituto Nacional de Antropología e Historia and Penn State University, Mexico City and University Park.

2003b   Urban Structure at Xochicalco. In *El Urbanismo en Mesoamerica*, edited by William Sanders, Alba G. Mastache, and Robert Cobean, 257–309. Instituto Nacional de Antropología e Historia and Penn State University, Mexico City and University Park.

2009a   Household, Workshop, Guild, and Barrio: The Organization of Obsidian Craft Production in a Prehispanic Urban Center. In *Domestic Life in Prehispanic Capitals: A Study of Specialization, Hierarchy, and Ethnicity*, edited by Linda R. Manzanilla and Claude Chapdelaine, 43–66. University of Michigan, Museum of Anthropology, Ann Arbor.

2009b   Housework and Domestic Craft Production: An Introduction. In *Housework: Craft Production and Domestic Economy in Mesoamerica*, edited by Kenneth G. Hirth, 1–12. Archaeological Papers of the American Anthropological Association no. 19, American Anthropological Association, Washington, DC.

2010   Finding the Mark in the Marketplace: The Organization, Development, and Archaeological Identification of Market Systems. In *Archaeological Approaches to Market Exchange in Ancient Societies*, edited by Chris P. Garraty and Barbara L. Stark, 227–247. University Press of Colorado, Boulder.

Hirth, Kenneth G., and Joanne Pillsbury

2013   Merchants, Markets and Exchange in the Pre-Colombian World. In *Merchants, Markets and Exchange in the Pre-Colombian World*, edited by Kenneth G. Hirth and Joanne Pillsbury, 1–22. Dumbarton Oaks Research Library and Collection, Washington, DC.

Hodder, Ian

1999   British Prehistory: Some Thoughts Looking In. *Cambridge Archaeological Journal* 9:376–380.

2006   *The Leopard's Tale: Revealing the Mysteries of Çatalhöyük*. Thames and Hudson, London.

Hole, Frank, Kent Flannery, and James Neely

1969   *Prehistory and Human Ecology of the Deh Luran Plain*. Museum of Anthropology, University of Michigan, Ann Arbor.

Horsfall, Gayel A.

1987   Design Theory and Grinding Stones. In *Lithic Studies among the Contemporary Highland Maya*, edited by Brian Hayden, 332–377. University of Arizona Press, Tucson.

Houston, Stephen D.

1993   *Hieroglyphs and History at Dos Pilas*. University of Texas Press, Austin.

1996   Symbolic Sweatbaths of the Maya: Architectural Meaning in the Cross Group at Palenque, Mexico. *Latin American Antiquity* 7:132–151.

1998a Classic Maya Depictions of the Built Environment. In *Function and Meaning in Classic Maya Architecture*, edited by Stephen D. Houston, 333–372. Dumbarton Oaks Research Library and Collection, Washington, DC.

2006 Impersonation, Dance, and the Problem of Spectacle among the Classic Maya. In *Archaeology of Performance: Theaters of Power, Community, and Politics*, edited by T. Inomata and L. S. Coben, 135–155. AltaMira Press, Lanham, MD.

2013 *The Life Within: Classic Maya and the Matter of Permanence.* Yale University Press, New Haven, CT.

2014 Courtesans and Carnal Commerce. Maya Decipherment: Ideas on Ancient Maya Writing and Iconography. https://decipherment.wordpress.com/tag/stephen-houston/.

Houston, Stephen D. (editor)

1998b *Function and Meaning in Classic Maya Architecture.* Dumbarton Oaks Research Library and Collection, Washington, DC.

Houston, Stephen D., Hector L. Escobedo, Mark Child, Charles Golden, and Rene Munoz

2003 The Moral Community: Settlement Transformation at Piedras Negras, Guatemala. In *Social Construction of Ancient Cities*, edited by Monica L. Smith, 212–253. Smithsonian Institution Press, Washington, DC.

Houston, Stephen D. and Takeshi Inomata

2009 *The Classic Maya.* Cambridge University Press, Cambridge.

Houston, Stephen D., David Stuart, and Karl Taube

2006 *The Memory of Bones: Body, Being and Experience among the Classic Maya.* University of Texas Press, Austin.

Houston, Stephen D., and Karl Taube

2000 An Archaeology of the Senses: Perception and Cultural Expression in Ancient Mesoamerica. *Cambridge Archaeological Journal* 10(2):261–294.

Howard, Ebenezer

1902 *Garden Cities of Tomorrow.* Sonnenschein and Sons, London.

Hudson, Bob

2000 The Origins of Bagan: New Dates and Old Inhabitants. *Asian Perspectives* 40:48–74.

Hutson, Scott R.

2000 Carnival and Contestation in the Aztec Marketplace. *Dialectical Anthropology* 25:123–149.

2002 Built Space and Bad Subjects: Domination and Resistance at Monte Albán, Oaxaca, Mexico. *Journal of Social Archaeology* 2(1):53–80.

2004 Dwelling and Subjectification at the Ancient Urban Center of Chunchucmil, Yucatan, Mexico. Ph.D. dissertation, Department of Anthropology, University of California, Berkeley.

2010 *Dwelling, Identity and the Maya: Relational Archaeology at Chunchucmil.* Altamira Press, Lanham, MD.

2015 Lowland Maya Ritual Labor. In *Religion and Politics in the Americas*, edited by Sarah Barber and Arthur Joyce. Routledge, New York.

Hutson, Scott R., and Miguel Covarrubias Reyna

2011 De Ucí hasta Kancab: Recorrido de una Calzada de Larga Distancia en Yucatán,

México. In *XXIV Simposio de Investigaciones Arqueológicas de Guatemala*, edited by Barbara Arroyo, 1221–1229. Museo Nacional de Arqueología y Etnología, Guatemala City.

Hutson, Scott R., Bruce H. Dahlin, and Daniel Mazeau

2010　Commerce and Cooperation among the Classic Maya: The Chunchucmil Case. In *Cooperation in Economy and Society*, edited by Robert Marshall, 81–103. Altamira Press, Lanham, MD.

Hutson, Scott R., and Gavin Davies

2015　Megalithic Materialities in the Northern Maya Lowlands. In *The Materiality of Everyday Life*, edited by Lisa Overholtzer and Cynthia Robin. Archaeological Papers of the American Anthropological Association, Washington, DC.

Hutson, Scott R., David Hixson, Aline Magnoni, Daniel E. Mazeau, and Bruce H. Dahlin

2008　Site and Community at Chunchucmil and Ancient Maya Urban Centers. *Journal of Field Archaeology* 33(1):19–40.

Hutson, Scott R., Bryan K. Hanks, and K. Anne Pyburn

2013　Gender, Power, and Politics in Early States. In *Companion to Gender Prehistory*, edited by Diane Bolger, 45–67. Blackwell, Oxford.

Hutson, Scott R., Aline Magnoni, Traci Ardren, Chelsea Blackmore, and Travis Stanton

2016　Chunchucmil's Urban Population. In *Ancient Maya Commerce: Multidisciplinary Research at Chunchucmil*, edited by Scott Hutson. University Press of Colorado, Boulder.

Hutson Scott R., Aline Magnoni, and Bruce H. Dahlin

2016　Architectural Group Typology and Excavation Sampling. In *Ancient Maya Commerce: Multidisciplinary Research at Chunchucmil*, edited by Scott Hutson. University Press of Colorado, Boulder.

Hutson, Scott R., Aline Magnoni, Daniel Mazeau, and Travis Stanton

2006　The Archaeology of Urban Houselots at Chunchucmil, Yucatan, Mexico. In *Lifeways in the Northern Lowlands: New Approaches to Maya Archaeology*, edited by Jennifer P. Mathews and Bethany A. Morrison, 77–92. University of Arizona Press, Tucson.

Hutson, Scott R., Aline Magnoni, and Travis Stanton

2004　House Rules?: The Practice of Social Organization in Classic Period Chunchucmil, Yucatan, Mexico. *Ancient Mesoamerica* 15:74–92.

Hutson, Scott R., Travis W. Stanton, Aline Magnoni, Richard E. Terry, and Jason Craner

2007　Beyond the Buildings: Formation Processes of Ancient Maya Houselots and Methods for the Study of Non-Architectural Space. *Journal of Anthropological Archaeology* 26:442–473.

Hutson, Scott R., and Jacob A. Welch

2014　Sacred Landscapes and Building Practices at Uci, Ucanha, and Kancab Yucatan, Mexico. *Ancient Mesoamerica* 25:421–439.

Iannone, Gyles, and Samuel V. Connell

2003　Perspectives on Ancient Maya Rural Complexity: An Introduction. In *Perspectives on Ancient Maya Rural Complexity*, edited by Gyles Iannone and Samuel V. Connell, 1–6. Cotsen Institute of Archaeology, University of California, Los Angeles.

Inomata, Takeshi

2004　The Spatial Mobility of Non-Elite Populations in Classic Maya Society and Its Political Implications. In *Ancient Maya Commoners*, edited by J. C. Lohse and F. J. Valdez, 175–196. University of Texas Press, Austin.

2006   Plazas, Performers and Spectators: Political Theaters of the Classic Maya. *Current Anthropology* 47:805–842.

Inomata, Takeshi, and Stephen D. Houston (editors)

2000   *Royal Courts of the Ancient Maya*. Westview Press, Boulder, CO.

Isbell, William

2009   Huari: A New Direction in Central Andean Urban Evolution. In *Domestic Life in Prehispanic Capitals: A Study of Specialization, Hierarchy, and Ethnicity*, edited by Linda R. Manzanilla and Claude Chapdelaine, 197–220. University of Michigan, Museum of Anthropology, Ann Arbor.

Isendahl, Christian, and Michael E. Smith

2013   Sustainable Agrarian Urbanism: The Low-Density Cities of the Mayas and Aztecs. *Cities* 31:132–143.

Jacobs, Jane

1961   *The Death and Life of Great American Cities*. Random House, New York.

1969   *The Economy of Cities*. Random House, New York.

Jacobs, L.

1979   Tell-i-Nun: Archaeological Implications of a Village in Transition. In *Ethnoarchaeology*, edited by Carol Kramer, 176–191. Columbia University, New York.

Janusek, John W.

2002   Out of Many, One: Style and Social Boundaries at Tiwanaku. *Latin American Antiquity* 13:35–61.

Janusek, John W., and Deborah E. Blom

2006   Identifying Tiwanaku Urban Populations: Style, Identity and Ceremony in Andean Cities. In *Urbanism in the Pre-Industrial World: Cross Cultural Approaches*, edited by Glenn Storey, 233–251. University of Alabama Press, Tuscaloosa.

Johnston, Kevin J.

2004   The Invisible Maya: Minimally Mounded Residential Settlement at Itzán, Petén, Guatemala. *Latin American Antiquity* 15(2):145–175.

Jones, Christopher

1996   *Excavations in the East Plaza of Tikal*. Tikal Report Number 16. The University Museum, University of Pennsylvania, Philadelphia.

2015   The Marketplace at Tikal. In *Ancient Maya Marketplaces: The Archaeology of Transient Space*, edited by Eleanor M. King and Leslie C. Shaw. University of Arizona Press, Tucson.

Joyce, Arthur A.

2009   Theorizing Urbanism in Ancient Mesoamerica. *Ancient Mesoamerica* 20:189–196.

Joyce, Arthur A., and Sarah B. Barber

2015   Ensoulment, Entrapment, and Political Centralization: A Comparative Study of Religion and Politics in Later Formative Oaxaca. *Current Anthropology*.

Joyce, Arthur A., Laura A. Bustamante, and Marc N. Levine

2001   Commoner Power: A Case Study from the Classic Period Collapse on the Oaxaca Coast. *Journal of Archaeological Method and Theory* 8(4):343–385.

Joyce, Arthur A., and Errin Weller

2007   Commoner Ritual, Resistance and the Classic to Postclassic Transition in Ancient Mesoamerica. In *Commoner Ritual and Ideology in Ancient Mesoamerica*, edited by Nancy Gonlin and Jon C. Lohse, 143–184. University Press of Colorado, Boulder.

Joyce, Arthur A., and M. Winter

1996   Ideology, Power, and Urban Society in Prehispanic Oaxaca. *Current Anthropology* 37(1):33–47.

Joyce, Rosemary A.

1993   Women's Work: Images of Production and Reproduction in Prehispanic Southern Central America. *Current Anthropology* 34(3):255–274.

1996   The Construction of Gender in Classic Maya Monuments. In *Gender and Archaeology*, edited by Rita P. Wright, 167–195. University of Pennsylvania, Philadelphia.

2000a   Heirlooms and Houses: Materiality and Social Memory. In *Beyond Kinship: Social and Material Reproduction in House Societies*, edited by Rosemary A. Joyce and Susan D. Gillespie, 189–212. University of Pennsylvania Press, Philadelphia.

2000b   Girling the Girl and Boying the Boy. *World Archaeology* 31(3):473–483.

Joyce, Rosemary A., and S. D. Gillespie (editors)

2000   *Beyond Kinship: Social and Material Reproduction in House Societies*. University of Pennsylvania Press, Philadelphia.

Kadushin, Charles

2012   *Understanding Social Networks: Theories, Concepts and Findings*. Oxford University Press, Oxford.

Keith, Kathryn

2003   The Spatial Patterns of Everyday Life in Old Babylonian Neighborhoods. In *The Social Construction of Ancient Cities*, edited by M. L. Smith, 56–80. Smithsonian Institution Press, Washington, DC.

Kemper, Robin V.

2002   Migration and Adaptation: Tzintzuntzeños in Mexico City and Beyond. In *Urban Life: Readings in the Anthropology of the City*, 4th ed., edited by George Gmelch and Walter P. Zenner, 193–204. Waveland Press, Prospect Heights, IL.

Kepecs, Susan, and Sylviane Boucher

1996   The Pre-Hispanic Cultivation of Rejolladas and Stone-Lands: New Evidence from Northeast Yucatan. In *The Managed Mosaic*, edited by Scott L. Fedick, 69–91. University of Utah Press, Salt Lake City.

King, Eleanor M.

2015   The Ethnohistoric Evidence for Maya Markets. In *Ancient Maya Marketplaces: The Archaeology of Transient Space*, edited by Eleanor M. King and Leslie C. Shaw. University of Arizona Press, Tucson.

King, Eleanor M., and Leslie C. Shaw (editors)

2015   *Ancient Maya Marketplaces: The Archaeology of Transient Space*. University of Arizona Press, Tucson.

Kintz, Ellen

1983   Neighborhoods and Wards in a Classic Maya Metropolis. In *Coba: A Classic Maya*

Metropolis, edited by William Folan, Ellen Kintz, and Larraine Fletcher, 179–190. Academic Press, New York.

Kintz, Ellen, and Larraine Fletcher

1983   A Reconstruction of the Prehistoric Population at Coba. In *Coba: A Classic Maya Metropolis*, edited by W. Folan, Ellen Kintz, and Larraine Fletcher, 191–210. Academic Press, New York.

Kolb, Michael J., and James Snead

1997   It's a Small World after All: Comparative Analysis of Community Organization in Archaeology. *American Antiquity* 62(4):609–628.

Kowalewski, Stephen A, Gary M Feinman, and Laura Finsten

1992   The Elite and Assessment of Social Stratification in Mesoamerican Archaeology. In *Mesoamerican Elites*, edited by Diane Z. Chase and Arlen F. Chase, 259–277. University of Oklahoma Press, Norman, OK.

Kowalski, Jeff K.

1987   *The House of the Governor: A Maya Palace at Uxmal, Yucatan, Mexico*. University of Oklahoma Press, Norman.

Kramer, Carol

1979   An Archaeological View of a Contemporary Kurdish Village: Domestic Architecture, Household Size, and Wealth. In *Ethnoarchaeology: Implications of Ethnography for Archaeology*, edited by Carol Kramer, 139–163. Columbia University Press, New York.

Kubler, George

1961   The Design of Space in Maya Architecture. In *Miscellanea Paul Rivet: Octogenario dicata*, 515–531. Universidad Nacional Autónoma de México, México, D.F.

Kunen, Julie

2004   *Ancient Maya Life in the Far West Bajo: Social and Environmental Change in the Wetlands of Belize*. Anthropological Papers of the University of Arizona, no. 69. University of Arizona Press, Tucson, AZ.

Kurjack, Edward B.

1974   *Prehistoric Lowland Maya Community and Social Organization: A Case Study at Dzibilchaltun, Yucatan, Mexico*. Middle American Research Institute 38. Middle American Research Institute, New Orleans, LA.

Kurtz, Donald V.

1974   Peripheral and Transitional Markets: The Aztec Case. *American Ethnologist* 1(4): 685–705.

Kurtzleben, Danielle

2011   The 13 Least Equal US Cities. *US News and World Report*, April 20. http://www.us-news.com/news/best-cities/slideshows/the-13-cities-with-the-greatest-economic-inequality. Accessed March 2014.

Lampard, Eric E.

1955   The History of Cities in the Economically Advanced Areas. *Economic Development and Culture Change* 3:81–136.

Law, Danny

2014   *Language Contact, Inherited Similarity and Social Difference: The Story of Linguistic Interaction in the Maya Lowlands*. John Benjamins Publishing Company, Amsterdam.

Lawrence, Denise, and Setha Low

1990   The Built Environment and Spatial Form. *Annual Reviews of Anthropology* 19:453–505.

Le Corbusier

1986   *Towards a New Architecture*. Translated by F. Etchells. Dover, New York.

1987   *The City of Tomorrow and Its Planning*. Translated by F. Etchells. MIT Press, Cambridge, MA.

LeCount, Lisa

1999   Polychrome Pottery and Political Strategies in Late and Terminal Classic Lowland Maya Society. *Latin American Antiquity* 10(3):239–258.

LeCount, Lisa, Jason Yaeger, Richard Leventhal, and Wendy Ashmore

2002   Dating the Rise and Fall of Xunantunich, Belize: A Late and Terminal Classic Lowland Maya Regional Center. *Ancient Mesoamerica* 13(1):41–63.

Lefebvre, Henri

1991   *The Production of Space*. Translated by D. Nicholson-Smith. Blackwell, Oxford.

Lemmonier, Eva

2012   Neighborhoods in Classic Lowland Maya Societies: Their Identification and Definition from the La Joyanca Case Study (Northwestern Peten, Guatemala). In *The Neighborhood as a Social and Spatial Unit in Mesoamerican Cities*, edited by M. Charlotte Arnauld, Linda Manzanilla, and Michael E. Smith, 181–201. University of Arizona Press, Tucson.

Lentz, David, Sally Woods, Angela Hood, and Marcus Murph

2012   Agroforestry and Agricultural Production of the Ancient Maya. In *Chan: An Ancient Maya Farming Community*, edited by Cynthia Robin, 89–109. University Press of Florida, Gainesville.

Leventhal, Richard

1979   Settlement Patterns at Copan, Honduras. Ph.D. dissertation, Department of Anthropology, Harvard University, Cambridge, MA.

Levi-Strauss, Claude

1982   *The Way of the Masks*. Translated by S. Modelski. Seattle, University of Washington Press.

Lewis, Oscar

1965   Further Observations on the Folk Urban Continuum and Urbanization with Special Reference to Mexico City. In *The Study of Urbanization*, edited by Philip M. Hauser and Leo F. Schnore, 441–503. Wiley and Sons, New York.

Littmann, Edwin R.

1958   Ancient Mesoamerican Mortars, Plasters, and Stuccos: The Composition and Origins of Sascab. *American Antiquity* 23:172–176.

Lohse, Jon C.

2004   Intra-Site Settlement Signatures and Implications for Late Classic Maya Commoner Organization at Dos Hombres, Belize. In *Ancient Maya Commoners*, edited by Jon C. Lohse and Fred Valdez, 117–145. University of Texas Press, Austin.

2007   Commoner Ritual, Commoner Ideology: (Sub-)Alternate View of Social Complexity in Prehispanic Mesoamerica. In *Commoner Ritual and Ideology in Ancient*

Mesoamerica, edited by Nancy Gonlin and Jon C. Lohse, 1–32. University Press of Colorado, Boulder.

Lohse, Jon C. (editor)

2013 *Classic Maya Political Ecology: Resource Management, Class Histories, and Political Change in Northwestern Belize*. Cotsen Institute, University of California at Los Angeles, Los Angeles.

Lohse, Jon C., and Fred Valdez

2004 Examining Ancient Maya Commoners Anew. In *Ancient Maya Commoners*, edited by Jon C. Lohse and Fred Valdez, 1–21. University of Texas Press, Austin.

Looper, Matthew G.

2001 Dance Performances at Quirigua. In *Landscape and Power in Ancient Mesoamerica*, ed. Rex Koontz, Kathryn Reese-Taylor, and Annabeth Headrick, 113–36. Westview Press, Boulder.

Lopiparo, Jeanne

2006 Crafting Children: Materiality, Social Memory, and the Reproduction of Terminal Classic House Societies in the Ulua Valley, Honduras. In *The Social Experience of Childhood in Mesoamerica*, edited by Traci Ardren and Scott R. Hutson, 133–170. University Press of Colorado, Boulder.

Lucero, Lisa J.

2003 The Politics of Ritual: The Emergence of Classic Maya Kings. *Current Anthropology* 44(4):523–558.

2007 Classic Maya Temples, Politics, and the Voice of the People. *Latin American Antiquity* 18(4):407–428.

Lynch, Kevin

1960 *The Image of the City*. MIT Press, Cambridge.

Maca, Allan L.

2006 Body, Boundaries, and "Lived" Urban Space: A Research Model for the Eighth-Century City at Copan, Honduras. In *Space and Spatial Analysis in Archaeology*, edited by E. C. Robertson, J. D. Seibert, D. C. Fernandez and M. U. Zender, 143–156. University of Calgary Press, Calgary.

Magnoni, Aline

2008 From City to Village: Landscape and Household Transformations at Classic Period Chunchucmil, Yucatán, Mexico. Ph.D. dissertation, Department of Anthropology, Tulane University, New Orleans, LA.

Magnoni, Aline, Traci Ardren, Scott R. Hutson, and Bruce H. Dahlin

2014 Urban Identities: Social and Spatial Production at Classic Period Chunchucmil, Yucatan, Mexico. In *Making Ancient Cities*, edited by Andrew T. Creekmore and Kevin D. Fisher, 145–180. Cambridge University Press, Cambridge.

Magnoni, Aline, Scott R. Hutson, and Bruce H. Dahlin

2012 Living in the City: Settlement Patterns and the Urban Experience at Classic Period Chunchucmil, Yucatan, Mexico. *Ancient Mesoamerica* 23:313–343.

Manzanilla, Linda R.

1997 Teotihuacan: Urban Archetype, Cosmic Model. In *Emergence and Change in Early Urban Societies*, edited by Linda Manzanilla, 109–132. Plenum, New York.

2009   Corporate Life in Apartment and Barrio Compounds at Teotihuacan, Central Mexico: Craft Specialization, Hierarchy, and Ethnicity. In *Domestic Life in Prehispanic Capitals: A Study of Specialization, Hierarchy, and Ethnicity*, edited by Linda R. Manzanilla and Claude Chapdelaine, 21–42. University of Michigan, Museum of Anthropology, Ann Arbor.

2012   Neighborhoods and Elite "Houses" at Teotihuacan, Central Mexico. In *The Neighborhood as a Social and Spatial Unit in Mesoamerican Cities*, edited by M. Charlotte Arnauld, Linda Manzanilla, and Michael E. Smith, 55–73. University of Arizona Press, Tucson.

Marcus, George

1983   Introduction. In *Elites: Ethnographic Issues*, edited by George Marcus, 3–6. University of New Mexico Press, Albuquerque.

Marcus, Joyce

1973   Territorial Organization of the Lowland Classic Maya. *Science* 180(4089):911–916.

1976   *Emblem and State in the Classic Maya Lowlands*. Dumbarton Oaks, Washington, DC.

1983   On the Nature of the Mesoamerican City. In *Prehistoric Settlement Patterns: Essays in Honor of Gordon Willey*, edited by Evon Z. Vogt and Richard Leventhal, 195–242. Peabody Museum of Archaeology, Cambridge, MA, and Ethnology and University of New Mexico Press, Albuquerque.

1992   Royal Families, Royal Texts: Examples from the Zapotec and Maya. In *Mesoamerican Elites*, edited by Diane Z. Chase, and Arlen F. Chase, 221–241. University of Oklahoma Press, Norman.

Marcus, Joyce and Jeremy A. Sabloff

2008   Introduction. In *The Ancient City: New Perspectives on Urbanism in the Old and New Worlds*, edited by Joyce Marcus and Jeremy A. Sabloff, 3–28. National Academy of Sciences, Washington, DC, and School of American Research, Santa Fe, NM.

Marken, Damien

2011   City and State: Urbanization, Rural Settlement, and Polity in the Classic Maya Lowlands. Ph.D. dissertation, Department of Anthropology, Southern Methodist University, Dallas.

Martin, Simon

2012   Hieroglyphs from the Painted Pyramid: The Epigraphy of Chiik Nahb Structure Sub 1-4, Calakmul, Mexico. In *Maya Archaeology 2*, edited by Charles Golden, Stephen D. Houston, and Joel Skidmore, 60–80. Precolumbian Mesoweb Press, San Francisco.

Martin, Simon, and Nikolai Grube

1995   Maya Superstates. *Archaeology* 48(6):41–46.

2000   *Chronicles of the Maya Kings and Queens*. Thames and Hudson, London.

Masson, Marilyn A.

2002   Introduction. In *Ancient Maya Political Economies*, edited by Marilyn A. Masson and David A. Freidel, 1–30. Altamira Press, Walnut Creek, CA.

Masson, Marilyn A., and David Freidel

2012   An Argument for Classic-Era Maya Market Exchange. *Journal of Anthropological Archaeology* 31:455–484.

2013   Wide Open Spaces: A Long View of the Importance of Maya Market Exchange. In

Merchants, Markets, and Exchange in the Pre-Columbian World, edited by Kenneth G. Hirth and Joanne Pillsbury, 201–228. Dumbarton Oaks Research Library and Collection, Washington, DC.

Masson, Marilyn A., Timothy S. Hare, and Carlos Peraza Lope

2006   Postclassic Maya Society Regenerated at Mayapán. In After Collapse: The Regeneration of Complex Societies, edited by Glenn M. Schwartz and John J. Nichols, 188–207. University of Arizona Press, Tucson.

2014   The Social Mosaic. In Kukulcan's Realm: Urban Life at Ancient Mayapan, edited by Marilyn A. Masson and Carlos Peraza Lope, 1–38. University Press of Colorado, Boulder.

Masson, Marilyn A., and Carlos Peraza Lope

2004   Commoners in Postclassic Maya Society: Social versus Economic Class Constructs. In Ancient Maya Commoners, edited by Jon C. Lohse and Fred Valdez, 197–223. University of Texas Press, Austin.

2014   Archaeological Investigations of an Ancient Urban Place. In Kukulcan's Realm: Urban Life at Ancient Mayapan, edited by Marilyn Masson and Carlos Peraza Lope, 1–38. University Press of Colorado, Boulder.

Mathews, Jennifer P., and James F. Garber

2004   Models of Cosmic Order: Physical Expression of Sacred Space among the Ancient Maya. Ancient Mesoamerica 15:49–59.

Mathews, Peter

1985   Maya Early Classic Monuments and Inscriptions. In A Consideration of the Early Classic Period in the Maya Lowlands, edited by Gordon R. Willey and Peter Mathews. Institute for Mesoamerican Studies, Albany, NY.

1991   Classic Maya Emblem Glyphs. In Classic Maya Political History: Hieroglyphic and Archaeological Evidence edited by T. Patrick Culbert, 19–29. Cambridge University Press and School of American Research, Cambridge.

Mathews, Peter, and John Justeson

1984   Patterns of Sign Substitution in Maya Hieroglyphic Writing: The Affix Cluster. In Phoneticism in Mayan Hieroglyphic Writing, edited by John S. Justeson and Lyle Campbell, 185–232. Institute for Mesoamerican Studies, State University of New York at Albany, Albany.

Maudslay, Alfred P.

1889–1902 Biologia Centrali-Americana: Archaeology. 5 vols. in 1. R. H. Porter and Dulau, London.

McAnany, Patricia A.

1992   A Theoretical Perspective on Elites and Economic Transformation in Classic Period Maya Households. In Understanding Economic Processes, edited by Sutti Ortiz and Susan Lees, 85–106. Monographs in Economic Anthropology. University Press of America, Lanham, MD.

1993a   Resources, Specialization and Exchange in the Maya Lowlands. In The American Southwest and Mesoamerica: Systems of Prehistoric Exchange, edited by Jonathan Ericson, and Timothy J. Baugh, 213–245. Plenum, New York.

1993b   The Economics of Social Power and Wealth among Eighth Century Maya Households. In *Lowland Maya Civilization in the Eighth Century A.D.*, edited by Jeremy A. Sabloff and John S. Henderson, 65–90. Dumbarton Oaks Research Library ad Collection, Washington, DC.

1995 *Living with the Ancestors: Kinship and Kingship in Ancient Maya Society*. University of Texas Press, Austin.

2010 *Ancestral Maya Economies in Archaeological Perspective*. Cambridge University Press, Cambridge.

McAnany, Patricia A., Ben Thomas, Steven Morandi, Polly A. Peterson, and Eleanor Harrison

2002 Praise the Ajaw and Pass the Kakaw: Xibun Maya and the Political Economy of Cacao. In *Ancient Maya Political Economies*, edited by Marilyn A. Masson and David A. Freidel, 123–139. Altamira Press, Walnut Creek, CA.

McIntosh, Roderick

2005 *Ancient Middle Niger: Urbanism and the Self-Organizing Landscape*. Cambridge University Press, Cambridge.

McKillop, Heather

2002 *Salt: White Gold of the Ancient Maya*. University Press of Florida, Gainesville.

McNeill, William Hardy

1976 *Plagues and Peoples*. Anchor Press/Doubleday, Garden City, NY.

Meskell, Lynn M., and Rosemary A. Joyce

2003 *Embodied Lives: Figuring Ancient Maya and Egyptian Experience*. Routledge, London.

Meskell, Lynn, and Robert Preucel (editors)

2004 *A Companion to Social Archaeology*. Blackwell, Malden, MA.

Miksik, John N.

1999 Water, Urbanization, and Disease in Ancient Indonesia. In *Complex Polities in the Ancient Tropical World*, edited by Elizabeth Bacus and Lisa Lucero, 167–184. American Anthropological Association, Arlington VA.

Milanovic, Branko

2009 *Global Inequality and the Global Inequality Extraction Ratio: The Story of the Past Two Centuries*. Policy Research Working Paper 5044. World Bank, Washington, DC.

Milbrath, Susan, and Carlos Peraza Lope

2003 Revisiting Mayapan: Mexico's Last Maya Capital. *Ancient Mesoamerica* 14:1–46.

Milgram, Stanley

1970 The Experience of Living in Cities. *Science* 167(3924):1461–1468.

Miller, Katherine A.

2015 Family, 'Foreigners,' and Fictive Kinship: A Bioarchaeological Approach to Social Organization at Late Classic Copan. Ph.D. dissertation, School of Human Evolution and Social Change, Arizona State University, Tempe.

Miller, Mary E.

1986 *The Murals of Bonampak*. Princeton University Press, Princeton, NJ.

1998 A Design for Meaning in Maya Archaeology. In *Function and Meaning in Classic Maya Architecture*, edited by Stephen D. Houston, 187–222. Dumbarton Oaks Research Library and Collection, Washington, DC.

1999 *Maya Art and Architecture*. Thames and Hudson, London.

Millet Cámara, Luis, and Rafael Burgos Villanueva

2006 Izamal: Una Aproximación a su Arquitectura. In *Los Mayas de Ayer y Hoy: Memorias del Primer Congreso Internacional de Cultura Maya*, vol. 1, edited by Alfredo Barrera Rubio and Ruth Gubler, 132–155. Gobierno del Estado de Yucatán, Mérida, México.

Millon, Rene

1976 Social Relations in Ancient Teotihuacan. In *The Valley of Mexico: Studies in Pre-Hispanic Ecology and Society*, edited by Eric Wolf, 205–248. University of New Mexico Press, Albuquerque.

1981 Teotihuacan: City, State and Civilization. In *Archaeology*, edited by Victoria Bricker and Jeremy A. Sabloff, 198–243. Vol. 1 of *Supplement to the Handbook of Middle American Indians*. University of Texas Press, Austin.

Millon, Rene, Bruce Drewitt, and George Cowgill

1973 *Urbanization at Teotihuacan, Mexico*. Vol. 1, *The Teotihuacan Map*. University of Texas Press, Austin.

Mills, Barbara J., Jeffery J. Clark, Matthew A. Peeples, Jr. W. R. Haas Jr., John M. Roberts, J. Brett Hill, Deborah L. Huntley, Lewis Borck, Ronald L. Breigere, Aaron Clauset, and M. Steven Shackley

2013 Transformation of Social Networks in the Late Pre-Hispanic US Southwest. *Proceedings of the National Academy of Sciences* 110(15):5785–5790.

Moholy-Nagy, Hattula

2003 The Hiatus at Tikal, Guatemala. *Ancient Mesoamerica* 14:77–83.

Monaghan, John

2000 Theology and History in the Study of Mesoamerican Religions. In *Ethnology*, edited by John Monaghan and Barbara Edmonson, 24–49. Vol. 6 of *Supplement to the Handbook of Middle American Indians*. University of Texas Press, Austin.

Moore, Jerry D.

1996 *Architecture and Power in the Ancient Andes: The Archaeology of Public Buildings*. Cambridge University Press, Cambridge.

2005 *Cultural Landscapes in the Ancient Andes: Archaeologies of Place*. University Press of Florida, Gainesville.

Morgan, Lewis H.

1880 A Study of the Houses of the American Aborigines. *Archaeological Institute of North America, Annual Report of the Executive Committee* 1:29–80.

Morley, Neville

1997 Cities in Context: Urban Systems in Roman Italy. In *Roman Urbanism: Beyond the Consumer City*, edited by Helen M. Parkins, 42–58. Routledge, London.

Morton, Shawn G., Meaghan Peuramaki-Brown, Peter C. Dawson, and Jeff D. Seibert

2012 Civic and Household Community Relationships at Teotihuacan, Mexico: a Space Syntax Approach. *Cambridge Archaeological Journal* 22:387–400.

2014 Peopling the Past: Interpreting Models for Pedestrian Movement in Ancient Civic-Ceremonial Centres. In *Mapping Spatial Relations, Their Perceptions and Dynamics*, edited by Susanne Rau and Ekkehard Schönherr, 25–44. Springer, Heidelberg.

Mouw, Ted

2006 Estimating the Causal Effect of Social Capital: A Review of Recent Research. *Annual Review of Sociology* 32(1):79–102.

Mumford, Lewis

1961   *The City in History*. Harcourt Brace and World, New York.

2011 (1937)   What Is a City? In *The City Reader*, edited by Richard LeGates and Frederic Stout, 92–95. Routledge, New York.

Narroll, Raoul

1962   Floor Area and Settlement Population. *American Antiquity* 27(587–589).

National Commission on Neighborhoods

1979   *People, Building Neighborhoods, Final Report to the President and Congress of the United States*. Government Printing Office, Washington, DC.

Navarrete, Carlos, María Jose Con, and A. Martínez Muriel

1979   *Observaciones Arqueológicas en Cobá, Quintana Roo*. Instituto de Investigaciones Filológicas, Universidad Nacional Autónoma de México, México D.F.

Netting, Robert M.

1982   Some Home Truths on Household Size and Wealth. *American Behavioral Scientist* 25(6):641–661.

Okoshi-Harada, Tsubasa

2012   Postclassic Maya "Barrios" in Yucatán: An Historical Approach. In *The Neighborhood as a Social and Spatial Unit in Mesoamerican Cities*, edited by M. Charlotte Arnauld, Linda Manzanilla, and Michael E. Smith, 286–303. University of Arizona Press, Tucson.

Ortiz, Isabel, and Matthew Cummins

2011   *Global Inequality: Beyond the Bottom Billion*. UNICEF Social and Economic Policy Working Paper. UNICEF, New York.

Ortman, Scott, Andrew H. F. Cabaniss, Jennie O. Sturm, and Luís M. A. Bettencourt

2014   The Pre-History of Urban Scaling. *PLOS One* 9(e87902).

2015   Settlement Scaling and Increasing Returns in an Ancient Society. *Science Advances*: 1–8.

Park, Robert E.

1925   The City: Suggestions for the Investigation of Human Behavior in the Urban Environment. In *The City*, edited by Robert E. Park, Ernest W. Burgess, and Roderick D. McKenzie, 1–46. University of Chicago Press, Chicago.

1952   *Human Communities*. Free Press, Glencoe, IL.

Parker Pearson, Parker, and Colin Richards

1994   Ordering the World: Perceptions of Architecture, Space and Time. In *Architecture and Order: Approaches to Social Space*, edited by M. Parker Pearson and C. Richards, 1–37. Routledge, London.

Pauketat, Timothy R.

2000   The Tragedy of the Commoners. In *Agency in Archaeology*, edited by Marcia-Anne Dobres and John Robb, 113–129. Routledge, London.

Pendergast, David M.

1967   *Palenque: The Walker-Caddy Expedition to the Ancient Maya City, 1839–1840*. University of Oklahoma Press, Norman.

Peraza Lope, Carlos, and Marilyn A. Masson

2014   Politics and Monumental Legacies. In *Kukulcan's Realm: Urban Life at Ancient Maya-*

pan, edited by Marilyn Masson and Carlos Peraza Lope, 39–104. University Press of Colorado, Boulder.

Petersen, Hans Christian, Jesper L. Boldsen, and Richard R. Paine

2006 Population Relationships in and around Medieval Danish Towns. In *Urbanism in the Pre-Industrial World: Cross Cultural Approaches*, edited by Glenn Storey, 110–120. University of Alabama Press, Tuscaloosa.

Peuramaki-Brown, Meaghan

2013 Identifying Integrative Built Environments in the Archaeological Record: An Application of New Urban Design Theory to Ancient Urban Spaces. *Journal of Anthropological Archaeology* 32:577–594.

Plank, Shannon E.

2004 *Maya Dwellings in Hieroglyphs and Archaeology: An Integrative Approach to Ancient Architecture and Spatial Cognition*. BAR International Series 1324. British Archaeological Reports, Oxford.

Poggi, Gianfranco

1993 *Money and the Modern Mind: Georg Simmel's Philosophy of Money*. University of California Press, Berkeley.

Polanyi, Karl

1944 *The Great Transformation: The Economic and Political Origins of Our Time*. Rinehart and Co., New York.

1957 The Economy as Instituted Process. In *Trade and Market in the Early Empires*, edited by K. Polanyi, Conrad M. Arensberg, and Harry W. Pearson, 243–270. Academic Press, New York.

Pollock, Harry E. D., Ralph Roys, Tatiana Proskouriakoff, and A. Ledyard Smith

1962 *Mayapan, Yucatan, Mexico*. Carnegie Institution Publication 619. Carnegie Institution of Washington, Washington, DC.

Portes, Alejandro

1998 Social Capital: Its Origins and Applications in Modern Sociology. *Annual Review of Sociology* 24(1):1–24.

Postgate, J. Nicholas

1992 *Early Mesopotamia: Society and Economy at the Dawn of History*. Routledge, London.

Pred, Allan

1990 *Lost Words and Lost Worlds: Modernity and the Language of Everyday Life in Late Nineteenth-Century Stockholm*. Cambridge University Press, Cambridge.

Proskouriakoff, Tatiana

1955 Mayapan: The Last Stronghold of a Civilization. *Archaeology* 7(2):96–103.

1962 Civic and Religious Structures of Mayapan. In *Mayapan, Yucatan, Mexico* edited by Harry E. D. Pollock. Carnegie Institution of Washington, Washington, DC.

1963 *An Album of Maya Architecture*. University of Oklahoma Press, Norman.

Pugh, Timothy

2003 The Exemplary Center of the Late Postclassic Kowoj Maya. *Latin American Antiquity* 14:408–430.

Puleston, Dennis

1974 Intersite Areas in the Vicinity of Tikal and Uaxactun. In *Mesoamerican Archaeology: New Approaches*, edited by Norman Hammond, 303–312. Duckworth, London.

1983   *The Settlement Survey of Tikal.* The Tikal Reports 13. The University Museum, University of Pennsylvania, Philadelphia.

Puleston, Dennis, and Donald Callendar Jr.

1967   Defensive Earthworks at Tikal. *Expedition* 9(3):40–48.

Putnam, Robert D.

2000   *Bowling Alone: The Collapse and Revival of American Community.* Simon and Schuster, New York.

Pyburn, K. Anne

1997   The Archaeological Signature of Complexity in the Maya Lowlands. In *The Archaeology of City-States: Cross-Cultural Perspectives,* edited by Thomas Charlton and Deborah Nichols, 155–168. Smithsonian Institution Press, Washington.

2004   Ungendering the Maya. In *Ungendering Civilization,* edited by P. K. Anne, 216–233. Routledge, New York.

2008   Pomp and Circumstance before Belize: Ancient Maya Commerce and the New River Conurbation. In *The Ancient City: Perspectives from the Old and New World,* edited by Joyce Marcus and Jeremy A. Sabloff, 247–272. National Academy of Sciences, Washington, DC, and School of American Research, Santa Fe, NM.

Pyburn, K. Anne, Boyd Dixon, Patricia Cook, and Anna McNair

1998   The Albion Island Settlement Pattern Project: Domination and Resistance in Early Classic Northern Belize. *Journal of Field Archaeology* 25:37–62.

Rands, Robert L., and Ronald L. Bishop

1980   Resource Procurement Zones and Patterns of Ceramic Exchange in the Palenque Region, Mexico. In *Models and Methods in Regional Exchange,* edited by Robert Fry, 19–46. Society for American Archaeology, Washington, DC.

Redfield, Robert

1941   *The Folk Culture of Yucatan.* University of Chicago Press, Chicago.

1955   *The Little Community: Viewpoints from the Study of a Human Whole.* University of Chicago Press, Chicago.

Redfield, Robert, and Alfonso Villa Rojas

1962   *Chan Kom: A Maya Village.* University of Chicago Press, Chicago.

Renfrew, Colin

1973   *Social Archaeology.* University of Southampton, Southampton.

1994   Concluding Remarks: Childe and the Study of Culture Process. In *The Archaeology of V. Gordon Childe: Contemporary Perspectives,* edited by David R. Harris, 121–133. University College of London Press, London.

Restall, Mathew

1997   *The Maya World: Yucatec Culture and Society, 1550–1850.* Stanford University Press, Palo Alto, CA.

Rice, Don S.

2006   Late Classic Maya Population: Characteristics and Implications. In *Urbanism in the Preindustrial World,* edited by Glenn R. Storey, 252–276. University of Alabama Press, Tuscaloosa.

Rice, Don S., and Prudence M. Rice

1990   Population Size and Population Change in the Central Peten Lakes Region, Guatemala. In *Pre-Colombian Population History in the Maya Lowlands*, edited by T. P. Culbert, and Don S. Rice, 123–148. University of New Mexico Press, Albuquerque.

Ricketson, Oliver G. J., and Edith B. Ricketson

1937   *Uaxactun, Guatemala, Group E, 1926–31*. Carnegie Institution of Washington, Publication 477. Carnegie Institution of Washington, Washington, DC.

Ringle, William M.

1999   Preclassic Cityscapes: Ritual Politics among the Early Lowland Maya. In *Social Patterns in Pre-Classic Mesoamerica*, edited by David C. Grove and Rosemary A. Joyce, 183–223. Dumbarton Oaks Research Library and Collection, Washington, DC.

Ringle, William M., and E. Wyllys Andrews V

1990   The Demography of Komchen, an Early Maya Town in Northern Yucatan. In *Precolumbian Population History in the Maya Lowlands*, edited by T. Patrick Culbert and Don S. Rice, 215–244. University of New Mexico Press, Albuquerque.

Ringle, William, and George J. Bey, III

2001   Post-Classic and Terminal Classic Courts of the Northern Maya Lowlands. In *Royal Courts of the Ancient Maya*. Vol. 2, *Data and Case Studies*, edited by Takeshi Inomata and Stephen D. Houston, 266–307. Westview Press, Boulder, CO.

Robertson, Ian G.

2004   *Mapping the Social Landscape of an Early City: Teotihuacan, Mexico*. University of Arizona Press, Tucson.

Robin, Cynthia

2002   Outside of Houses: The Practices of Everyday Life at Chan Nòohol, Belize. *Journal of Social Archaeology* 2(2):245–267.

2004   Social Diversity and Everyday Life within Classic Maya Settlements. In *Mesoamerican Archaeology: Theory and Practice*, edited by Julia A. Hendon and Rosemary A. Joyce, 148–168. Blackwell, Malden, MA.

2006   Gender, Farming and Long-Term Change. *Current Anthropology* 47(3):409–433.

2012   Learning from an Ancient Maya Farming Community. In *Chan: An Ancient Maya Farming Community*, edited by Cynthia Robin, 311–341. University Press of Florida, Gainesville.

2013   *Everyday Life Matters: Maya Farmers at Chan*. University Press of Florida, Gainesville.

Robin, Cynthia, James Meierhoff, and Laura J. Kosakowsky

2012   Nonroyal Governance and Chan's Community Center. In *Chan: An Ancient Maya Farming Community*, edited by Cynthia Robin, 133–149. University Press of Florida, Gainesville.

Rotenberg, Robert

2002   The Metropolis and Everyday Life. In *Urban Life: Readings in the Anthropology of the City*, 4th ed., edited by George Gmelch and Walter P. Zenner, 93–105. Waveland Press, Prospect Heights, IL.

Roys, Ralph L.

1943   *The Indian Background of Colonial Yucatan*. Carnegie Institution of Washington, Washington, DC.

1957   *The Political Geography of the Yucatan Maya*. Carnegie Institute of Washington Publication 613. Carnegie Institution of Washington, Washington, DC.

Ruppert, Karl

1943   *The Mercado, Chichen Itza, Yucatan*. Carnegie Institution of Washington Publication 546. Carnegie Institution of Washington, Washington, DC.

Ruppert, Karl, and John H. J. Denison

1943   *Archaeological Reconnaissance in Campeche, Quintana Roo, and Peten*. Carnegie Institution of Washington Publication 543. Carnegie Institution of Washington, Washington, DC.

Russell, Bradley

2008   Postclassic Maya Settlement on the Rural-Urban Fringe of Mayapan, Yucatan, Mexico. Ph.D. dissertation, Department of Anthropology, State University of New York at Albany.

Russell, Josiah C.

1958   *Late Ancient and Medieval Population. Transactions of the American Philosophical Society* 48(3:1–152.

Sabloff, Jeremy A., and Robert E. Smith

1969   The Importance of Both Analytic and Taxonomic Classification in the Type-Variety System. *American Antiquity* 34(3):278–285.

Sabloff, Jeremy A. and Gair Tourtellot

1991   *Ancient Maya City of Sayil: The Mapping of a Puuc Region Center*. Middle American Research Institute, New Orleans, LA.

Sahagún, Bernadino de

1950–1982 *General History of the Things of New Spain: Florentine Codex*. Monographs of the School of American Research no. 14. School of American Research, Santa Fe, NM, and University of Utah, Salt Lake City.

Saitta, Dean J.

1994   Class and Community in the Prehistoric Southwest. In *The Ancient Southwestern Community: Models and Methods for the Study of Prehistoric Social Organization*, edited by Wirt H. Wills and Robert D. Leonard, 25–44. University of New Mexico Press, Albuquerque.

Sanders, William T.

1962   Cultural Ecology of the Maya Lowlands, Part I. *Estudios de Cultura Maya* 2:79–121.

1963   Cultural Ecology of the Maya Lowlands, Part II. *Estudios de Cultura Maya* 3:203–241.

1973   The Cultural Ecology of the Lowland Maya: A Reevaluation. In *The Classic Maya Collapse*, edited by T. P. Culbert, 325–365. University of New Mexico Press, Albuquerque.

1981   Classic Maya Settlement Patterns and Ethnographic Analogy. In *Lowland Maya Settlement Patterns*, edited by W. Ashmore, 351–369. University of New Mexico Press, Albuquerque.

1989   Household, Lineage and State in 8th Century Copan. In *House of the Bacabs: A Study of the Iconography, Epigraphy, and Social Context of a Maya Elite Structure*, edited by David L. Webster, 89–105. Dumbarton Oaks Research Library and Collection, Washington, DC.

1992   Ranking and Stratification in Prehispanic Mesoamerica. In *Mesoamerican Elites*, edited by Diane Z. Chase, and Arlen Chase, 278–291. University of Oklahoma Press, Norman.

Sanders, William T., and J. W. Michels

1977   *Teotihuacan and Kaminaljuyu: A Study in Prehistoric Contact*. Pennsylvania State University Press Monograph Series. Pennsylvania State University Press, University Park.

Sanders, William T., and Barbara J. Price

1968   *Mesoamerica: The Evolution of a Civilization*. Random House, New York.

Sanders, William T., and David L. Webster

1988   The Mesoamerican Urban Tradition. *American Anthropologist* 90:521–546.

Saul, Frank P.

1972   *The Human Skeletal Remains of Altar de Sacrificios: An Osteobiographic Analysis*. Papers of the Peabody Museum of Archaeology and Ethnology, 63, no. 2. Harvard University Press, Cambridge, MA.

Scarborough, Vernon

2005   Landscapes of Power. In *A Catalyst for Ideas: Anthropological Archaeology and the Legacy of Douglas W. Schwartz*, edited by V. Scarborough, 209–228. School of American Research Press, Santa Fe.

Scarborough, Vernon L., and Fred Valdez Jr.

2009   An Alternative Order: The Dualistic Economies of the Ancient Maya. *Latin American Antiquity* 20:207–227.

Schele, Linda

1998   The Iconography of Maya Architectural Facades during the Late Classic Period. In *Function and Meaning in Classic Maya Architecture*, edited by Stephen D. Houston, 479–517. Dumbarton Oaks Research Library and Collection, Washington, DC.

Schele, Linda, and David A. Freidel

1990   *A Forest of Kings: The Untold Story of the Ancient Maya*. William Morrow, New York.

Schele, Linda and Mary E. Miller

1986   *The Blood of Kings*. George Braziller, New York.

Scholes, France V., and Ralph L. Roys

1948   *The Maya Chontal Indians of Acalan-Tixchel*. 2nd ed. University of Oklahoma Press, Norman.

Scott, James C.

1985   *Weapons of the Weak*. Yale University Press, New Haven, CT.

1990   *Domination and the Arts of Resistance*. Yale University Press, New Haven, CT.

Sewell, William H., Jr.

1992   A Theory of Structure: Duality, Agency and Transformation. *American Journal of Sociology* 98:1–29.

Shafer, Harry J., and Thomas R. Hester

1983   Ancient Maya Chert Workshops in Northern Belize, Central America. *American Antiquity* 48:519–543.

Sharer, Robert J., and Charles W. Golden

2004   Kingship and Polity: Conceptualizing the Maya Body Politic. In *Continuities and*

Changes in Maya Archaeology, edited by Charles W. Golden and Gregory Borgstede, 23–50. Routledge, New York.

Sharer, Robert J., and Loa Traxler

2006 *The Ancient Maya.* 6th ed. Stanford University Press, Palo Alto.

Shaw, Justine M.

2008 *White Roads of the Yucatan: Changing Social Landscapes of the Yucatec Maya.* University of Arizona Press, Tucson.

Shaw, Leslie C.

2012 The Elusive Maya Marketplace: An Archaeological Consideration of the Evidence. *Journal of Archaeological Research* 20(2):117–155.

Shaw, Leslie C., and Eleanor M. King

2015 The Maya Marketplace at Maax Na, Belize. In *Ancient Maya Marketplaces: The Archaeology of Transient Space*, edited by Eleanor M. King and Leslie C. Shaw. University of Arizona Press, Tucson.

Sheets, Payson

2000 Provisioning the Ceren Household. *Ancient Mesoamerica* 11:217–230.

Shenk, Mary K., Monique Borgerhoff Mulder, Jan Beise, Gregory Clark, William Irons, Donna Leonetti, Bobbi S. Low, Samuel Bowles, Tom Hertz, Adrian Bell, and Patrizio Piraino

2010 Intergenerational Wealth Transmission among Agriculturalists: Foundations of Agrarian Inequality. *Current Anthropology* 51(1):65–83.

Shook, Edwin M.

1952 *The Great Wall of Mayapan.* Department of Archaeology, Current Reports, No. 2. Carnegie Institution of Washington, Washington, DC.

Siemens, Alfred H.

1996 Benign Flooding on Tropical Lowland Floodplains. In *The Managed Mosaic*, edited by Scott Fedick, 132–144. University of Utah Press, Salt Lake City.

Simmel, Georg

1950 *The Sociology of Georg Simmel.* Free Press, New York.

2002 The Metropolis and Mental Life. [1903]. In *The Blackwell City Reader*, edited by G. Bridge and A. A. Watson, 11–19. Blackwell, Malden MA.

Sjoberg, Gideon

1960 *The Preindustrial City.* Free Press, New York.

Smith, A. Ledyard

1962 Residential and Associated Structures at Mayapan. In *Mayapan, Yucatan, Mexico*, edited by Harry E. D. Pollock, Ralph L. Roys, T. Proskouriakoff, and A. Ledyard Smith, 165–320. Carnegie Institution of Washington, Washington, DC.

Smith, Adam T.

2003 *The Political Landscape: Constellations of Authority in Early Complex Polities.* University of California Press, Berkeley.

Smith, Eric A., Kim Hill, Frank W. Marlowe, David Nolin, Polly Wiessner, Mike Gurven, Samuel Bowles, Monique Borgerhoff Mulder, Tom Hertz, and Adrian Bell

2010 Wealth Transmission and Inequality among Hunter Gatherers. *Current Anthropology* 51(1):19–34.

Smith, Michael E.

1987   Household Possessions and Wealth in Agrarian States: Implications for Archaeology. *Journal of Anthropological Archaeology* 6(4):297–335.

1989   Cities, Towns, and Urbanism: Comment on Sanders and Webster. *American Anthropologist* 91:454–461.

1996   *The Aztecs.* Blackwell, Malden, MA.

2003   Can We Read Cosmology in Ancient Maya City Plans? Comment on Ashmore and Sabloff. *Latin American Antiquity* 14(2):221–228.

2004   The Archaeology of Ancient State Economies. *Annual Review of Anthropology* 33:73–120.

2005   Did the Maya Build Architectural Cosmograms? *Latin American Antiquity* 16(2):217–224.

2007   Form and Meaning in the Earliest Cities: A New Approach to Ancient Urban Planning. *Journal of Planning History* 6:3–47.

2008   *Aztec City-State Capitals.* University of Florida Press, Gainesville.

2009   Gordon Childe and the Urban Revolution: A Historical Perspective on a Revolution in Urban Studies. *Town Planning Review* 80:3–29.

2010   The Archaeological Study of Neighborhoods and Districts in Ancient Cities. *Journal of Anthropological Archaeology* 29(2):137–154.

2011   Classic Maya Settlement Clusters as Urban Neighborhoods: A Comparative Perspective on Low-Density Urbanism. *Journal de la Societe des Americanistes* 97:51–73.

2015   Quality of Life and Prosperity in Ancient Households and Communities. In *The Oxford Handbook of Historical Ecology and Applied Archaeology*, edited by Christian Isendahl and Daryl Stump. Oxford University Press.

Smith, Michael E. and Juliana Novic

2012   Introduction: Neighborhoods and Districts in Ancient Mesoamerica. In *The Neighborhood as a Social and Spatial Unit in Mesoamerican Cities*, edited by M. Charlotte Arnauld, Linda Manzanilla, and Michael E. Smith, 1–26. University of Arizona Press, Tucson.

Smith, M. G.

1972   Complexity Size and Urbanization. In *Man, Settlement, and Urbanism*, edited by Peter J. Ucko, Ruth Tringham, and George W. Dimbleby, 567–574. Duckworth, London.

Smith, Monica L.

2003   Introduction. In *The Social Construction of Ancient Cities*, edited by Monica L. Smith. Smithsonian Institution Press, Washington, DC.

2006   The Archaeology of South Asian Cities. *Journal of Archaeological Research* 14:97–142.

Smith, Robert E.

1971   *The Pottery of Mayapan.* Papers of the Peabody Museum of Archaeology and Ethnology, Vol. 66. Harvard University, Cambridge.

Smyth, Michael P., Chris C. Dore, and Nicholas P. Dunning

1995   Interpreting Prehistoric Settlement Patterns: Lessons from the Maya Center of Sayil, Yucatan. *Journal of Field Archaeology* 22:321–347.

Smyth, Michael P., and David Ortegón Zapata

2006 Foreign Lords and Early Classic Interaction at Chac II, Yucatan. In *Lifeways in the Northern Lowlands: New Approaches to Maya Archaeology*, edited by Jennifer P. Mathews and Bethany A. Morrison, 119–141. University of Arizona Press, Tucson.

Smyth, Michael P., and Daniel Rogart

2004 A Teotihuacan Presence at Chac II, Yucatan, Mexico. *Ancient Mesoamerica* 15:17–47.

Soja, Edward

2000 *Postmetropolis*. Blackwell, Malden, MA.

Spence, Michael

1991 Tlailotlacan: A Zapotec Enclave in Teotihuacan. In *Art, Ideology, and the City of Teotihuacan*, edited by Janet C. Berlo, 59–88. Dumbarton Oaks Research Library and Collection, Washington, DC.

Stanton, Travis W.

2005 Taluds, Tripods, and Teotihuacanos: A Critique of Central Mexican Influence in Classic Period Yucatan. *Mayab* 18:17–35.

Stanton, Travis, and Scott R. Hutson

2012 "Patrones de crecimiento urbano: albarradas y grupos domésticos en el Clásico Temprano en Chunchucmil, Yucatán. In *VII Coloquio Pedro Bosch Gimpera*, edited by Guillermo Acosta Ochoa, 299–316. UNAM, Mexico City.

Stark, Barbara L., and Chris P. Garraty

2010 Detecting Marketplace Exchange in Archaeology: A Methodological Review. In *Archaeological Approaches to Market Exchange in Ancient Societies*, edited by Chris P. Garraty and Barbara L. Stark, 3–32. University Press of Colorado, Boulder.

Stark, Barbara L., and Alanna Ossa

2007 Ancient Settlement, Urban Gardening, and Environment in the Gulf Lowlands of Mexico. *Latin American Antiquity* 18:385–406.

Stephens, John L.

1841 *Incidents of Travel in Central America, Chiapas, and Yucatan*. Harper and Brothers, New York.

Stockton, Trent

2013 An Archaeological Study of Peripheral Settlement and Domestic Economy at Ancient Xuenkal, Yucatan, Mexico. Ph.D. dissertation, Department of Anthropology, Tulane University, New Orleans, LA.

Stone, Elizabeth C.

1987 *Nippur Neighborhoods*. University of Chicago Press, Chicago.

Storey, Glenn

1997 Estimating the Population of Ancient Roman Cities. In *Integrating Archaeology: Multidisciplinary Approaches to Prehistoric Population*, edited by Richard R. Paine, 101–130. Center for Archaeological Investigations, Southern Illinois University at Carbondale, Carbondale.

Storey, Rebecca

1992a *Life and Death in the Ancient City of Teotihuacan*. University of Alabama Press, Tuscaloosa.

1992b The Children of Copan: Issues in Paleopathology and Paleodemography. *Ancient Mesoamerica* 3(1):161–168.

Stuart, David

1987   *Ten Phonetic Syllables*. Research Reports on Ancient Maya Writing 14. Center for Maya Research, Washington, DC.

1998   "The Fire Enters His House": Architecture and Ritual in Classic Maya Texts. In *Function and Meaning in Classic Maya Architecture*, edited by Stephen D. Houston, 373–425. Dumbarton Oaks Research Library and Collection, Washington, DC.

2006   The Inscribed Markers of the Coba-Yaxuna Causeway and the Glyph for *Sakbih*. http://www.mesoweb.com/stuart/notes/Sacbe.pdf.

Stuart, David, and Stephen D. Houston

1994   *Classic Maya Place Names*. Studies in Pre-Columbian Art and Archaeology. Dumbarton Oaks Research Library and Collection, Washington, DC.

Stuart, George, John C. Scheffler, Edward B. Kurjack, and John W. Cottier

1979   *Map of the Ruins of Dzibilchaltun, Yucatan, Mexico*. Middle American Research Institute Publication Number 47. Middle American Research Institute, New Orleans, LA.

Sullivan, K. S.

2006   Specialized Production of San Martin Orange Ware at Teotihuacan, Mexico. *Latin American Antiquity* 17:23–53.

Suttles, Gerald D.

1972   *The Social Construction of Communities*. University of Chicago Press, Chicago.

Taube, Karl A.

1992   *The Major Gods of Ancient Yucatan*. Studies in Pre-Columbian Art and Archaeology 32. Dumbarton Oaks Research Library and Collection, Washington, DC.

1998   The Jade Hearth: Centrality, Rulership, and the Classic Maya Temple. In *Function and Meaning in Classic Maya Architecture*, edited by Stephen D. Houston, 427–478. Dumbarton Oaks Research Library and Collection, Washington, DC.

2004   Flower Mountain: Concepts of Life, Beauty, and Paradise among the Classic Maya. *RES: Anthropology and Aesthetics* 45:69–98.

Tedlock, Dennis (translator)

1985   *Popol Vuh: The Definitive Edition of the Mayan Book of the Dawn of Life and the Glories of God and Kings*. Simon and Schuster, New York.

Thomas, Prentice

1981   *Prehistoric Maya Settlement Patterns at Becan, Campeche, Mexico*. MARI Publication 45. Middle American Research Institute, New Orleans, LA.

Thompson, J. Eric S.

1931   *Archaeological Investigations in the Southern Cayo District, British Honduras*. Field Museum of Natural History Publication 301. Field Museum of Natural History, Chicago.

1950   *Maya Hieroglyphic Introduction: An Introduction*. Carnegie Institute of Washington Publication 589. Carnegie Institute of Washington, Washington, DC.

1971   Estimates of Maya Population: Deranging Factors. *American Antiquity* 36:214–216.

Tobler, Waldo

1970   A Computer Movie Simulating Urban Growth in the Detroit Region. *Economic Geography* 46(2):234–240.

Tokovinine, Alexandre

2013   *Place and Identity in Classic Maya Narratives*. Dumbarton Oaks Pre-Columbian Art and Archaeology Studies Series. Dumbarton Oaks Research Library and Collection, Washington, DC.

Tokovinine, Alexandre, and Dmitri Beliaev

2013   People of the Road: Trade and Travelers in Ancient Maya Words and Images. In *Merchants, Markets and Exchange in the Pre-Colombian World*, edited by Kenneth G. Hirth and Joanne Pillsbury, 169–200. Dumbarton Oaks Research Library and Collections, Washington, DC.

Tokovinine, Alexandre, and Marc Zender

2012   Lords of Windy Water: The Royal Court of Motul de San Jose. In *Motul de San Jose: Politics, History, and Economy in a Classic Maya Polity*, edited by Antonia E. Foias and Kitty F. Emery, 30–66. University Press of Florida, Gainesville, FL.

Torquemada, Fray Juan de

1943   *Monarquia Indiana*. Vol. 2. Salvador Chavez Hayhoe, Mexico City.

Tourtellot, Gair

1988   Developmental Cycles of Households and Houses at Seibal. In *Household and Community in the Mesoamerican Past*, edited by Richard Wilk and Wendy Ashmore, 97–120. University of New Mexico Press, Albuquerque.

1993   A View of Ancient Maya Settlements in the Eighth Century. In *Lowland Maya Civilization in the Eighth Century A.D.*, edited by Jeremy A. Sabloff and John S. Henderson, 219–241. Dumbarton Oaks Research Library and Collection, Washington, DC.

Tourtellot, Gair, Kelli Carmean, and Jeremy A. Sabloff

1992   "Will the Real Elites Please Stand Up?": An Archaeological Assessment of Maya Elite Behavior in the Terminal Classic Period. In *Mesoamerican Elites: An Archaeological Assessment*, edited by Diane Z. Chase and Arlen F. Chase, 80–98. University of Oklahoma Press, Norman.

Tourtellot, Gair, Michael P. Smyth, and Jeremy A. Sabloff

1990   Room Counts and Population Estimation for Terminal Classic Sayil in the Puuc Region, Yucatan, Mexico. In *Precolumbian Population History in the Maya Lowlands*, edited by T. Patrick Culbert and Don S. Rice, 245–261. University of New Mexico Press, Albuquerque.

Tourtellot, Gair, Marc Wolf, Scott Smith, Kristen Gardella, and Norman Hammond

2002   Exploring Heaven on Earth: Testing the Cosmological Model at La Milpa, Belize. *Antiquity* 76(293):633–634.

Tozzer, Alfred M.

1941   *Landa's Relacion de las Cosas de Yucatan: A Translation*. Papers of the Peabody Museum of American Archaeology and Ethnology, Harvard University, vol. 17. Peabody Museum of American Archaeology and Ethnology, Cambridge, MA.

Trigger, Bruce

1972   Determinants of Urban Growth in Pre-Industrial Societies. In *Man, Settlement, and Urbanism*, edited by Peter J. Ucko, Ruth Tringham, and George W. Dimbleby, 575–599. Duckworth, London.

1990   Monumental Architecture: A Thermodynamic Explanation of Symbolic Behavior. *World Archaeology* 22:119–132.

2003   *Understanding Early Civilization: A Comparative Study*. Cambridge University Press, New York.

Tuan, Yi-Fu

1977　*Space and Place: The Perspective of Experience.* University of Minnesota Press, Minneapolis.

Turner, Margaret H.

1992　Style in Lapidary Technology: Identifying the Teotihuacan Lapidary Industry. In *Art, Ideology, and the City of Teotihuacan,* edited by Janet C. Berlo, 89–112. Dumbarton Oaks Research Library and Collection, Washington, DC.

United Nations Human Settlement Programme

2010　*State of the World's Cities 2010/2011: Cities for All: Bridging the Urban Divide.* UN HABITAT, Nairobi.

Vail, Gabrielle, and Christine Hernandez

2013　*Re-Creating Primordial Time: Foundation Rituals and Mythology in the Postclassic Maya Codices.* University of Colorado Press, Boulder.

Varela Torrecilla, C.

1998　*El Clásico Medio en el Noroccidente de Yucatan.* BAR International Series 739, Archaeopress, Oxford.

Varien, Mark, and James Potter (editors)

2008　*The Social Construction of Communities: Agency, Structure, and Identity in the Prehispanic Southwest.* Altamira Press, Lanham, MD.

Vogt, Evon Z.

1961　Some Aspects of Zinacantan Settlement Patterns and Ceremonial Organization. *Estudios de Cultura Maya* 1:131–145.

1969　*Zinacantan: A Maya Community in the Highlands of Chiapas.* The Belknap Press of Harvard University Press, Cambridge, MA.

1976　*Tortillas for the Gods.* Harvard University Press, Cambridge, MA.

Waldeck, Jean-F.

1838　*Voyage Pittoresque et Archéologique dans la province d'Yucatan pendant les années 1834 et 1836.* Bellizard Dufour et cie, Paris.

Watanabe, John M.

2004　Some Models in a Muddle. *Ancient Mesoamerica* 15:159–166.

Watanabe, Takeshi

2000　Form and Function of Metates in Chunchucmil, Yucatan, Mexico. Master's Thesis, Anthropology Department, Florida State University, Tallahassee.

Wauchope, Robert

1938　*Modern Maya Houses: A Study of Their Archaeological Significance.* Carnegie Institution of Washington Publication 502. Carnegie Institution of Washington, Washington D. C.

Weber, Max

(1921) 1958　*The City.* Translated by D. Martindale and G. Neuwirth. Free Press, New York.

Webster, David L.

1976　*Defensive Earthworks at Becan, Campeche Mexico: Implications for Maya Warfare.* Middle American Research Institute Publication 41. Middle American Research Institute, New Orleans, LA.

1979   *Cuca, Chacchob, Dzonot Aké: Three Walled Northern Maya Centers*. Occasional Paper in Anthropology 11. Pennsylvania State University Press, State College, PA.

1992   Maya Elites: The Perspective from Copan. In *Mesoamerican Elites*, edited by Diane Z. Chase and Arlen F. Chase, 135–156. University of Oklahoma Press, Norman.

1997   City-States of the Maya. In *Archaeology of City-States: Cross-Cultural Approaches*, edited by Thomas H. Charlton and Deborah L. Nichols, 135–154. Smithsonian Institution Press, Washington, DC.

2002   *The Fall of the Ancient Maya*. Thames and Hudson, New York.

2008   The Regional Setting of the 8th Century Copan Polity: Implications for Maya Urbanism. In *El Urbanismo en Mesoamérica/Urbanism in Mesoamerica*, edited by Alba G. Mastache, Robert H. Cobean, Ángel García Cook, and Kenneth G. Hirth, 227–258. Pennsylvania State University, University Park, and Instituto Nacional de Antropología e Historia, Mexico City.

Webster, David L., and Nancy Gonlin

1988   Household Remains of the Humblest Maya. *Journal of Field Archaeology* 15:169–190.

Webster, David L., and Stephen D. Houston

2003   Piedras Negras: The Growth and Decline of a Classic Maya Center. In *El Urbanismo en Mesoamerica*, edited by William T. Sanders, Alba G. Mastache, and Robert H. Cobean, 427–449. Instituto Nacional de Antropología e Historia, Mexico City.

Webster, David L., Tim Murtha, Kirk D. Straight, Jay Silverstein, Horacio Martinez, Richard Terry, and Richard Burnett

2007   The Great Tikal Earthwork Revisited. *Journal of Field Archaeology* 32(1):41–64.

Wheatley, Paul

1971   *The Pivot of the Four Corners: A Preliminary Inquiry into the Origins and Character of the Chinese City*. Aldine Publishing Company, Chicago.

1972   The Concept of Urbanism. In *Man, Settlement, and Urbanism*, edited by Peter J. Ucko, Ruth Tringham, and George W. Dimbleby, 601–637. Duckworth, London.

Whitby, Michael

1998   The Grain Trade of Athens in the 4th Century BC. In *Trade, Traders, and the Ancient City*, edited by Helen M. Parkins and Christopher Smith, 102–128. Routledge, London.

Whittington, Stephen L.

1989   Characteristics of Demography and Disease in Low Status Maya from Classic Period Copan, Honduras. Ph.D. dissertation, Department of Anthropology, Pennsylvania State University, State College.

Widmer, Randolph J.

1991   Lapidary Craft Specialization at Teotihuacan: Implications for Community Structure at 33:S3W1 and Economic Organization in the City. *Ancient Mesoamerica* 2(1):131–147.

Widmer, Randolph J., and Rebecca Storey

2012   The "Tlajinga Barrio": A Distinctive Cluster of Neighborhoods in Teotihuacan. In *The Neighborhood as a Social and Spatial Unit in Mesoamerican Cities*, edited by M. Charlotte Arnauld, Linda Manzanilla, and Michael E. Smith, 102–116. University of Arizona Press, Tucson.

Wilk, Richard

1983   Little House in the Jungle: The Cause of Variation in House Size among Modern Maya. *Journal of Anthropological Archaeology* 2:99–116.

Wilkinson, Richard G., and Kate Pickett

2009   Income Inequality and Social Dysfunction. *Annual Review of Sociology* 35:493–511.

Willey, Gordon R.

1956a   Problems Concerning Prehistoric Settlement Patterns in the Maya Lowlands. In *Prehistoric Settlement Patterns of the New World*, edited by Gordon R. Willey, 107–114. Wenner Gren Foundation for Anthropological Research, New York.

1956b   The Structure of Ancient Maya Society: Evidence from the Southern Lowlands. *American Anthropologist* 58:777–782.

1962   Review of Map of the Ruins of Tikal, El Peten, Guatemala by Robert F. Carr, James E. Hazard. *American Antiquity* 28(1):117–118.

Willey, Gordon R., and William J. Bullard

1965   Prehispanic Settlement Patterns in the Maya Lowlands. In *Archaeology of Southern Mesoamerica, Part 1*, edited by Gordon R. Willey, 360–377. Vol. 2 of *Handbook of Middle American Indians*. University of Texas Press, Austin.

Willey, Gordon R., J. William J. Bullard, John B. Glass, and James C. Gifford

1965   *Prehistoric Maya Settlement in the Belize Valley.* Paper of the Peabody Museum of Archaeology and Ethnology, Harvard University 54. Peabody Museum of Archaeology and Ethnology, Harvard University, Cambridge, MA.

Willey, Gordon R., and Richard M. Leventhal

1979   Prehistoric Settlement at Copan. In *Maya Archaeology and Ethnohistory*, edited by Norman Hammond and Gordon R. Willey, 75–102. University of Texas Press, Austin.

Willey, Gordon R., Richard M. Leventhal, and William Fash

1978   Maya Settlement in the Copan Valley. *Archaeology* 31:32–43.

Williams, Raymond

1973   *The Country and the City*. Oxford University Press, New York.

Wirth, Louis

1925   A Bibliography of the Urban Community. In *The City*, edited by Robert E. Park, Ernest W. Burgess, and Roderick D. McKenzie, 161–228. University of Chicago Press, Chicago.

1938   Urbanism as a Way of Life. *American Journal of Sociology* 44:1–24.

1940   The Urban Society and Civilization. *American Journal of Sociology* 45(5).

Wisdom, Charles

1940   *The Chorti Indians of Guatemala*. University of Chicago Press, Chicago.

Wolf, Eric

1955   Types of Latin American Peasantry: A Preliminary Discussion. *American Anthropologist* 57(3):452–471.

1966   *Peasants*. Prentice Hall, Englewood Cliffs, NJ.

Woolley, Leonard

1976   *Ur Excavations*. Vol. 7, *The Old Babylonian Period*. British Museum, London.

World Bank

2014 Gini Index (World Bank Estimate). http://data.worldbank.org/indicator/SI.POV. GINI?page=1. Accessed March 2014.

Wright, Lori E., and Christine D. White

1996 Human Biology in the Classic Maya Collapse: Evidence from Paleopathology and Paleodiet. *Journal of World Prehistory* 10(2):147–198.

Wrigley, Edward Anthony

1969 *Population and History.* McGraw Hill, New York.

Wurtzburg, Susan

1991 Sayil: Investigations of Urbanism and Economic Organization at an Ancient Maya City. Ph.D. dissertation, Department of Anthropology, State University of New York, Albany.

2015 Contemporary Maya Marketplaces: Gender, Social Change, and Implications for the Past. In *Ancient Maya Marketplaces: The Archaeology of Transient Space,* edited by Eleanor M. King and Leslie C. Shaw. University of Arizona Press, Tucson.

Yaeger, Jason

2000 The Social Construction of Communities in the Classic Maya Countryside: Strategies of Affiliation in Western Belize. In *The Archaeology of Communities: A New World Perspective,* edited by Marcello A. Canuto and Jason Yaeger, 123–141. Routledge, London.

2003 Small Settlements in the Upper Belize River Valley: Local Complexity, Household Strategies of Affiliation, and Changing Organization. In *Perspectives on Ancient Maya Rural Complexity,* edited by Gyles Iannone and Samuel V. Connell, 43–58. Cotsen Institute, University of California at Los Angeles, Los Angeles.

2010 Landscapes of the Xunantunich Hinterlands. In *Classic Maya Provincial Politics: Xunantunich and Its Hinterlands,* edited by Lisa J. Lecount and Jason Yaeger, 233–249. University of Arizona Press, Tucson.

Yaeger, Jason, and Marcello A. Canuto

2000 Introducing an Archaeology of Communities. In *The Archaeology of Communities: A New World Perspective,* edited by Marcello A. Canuto and Jason Yaeger, 1–15. Routledge, London.

Yaeger, Jason, and Cynthia Robin

2004 Heterogeneous Hinterlands: The Social and Political Organization of Commoner Settlements near Xunantunich, Belize. In *Ancient Maya Commoners,* edited by J. C. Lohse and F. J. Valdez, 148–173. University of Texas Press, Austin.

York, Abigail, Michael E. Smith, Benjamin Stanley, Barbara L. Stark, Juliana Novic, Sharon Harlan, George L. Cowgill, and Christopher Boone

2011 Ethnic and Class-Based Clustering through the Ages: A Transdisciplinary Approach to Urban Social Patterns. *Urban Studies* 48:2399–2415.

Zaro, Gregory, and Jon C. Lohse

2005 Agricultural Rhythms and Rituals: Ancient Maya Solar Observation in Hinterland Blue Creek, Northwestern Belize. *Latin American Antiquity* 16(1):81–98.

Index

Page numbers in *italics* refer to illustrations.

Abrams, Elliott, 143, 149

Actuncan, Belize, 54

Adams, Richard, 57, 142

Addis Ababa, Ethiopia, 75

Agency, 7, 9, 181, 203

Agriculture: within cities, 11, 53, 83–84, 199; extensive forms, 53; intensive forms, 53

Aguateca, Guatemala, 188

Aké, Mexico, 35

Albion Island, Belize, 166

Altepetl, 15

Ancestor shrines, 173

Andrews, E. Wyllys, IV, 38

Andrews, George, 181–82, 184

Angkor, Cambodia, 52, 54

Anomie, 3, 20

Anuradhapura, Sri Lanka, 54

Apartment compounds. *See under* Teotihuacan, Mexico

Architecture: aesthetics, 181–82, 184; orientation, 91, 122–24; salience, 185

Arnauld, Charlotte, 82

Arnold, Jeanne, 150, 161–63

Ashmore, Wendy, 38, 80, 176

Asty, 15

Axial analysis, 190

Axis mundi, 23, 179–80

Aztecs, 197

Babylon, 199; neighborhoods within, 90

Bagan, Myanmar, 54

Barnhart, Edwin, 42, 157

Barthel, Thomas, 51

Barton Ramie, Belize, 32–33, 37

Basin of Mexico, 10, 63, 66

Becan, Mexico, 35, 52

Becker, Marshall, 31, 38, 89–90

Beijing, China, 154

Belize, 8, 149

Belize River Valley, 32–33

Betz, Virginia, 14, 184, 191

Bioarchaeology, 3–4

Blue Creek, Belize, 195

Bonampak, Mexico, 192, 201

Boundaries. *See under* Neighborhoods

Brown, Clifford, 51, 87, 130, 154–59

Buenavista del Cayo, Belize, 65, 84

Built form, 14, 23–24, 170–201

Bullard, William, 32–33, 37, 54, 74, 141

Burgess, Ernest, 9, 164

Calakmul, Mexico, 38, 40, 58; Chiik Nahb murals, 66, 196; marketplace, 65–66, 195–96; relations with subordinate rulers, 172

Calendar, Maya, 178

Caracol, Belize, 38, 40; Caana acropolis, 164, 166, 190; circulation within, 186, *187*, 191, 198; distribution of wealth within, 164–65; marketplace, 65; plazas, *189*, 190; political alliances, 58, 76; settlement density, 53; shrines, 89; social identity, 87

Cargo system, 32

Carmean, Kelli, 158

Carr, Robert, 33
Cartesian dualisms, 183
Catal Hoyuk, Turkey, 10
Causeways. *See* Sacbes
Cave, 57, 119, 192
Ceiba tree, 179
Center, as a unit of settlement, 13
Central Mexico. *See* Basin of Mexico
Centricity, 188
Ceremonies, 192–95
Ceren, El Salvador, 61
Chac, Mexico, 89
Chacchob, Mexico, 35
Chan, Belize, 54, 171, 195
Chase, Arlen, 87, 89, 164
Chase, Diane, 87, 89, 163–64
Ch'e'n. *See* Wells
Chiapas, Mexico, 32, 76, 117
Chicago, 42, 51, 164
Chicago School of Sociology, 3, 198, 204
Chichbes, 120–22
Chichen Itza, Mexico, 65, 68, 169, 186, 187,
    193, 201
Chichicastenango, Guatemala, 31
Chi'ich mounds, 44
Childe, Gordon, 4, 9, 11, 38, 185
Children, ancient Maya, 160, 192–93
Cholera, 3
Cholula, Mexico, 91
Chora, 15
Chunchucmil, Mexico: Aak compound,
    129–30; building orientations, 122–24;
    chronology, 99; circulation patterns within,
    105, 185–86; cooperation among residents,
    199–200; craft specialization within, 133–35;
    defensive barricade in, 35; distribution of
    wealth within, 145, 146, 163, 168; excava-
    tion sampling strategy, 124, 125; inequality
    within, 154–55; large structures within, 109,
    110, 111; map, 45; marketplace, 66, 115, 128,
    195–96; migration toward, 120; neighbor-
    hoods within, 97–138; open spaces within,
    115, 117, 118; Pich compound, 111, 130; pot-
    tery, 99, 128–31; preservation conditions,
    98; quadrangles, 110–11, 113; settlement
    density, 44–45, 99; settlement zones, 99;
    site planning, 176; spoke clusters within,
    103, 105–14; walls, 74, 98; wells, 117–19

City: circulation within, 100–105, 101, 186–87;
    concentric zonation within, 160–66;
    definitions, 9, 12, 15–17; as distinct from
    villages, 19, 171; grid patterns within,
    91, 100–103, 101; identification with, 14,
    193; low-density cities, 16; as opposed
    to centers, 13; relationship to urbanism,
    17; researching social inequality, 145–46;
    specialized functions within, 12–13, 38–39
City-states: definition, 55; Greek, 11, 55, 60,
    204; Maya cities as city-states, 55–58
Class, social, 19, 21, 142–44
Clendinnen, Inga, 197
Cluster. *See* Settlement cluster
Coba, Mexico, 38, 40; circulation within,
    186, 187, 191; distribution of wealth within,
    162–63, 168; focal nodes, 80, 108; Group
    B/Iglesia/Coba Group, 166, 190; mar-
    ketplace, 65; plazas, 190; population and
    settlement density, 46, 47; social organiza-
    tion, 166–67; spatial clusters, 75–78, 79
Coe, William, 38
Coercion, 6, 171–72
Colha, Belize, 90
Colonialism. *See* Spanish contact and
    colonialism
Commerce. *See* Marketplaces
Commoners, 7, 82, 143, 168, 173, 181, 201–3;
    and Maya religion, 195
Community, 72, 188, 193
Concentric zonation. *See under* City
Cooperation, 199–200
Copan, Honduras, 40, 149; circulation
    within, 191; early exploration of, 29;
    Group 9N-8, 143, 147, 166–67; health
    problems and, 4; map, 50; neighbor-
    hoods within, 106; Penn State excavations
    within, 143, 147; plazas, 188, 190; Principal
    Group, 143, 162, 166; regional politics, 58;
    settlement density, 50–51; social organiza-
    tion within, 74, 143; and Teotihuacan, 89;
    wealth differences within, 152, 162
Corporate groups, 82, 86
Courts, royal, 8, 39–40. *See also* Palaces
Cowgill, George, 4, 16–17, 24, 87, 92, 95, 172
Craft specialization, 4, 10–11, 25, 90; at
    Chunchucmil, 128, 131–36; at Teotihuacan,
    93–94; at Tikal, 90

Creation mythology, 178; three stone hearths, 179–80
Crime, 3
Cuca, Mexico, 35
Culbert, T. Patrick, 35

Dahlin, Bruce, 196
De Borhegyi, Stefan, 31
Del Rio, Antonio, 29
Demarest, Arthur, 194
Demography, 3, 18, 30, 170
de Montmollin, Olivier, 171
Density. See Settlement density
Diaz del Castillo, Bernal, 197
Disease, 3
Distance measures (for delimiting neighborhood boundaries), 75–81
Distributional approach. See under Marketplaces
District, 72, 86, 93–94, 106–8, 122
Dos Pilas, Guatemala, 35, 76
Drama, 23. See also Ceremonies
Durán, Diego, 197
Durkheim, Emil, 11
Dzibilchaltun, Mexico: circulation within, 186; distribution of wealth within, 164–68; focal nodes, 84–86; inequality within, 157–58; plazas, 188–89; population and settlement density, 47–48, 54; settlement history, 46; site map, 30, 37; social differentiation within, 37–38; spatial clusters within, 75, 75

Economy: degree of commercialization, 60; dual economies of ancient Maya, 61; economic efficiency, 24–25, 195; exchange, 26; relations between cities and hinterlands, 61. See also Marketplaces
Egalitarianism, 32–33, 141
Ek Balam, Mexico, 35
El Cayo, Mexico, 173
Elites, 7, 82, 143–44, 160, 201–2
El Peru/Waka', Guatemala, 50, 66, 161
Emberling, Geoff, 88
Emblem glyphs, 56
Encounters between people. See Face-to-face interactions
Energetics, 149–52

Ethnic enclaves, 92–93
Ethnic identity, 87–89
Ethnohistory, 67

Face block, 101–3
Face-to-face interactions, 10, 21–22, 71–72, 80, 84, 96, 117–19, 167, 169
Farming. See Agriculture
Fash, William, 74, 86, 106
Feasts, 8, 84–86
Finley, Moses, 11
Flintknapping, 90
Focal nodes, 80, 108, 115
Foias, Antonia, 59
Folan, William, 46, 161–63, 166–67
Ford, Anabel, 150, 161–63
Fox, Richard, 39, 62
Freidel, David, 64–65, 169, 178
Freiwald, Carolyn, 88
Fried, Morton, 142
Fry, Robert, 87

Garden. See Agriculture
Garden city, 20, 53, 104
Gender inequalities, 141
Gentrification, 21
Geographic Information Systems (GIS), 163
Giddens, Anthony, 7
Gini coefficient, 153–55, 168
Glaeser, Louis, 10
Gods, Maya, 177–80; God L, 66; Maize God, 178. See also Palenque
Goffman, Erving, 20
Golden, Charles, 8
Gómez Chávez, Sergio, 94–95
Graffiti, 160, 183
Greek city-states. See City-states
Grid pattern. See City
Grube, Nikolai, 58–59, 192
Guatemala City, 154

Hammond, Norman, 143, 198
Hannerz, Ulf, 22, 27
Hansen, Mogens, 11, 13, 55
Hanson, Julienne, 186
Hare, Timothy, 78, 86, 90
Harrison, Peter, 161, 174

Harvey, David, 21
Haussmann, Baron Von, 21
Haviland, William, 35, 37, 143, 150, 161–62, 167
Hazard, James, 33
Health problems, 3–4, 10, 18, 51, 87
Hillier, Bill, 186
Hinterlands, 55, 128, 171; interdependence
    with cities, 61, 68, 82
Hirth, Kenneth, 15, 55, 62, 68
Homophily, 22
Households, 6–11, 21, 28, 38–39, 68–69, 76,
    136–37; population estimates, 106; wealth
    and status within, 143–52
House lots, 105–8, 118–24, 199
Housemounds, 31–32
House societies, 120, 147, 167
Houston, Stephen, 8, 183
Howard, Ebenezer, 20, 104
Hub-and-spoke city layout, 102–4

Inequality. See Social inequality
Innovation, 25
Inomata, Takeshi, 88, 114, 188, 192
Invisible Maya, 98, 151

Jacobs, Jane, 10, 104–5, 136
Jacobs, Linda, 151
Janusek, John, 24, 87–88
Jasaw Chan K'awiil, 174–75, 188, 196
Jones, Christopher, 196
Joyce, Arthur, 7, 198
Joyce, Rosemary, 159

Kaloomte, 59
Kekchi Maya, 149, 151
Kemper, Robin, 87
Kings, 8, 56, 172–76
Kinship, 19–20, 85, 167, 197
Kintz, Ellen, 46, 75–78, 80, 82, 108
Kowoj, 89
Kramer, Carol, 151
Kubler, George, 181
K'uhul Ajaw, 56, 58–59, 172
Kurjack, Edward, 47–48, 85, 157, 164–65, 167

La Joyanca, Guatemala, 80–81
Lakamha, 57. See also Palenque
La Mar, Mexico, 173

La Milpa, Belize, 171
Lampard, Eric, 24
Landa, Bishop Diego de, 67, 99, 140–41, 160,
    164, 192
Landesque capital, 173
Landmarks, 24
Languages, Maya, 55–56
La Pasadita, Guatemala, 172–73
Law of Urban Natural Decrease, 3
Le Corbusier, 20, 182
Lecount, Lisa, 152
Lemmonier, Eva, 80–81
Levelling mechanisms, 33, 141
Leventhal, Richard, 74, 143
Levi-Strauss, Claude, 82, 147
Lewis, Oscar, 20
Lineages, 82, 120, 147, 166
Lohse, Jon, 195
London, 3–4, 10
Los Angeles, California, 154
Lubaantun, Belize, 198
Lucero, Lisa, 173
Lynch, Kevin, 24, 184–85

Maax Na, Belize, 65
Madrid codex, 179
Magnoni, Aline, 156
Maine, Henry, 19
Maize God. See under Gods, Maya
Manila, Philippines, 154
Manzanilla, Linda, 92, 94–95
Marcus, Joyce, 15, 57, 59, 142, 165
Marketplaces, 12, 26, 51, 60–61; among the
    ancient Maya, 62–64, 67–68, 159; benefits
    to leaders, 26, 64, 198; at Calakmul, 65–66,
    195; at Chunchucmil, 128, 195; distribu-
    tional approach, 66, 128, 196; efficiencies
    within, 195; items available within, 152;
    social aspects of, 195–98; at Tikal, 65–66,
    195
Martin, Simon, 58
Marxism, 144
Masson, Marilyn, 78, 86, 90, 166
Mathews, Peter, 57
Maudslay, Alfred, 29
Mayapan, Mexico, 33–35, 51, 63, 65, 68, 78,
    86; craft production within, 90; distribu-
    tion of wealth within, 163–64, 166; forced

relocation to, 172; inequality within, 158; map, 34; pottery within, 130; social identity, 87

Mayapan Confederacy, 196

McAnany, Patricia, 142

McIntosh, Roderick, 7, 13, 169

Mellart, James, 10

Men, ancient Maya, 160, 192, 197–99

Mercantile centers, 62

Merchants, 66

Merchants Barrio at Teotihuacan, 92

Mesopotamia, 37, 72, 84, 88, 204

Metates, 131–32

Mexico City, 20–21, 87, 154

Microcosms, 179

Migration, 4, 19–20, 87–88, 120, 170–71

Milgrim, Stanley, 17

Miller, Katherine, 88

Miller, Mary, 192

Millon, Rene, 91

Moche, Peru, 88

Monte Albán, Mexico, 40

Monumental architecture, 32, 80–81, 110–12, 137, 181, 184; salience of pyramids, 185

Moon Pyramid, Teotihuacan, 92

Mopan Maya, 149

Moral order, 8

Morgan, Lewis Henry, 19, 29

Morley, Sylvanus, 31

Mortality rates, 3–4

Morton, Sean, 190

Motul de San José, Guatemala, 58–59, 65, 66

Multiplicity, 21–22, 104, 140, 168–69, 194, 201

Mumford, Lewis, 12, 20, 22–23, 181, 183

Nah (house), 177

Nahua, 15

Naranjo, Guatemala, 176

Neighborhoods, 19–21; boundaries, 74–76; at Chunchucmil, 97–138; city plans and, 100–104; craft specializations within, 90, 131–36; definition, 71; difficulties in specifying neighborhoods, 95; identifying neighborhoods, 73–82; spatial clusters, 73–79, 100–104; at Teotihuacan, 90–96; wealth-based, 92, 160–66

Netting, Robert, 151

Neuroscience, 184

New York City, 42, 154, 159

Niger, 6

Nucleation of population, 41, 51, 64

Oaxaca Barrio at Teotihuacan, 92, 120

Obsidian, 134–35

Occupational specialization. See Craft specialization

Okoshi-Harada, Tsubasa, 76

Open space, 115–16

Ostia, Italy, 42

Otoot, 177

Palaces, 161–62, 183, 191

Palenque: cooperation among residents, 199; Cross Group, 57, 177; early exploration of, 29; inequality within, 154, 157; map, 43; palace, 191; plazas, 188; population, 44; pottery exchange, 61; settlement history, 42; site planning within, 176; temple, 176; triad of gods, 57, 177

Paris, France, 21

Park, Robert, 1, 3, 12, 198

Parker, Joy, 178

Parker Pearson, Michael, 181

Parthenon, Greece, 182

Pathways within cities, 100, 120–21, 136, 185–87

Patios, 112–14

Permeability, 185–86

Peuramaki-Brown, Meaghan, 84–85

Phenomenology, 182

Piedras Negras, Guatemala, 8, 60, 88, 172–73

Pillsbury, Joanne, 68

Plaza Plan II, 89

Plazas, 188–92

Plazuela, 52

Polanyi, Karl, 62–64

Polis, 15

Political organization, 55–59, 82

Pompeii, Italy, 42

Popol Vuh, 178

Postgate, Nicholas, 72

Pottery, 25, 66, 87; at Chunchucmil, 128–31; at Teotihuacan, 92–93; as wealth, 152

Pred, Allan, 19, 21
Privacy, 51, 53
Processions, 193
Proskouriakoff, Tatiana, 31, 181–82
Puleston, Dennis, 31–32, 37
Puuc Hills, Mexico, 173
Pyburn, Anne, 166
Pyramids. *See* Monumental architecture

Quadripartite forms, 179, 195
Quality of life, 141
Quarries, 132–33, 135
Quirigua, 29

Redfield, Robert, 178
Redistribution, 26
Regal-ritual city, 30, 39–40, 138
Relational perspective, 8
Resource diversity among the Maya low-
    lands, 65
Rice, Don, 41, 88
Rice, Prudence, 88
Richards, Colin, 181
Ricketson, Oliver, 31–32, 54
Rio Bec, Mexico, 82, 83, 95
Robertson, Ian, 92
Robin, Cynthia, 177, 195, 199
Rome, 3–4, 87
Rotenberg, Robert, 14
Royal courts. *See* Courts, royal
Roys, Ralph, 67
Rural settlement, 6, 68, 170–71, 195,
    200–202

Sabloff, Jeremy, 48, 59, 176
Sacbes, 100, 108–9, 185, 191; for processions,
    193
Sajal, 172–73
Salience. *See* Architecture
Salt, 99
Sanders, William, 39–40, 143
San Francisco, California, 10, 42
San Lorenzo, Belize, 84, 85
San Martin Orange pottery, 93
Sascab/Sascaberas, 100, 119, 132–33
Sayil, Mexico, 48, 53, 65, 150; distribution of
    wealth within, 163; inequality within, 158;
    map, 49

Scarborough, Vernon, 61–62, 171
Schele, Linda, 169, 178–79
Scherer, Andrew, 8
Servants, 143, 167–68
Settlement cluster, 70, 72–75
Settlement density, 10, 16, 31–35, 42–43,
    51–53, 161, 200
Settlement survey, 31
Shook, Ed, 31
Sian otot, 74, 86, 106
Simmel, Georg, 2, 12, 197
Sjoberg, Gideon, 17, 22, 88, 140, 160
Skeletal analysis. *See* Bioarchaeology
Slash-and-burn agriculture. *See* Agriculture
Smith, A. Ledyard, 51, 78
Smith, Adam, 180
Smith, Michael, 13, 23, 71–72, 152
Smith, Monica, 7, 13, 16, 198
Smyth, Michael, 89, 141, 164
Social archaeology, 202–3
Social capital, 22
Social class: Urban Revolution and, 6
Social contact. *See* Face-to-face interactions
Social differentiation, 11, 29; among the
    Classic Maya, 37–38; in early Maya
    research, 31–32
Social inequality, 6, 140–41
Social networks, 22, 140, 152, 194; and pot-
    tery, 157
Social organization, 74, 82, 84–85, 166–67
Social relations, 19
Soja, Edward, 11
Solola, Guatemala, 31
Spanish contact and colonialism, 32, 63, 67,
    88, 172, 178, 187, 196
Spatial clusters. *See under* Neighborhoods
Spectacle, 192–93, 197, 201
Spoke clusters. *See under* Chunchucmil,
    Mexico
Sprawl, 54
States, 13; Urban Revolution and, 6
Status, 141–42
Stevens, John, 29
Stockholm, Sweden, 19, 21
Storey, Glenn, 42, 51
Storey, Rebecca, 4, 93–94
Street of the Dead, Teotihuacan. *See under*
    Teotihuacan, Mexico

Stuart, George, 35
Stylistic clustering, 87–89; at Chunchucmil, 119–22
Suttles, Wayne, 100
Symbolic meaning, 23, 175–80, 182–83

Taube, Karl, 180
Tecolote, Guatemala, 173
Temples, 80, 174–80
Tenochtitlan, Mexico, 3, 40, 67, 91, 196–97
Teotihuacan, Mexico, 40, 120; apartment compounds, 91–92; building orientations and orthogonal layout, 91, 122; connections with the Maya lowlands, 89; health problems in, 4; La Ventilla, 94–95; migration, 87, 171–72; neighborhoods within, 90–96; pyramids of, 24; settlement density, 33, 42; status distinctions within, 92; Street of the Dead, 91, 94; Teopancazco, 94–95; Tlajinga, 93, 93–94, 132
Theater. See Ceremonies
Thompson, Eric, 31, 57
Three stone hearths. See under Creation mythology
Ticul, Mexico, 40
Tikal, Guatemala, 40: causeways, 191; Central Acropolis, 166; cost of architecture, 150; craft specialization within, 90; earthworks, 54; East Plaza, 196; ethnicity, 89; health problems, 4; map and settlement survey, 30–37, 36, 52–53, 54; marketplace, 65–66, 195–96; migration, 88; musical hammocks, 150; palaces, 161–62; plazas, 188; political alliances, 58–59, 76, 172; pottery exchange, 61, 87; site planning within, 174, 175, 191, 199; social differentiation within, 37–38, 143, 167; temples, 174, 188; and Teotihuacan, 89; twin temple group, 179; wealth distribution within, 161–62
Tiloom, 172–73
Tiwanaku, Bolivia, 20, 24, 87–90
Tlajinga. See under Teotihuacan, Mexico
Tlatelolco, Mexico, 63, 66, 196–97
Tobler's Law, 76, 78
Tokovinine, Alex, 57, 192
Tourtellot, Gair, 48, 88, 158

Toynbee, Arnold, 22
Transect survey. See Settlement survey
Trigger, Bruce, 7, 12–14, 25, 167
Trinidad de Nosotros, Guatemala, 65
Tula, Mexico, 40
Tulum, Mexico, 35
Type-variety classification, 128

Uaxactun, Guatemala, 30–32
Ur, Iraq, 84, 108
Urbanism: definition of, 2, 17, 204; state of mind, 2
Urbanization, 12, 17, 51
Urban planning, 20
Urban Revolution, 4
Uruk, Iraq, 171
Usumacinta River, 8
Uxmal, Mexico, 29, 35

Vacant ceremonial center, 31, 140
Valdez, Fred, 61–62, 171
Valley of Oaxaca, 92
Vaulted architecture, 54, 153, 157–58, 165
Veracruz, Mexico, 92–93
Villages, 12, 19, 74, 82, 104, 136, 151, 200–202. See also Hinterlands
Villa Rojas, Alfonso, 178
Vogt, Evon, 32, 76

Waka'. See El Peru/Waka', Guatemala
Waldeck, Jean, 29
Walker and Caddy expedition, 29
Walls: delimiting house lots, 51, 74, 98; delimiting larger areas within cities, 73–74; delimiting paths, 78, 98; at Teotihuacan, 91
Ward, 72, 86, 91, 106–8
Wealth, 141–42; as measured by architecture, 148–49; as measured by portable goods, 152; spatial distribution in cities, 160–66
Wealth-based neighborhoods. See under Neighborhoods
Weber, Max, 1, 9, 11–12, 39
Webster, David, 39–41, 51–52
Wells, 57, 70, 117
Wheatley, Paul, 23
White, Christine, 4

Widmer, Randolph, 93–94
Wilk, Richard, 149, 151
Willey, Gordon, 32–33, 38, 54, 141, 143
Williams, Raymond, 19
Wirth, Louis, 17, 51
Wisdom, Charles, 74, 106
Wolf, Eric, 24
Women, ancient Maya, 159, 192, 197–99
Woolley, Leonard, 84
Wright, Lori, 4

Xochicalco, Mexico, 73, 90
Xunantunich, Belize, 8, 54, 84, 86, 152, 176, 198

Yaeger, Jason, 84–86
Yaxchilan, Mexico, 60, 172–73, 192
Yax Nuun Ayiin II, 175
Yaxun B'alam, 172–73
Yik'in Chan K'awiil, 175
Yucatan, Mexico, 32, 63, 67, 98, 172, 178

Zinacantan, Mexico, 32

Scott R. Hutson, professor of anthropology at the University of Kentucky, is the author of *Dwelling, Identity, and the Maya: Relational Archaeology at Chunchucmil* and editor of *Ancient Maya Commerce: Multidisciplinary Research at Chunchucmil.*

Edited by Michael E. Smith, Arizona State University;
Marilyn A. Masson, University at Albany, SUNY;
John W. Janusek, Vanderbilt University

Aztec City-State Capitals, by Michael E. Smith (2008)
Tenochtitlan: Capital of the Aztec Empire, by José Luis de Rojas (2012; first paperback edition, 2014)
Cusco: Urbanism and Archaeology in the Inka World, by Ian Farrington (2013; first paperback edition, 2014)
Ancient Maya Cities of the Eastern Lowlands, by Brett A. Houk (2015; first paperback edition, 2016)
The Ancient Urban Maya: Neighborhoods, Inequality, and Built Form, by Scott R. Hutson (2016; first paperback edition, 2018)
The Casma City of El Purgatorio: Ancient Urbanism in the Andes, by Melissa A. Vogel (2016)

www.ingramcontent.com/pod-product-compliance
Lightning Source LLC
Chambersburg PA
CBHW020528270326
41927CB00006B/484